ABSTRACTS
from
The EDENTON GAZETTE
and
FARMER'S PALLADIUM

CHOWAN COUNTY
NORTH CAROLINA
- 1830 -1831 -

Compiled by:
Raymond Parker Fouts

Southern Historical Press, Inc.
Greenville, South Carolina

This volume was reproduced
from a personal copy located in
the Publishers private library

Please direct all correspondence and book orders to:
SOUTHERN HISTORICAL PRESS, Inc.
PO Box 1267
Greenville, SC   29602-1267

Copyright 2006 by: Raymond Parker Fouts
Copyright Transferred 2023 to:
               Southern Historical Press, Inc.
ISBN #978-1-63914-208-8
Printed in the United States of America

PREFACE

These abstracts and extracts were compiled from microfilm images of the original newspapers, available from the North Carolina State Archives, Raleigh, NC. The issues included in this work are from Reel #EdEGw-2, Edenton Gazette Jan. 12, 1819-Dec. 21, 1831.

This was a weekly, four-page newspaper, published in the town of Edenton, North Carolina. Edenton is the county seat of Chowan County, but "local" news also included numerous items from the surrounding counties of Bertie, Gates, Halifax, Hertford, Northampton, Perquimans, Tyrrell and Washington. State news was gathered from other North Carolina newspapers. National and international news came from papers published in the large American ports and was located on the first two pages. The third page contained advertisements, obituaries and marriage announcements, while the fourth page was usually devoted to arts and entertainment

Several marriages found in these papers were never recorded in the appropriate county records. The newspaper often provides greater detail than the county record of those that were recorded. Obituaries occasionally record nativity and the cause of death, as well as the date and location. North Carolina did not record vital statistics until 1913, thus causing the newspaper accounts to become the sole source for this information, other than scattered Bible records. Numerous deaths of infants and young children are recorded in the newspaper and most often provide the sole surviving record of their existence.

This newspaper became the *Edenton Gazette and Farmer's Palladium* as of 15 July 1830. The Editor customarily allowed his staff a holiday at Christmas and New Year's and no issues were printed until the first Thursday in January. The last issue in 1830 was published 23 December. The final issue of the *Edenton Gazette and Farmer's Palladium* was published 21 December 1831, after 27 years of operation. It changed hands and became *The North-Carolina Miscellany*, under the management of Thos. **MEREDITH** and Wm. E. **PELL**, as described in Item #742.

Items that contain a city dateline are from that city, unless otherwise noted. Advertisements have been transcribed only from the first extant issue in which they appear. All newspapers mentioned in articles are included in the Miscellaneous Index.

Every name appears in the Name Index, including all variant spellings. A supplementary index of female given names is included. In the case of marriages, both maiden and married names appear in this index, even though the married name, i. e., "Fanny (**JONES**) **WALTON**, may not appear in the text. Widows marrying again are listed with both married surnames in caps, i. e., "Mary **WALTON GRIMES**," facilitating her identification after her marriage. All female maiden names also appear in the main Name Index.

The slave insurrection known as the "Nat **TURNER** Rebellion," is reported herein. The names of many of the fatalities on both sides are included, being of value to the historian, as well as the genealogist.

Geographic names used to describe products, i.e., "St. Croix Salt," "Gates County Brandy," are not indexed. All deaths, either by accident, illness, murder, execution or suicide, are indexed under "Deaths," within the Miscellaneous Index. Various forms of "North Carolina" have all been indexed under that heading, within the Location Index. Spelling and punctuation have been transcribed verbatim. Each item has been assigned a number, within brackets. The indices refer to these numbers, *not* the page numbers. Not all issues are clear and legible. Underlined letters emphasize verbatim spelling. Missing or illegible letters or words are denoted by "___," or "?".

CONTENTS

1830 1
    Filmed from originals in the Cupola House, Edenton, NC. Issue of 9 January is the only issue missing.

1831 66
    Filmed from originals in the Cupola House, Edenton, NC. No missing issues.

Female Index 123

Name Index 127

Miscellaneous Index 151

Location Index 155

ABSTRACTS FROM THE EDENTON GAZETTE

AND FARMER'S PALLADIUM

EDENTON, NORTH CAROLINA

1830-1831

Edenton Gazette.
Vol. XXVI.....No. 1. Edenton, N. C. Saturday Morning, January 2, 1829/30/. Whole No. 1200+1.

[1] [p. 1] Printed every Saturday by Wm. E. **PELL**, for the proprietor. Terms—Three Dollars per year, payable in advance. Subscribers will be continued on the list, and be considered liable for payment to an indefinite period, unless a wish be signified to withdraw their names.

Advertisements inserted at fifty cents per square for the first, and twenty five cents for every subsequent insertion. Eloped wives or discarded husbands, $10. Letters to the Editor, must be post paid.

[2] [p. 3] Summary. The Portsmouth Journal says the Rev. John N. **MAFFIT** of the M[et]hodist Episcopal Church, has be[en] appointed a chaplain in the N[av]y. An application is expected to be sent to Congress for the admission of Florida into the Union as a State. ...

[3] Edenton: Saturday, January 2, 1829. [sic] We understand that the store of Mr. *David* **PICKARD** of this County, with a quantity of goods and other articles were entirely consumed by fire, on Sunday night last. It is supposed to be the act of an incendiary.

[4] Gen. *GAINES* of the U. S. Army arrived in this place on the 24th ult on his way to Washington City, and took lodgings at Mrs. **WILLS**' he resumed his journey on the 25th.

The following gentleman have been re-elected to their former offices, by the Legislature, without opposition:--*Wm.* **HILL**, Secretary of State. *Wm.* **ROBARDS**, Public Treasurer. *Jas.* **GRANT**, Comptroller.

Peter O. **PICOT**, Esq. of Plymouth, has been elected, after several ballotings, Brigadier General of the 13th Brigade of North Carolina Militia.

Councillors of State.—The following gentlemen have been elected Councillors of State for the ensuing year: George W. **JEFFREYS**, Gideon **ALSTON**, Thomas **KENAN**, Alexander **GRAY**, Archibald **M'BRYDE**, Daniel M. **FORNEY** and Joseph B. **OUTLAW**.

[5] Congress. There has not been as yet, much business of moment to our readers, transacted in either House of Congress; our selections are therefore scanty. Our Senator Gen. **IREDELL** on the 14th ult. presented the petition of Lewis **LEROY**, Esq. of Washington, N. C. praying a remission of the additional duties imposed by the Tariff of 1828, on a certain quantity of Molasses imported by him; referred to the committee on Finance. ... Mr. **BARRINGER** announced the death of Gabriel **HOLMES** a member of the 20th, and member elect of the 21st Congress, and moved the usual testimony of respect to his memory.

[6] MARRIED, In this Town on Tuesday evening last, by the Rev. James **DEY**, Capt. Stewart **DEAN** to Miss Isabella **NEIL**, daughter of Mr. Horatio **NEIL**, deceased.

In this county on the 22d ult. by the same, Mr. Theophilus **ELLIOTT** of Perquimans county to Mrs. Sarah **WILDER**, widow of Thomas **WILDER**, deceased.

[7] DIED, On Saturday morning the 19th ult. William C. **ROBERTS**, Esq. a respectable farmer of this county. In this town on the 29th ult. James **MOFFATT**, Esq. Register of this county, in the 51st year of

Edenton Gazette 2 January 1830

his age. Mr. **M.** was a native of Scotland, but for 30 years past a respectable citizen of this place.

OBITUARY. Departed this life on Friday the 25th ult. after a severe and protracted indisposition, Mrs. Catharine **HANKINS**, consort of Mr. John G. **HANKINS** of this town. In recording the death of this amiable woman, we do so with the strongest emotions of grief; but we are consoled in the full assurance that she has gone to the "bosom of her Father and her God." During her severe illness, though her sufferings were great, yet she bore them with that meekness and fortitude, so apparent in the Christian character; not a murmur or complaint escaped her lips, but firmly relying on the merits of her blessed Redeemer, she calmly resigned her pure spirit into the hands of Him who gave it. Not many hours before her dissolution, she cast her eyes around the room and said "all my friends are with me, Now! now my Saviour receive me." We have been acquainted with the subject of these remarks for some years, and had an opportunity of observing her in sickness and in health, and in no case did she deviate from that strict regard which she had for the religion of our lord and Saviour Jesus Christ, of which she was professedly and practically an humble follower. As a member of the Baptist Church, she was regular in her attendance when an opportunity offered, and strict in her adherence to its tenets. As a fond, dutiful and obedient wife, an affectionate mother, a warm-hearted friend, her memory will long be cherished by her afflicted relatives and friends: And though thou must repose for a season in the dark and gloomy mansions of the dead, 'Yet of all thy grave with rising flow'rs be drest, 'And the green turf lie lightly on thy breast.' And on the glorious morn of the resurrection, thou wilt arise resplendent in beauty, and receive from Him, in whom thou didst put thy trust, a crown of unfading lustre.—"Let me die the death of the righteous, and let my last end be like his."

[8] *NOTICE.* On Monday the 18th January next, will be sold at the late residence of Mr. *Wm. C.* **ROBERTS**, dec'd, all his perishable Estate consisting of Household and kitchen FURNITURE, Farming Utensils, his Stock of *Horses, Cattle, Sheep* and from forty to sixty well fatted HOGS, besides Sows and Pigs. Also, from 4 to 500 barrels CORN, and from 50 to 60,000 pounds of COTTON IN SEED. At the same time and place, will be hired out until the 1st January 1831, from Forty to Fifty likely Negroes, a large proportion of which are boys and girls well calculated for a Cotton crop. Also, will be rented all his LANDS, for the balance of the ensuing year. Terms, generally, will be made known on the day of sale by the ADMINISTRATOR. Dec. 26th 1829.

[9] *The subscriber has for Sale, at his store upon the wharf,* 16 Hhds. Guad. Molasses, 10 bbls. Baltimore How'd St. Flour, which he will sell low. Jona. H. **HAUGHTON**.

[10] The Officers and members o[f] Unanimity Lodge, No. 54 Edenton, are requested to wear the usual badge of mourning for the space of thirty days, from the 21st ult. as a token of respect for their deceased brother, *James MOFFATT.* By order of the Lodge, J. I. **TREDWELL**, *Sec'y.* Jan. 2nd 1830.

[11] State Bank Of North Carolina, *Edenton Branch*, 31st Dec. 1829. BILLS of Exchange hereafter offered for discount at this Bank must be put in by 9 o'clock, A. M. on Tuesday and Saturday mornings, and on Thursdays the regular discount day, at which times they will be acted on. D. W. **STONE**, *Cashier*. Edenton, Jan. 2.

[12] Those who may be desirous of purchasing the property offered for sale by the Subscriber, and described in the numbers of this Gazette published in December, have still an opportunity. All persons indebted to the subscriber, are expected to pay their accounts without delay. James **NORCOM**. Jan. 1st 1830.

[13] Lake Drummond HOTEL. This House of entertainment is situated on the *Dismal Swamp Canal,* half way from Norfolk to Elizabeth City, immediately on the N. Carolina and Virginia line, one half of the building in each State. The subscriber having erected this establishment at considerable expense during the present year, is now prepared to entertain travellers and boarders in a style which he thinks will give satisfaction. His house is large and commodious, being 128 feet long and having eight separate chambers with fire places, so that families travelling or parties of pleasure can be accommodated with distinct apartments if they wish. His table will always be supplied with the substantials of the Norfolk

Edenton Gazette 2 January 1830

and other neighboring markets. He has an extensive range of stables, well supplied with good provender, and attended by careful ostlers. In addition to the improvements already made, he is now building a large Carriage House, which will be completed in a few weeks; and he intends providing boats for the convenience of persons wishing to visit the Lake. His prices will be moderate, and he hopes with all these comforts and his own unremitted attention to please his guests, to merit and receive a share of the public patronage. Isaiah **ROGERSON**. Dec. 23. 1829.

[14] FEMALE SCHOOL. Mrs. **HARVEY** begs leave to inform her friends and the public in general, that her School for young Ladies will be resumed again at Hyde Park, on the 12th day of January next. The charges for the highest Branches and Sciences, $10 per sess. For the lower $7 Music on the Piano, $15 Drawing & Painting, $4 Board can be obtained at $30 per session. Those who may feel disposed to patronise the school, will please address a line post paid to Eliza J. **HARVEY**, *Hyde Park, Halifax Co. N. C. December,* 10. 1829.

[15] [p. 4] Land For Sale. By an order of the Court of Equity for the County of Chowan, made (on the petition of James **NORCOM**, Henderson, William and Elizabeth **SUTTON**, for the sale of Land for a division) at the last term of said Court, I will proceed to sell on the 1st day of January next, before the tavern of Mr. Edmund **HOSKINS** in the town of Edenton, A Valuable Tract of LAND, lying and being in the county of Chowan and adjoining the lands of James **NORCOM**, Thomas **BENBURY** and Frederick **NORCOM**'s heirs, containing about 30 Acres, the same being a part of the Sandy Point plantation formerly owned by James **SUTTON**, deceased. A credit of twelve months will be allowed, the purchaser giving bond with a good and sufficient security. James **BOZMAN**, C. & M. E. Nov. 21.

[16] NOTICE. Those persons indebted to this Office, for Subscription or Job Work, are respectfully requested to call on *Mr. Wm.* **GRIMES** and close their accounts, as he is fully authorized to receive payment and give receipts.

[17] James **BOZMAN** *Has just received at his store in Edenton a fresh supply of* **LEE**'s tried and highly approved Valuable Medicines. Prevention better than Cure. **LEE**'s famous Anti-Bilious Pills. 25 and 50 cents per box. The operations of these Pills is perfectly mild, so as to be used in safety by persons in every situation, and of every age. The proprietor confidently recommends the timely use of these pills, as a preventive and cure of Billious, Yellow, and Malignant Fevers.

Please inquire for 'LEE'S ANTI-BILLIOUS PILLS,' with the signature of Noah **RIDGELY**, (late Michael **LEE** & Co.) *as none other are genuine.* *Lee's Worm Destroying Lozenges...Lee's Elixir...Lee's Nervous Cordial...Lee's Essence of Mustard... Lee's Ague and Fever Drops... Lee's Sovereign Ointment... Lee's Persian Lotion... Lee's Vegetable Indian Specific... Lee's Tooth-ache Drops... Lee's Tooth Powder... Lee's Eye Water... Lee's Anodyne Elixir... Lee's Corn Plaster...* Dec. 5. 1829.

[18] Notice. The subscriber having come to the determination to quit this section of country, will offer for sale at 6 months credit, on the 28th January next, all his property of every description, consisting of Household and kitchen FURNITURE, FARMING UTENSILS, HORSES, CATTLE, HOGS, SHEEP. &c. &c. notes with approved security will be required. All persons to whom I am in any way indebted, are requested to attend on the above day, when arrangements will be made to discharge the same; and those indebted to me are requested to make payment, on or before said day. Joseph M. **HAUGHTON**. Dec. 19.

[19] SALT. Liverpool, Cadiz, St. Ubes and Turks Island at Retail, at 60 cents per bushel for Cash, by Samuel **FOWLER**. Dec. 12.

[20] Call and see and judge for yourselves! NOTICE. The subscriber has received by several recent arrivals from New York, an assortment of Cloths. Cassimeres, &c. &c.; among them are the following, viz: Super blue Cloths and Cassimeres, Fine and Common do. do. ... Fine blue Palisse cloth & trimmings for do....Bang-up cord; several pieces of low priced drab Casimere of various shades; super white Swan-skin Flannel...an assortment of Suspenders, from 12½ cents to $2 50 per pair; an assortment of Buttons, gilt

Edenton Gazette 2 January 1830

and plated, also covered buttons of all the colors generally used...all or any part of which, I will sell at a very small advance on *costs* for Cash, or good notes in *advance*. Joseph **MANNING**. Merchant Tailor. ... Edenton, Dec. 5th.

[21] *FOR SALE* BY THE SUBSCRIBER, 18 Hhds Molasses, 4 do. Sugar, 35 bags Coffee, 100 kegs Nails, 100 casks Lime, 25 do. Tobacco, 50 bbls. Gates County Apple Brandy, 40 pieces Cotton Bagging 42 inch. Domestic Goods. Satinetts, Sheetings and Shirtings bleached and unbleached, Prints, Wool and Napt [sic] Hats, *&c*. Salt, Twine & Rope in large or small quantities for Fisheries, on the most accommodating terms. Samuel **FOWLER**. Oct. 31.

[22] *NOTICE*. The subscriber begs leave to inform his friends and the public, that he has lately returned from New York, with a general assortment of GOODS suitable for the season, which he offers for sale on accommodating terms, at his store on the wharf two doors below Thos. I. **CHARLTON**, Esq. His stock consists of DRY GOODS, *Groceries*, Hardware and Crockery, also an assortment of Drugs & Medicines, among which is a supply of choice French Quinine. Nat. J. **BEASLEY**. P. S. The subscriber also gives notice to the public, that his Foot and Horse BOATS are in complete order, and that he will be ready to convey passengers to any of the Ferries, at the shortest notice. N. J. **B**. Edenton, Dec. 5.

[23] R. H. **MIDDLETON** *At his old stand near the market on Water Street, has just received from New York per Schooner Ocean, an additional supply of DRY GOODS, suitable for the present Season, together with his former stock makes his assortment pretty general. viz* Fine and coarse Satinetts; 4 & 4½ point Blankets; worsted Hose and ½ Hose; white and red Flannel; Ladies & Gentlemen white cotton Hose; cotton Cambrics; Prints of the latest fashions; flag & silk bandannoe Hdkfs; Cravats for gentle'n cotton Hdkfs; do. Shawls; Spun Cotton; 3-4, 4-4 & 6-4 bleached & unbleached Cottons...ladies Shoes; fine and coarse Hats for men and boys; Powder & Shot; *Glass and Crockery-Ware* assorted. CUTLERY &c. ... GROCERIES... Edenton, Dec. 5th 1829.

[24] New Goods. *By the arrival of the Schr. Ocean, I am enabled to offer the following articles,* viz: White lambs-wool ½ Hose...Cotton Yarn from No. 5 to 10; Bl'k Sinchews; Satin Levantines; Nankin Crape; white Purlings; Fig'd swiss Muslins; super H. Skin Gloves; Leghorns very cheap; Hooks & Eyes; Negro Shoes; Brogans; men's lined & bound Shoes Men's best calf-skin latest fashion; Women's leather Shoes; women's best seal-skin do. thick soles... GROCERIES. Old Sherry Wine, Sugar, Saltpeter, Raisins in ½ boxes; Cheese; Rice; Gunpowder Tea, Goshen Butter, Sperm Oil; Mace; Snuff and 10 barrels and ½ bbls. Flour. James **GORHAM**. Edenton, Dec. 5.

[25] *New Goods*. I have just received and now opening at my store on the wharf, the following GOODS, which together with late importations and the former stock, comprises one of the largest and best assortments now offered in this Town, and will be sold to customers on my usual terms. Navy blue Satinetts very fine, do. mixed do. ... Red Flannels, 3-4 Checks, 4-4 do., Point Blankets, Castor Oil in quart and pint bottles, Quinine, Sperm Oil winter strained, Linseed do., Litherage, English White Lead No. 1. Sugar and Molasses, Butter and Cheese, prime green Coffee, Onions, &c. &c. Tho. J. **CHARLTON**. Oct. 29.

[26] New Goods. *The subscriber has just received from New York*...Blue merino Circassian for ladies Cloaks, Camblet Plaid for gent's ditto, Sattinets, white Flannels, Black & blue Bombazettes, Tooth Brushes, self sharpning Pencil cases with 1 doz. extra pencils, Table Salt, Pearl-ash, Ginger, Lamp Oil... James **WILLS**. Nov. 28. ... Dec. 12.

[27] $15 Reward Will be paid for the apprehension and delivery to me, or confining in jail so that I get him, negro man **HENRY**; belonging to the estate of the Rev. Henry **HOLMES** dec'd; said fellow is so *well* known in this place and its *neighbourhood*, as an excellent Sawyer, a description is deemed unnecessary. It is believed that he is lurking in the neighbourhood of Gen. Richard T. **BROWNRIGG**, where he has a sister living: or in the neighbourhood of Bear Swamp. All persons are forwarned harboring or employing him. Wm. B. **ROBERTS**, *Executor*. Edenton, Dec. 19.

[28] $100 Reward. Runaway from the subscriber, his negro men **BILL** and **GILES**; **BILL** is about 22 or

Edenton Gazette 2 January 1830

23 years of age, 5 feet 6 inches high, very black and was formerly the property of Samuel **GREGORY**, Esq. deceased. **GILES** is about 35 years of age, 5 feet 6 inches high, dark complexion and very grey. **BILL** runaway on Wednesday 15th inst. and **GILES** about the middle of May last, and I have reason to believe they are lurking about the Town of Edenton and neighbourhood.—I will give Fifty Dollars reward for each of them if taken out of the State, or Twenty Five Dollars for each if taken within it. James **COFFIELD**. Chowan Co. July 28th. N. B. **BILL**, named in the above advertisement has come in. Sept. 22d.

[29] Notice to Fishermen. *The subscriber has received a large supply of* RIGGING, TWINE, CORK-WOOD and SALT, and will furnish fishermen with the above articles in such quantities as may be wanted on the most libe___ terms both as regards price ___ time of payment. Sam'l **FOWLER**. Dec. 12.

Edenton Gazette.
Vol. XXVI.....No. 3. Edenton, N. C. Saturday Morning, January 16, 1830. Whole No. 1203

[30] [p. 1] Miscellaneous. New York, Dec. 24. The fire yesterday morning, is said to have commenced in Mr. **HAYDOCK**'s crockery store, No. 1 Burling slip, which was destroyed, with most of the goods it contained. The house No. 3, occupied by S. **HUNTINGTON**, grocer, and W. **STROUGHTENBOROUGH**, wire manufacturer, was nearly destroyed, and only a small portion of the goods saved. The house on the corner of Pearl Street, occupied by Thos. **RICHARDS**, watch maker and jeweller, and by Chas. **JUDSON**, Esq. counsellor at law, and the adjoining store, No. 242 Pearl st, occupied by **PLATT & FAULKNER**, merchant tailors, were also destroyed. Most of the goods in the latter store, and the most valuable part of those of Mr. **RICHARDS**, were saved.—The upper stories of the two last mentioned buildings were occupied by Mr. Wm. A. **MERCEIA**, whose extensive stock of printing materials, together with an edition of the life of the Rev. Mr. **SUMMERFIELD**, just completed, and a quantity of printing paper, were wholly consumed. It is said the principal part of the property was insured.

[31] Flour, Beef, &c. 20 Bbls Superfine FLOUR, 20 bbls prime Beef, 10 bbls prime Pork. 50 boxes Soap, 20 do. Candles, 800 Bushels Irish Potatoes, received...& for sale, by Samuel **FOWLER**. Dec. 12.

[32] [p. 2] State Legislature. From the Raleigh Star, of Jan. 7th. Legislature. ... In the *House of Commons*, on Wednesday the 30th ultimo, the bill vesting the election of Sheriffs in the free white men of the State, was ordered to be enrolled, and is, consequently, a law. On Thursday, William R. **HILL**, was reappointed Librarian for the ensuing year. On the same day, the resolution authorising the engraving and publication of a Map of the State, was rejected. ...

[33] Domestic News. From the Raleigh Register, Dec. 31. *Tragical Affair.*—A certain Thomas **THOMPSON**, Of Elizabeth City, two or three years ago, succeeded in obtaining the hand of an amiable and respectable young lady of Beaufort, Carteret county. In a short time after their marriage, his conduct towards her became so brutal that her friends separated her from him. He has professed to feel extremely unhappy in consequence, and has endeavored to prevail upon her to return to him, but without effect. For nearly or quite two years this has been his course, until within the last few months, when he has been less heard of. It seems however, that he was only slumbering to make a more deadly spring. On Saturday the 16th inst. he arrived at Beaufort armed with pistols and a dirk, and entered the dwelling of his unfortunate wife, caught her in his arms and endeavored to persuade her to go with him. The family became alarmed, and despatched a messenger for the brother of the wife, who was at Fort Macon (two miles off.) On his arrival he demanded his sister. **THOMPSON** refused, and threatened any man with instant death who should touch either him or his wife. The brother, however, agreeing to leave it to the lady to choose, and she preferring to remain, **THOMPSON** snapped one pistol at the young man, and stabbed his wife once in her breast and twice in her arm—and likewise, a Justice of the Peace, who attempted to stop him. He then made his escape, and though vigilant measures were adopted, the Police have not succeeded as yet, in taking him.

Edenton Gazette 16 January 1830

[34] [p. 3] Edenton: Saturday, January 16, 1830. We have received several numbers of a paper published in Norfolk, by Jas. C. **WEST** called "The People's Free Press"—it is neatly printed and will no doubt be ably edited, we wish it success...

[35] Henry **BALDWIN**, Esq. of Pennsylvania, has been appointed to supply the vacancy on the Bench of the Supreme Court of the United States, occupied by the decease of Judge **WASHINGTON**.

Cadwallader **JONES**, David L. **SWAIN** and James **MORGAN**, Esqrs. have been elected members of the Board of Internal Improvement for the present year.

[36] Summary. The small pox is said to be raging in Trenton, N. J. and its vicinity to an alarming extent. Capt. Henry E. **BALLARD**, now on the Baltimore station has been appointed to command the U. S. frigate Brandywine, now fitting out in New York. He is succeeded in the command at Baltimore, by Com. Jacob **JONES**.

The subscriptions at New-York for a statute [sic] to the memory of Alexander **HAMILTON**, is said to be nearly adequate to the object. The site selected is the centre of the large room in the exchange.

William S. HAMILTON declines accepting the office of Surveyor General of Louisiana, conferred upon him by the President.

On Saturday the 9th inst. the Legislature of Virginia elected General John **FLOYD** Governor of that State, vice Wm. B. **GILES**, Esq.

Thomas King CARROLL, Esq. has been elected Governor of Maryland for the ensuing year.

[37] Mansion House Plymouth, N. C. The subscriber having taken the above pleasant and commodious House, has opened it as a House of Public ENTERTAINMENT, for the reception of all such travellers and boarders as may favour him with their custom. He will have his rooms well furnished, and promises to supply his Table with the best, the Country and seasons afford. Gentlemen travelling with their families, can be accommodated with private and retired apartments, and Gentlemen of the Bar during the Courts, with exclusive rooms, (a suitable building having been erected for that purpose.) In order to make this a desirable resting place for travellers and others, the subscriber has spared no pains in procuring trusty servants, to attend in the House as well as in the Stables. ... He will also keep conveyances ready for persons who are travelling by land, at a moderate price. John D. **BENNETT**. Plymouth, N. C. Jan. 1st.

[38] State of North-Carolina, *Hertford County.* Court of Pleas & Quarter-Sessions, November Term 1829. John K. **RANSOM**, Elisha H. **SHARP** in fact vs. The heirs and devisees of Elenor **MONTGOMERY** deceased.} Sci. Fa. vs. heirs & devisees, to sell Land. It appearing to the Court, that James C. **JONES** and Lavinia **JONES** his wife, devisees of Elenor **MONTGOMERY**, dec'd, are not inhabitants of this State. The Court therefore order publication to be made in the Edenton Gazette for six weeks, giving notice to the said James C. & Lavinia **JONES**, to appear at the next term of this Court to be held for the County of Hertford, at the Court-House in Winton on the fourth Monday in February next, then and there to answer, plead or demur; or Judgment *pro confesso* will be entered up against them. Test, L. M. **COWPER**, Cl'k. Jan. 16.

[39] State of North-Carolina, *Hertford County.* Court of Pleas & Quarter-Sessions, November Term 1829. James C. **JONES** James S. **JONES** in fact vs. The heirs and devisees of Elenor **MONTGOMERY** deceased.} Sci. Fa. vs. heirs & devisees, to sell Land. It appearing to the Court, that James C. **JONES** and Lavinia **JONES** his wife, devisees of Elenor **MONTGOMERY**, dec'd, are not inhabitants of this State. The Court therefore order publication to be made in the Edenton Gazette for six weeks, giving notice to the said James C. & Lavinia **JONES**, to appear at the next term of this Court to be held for the County of Hertford, at the Court-House in Winton on the fourth Monday in February next, then and there to answer, plead or demur; or Judgment *pro confesso* will be entered up against them. Test, L. M. **COWPER**, Cl'k. Jan. 16.

[40] Carolina and Virginia HOTEL. The subscriber begs leave to inform his friends and the public, that he has opened a house of ENTERTAINMENT in Portsmouth, Va. and is now prepared to accommodate

Edenton Gazette 16 January 1830

travellers and boarders. His table shall be supplied with the best the market affords, his bar with choice liquors, his stable with good provender and attentive Ostlers, and his charges moderate. This house so well known as a public one, needs nothing further than to say, it is the most convenient to business, of any in Portsmouth. ... Richard WYATT. *Portsmouth, Va.* Jan. 16th.

[41] CANAL COMMERCE. The Canal Boat Favorite, Capt. DEAN, will trade regularly between this place and Norfolk. She is 20 tons burthen and carries 10 M. staves, she is also well fitted to carry cotton, corn &c. For freight inquire of A. SPENCE or Nat. J. BEASLY. Edenton, Jan. 9.

[42] $10 Reward. Runaway from the subscriber on the 31st December last, negro man **JIM**, by trade a black smith, belonging to the **DAVIS** Estate, Said fellow has a wife at *Sam'l SUTTON's* in Perquimans County, and it is supposed he is lurking in that neighbourhood; he is well known in this and Perquimans County, and a description of him, is deemed unnecessary. I will give the above reward and pay all reasonable expenses, to any one who will deliver the said fellow to me or confine him in jail so that I get him. Richard **BEASLEY**. Chowan Co. Jan. 3th [sic] 1830.

[43] [p. 4] List of Letters *Remaining in the Post Office at Edenton,* 31st *December* 1829. **A.**—Wm. **ARMISTEAD**, Benjamin **ALFORD**, Nathan **ALEXANDER**. **B.**—Charles **BOZMAN**, Richard **BEASLEY**, Thos. R. **BARNSWELL**, C. C. **BISHOP**, John C. **BRIDSON**, Nathan E. **BRICKHOUSE**, Martha Ann **BATEMAN**, Darcise **BENBURY**, Mary A. **BISSELL**. **C.**—Jeremiah **CHASE**, Capt. Jno. D. **COOK**, Alfred **CHURTON** 2, Emily E. **CHRISTIAN**. **D.**—Sam'l **DAMERON** 2, Stephen **DOLBY**. **F.**—Sam. **FOWLER**, Henry **FLURY**. **G.**—John **GOODWIN**, Wm. **GREGORY** 2, Nathan D. **GREGORY**. **H.**—Stephen **HARRISON**, Capt. Jas. **HACKETT**, Polly **HARRIS**. **K.**—Robert **KEATING**, sen. **L.**—Thomas H. **LEARY** 3, Capt. John **LAMBERT**, Hester C. **LEE**. **M.**—Jas. **MOFFATT**, Wm. **M'NIDER**. **N.**—Elijah **NIXON**, Nancy **NEWSAM**. **P.**—Adoris **PARRIMORE**, Sally **PERKINS** 2, Sarah **PETTIJOHN**. **R.**—Wm. **ROBERTS**. **S.**—**SAWYER** & **CLEVELAND**, Jas. **SUTTON**, Josiah **SKINNER** 2, David **SMALL**, Edmund B. **SKINNER**, Lemuel **SKINNER**, Betsey **SKINNER**. **V.**—Wm. **VEZZEN**. **W.**—John M. **WOODARD**, Rich'd **WILDER**, Nathaniel **WILDER**. N. BRUER, P. M. Jan. 1st 1830.

[44] 'HOLD SO.' The subscriber has removed to the dwelling house lately occupied by Gen. James **IREDELL**, on King street, and will hereafter carry on his trade in the apartment formerly used by him as an Office. He is prepared to carry on business in his line, in a manner to satisfy his friends and the public; and will take pleasure in executing their commands with fidelity and despatch. Nath'l. **HOWCOTT**. N. B. He hopes that those persons who are indebted to him for work, will have the consideration to reflect that he has a family to support, whose comfort depends upon the labour of his hands. If with all his industry and application to business he can barely make out to live, how can he subsist if a large part of his time is consumed in running about after little accounts. More punctuality is therefore requested from those who may find it inconvenient to pay cash for work, of which he would be glad to have the number as small as possible. N. H. Edenton, Jan. 9 1830. [Nathaniel **HOWCOTT** was a "clock and watch maker." There is a depiction of a timepiece at the top of this advertisement. rpf]

[45] NOTICE. Will be sold in the town of Edenton on the 12th day of February next, the real estate conveyed by *James R. CREECY*, by deed of trust dated Sept. 15, 1829, consisting of Lots of ground in the said town and several *Tracts of Land* lying in Chowan County below the town of Edenton. Terms made known on the day of sale, by the Trustee. Edenton, Jan. 8.

[46] *To the lovers of Good Tea!* Fresh Teas. Gunpowder, Imperial and Hyson TEAS *of superior quality,* are received and for sale by Wm. F. **BENNETT**. Edenton, Oct. 24th.

Edenton Gazette.
Vol. XXVI.....No. 4. Edenton, N. C. Saturday Morning, January 23, 1830. Whole No. 1204

[47] [p. 1] Captions Of The Laws Enacted by the General Assembly of North Carolina, at its session in

Edenton Gazette 23 January 1830

1829-30. PUBLIC ACTS. ... 2 Amending the act of 1827, prescribing upon what evidence the Public Treasurer shall receive the purchase money for vacant and unappropriated lands. [Provides that the Secretary of State shall issue grants for vacant lands upon a certificate taken from the copy of entry books returned to his office, in the same manner as he now does from warrants and surveys.] 3. Amending the 10th section of the act of 1819, prescribing the mode of surveying and selling the lands acquired by treaty from the Cherokee Indians. ... 5. Amendatory of the law respecting the crime of Bigamy. [Provides that persons convicted of Bigamy shall be entitled to the benefit of clergy for the first offence; and that the court may sentence the offender to be fined and imprisoned, to receive one or more public whippings, and to be branded on the left cheek with the letter B. If the offender be a female, it shall be discretionary with the court to inflict all or any of the aforesaid punishments, branding excepted.] 6. Vesting the right of electing Sheriffs in the several counties within the State in the free white men thereof.—[Provides that the Sheriffs shall be elected by the free white men who are entitled to vote for members of the House of Commons, every two years, at the same times and places that members of the General Assembly are elected. ... No person to be eligible to the office of Sheriff who has not attained the age of 21 years, resided in his county one year immediately preceding the election, and be possessed of a freehold of 100 acres of land. 7 Directing the removal of certain papers from the office of the Treasurer to that of the Secretary of State. [Provides for the removal of the papers relative to the Tuscarora lands.] ... 12 Vesting in the superior and county courts jurisdiction of applications for the legitimation of bastard children. ... 16 Concerning the cross canal leading from the Great Dismal Swamp Canal, near the head of the woods in Camden county, to the White Oak Spring Marsh in Gates county. [Allows a farther time of seven years to complete said canal; authorises the company to erect locks and collect tolls, and provides that the charter of the company shall remain in force for 33 years from Jan. 1, 1830.] ... 18 Exempting the members of fire companies from performing military duty. ...

PRIVATE ACTS. ... 2 Legitimating Alexander **CHESHIRE**, of Edenton. ... 6 Altering the names of Ezekiel H. **WALL** and Elizabeth A. **WALL**, of Columbus. ... 16 Compelling the clerk of the county court of Gates to keep the whole of the records, books, papers, &c. belonging to his office, in the office at the court house. ... 20 To revive and continue in force the act of 1827, authorising Thomas **BROWN**, of Haywood (now Macon) county, to erect two gates on a public road. 21 Authorising Matthew M. **HUGHES**, of Surry, to erect a dam across **FISHER**'s river. ... 25 Authorising James **M'KEE**, sheriff of Haywood, to collect certain taxes. ... 27 Incorporating the Vance Circulating Library Society of Asheville. ... [p. 2] 36 Authorising Rich'd T. **BRUMLY**, of Lincoln, to erect a gate on his lands. ...53 Empowering the county court of Onslow to authorise Solomon E. **GRANT** to erect a gate across the main road at Onslow court house. ... 62 Authorising Nat. G. **BLOUNT** to erect a spiral wheel in Neuse river. ... 77 Authorising Alexander, William and Duncan **MURCHISON** to erect a bridge across Lower Little river, in Cumberland county. ... 85 For the relief of James D. **JUSTICE**, of Buncombe county. ... 88 Authorising Andrew **WELCH** and William **THOMAS**, of Macon county, to erect certain gates. ... 90 Authorising Thomas L. **COWAN** of Rowan, to erect certain gates. ... 108 Authorising the county court of Burke to appoint commissioners to run and lay off a turnpike road from the Lincoln line to Jacob **MALL**'s mill. ...

RESOLUTIONS. ... 3 Concerning Miss Edney M. **BLAKELY**. [Discontinuing the appropriation for her support and education.] ... 9 In favor of James **RILEY**, of Davidson. 10 In favor of George **RISH**. 11 In favor of Absalom **WILLIAMS**, of Davidson. 12 In favor of Archibald S. **BROWN**. 13 In favor of the late John L. **TAYLOR**. 15 [sic] In favor of John **LOWRIE**, of Burke. [Number 14 was omitted.] 15 In favor of Stephen **PEARSON**, of Wake. 16 In favor of George **MILLER**. 17 In favor of Ransom **HINTON**. 18 In favor of Isaiah **ROGERSON**. ... 20 In favor of John **BLACK**, sheriff of Cumberland. 21 In favor of Presley C. **PERSON**, of Franklin. 22 In favor of Edward **WARD** of Onslow. 23 In favor of Thomas **WALKER**, of Mecklenburg. 24 In favor of Alex. **NICHOLSON**. 25 In favor of James **BRYSON**. 26 Appointing William R. **HILL** Librarian. ... 29 In favor of D. **LINDEMAN**. ... 32 In favor of David **GRAYHEAL**. 33 In favor of Merritt **HUTCHINS**. 34 In favor of Benj. H. **BLOUNT**. 35 In favor of Ezekiel **ELLIS**. ...

[48] [p. 3] Edenton: Saturday, January 23, 1830. ... A negro girl belonging to the estate of the late Mr. *Wm. C.* **ROBERTS**, of this County, was so badly burnt a few days past, by her clothes coming in contact with the fire, that she survived but a short time.

Edenton Gazette 23 January 1830

[49] *Supreme Court.*—Judge **RUFFIAN** [sic] qualified and took his seat on the Bench as a Judge of this Court, on the 9th inst. The following gentlemen have been admitted to the practice of law in the County Courts, viz: Jno. B. **MUSE**, of Pasquotank; Charles **SHEPARD**, of Newbern; Ezekiel H. **M'CLURE**, of Buncombe; and Thomas S. **HOSKINS**, of Edenton.

[50] It is with regret we state, (says the Raleigh Star,) that on Friday morning last, as Gen. *Bridjer J. MONTGOMERY*, the Senator from Hertford county, was taking his departure for home, his horse took flight and ran away; and, in attempting to escape from the gig by leaping out, the General's leg was struck by the wheel, and considerably fractured. He was immediately conducted back to his lodgings, where he at present remains. He is now, however, in a fair way of recovering from his wounds, and it is hoped will, in a short time, be able to resume his journey.

[51] We understand, that the resolution of the late General Assembly, directing the Governor to send some fit person as agent to Washington City, to adjust and settle all the claims of the State against the Uninited [sic] States for expenditures made in defence of the country during the late war, has been complied with by conferring the commission on *William M. SNEED*, Esquire, of Granville. *Ibid.*

[52] RESIGNATION. Plymouth, 17th. Nov. 1829. *To the Honorable Speaker of the House of Commons.* Feeling as I ought, abundantly grateful for the honor conferred on me by the Legislature of this State, as one of the Magistrates of the County of Washington; but, sensible of the great redundancy of that class of our fellow-citizens in attendance on our common Courts of Pleas and Quarter Sessions through this Commonwealth——Satisfied also, that if not at this present time, at *one* not far distant, it will merit legislative correction and interposition, in order to reduce this great engine of electioneering to a *proper* standard and constitutional policy—a system, *sir*, that is never right, excluding *positively* all ideas of intelligence, honor and of reason, and forever associated with what is wrong—an office in which there is too much *honor*, and for 50 years the object of eternal criticism. Unable, sir, to bear any longer the weight of the responsibility attached to that undignified, mischievous, and empyrical way of administering the law, I respectfully tender you my resignation—hoping at the same time *that* though I withdraw myself from this "comedy of eternal errors," I will see the happy time in anticipation of a great reform and amendment in that part of our Judicial system. ... Julian **PICOT**. The above resignation we are told, caused more debate and *fun* in the Legislature, than any thing that occurred during the session. ...

[53] From the U. S. Telegraph. A CARD. The production of some letter writer from Washington is going the round of the opposition presses, implicating the undersigned in regard to a supposed defalcation of Purser **TIMBERLAKE**, deceased. A liberal public cannot expect that the anonymous imputations of the retailers of ribaldry and scandal in shape of letters from Washington, should receive a more particular notice from those who are intended to be affected by them, than is done in the present instance; which is to say, that whenever a responsible name is vouched, in support of the charges referred to, measures will be forthwith taken to unveil the conspiracies by which they have been produced and to prove that the author is a base calumniator. J. H. **EATON**. January 4, 1830.

[54] Summary. Hon. Walter **BOWNE** has been re-elected Mayor of the city of New York, for the present year. ... The venerable Ex-President James **MONROE**, is now on a visit to Washington City. His health continues very feeble.

Judge **WILLIAMS** of Tennessee, who was impeached by the Legislature of that State, some time since, has been acquitted. Harmer **DENNY**, Esq. of Pittsburg, Pa., has been elected to Congress, to supply the vacancy occasioned by Judge **WILKIN**'s resignation. ...

[55] CASH! CASH!! Cash will be given for Fifty Bales of COTTON on delivery, at a fair price, or upon the receipt of Bills of Lading, where the Cotton has been shipped to New York. Alex. **CHESHIRE**. Jan. 23.

[56] *Attention!* The subscriber keeps constantly on hand, a general assortment of Dry Goods, Hard-Ware, Crockery & Groceries, and would be pleased to accommodate his friends and the public, with any

Edenton Gazette 23 January 1830

article in his line, at moderate prices. R. H. **MIDDLETON**. N. B. He respectfully and earnestly requests all persons indebted to him, to call and liquidate their notes and accounts forthwith, as the indulgence given has been sufficient, and longer ought not to be asked. R. H. M. Jan. 23.

[57] State of North Carolina, *Gates County*. Court of Pleas & Quarter Sessions, November Term 1829. David **PARKER** vs. James **WASHINGTON**.} Original Attachment, Levied on Land. It appearing to the satisfaction of the Court, that James **WASHINGTON** is not an inhabitant of this State—It is therefore ordered that publication be made in the Edenton Gazette, for six weeks, that unless the said James **WASHINGTON** do appear at the next Court to be held for said County, at the Court House in Gates, on the third Monday of February next, and replevy, that Judgment will be entered against him &c. Test, J. **SUMNER**, Clerk. Jan. 23.

[58] Seine Twine. FISHERMEN can be supplied with Seine Twine, at 35 cents per pound, payable 1st June next. J. & J. **BRYAN**. *Windsor*, Jan. 4th 1830.

Edenton Gazette.
Vol. XXVI.....No. 5. Edenton, N. C. Saturday Morning, January 30, 1830. Whole No. 1205

[59] [p. 3.] Edenton: Saturday, January 30, 1830. *Distressing Occurrence.*—On Friday the 22d inst. a kitchen on the farm of Clement H. **BLOUNT**, Esq. of this county, and a coloured infant child within it, was entirely consumed by fire. It is supposed that the fire was communicated to some clothes, by a spark falling, as a boy was passing out of the door with a torch in his hand, during the prevalence of a high wind. So rapid was the flame that all attempts to save the infant, proved ineffectual, and no one could have entered the premises, without the forfeit of his life.

[60] Maj. Gen. *E. P. GAINES*, of the U. S. Army, arrived at this place on the 27th inst. and took lodgings at Mrs. **WILLS**'; on the 28th he departed for Washington, N. C. where we believe his family is at present.

[61] Summary. The National Intelligencer contradicts the report of the removal of Philip S. **MARKLY** as Attorney General of Pennsylvania. ...

    John Q. **ADAMS** has been elected a member of the Board of Overseers of Harvard University, in place of Josiah **QUINCY**, elected President.

    A young chemist of Philadelphia, after experiments, thinks the poppy for opium, may be profitably cultivated in the Carolinas and Georgia.

    The Louisville Public Advertiser announces the establishment by the authorities of that city of a school at the public expense, which is stated to be the first south of the Ohio. It is opened to the children of all the citizens, and has two teachers. The number of pupils entered is 300. The building, which is erected at the public expense, is 94 feet long and 42 wide, and three stories high.

    Thomas **NORMAN**, convicted last Fall Circuit, at Guilford Superior Court, of Bigamy, has been pardoned by the Governor. The idle ceremony, of taking him to the Gallows and placing the rope around his neck, was enacted.

    William **CLARK**, who was to have been hung for horse stealing, at Edgefield Court House on Friday the 1st inst. has been pardoned by the Governor.

    Gen. *Samuel HOUSTON*, late Governor of Tennessee, is on a visit to Washington City.

    Suicide.—A dreadful and novel mode of committing this crime was put in practice by a man named **FELLOW**, in Worburn, Delaware, on the 16th ult. He placed a barrel of vinegar in such a manner on the steps of his cellar, that it must roll down: then placing his head on the lowest step, he contrived to set the barrel a going—it of course crushed his head to pumice.

    Arnold NAUDAIN has been chosen a Senator of the United States from the State of Delaware, to fill the [v]acancy occasioned by the resignation of Mr. **MC LANE**, now Minister of England.

[62] MARRIED, In Newbern, on the 13 [?] th inst. John P. **DAVES**, Esq. to Miss Elizabeth B. **GRAHAM**, daughter of Edward **GRAHAM**, Esq.

Edenton Gazette 30 January 1830

On the 21st inst. in Murfreesborough, N. C. by the Rev. Mr. **NIELL**, William B. **WYNNS**, Esq. of Hertford County, to Miss Mary **PIPKIN**, of the former place.

[63] Lavallee Academy, *Sixteen miles immediately above the town of Halifax.* Mrs. Lydia **PHILLIPS** respectfully informs her friends and the public, that the exercises of this institution will be resumed on the 11th day of February.

Having had the benefit of an experience of nearly 18 years in different parts of the U. S. in this employment, she will teach all the branches of education usually taught in the best female Seminaries, viz: Orthography, Reading, Writing, Arithmetic, English Grammar, Geography, Ancient and Modern History, Rhetoric, Natural Philosophy, Astronomy, Chemistry and Botany, Composition, plain and ornamental needle Work and embroidery, drawing, painting, and music on the Piano.—She will also teach French if required. ...

Mrs. **PHILLIPS** thinks it not amiss, to subjoin the following certificate. Bristol, Nov. 1st, 1827. We hereby certify, to all whom it may concern, that Mrs. Lydia **PHILLIPS** is a lady of respectable and unblemished character, that she is, we believe, well qualified to be the instructress of young ladies, an occupation to which she prefers devoting her time and talents, and whatsoever she engages to do, she will faithfully perform; and she is hereby recommended to the favour and patronage of those who may need the services of such a teacher. Alex'r V. **GRISWOLD**, Bishop of the eastern Diocese. Clarkson **DENN**, Rector of Christ Church.

The subscriber informs his friends and the public, that having rented that large and commodious dwelling house, formerly the property of Col. Nevil **GEE** deceased, will be prepared to take boarders for the above seminary at $30 per session of five months, two thirds payable in advance. Every exertion will be made on his part to give satisfaction to those who think proper to put their children or wards under his care. Tippo S. **BROWNLOW**. Halifax, Jan. 15, 1830.

[64] NOTICE. The subscribers will supply Fishermen, & others who want, *SEINE TWINE* of an excellent quality, at 35 cents per pound, payable 1st June. ... They have on hand...a few half-pipes & quarter Casks old London particular Madeira Wine, of a very superior quality imported direct from Madeira... Daily expected from 5 to 10,000 bushels TURKS ISLAND SALT, which they will sell deliverable at any of the Fisheries on the Chowan, Roanoke or Cashie Rivers. **MORGAN, COWPER & CO.** Murfreesboro, Jan. 20.

[65] *HUE AND CRY!* Whereas one Thomas W. **BAKER** committed to the Jail of Chowan County, for a violation of the Revenue Law of the United States, did escape from said Jail on Sunday night last: this is therefore to require all Coroners, Sheriffs, Constables and other officers of this State, to arrest the said *Thomas W. BAKER*, if to be found in their jurisdiction, and commit him again, so that he may be forthcoming to answer said charge. *Thos. W. BAKER* is a resident of the town of Dennis, Massachusetts, aged 25 years, 5 feet 6 inches high, light complexion, dark hair, has a very simple look and to appearance possesses great simplicity of character. Wm. D. **RASCOE**, *Sheriff*. Edenton, Jan. 30th

Edenton Gazette.
Vol. XXVI.....No. 6. Edenton, N. C. Saturday Morning, February 6, 1830. Whole No. 1206

[66] [p. 2] AFRICAN COLONY—We are informed that the brig Liberia, Captain **SHERMAN**, which sailed from this port, the other day, for Monrovia, took out about sixty emigrants for the interesting colony at that place. Of these, we understand fourteen were liberated by Robert **BRADEN** dec'd. of Loudoun county; five by John **BRADEN** of do.: one by Albert **HEATON** of do; one by Townsend **HEATON** of do.; one by Mr. **BLACKFORD** of Fredericksburg; five by Mr. **WINSTON** of Richmond; one by J. **SCOTT** of Murfreesborough, North Carolina; and the rest were free people of color, nine of whom were from Loudon, and seven from Lynchburg. Among them, was a preacher by the name of **ERSKINE**, of good character for piety and talent, with his whole family, twelve in all. In addition to those, there were about thirty liberated by Joseph **EARLY**, Esq. of Greensborough, Georgia who were to have sailed in this vessel, but who arrived here a little too late; and are now in town waiting for the next opportunity.

Edenton Gazette 6 February 1830

We are gratified to learn, also, that two missionaries from the Missionary Society, of Basle, in Switzerland, Rudolf **DIETSCHY**, and H. **GRANOR**, went out in the brig, to join another of their brethren at the settlement. The whole accompanied by a physician, Dr. J. **ANDERSON**, will be valuable reinforcement to the flourishing colony which has been so happily planted at the Cape. [*Nor. Her.*

[67] [p. 3] Edenton: Saturday, February 6, 1830. ... On the morning of the 3rd inst. an inquest was held over the body of Mr. Absalom **PRITCHARD**, of this county—verdict of the jury, that he came to his death in consequence of having broken a blood-vessel, while in a violent fit of coughing.

[68] *Supreme Court.* Wm. E. **PUGH**, of Gates County, and Joseph W. **TOWNSEND** of Perquimans, have obtained license to practice law in the County Courts of this State.

[69] By a proof slip received at Norfolk from the editor of the New Orleans Bee, we learn that a Fire broke out in New Orleans on the 13th ult. in the Horse press and Cotton Warehouse, occupied by Messrs. N. & B. **HART**. It is understood that 8,000 bales of Cotton were consumed, together with the buildings—the loss is estimated at $300,000.

[70] *Richard BUSH*, Esq. who has been negociating loans in Europe for the Ohio and Chesapeake Canal has returned in the packet ship Canada.

[71] MARRIED, In Tarborough on the 19th Jan. Mr. James H. **HARTMUS**, formerly of this place, to Mrs. Frances **OUTLAW**, of the former place.

[72] DIED, In this County on the 25th ult. after a short indisposition Mrs. Lavinia **WELCH**, consort of Mr. John **WELCH**, leaving her relations and friends to mourn their irreparable loss.

In this County on Saturday last after a short illness Mrs. Elizabeth **EVANS**, consort of the Rev. Zachariah **EVANS**.

[73] *LOOK HERE Farmers & Merchants!* William **COFFIELD**, at No. 16, Market Square, Norfolk, VA. Will take pleasure in selling and purchasing all kinds of PRODUCE, to the best advantage for his friends and the Public.—Punctuallity shall guide him, as an increase of business, is his most ardent desire. W. C. keeps for sale at the above named place, a general and handsome assortment of Fancy and other DRY GOODS, at the most reduced prices. Feb. 6.

[74] NOTICE. The subscriber at the last December Term of Chowan County Court, qualified as Administrator on the estate of *William C. ROBERTS*, deceased, and hereby requests all persons indebted to the estate, to come forward and make payment without delay; those to whom the estate is indebted, are requested to present their claims duly authenticated, for payment, within the time prescribed by law; or this notice will be plead in bar of a recovery. Jos. H. **SKINNER**, *Adm'r.* Feb. 6.

Edenton Gazette.
Vol. XXVI.....No. 7. Edenton, N. C. Saturday Morning, February 13, 1830. Whole No. 1270. [sic]

[75] [p. 2] The U. S. Ship *Natchez*, Capt. Alexander **CLAXTON**, bearing the broad pennant of Com. John Orde **CREIGHTON**, late comander in chief of the Naval Forces on the Brazilian station, arrived in Hampton Roads on the 3d inst. *Norfolk paper.*

[76] Summary. The Wilmington Reporter of the 26th ult. states that the Small Pox, recently reported to have broken out there, has entirely disappeared. ...

The Hon. G. M. **TROUP** arrived in Augusta from Washington on the 27th ult. We regret to state that he left his seat in the senate in consequence of the illness of one of his family.

Small Pox.—It is with regret we learn that there are several cases of the Small Pox in Newbern. The commissioners of that town, we understand, have taken the necessary measures to prevent the spread of the disease, and that hopes are entertained that in a short time all danger from its contagion will be re-

Edenton Gazette 13 February 1830

moved.

The Cherokees.—The Editor of the Cherokee Phenix, states that he has the signatures of 1000 Indians to a memorial about to be presented to Congress, deprecating a removal to the western wilderness.

Peter FORCE, Esq. late proprietor has disposed of the establishment of the "National Journal," to George **WALTERSTON**, Esq. of Washington, (late Librarian to Congress,) by whom it will be published hereafter.

New-Hampshire. The election of Governor in New-Hampshire takes place early in March. The candidates in nomination for the office are Gen. Timothy **UPHAM**, late Collector of Portsmouth; who will be supported by the anti-**JACKSON** party; and Hon. Matthew **HARVEY**, who is the candidate of the friends of the national administration.

Rhode Island.—There are two candidates in nomination in this state for the office of Governor, viz: His Excellency James **FENNER**, and Dr. Asa **MESSER**, late President of Brown University.

[77] [p. 3] Edenton: Saturday, February 13, 1830. ... Our Town for a few days past, has shown more the appearance of business (though in fact no real change has taken place) than is usual, growing out of the curiosity excited in our good citizens, to see the Menagerie of Animals now exhibiting in this place. Money is scarce and we dislike to hear of any of the small quantity in circulation among us, being carried away; yet those who have a spare quarter will get the value of their money, in viewing these wonders of nature.

[78] It is stated in an Alabama paper, that the Rev. William **HOOPER**, at present one of the Faculty of our University, has been elected Professor of Languages in the University of Alabama. The Fayetteville Observer says, he has accepted the appointment.

[79] *Departure of the Steam Boat N. Carolina.*—The Norfolk Beacon of the 6th says, this fine boat, so well adapted by her light draft of water, for navigating the waters of the upper Roanoke left that place on Wednesday evening last, coastwise, for Elizabeth City, N. C. to assume her duties as a passage and tow Boat on the Roanoke. She is owned by the Virginia and North Carolina Transportation Company, and commanded by Capt. **PEDRICK**.

[80] Congressional. SENATE. *Jan.* 25. Mr. **BROWN** presented a resolution of the Legislature of North-Carolina, instructing the Delegation from that State in Congress to procure the repeal of the duty on Salt. Referred to the Committee on Finance. ... Mr. **IREDELL** also presented a petition from Sam'l. **SIMPSON** of Newbern, for a remission of the additional duties on certain goods imported by him on the 1st July, 1828.

[81] DIED, In this town on the 5th inst. Thomas Cox, infant son of Mr. John **CHESHIRE** of this place.

[82] LIST OF LETTERS Remaining in the Post Office Plymouth, N. C. Jan'y 1st 1830, and if not taken out, will be sent to the General Post Office, April 1st next as Dead Letters. James **BLOUNT**, jr. Capt. Reuben F. **DODGE**, William S. **ELLIS**, Mrs. Patsey **GREEN**, Henry **HARDY**, Abner S. **JACKSON**, John C. **PETTIJOHN**, Jordan J. **PHELPS**, Chas. H. **PHELPS**, Thos. W. **RASCOE**, Peter **RAYMOND**, Capt. Jos. **STARR**, Uriah W. **SWANNER**—3. W. A. **TURNER**, P. M. Feb. 4.

Edenton Gazette.
Vol. XXVI.....No. 8. Edenton, N. C. Saturday Morning, February 21, 1830. Whole No. 1208

[83] [p. 2] A General Naval Court Martial assembled in Washington on Monday last, for the trial of such officers as may be brought before it. The Court is composed as follows: Capt. Charles G. **RIDGELY**, Prest. Capt. Joseph l. **NICHOLSON**, Capt. Edmund P. **KENNEDY**, Capt. Thomas Ap. Catesby **JONES**. Master Com. Wm. B. **SHUBRICK**, Master Com. Chas. W. **MORGAN**, Master Com. Beverly **KENNON**, Lieutenant Isaac **M'KEVER**, Lieutenant Charles S. **M'CAULEY**. H. M. **MORFITT**, Esq. Judge Advocate. ... *Nat. Int.*

Edenton Gazette 21 February 1830

[84] PROCEEDINGS OF THE CONVENTION. At a meeting of Delegates assembled at *Edenton*, N. C. on Monday the 15th February 1830, for the purpose of memorializing Congress on the subject of re-opening Roanoke Inlet at or near Naggs Head. Doctor James **NORCOM** was called to the chair, and Thomas **COX** appointed Secretary.

The following gentlemen appeared as representatives from the Counties herein after named, viz: Malachi S. **LEWIS**, Thomas **DOZIER**, *from Camden*; Jordan A. **WRIGHT**, Exum **NEWBY**, *from Pasquotank*; Josiah **COLLINS**, Wm. R. **NORCOM**, Joseph B. **SKINNER**, Joseph H. **SKINNER**, James **NORCOM**, Richard T. **BROWNRIGG**, *from Chowan*, Jeptha **FOWLKES**, Edward R. **HUNTER**, Richard H. **PARKER**, *from Gates;* James **MORGAN**, John A. **ANDERSON**, John H. **WHEELER**, *from Hertford*; Stark **ARMISTEAD**, Alexander W. **MEBANE**, *from Bertie*; Thomas B. **HAUGHTON**, Thomas **COX**, *from Washington*; Daniel N. **BATEMAN**, John **HAUGHTON**, *from Tyrrell;* D. W. **BAGLEY**, Thomas W. **WATTS**, Asa **BIGGS**, *from Martin*.

On motion. *Resolved*, that a Committee consisting of two of the Delegates from each County, be formed for the purpose of preparing an exhibit, showing the annual loss sustained by the Counties interested in the commerce of Albemarle, for the want of a direct communication with the Ocean.

Resolved further, that the said committee, prepare a memorial to Congress on this subject, and make report to this Convention.

Resolved also, that the chairman appoint this committee, and that he be further authorized, in the event of any delegates arriving from other counties not now represented in this convention, to add to this committee, two members from each county, whose delegates may hereafter arrive.

The committee so appointed consisted of Messrs. Malachi S. **LEWIS**, Thomas **DOZIER**, *from Camden*; Jordan A. **WRIGHT**, Exum **NEWBY**, *from Pasquotank*; Wm. R. **NORCOM**, Joseph B. **SKINNER**, *from Chowan*, Jeptha **FOWLKES**, Edward R. **HUNTER**, *from Gates;* James **MORGAN**, John A. **ANDERSON**, *from Hertford*; Stark **ARMISTEAD**, Alexander W. **MEBANE**, *from Bertie*; Thomas B. **HAUGHTON**, Thomas **COX**, *from Washington*; Daniel N. **BATEMAN**, John **HAUGHTON**, *from Tyrrell;* D. W. **BAGLEY**, Thomas W. **WATTS**, Asa **BIGGS**, *from Martin*.

Resolved, that this Meeting adjourn until to-morrow 10 o'clock.

Tuesday, Feb. 10. The Convention met according to adjournment, and the proceedings of yesterday were read and approved. The Committee appointed yesterday...reported a memorial for that purpose; which report and memorial were read and approved.

Resolved, that 50 Copies of the proceedings of this meeting of delegates be printed, and that a copy be sent to each of our Senators and Representatives in Congress; and that our Senators be requested, and our Representatives instructed, to use their best endeavours to procure from Congress, such appropriations as may be necessary to open an Inlet at or near Naggs Head, as prayed for in our memorial.

Resolved, that 500 copies of the proceedings of this meeting be printed, and that ten copies thereof, be sent to each of the following Counties, viz: Currituck, Camden, Pasquotank, Perquimans, Gates, Chowan, Hertford, Bertie, Washington, Tyrrell, Martin, Northampton, Halifax, Edgecombe, Nash, Warren, Franklin, Wake, Granville, Person, Orange, Caswell, Guilford, Rockingham, Stokes and Surry, in North Carolina; and the Counties of Southampton, Sussex, Greensville, Brunswick, Nansemond, Franklin, Patrick Henry, Bedford, Pittsylvania, Halifax, Charlotte, Lunenburg, Mecklenburg, Montgomery, Botetourt, Campbell, Nottaway, Isle of Wight, Grayson, Washington and Wythe, in Virginia... requesting such Counties as are not represented in this Convention, to co-operate with us, in soliciting the aid of Congress, to open an Inlet at or near Nagg's Head; and that they take speedy measures to make known their proceedings to Congress. ... Whereupon the Convention adjourned *sine die*. James **NORCOM**, *Chairman*. Thomas **COX**, *Secretary*. ...

[85] [p. 3] Edenton: Saturday, February 20, [sic] 1830. ... *State Bank of North Carolina*. At a meeting of the Directors of this institution at their Banking house in Raleigh on the 8th inst. agreeably to the terms of the extension of their charter, by the last Legislature, they proceeded to reduce the Directors at the several branches, from thirteen to seven; those appointed to conduct the Branch in this place are as follows. George W. **BARNEY**, *President*. James **BOZMAN**, Jos. **MANNING**, John **COX**, James **WILLS**, J. B. G. **ROULHAC**, and Charles W. **MIXSON**. We learn from a gentleman recently from Fayetteville, that the branch of the State Bank at that place, has been discontinued.

Edenton Gazette 21 February 1830

[86] We stated in our last on the authority of the Newbern Spectator, that several cases of the Small Pox had occurred in that place; we learn since from the same source, that the Faculty have pronounced the disease to be the *Varioloid*. If this disease is as fatal as it was in some of the nothern cities a few years since, it is as much to be dreaded as the Small Pox. The Commissioners of the town of Beaufort, are so apprehensive of danger, that they have ordered all communication between Newbern and that place, to be suspended.

[87] *Case of Rowland STEPHENSON.*—We learn from our correspondent of the Savannah Republican office, that Geo. **MILLEN** and William **WILLIAMS**, the parties who entered the plea of guilty to the indictment against them in the affair of Rowland **STEPHENSON**, were sentenced by Judge **HOLT**, on the 1st instant, the former to a fine of one thousand dollars and six months imprisonment—the latter to a fine of five hundred dollars, and imprisonment for three months.—*Ch. Cour.*

[88] MARRIED, In Bertie County, on Thursday the 4th inst. by the Rev. Mr. **LAWRENCE**, Mr. Richard **WILDER** of this County, to Miss Harriet **HARDY** of the former County.

[89] DIED, At his residence in this Town on Wednesday last, John **CHESHIRE**, Esq. who [?] ___ respectable and useful member of our community, leaving a wife and several children to mourn their severe bereavement.

[90] Trust Sale. On the 2d day of March next in the town of Plymouth, all the real and personal estate of Messrs. *Thos. & Wm. A. TURNER*, will be sold on a credit, by virtue of a deed in trust executed by them to *Stark ARMISTEAD* for certain purposes therein set forth. The terms will be more fully made known on the day of sale by The Trustee. Windsor, Feb. 10, 1830.

[91] To Merchants, Planters And *MANUFACTURERS*. Nathaniel F. **WILLIAMS** tenders his services to his friends and the public, to transact business on Commission, and respectfully refers to the gentlemen named below, for his qualifications. References. Hon. *Sam'l SMITH*, Hon. *E. F. CHAMBERS*, Senators in Congress from Maryland. Hon. *John FORSYTH*, Senator in Congress from Georgia. Hon. *Daniel WEBSTER*, Senator in Congress from Massachusetts. Hon. *Lewis WILLIAMS*, Representative in Congress from North Carolina. Hon. *Warren R. DAVIS*, Representative in Congress from South Carolina. Messrs. *MACDONALD & RIDGELY*, *William LORMAN*, esq. *Luke TIERNAN*, esq. *Isaac M'KIM*, esq. of Baltimore. Baltimore Feb. 1830

Edenton Gazette.
Vol. XXVI.....No. 9. Edenton, N. C. Saturday Morning, February 27, 1830. Whole No. 1209

[92] [p. 2] Summary. Thomas **BIDDLE**, Esq. of Philadelphia, has offered to loan to Pennsylvania, 4,000,000 for 25 years, at 5 per cent.

It is said that Col. R. M. **JOHNSON**, of the House of Representatives, will in a few days, make a report to the house upon the many petitions presented to Congress relative to the transportation of the mail on Sunday.

Fanny **WRIGHT** has chartered a vessel at New-Orleans for the transportation of herself and thirty slaves to St. Domingo, where she proposes to settle and establish them in freedom.

Robert H. **ANDERSON**, Esq. has been elected U. S. Senator from Mississippi, to supply the vacancy occasioned by the death of Thomas B. **REID**, Esq.

Tobias WATKINS.—The petition of this individual for a writ of habeas corpus, has been rejected by the Supreme Court of the United States.

Gen. *Geo. RUST*, of Loudon county, VA. has been appointed Superintendent of the United States Armory at **HARPER**'s Ferry, in the place of Colonel **DUNN**, an account of whose assassination was given in our last paper.

J. M. GOODENOW, a representative in Congress, and Elijah **HAYWARD**, of Cincinnati, have been elected Judges of the Supreme Court of Ohio.

John G. **HUNTOON** Esq. has been elected Governor of the State of Maine.

Edenton Gazette 27 February 1830

[93] [p. 3] Edenton: Saturday, February 27, 1820. ... Washington, Feb. 13. *Appointments by the President, by and with the advice and consent of the Senate.* Louis **MC LANE**, of Delaware, to be Envoy Extraordinary and Minister Plenipotentiary of the United States, at the Court of the United Kingdom of Great Britain and Ireland, vice James **BARBOUR**.

William C. RIVES, of Virginia, to be Envoy Extraordinary and Minister Plenipotentiary of the United States to the Court of His Most Christian Majesty the King of France and Navarre, vice James **BROWN**, resigned.

William Pitt PREBLE, of Maine, to be Envoy Extraordinary and Minister Plenipotentiary of the United States at the Court of His Majesty the King of the Netherlands.

Cornelius P. VAN NESS, of Vermont, to be Envoy Extraordinary and Minister Plenipotentiary of the United States at the Court of His Catholic Majesty, in the place of Alexander H. **EVERETT** recalled.

Washington IRVING, of N. York, to be Secretary of Legation of the United States to his Britannic Majesty, in place of William Beach **LAWRENCE**.

Charles Carroll HARPER, of Maryland, to be Secretary of Legation of the United States to His Majesty the King of France and Navarre, in place of John Adams **SMITH**.

Auguste DAVEZAC, of Louisiana, to be Secretary of Legation of the United States of America at the Court of His Majesty the King of the Netherlands.

J. C. PICKETT, of Virginia, to be Secretary of Legation of the United States to the Republic of Colombia.

William J. DUANE, of Philadelphia, to be Director of the Bank of the United States, in the place of Nicholas **BIDDLE**, who declined accepting the commission transmitted to him by the Government, having been previously elected by the Stock holders of the Bank a Director.

James CAMPBELL, of New-York, to be a Director of the Bank of the United States, Benjamin **BAILY** having declined the appointment.

Richard W. GREEN, of Rhode Island, to be Attorney of the United States for the District of Rhode-Island.—[*U. S. Telegraph.*

[94] The Columbian (Georgetown, D. C.) Gazette, of Saturday, says, "We understand, on good authority that the Senate yesterday rejected the nomination of Henry **LEE**, as Consul General to Algiers.

[95] *Something new under the Sun.*—Silvanus **MILLER**, who holds the office of public administrator of New York, has laid before the city authority, a communication in which he states, that the salary, allowed by the revised statutes, for his office is quite too large.

[96] MARRIED, In Perquimans on Wednesday 17th inst. by the Rev. B. **NIXSON**, Mr. Sam'l **NEWBY** to Miss Martha Ann **PERRY**, daughter of Josiah **PERRY**, Esq.

At Mr. Myles **ELLIOTT**'s in the town of Hertford, on Thursday the 18th inst. by Henry **SKINNER** Esq. Mr. Exum **ELLIOTT** to Miss Eliza **POOL**, all of that place.

In Jackson County, Florida, on Thursday, the 7th January last by the Rev. Richard **HOLMES**, Mr. Thomas H. **EVERETT**, formerly of this County, to Miss Rebecca G. **SPEARS** of the former place.

[97] DIED, In Perquimans County, on the 22d inst. Mrs. Martha **WHITE**, consort of Mr. Andrew **WHITE** of that county.

[98] Trust Sale. By virtue of a Deed of Trust, executed by Clement H. **BLOUNT**, for certain purposes therein mentioned; the subscriber will offer for sale before the Court House door in the town of Edenton, on the 27th day of April next, from 10 to 20 likely NEGROES, the property of said **BLOUNT**. Terms Cash. Wm. R. **NORCOM**, *Trustee.* Edenton, Feb. 27th.

[99] New Goods. The Subscriber has just received from New-York...Fine Linen Tapes; Oil Cloth; Bedtick; Spool Cotton; Loaf and Lump Sugar; Family Flour and Soap; ALSO, An elegant mantle Looking-Glass, which he will sell low. James **WILLS**. Edenton, Feb. 27.

Edenton Gazette.
Vol. XXVI.....No. 10.   Edenton, N. C. Saturday Morning, March 6, 1830.   Whole No. 1210

Edenton Gazette 6 March 1830

[100] [p. 2] CONGRESSIONAL. *Tuesday, Feb.* 23. ... A petition was also presented by Mr. **WHITTLESEY**, from *Eleza* **BASSETT**, of Ohio, for a pension, on account of having served nine months as a soldier during the War of the Revolution. ...*Telegraph.*

[101] From the National Intelligencer of Thursday. The Army Court Martial, of which Gen. **ATKINSON** is President, which was to have assembled in this city on Monday last, did not form a quorum till yesterday, owing to the non-arrival of some of the members. We understand that this Court convenes for the trial of Col. *Roger* **JONES** Adjutant General of the Army upon a charge, preferred by the Commanding General, of official mis-conduct, or breach of Army Regulation, which consists in his having signed certain general orders as by order of the Secretary of War, instead of as by order of the Commanding General. ...

[102] [p. 3] Edenton: Saturday, March 6, 1830. ... *Melancholy.*—We learn that captain *James* **HACKETT**, master of the Sch'r Flag of Truce of this port, while on his passage from this place to Baltimore, fell overboard at sea and was drowned.

[103] Among the appointments made by the President, by and with the advice and consent of the Senate, we observe the following: Henry **MUSE**, Surveyor and Inspector of the port of Urbanna, Va. from 29th of Jan. 1830. Levi **FAGAN**, Collector and Inspector of the port of Plymouth, N. C. from 19th of Feb. 1830. Thomas H. **BLOUNT**, Collector and Inspector for the port of Washington, N. C. from 19th of February 1830.

[104] Summary. The National Intelligencer of Friday states—"it is rumored and believed, that on Wednesday, the nomination of Mr. **WILLIAMS**, to be Collector of the port of N. Bedford, vice Russell **FREEMAN**, removed, was rejected, by a vote of 34 to 11."

[105] MARRIED, In Raleigh on the 15th ult. by Rev. Geo. W. **FREEMAN**, John S. **BRYAN**, Esq. merchant, of Plymouth, to Miss Lucy D. **HAYWOOD**, daughter of Sherwood **HAYWOOD**, dec'd.

[106] DIED, In the city of New York on the 17th ultimo Colonel Henry **RUTGERS**, in the 85th year of his age.

Edenton Gazette.
Vol. XXVI.....No. 11. Edenton, N. C. Saturday Morning, March 13, 1830. Whole No. 1211

[107] [p. 2] The Methodist Conference. Richmond, *Feb.* 27. For several days our city has been the resort of a multitude of persons of both sexes, who have come from different quarters to attend the *Methodist Conference.* ... The conference commenced on Wednesday the 17th inst, and was concluded on Thursday the 25th inst. We have been favored with the following appointment of the Preachers, (made during the Conference,) for the present year: *James River District*—Lewis **SKIDMORE**, P. E. *Richmond*, Shockoe Hill, Wm. J. **WALLER**; Trinity, W. A. **SMITH**. *Williamsburg*, Samuel **HARRELL**, David **WOOD**. *Gloucester*, Geo. A. **BAIN**, Robert J. **CARSON**. *Caroline*, Josh. **LEIGH**, J. E. **DAVIDSON**. *Hanover*, Philip **ANDERSON**, Joseph A. **BROWN**. *Culpeper*, Robt. **BAILY**, Wm. B. **ROWZEC**. *Charlottsville*, John A. **MILLER**, Lorenzo **LEA**. *Amherst*, J. **BOYD**, H. S. **PEYTON**. *Columbia*, Robert **SCOTT**, Rufus **LEDBETTER**, *supernumerary*. *Meherrin District*, John **EARLY**, P. E. *Lynchburg*, Martin P. **PARKS**. *Petersburg*, Bennet T. **BLAKE**. *Bedford*, H. **ALLEY**, J. **POWERS**. *Campbell*, C. **LEACH**, I. **SOULE**. *Buckingham*, Bennett T. **MAXEY**, Albert G. **BURTON**. *Greensville*, Wm. H. **STARR**, Anthony **DIBBLE**. *Mecklenburg.* John W. **CHILDS**, Rowland G. **BASS**. *Brunswick*, Jas. **MC ADEN**, Wm. W. **KEININGHAM**. *Amelia*, John W. **WHITE**, Geo. W. **LANGHORN**. *Chesterfield*, John **KERR**, Samuel T. **MOORMAN**. *Sussex*, George **MAHOOD**, James **M'DONALD**. *Neuse District*, Jos. **CARSON**, P. E. *Newbern*, Leroy M. **LEE**. *Raleigh City*, Abram **PENN**. *Raleigh Circuit*, Wm. **COMPTON**. *Trent*, A. **NORMAN**, D. **WATERS** jr. *Beaufort*, John D. **HOLSTEAD**. *Straights*, Henry J. **EVANS**. *Black River*, Jos. W. **BELL**, John J. **CARTER**. *Tar River*, Henry **SPECK**, Henry D. **WEATHERLY**. *Topsail Inlet*, Isaac **HAYNES**.

Edenton Gazette 13 March 1830

Haw River, J. **REID**, J. J. **HICKS**. *Snow Hill*, William **ANDERSON**, Thomas S. **RANSON**. *Yadkin District*, M. **BROCK**, P. E. *Yadkin Circuit*, Stephen W. **WINBOURNE**, Joshua **BETHELL**. *Iredell*, J. **GOODMAN**, T. J. **STARR**. *Salisbury*, Benjamin **KIDD**. *Shallow Ford*, Samuel D. **TOMPKINS**, Henry D. **FORD**. *Franklin*, B. **FIELD**, Jas. N. **LEA**. *Guilford*, Peter **DOUB**. *Caswell*, Jno. W. **WATSON**, Jno. J. **HEAD**. *Bannister*, Phails **MC DONALD** *Orange*, Charles P. **MOORMAN**. *Norfolk District*, Thos. **CROWDER**, P. E. *Norfolk*, George W. **NOLLY**. *Portsmouth*, Abram **HARRELL**. *Edenton*, Thomas **BARNUM**. *Elizabeth City*, Vernon **ESKRIDGE**. *Murfreesboro*, James **DEY**. *Gates and Bertie*, Jas. **MORRISON**, *one to be supplied*. *Suffolk*, Irwin **ATKINSON**. *Princess Anne*, Thos. V. **WEBB**, Horatio N. **BUCTROUT**. *Camden*, Jonathan **WILLIAMS**. *Surry*, S. **NORMAN**, D. **FISHER**. *Roanoke District*, Benj. **DEVANY**, P. E. *Roanoke Circuit*, T. R. **BRAME**, James **JENISON**. *Granville*, Wm. **HOLMES**, George W. **DYE**. *Washington*, George N. **GREGORY**. *Plymouth*, Wilson **BARCLIFF**. *Albemarle Sound*, William M. **SCHOOLFIELD**. *Banks and Islands*, Miles **FOY**. *Portsmouth and Ocracock*, Raymond R. **MINOR**. *Mattamuskeet*, David S. **DOGGETT**. *Neuse and Pamplico*, Thompson **GARRARD**, Benjamin M. **BARNES**. *Halifax*, Stephen W. **JONES**. Dan. [?] **HALL**, Conference Missionary Agent. William **HAMMETT**, not returned from Ireland. Hez. G. **LEIGH**, College Agent. The next Conference to be held at Newbern, Feb. 16th, 1831. *Compiler*.

[108] [p. 3] Edenton: Saturday, March 13, 1830. ... The editor of the Freeman's Echo, Washington, N. C. has given notice to his patrons and the public, that he has entered into copartnership with Mr. Wm. C. **CARRINGTON**, and that arrangements have been made to procure the necessary materials for enlarging and improving a newspaper, to be issued as soon as the materials shall arrive, under title of the "*Washington Times*," after which he intends discontinuing the Echo. ...

[109] MARRIED, In this county on the 18th ult. by William **GREGORY**, Esq. Mr. John **BEASLEY**, to Miss Elizabeth **WOOD**, daughter of Mr. Rich'd **WOOD**.

In Washington City, on the 25th ult. by the Rev. Mr. **JOHNS**, the Hon. Augustine H. **SHEPPARD**, a representative in congress from this State, to Miss Martha **TURNER**, youngest daughter of Mrs. Mary **TURNER**, of that city.

At Norfolk on the 4th inst. by the Rev. Dr. **DUCACHET**, Clark **LILLYBRIDGE**, M. D. to Miss Clarissa **COFFIELD** of that place.

[110] DIED, In Elizabeth City, N. C. on the 3rd inst. after an illness of several months, Miss Mary **CLUFF**, youngest sister of Matthew **CLUFF**, Esq. merchant of that place.

[111] Sale of Law and other BOOKS. Will be offered for sale at the Court-House at Winton on the 22d inst., being the first day of the Superior Court of Law and Equity, the LAW LIBRARY and the valuable collection of Historical, Classical and other *Miscellaneous Works*, belonging to the late *Henry W. LONG*, Esq. The Law Library is inferior to none in the State, and well merits the attention of the gentlemen of the Bar. Terms of sale, on a credit of six months by the purchasers giving bond, with approved security. R. G. **COWPER**, *Adm'r. Hertford Co. March 8th*.

[112] $15 Reward. Escaped from the Jail of Beaufort County on the night of the 24th inst. Miles **SPIER**, Churchill **PURSER**, & Thos. **PERRY**. The sum of ten dollars will be given for the apprehension of **SPIER**, five dollars for **PERRY**, and five cents for **PURSER**. **SPIER** is a brother to Robert **SPIER** who was tried at Newbern for the murder of John **WILLIAMS**. SPIER is a man of small stature, thin visage, sallow complexion, and has a down look when spoken to. He was born and raised in Pitt County, but has latterly resided in Beaufort; he is well known in both Counties. He was committed at the last Term of Beaufort County Court on a charge of grand larceny. **PERRY** is about 18 years of age, thick set, light complexion, and speaks quick. He is a native of Currituck County, and was committed under a *Capias* on a charge of *Assault* and *Battery*. **PURSER** is so well known in this County, that a particular description of him is deemed unnecessary. Allen **GRIST**, *Sh'ff*. Washington, Feb. 25th.

Edenton Gazette.
Vol. XXVI.....No. 12. Edenton, N. C. Saturday Morning, March 20, 1830. Whole No. 1212

Edenton Gazette 20 March 1830

[113] [p. 2] *Rice Flour.*—There has been left with us for public inspection, a sample of Rice Flour ground at the mill of Elias **HORRY**, Esq. on Santee; a small supply of which has been received for sale, by Messrs. **CHISOLM** and **TAYLOR**, at the rate of 3 cents per pound. It is very finely bolted, and does not suffer in appearance when compared with superfine wheat flour. ... *Charleston Courier.*

[114] *Distressing Accident.*—The Norfolk papers announce the death of Mr. *John HARRELL*, of Hertford county, under the following afflicting circumstances: Mr. **HARREL** [sic] was returning home from court on Monday, the 22d ultimo, with his little son in a gig; when the horse took fright, and, whilst endeavoring to pull him in the reins broke. Having thus lost all control over the horse, Mr. **H**. desired his son to jump out, who did so, and escaped without injury. The father then attempted to escape from the vehicle in the same manner, but, unfortunately, the wheel came in contact with his head, and fractured the temple bone. He lingered until the following evening, when he expired.

[115] [p. 3] Edenton: Saturday, March 20, [sic] 1830. ... The Halifax Minerva has altered its name to that of the *Roanoke Advocate*.

[116] LAW CASE. Important Legal Decision. The Supreme Court of the United States have, at their present term, settled an important and hitherto embarrassing question, in the case of Samuel D. **HARRIS**, Marshal of Massachussetts, plaintiff in error, *v.* James **DENNIE**, Deputy Sheriff of the county of Suffolk. It was a writ of error from the Supreme Judicial Court of Massachusetts, and the question was respecting the validity of attachments under the State laws of goods imported *before entry*, and while in the custody of the custom house officers under the lien of the United States for the duties.—The cause was argued by the District Attorney for Massachusetts and the Attorney General of the United States for the Marshal, and by Mr. **WEBSTER** for the defendant in error; and the Supreme Court...have reversed the judgment of the Supreme Judicial Court of Massachusetts, upon the grounds stated in the following letter from the Reporter:--*Washington City Feb 22, 1830: Chamber of the S. C. U. States.}* Andrew **DUNLAP**, Esq. Boston:--Dear Sir—The Court this day decided the case of *HARRIS* v. *DENNIE*, reversing the judgement of the State Court, and ordering a mandate "to that Court, with directions to enter judgment upon the special verdict in favor of the original defendant." ... Richard **PETERS**, Reporter.

[117] Summary. ... On Friday last, Gen. John **FLOYD** took the oaths of office, and entered upon the duties of Governor of Virginia. ... The Rev. Sidney **WELLER** has been appointed Post Master at Brinleyville [sic] in Halifax County—the Office is kept at the Brinkleyville Academy. ...

[118] DIED, On Friday the 5th inst. at Raleigh, the Right Reverend John S. **RAVENSCROFT**, D. D. Bishop of the Diocess of North Carolina. In the death of this good and great man, the cause of pure and undefiled religion has lost an able and zealous advocate—the Episcopal Church of North Carolina has lost its brightest ornament, its pious and venerated head—society has lost its friend, its guide, its instructor, and the tongue of the most eloquent preacher of the day, is laid low in the dust. It is hoped, that some friend possessed of the materials, will furnish the public with a correct biographical sketch of the life of Bishop **RAVENSCROFT**.

[119] The High Blooded Horse ARCHIE, Belonging to *Jas. C. JOHNSTON*, will stand this season, which will commence the 10th of March and close the 10th of June next, at the residence of the owner in Chowan, and on his farm in Pasquotank County, at the following price viz: $5 for the single leap and $10 for the season, if paid by the 10th of June next—if paid after the expiration of that time, $6 and $12 will be required, with an addition of 37½ cents on each mare for the groom. James **PALMER**. Pasquotank, March 5.

Edenton Gazette.
Vol. XXVI.....No. 13. Edenton, N. C. Saturday Morning, March 27, 1830. Whole No. 1213

[120] [p. 2] Summary. Miss Frances **WRIGHT** arrived at Port au Prince, in a vessel from New Orleans. She has with her, 21 liberated slaves, and a cargo of provisions; which she intends selling for their benefit...

Edenton Gazette 27 March 1830

[121] Within the last year, the office of the Bank of the United States in Fayetteville, (N. C.) has received from dealers $30,863 in gold, (bars) the produce of the North Carolina mines.

Robert **LUCAS**, Speaker of the Senate of Ohio, has been nominated as the **JACKSON** candidate for the office of Governor.

We understand says the National Journal of Saturday, that the Senate has confirmed the nomination of James A. **HAMILTON**, of N. York, to be United States Attorney in the state of New York, in the place of John **DUER**; of David **PORTER**, to be Consul General at Algiers; of William B. **LEWIS**, to be Second Auditor, and of several Collectors.

[122] New Goods. *James GORHAM* Has just received from New York the following articles, calculated for the present and approaching seasons, and further supplies are expected by the first arrivals. Rich gauze Ribbons; gro de nap do. Black Tafeta do; col'd fringed do. White Italian do. ... Tambored Caps; Elegant worked Lace do. Ladies Gloves...Black & White silk Hose for ladies; Gentlemens white Silk ½ do.... March, 23.

[123] [p. 2] Edenton: Saturday, March 27, 1830. [This column usually appears on page 3.] [p. 3] *Longevity.*—There is living near Chambersburg, Pa. a man of the name of John **HILL**, who, from the best information that can be obtained from himself and others, is between 120 and 130 years of age! He served George the I, II and III, as a soldier—the latter, the last time in this country, under General **BRADDOCK**, and was considered too old for a soldier when our revolutionary war broke out! He enjoys pretty good health at present, and appears likely yet to have some years in store.

[124] Trust Sale. By virtue of a deed of Trust executed to the subscriber by *Thomas V. HATHAWAY*, to secure certain debts therein named, I will expose to public sale, on Monday the 5th day of April next, before the Court House in the town of Edenton, between Twenty And Thirty *LIKELY NEGROES*, consisting of men, women, boys and girls, among which is an excellent Blacksmith and several first rate house-servants. At the same time and place will be sold a House and part of a lot, adjoining the property of Malachi **HAUGHTON**, Esq. on the corner of Church and Oakum streets, also about 74 Acres of LAND in the county of Chowan, adjoining the lands of Jos. **M'KEEL** and Thomas M. **CARTER**, Esquires. Terms made known on the day of sale. N. **BRUER**, *Trustee*. Edenton, Mar. 17, 1830.

[125] United States of America, *North Carolina District.*} *ss.* Whereas the Attorney for the United States, for the District aforesaid, hath exhibited his libel to the Honorable the District Judge for the said District, setting forth that *Charles GRICE*, Esq. Collector of the District of Camden, on the 10th day of March, one thousand eight hundred and thirty, at the Port of Elizabeth City, in the district of Camden, seized as forfeited to the United States, eleven barrels of Coffee, for these causes to wit: that the said eleven barrels of Coffee were, between the seventh day of March, one thousand eight hundred and thirty and the fileing of this libel, imported and brought in a certain schooner or vessel called the Harriet Eliza, of Boston, belonging in whole or in part to a citizen or citizens of the United States, from a foreign Port or place, to wit: the Islands of Porto Rico and Turks Island, to a Port...and that the said eleven barrels of Coffee were not included in the Manifest of the goods...and merchandize imported into the United States...and praying that the said Coffee may for the said causes, set forth in his said Libel, be condemned and remain forfeited to the United States. And his Honor having appointed to hear and determine on the said libel, at the next District Court of the United States, to be held at Edenton, for the District of Albemarle, on the third Monday of April next; notice is hereby given to all persons who claim...any interest in the said Coffee, to appear at the time and place, and shew cause if any they can, wherefore the same should not for the causes aforesaid, be condemned and remain forfeited to the United States. J. W. **LITTLEJOHN**. *Register of U. S. Court of Admiralty for Albemarle District.* Edenton, Mar. 24th 1830.

[126] United States of America, *North Carolina District.*} *ss.* Be it known unto all whom it may concern, that information hath been filed in the District Court of the United States, directed to be held at Edenton, within and for the District of Albemarle, by *Thomas P. DEVEREAUX*, Esq. Attorney of the United States for the District of North Carolina, against a quantity of Salt, one Quarter Cask and one half Quarter Cask of Madeira Wine, seized by *Duncan M'DONALD*, Esq. Collector of the Customs for the District of

Edenton Gazette 27 March 1830

Edenton, on the 28th day of December, one thousand eight hundred and twenty nine, and on the [blank] day of January last; the same having been imported into the district aforesaid, from a foreign Port in a certain vessel or schooner called the Thankful Winslow, Thomas W. **BAKER**, master, contrary to the Laws of the United States in such cases made and provided.

    Notice is hereby given to all persons who may have any interest in the said Salt and Wine, that at a stated Court of the United States to be held at the Court House in the Town of Edenton for the District of Albemarle, on the third Monday in April, one thousand eight hundred and thirty, the said Salt, together with the...Madeira Wine, will be adjudged as forfeited to the United States, unless they then and there appear, and appearing do alle_dge_ in due form, concludent in law, a reasonable and lawful cause to the contrary. J. W. **LITTLEJOHN**. *Register, U. S. Court of Admiralty, for Albemarle District.* Edenton, Mar. 24th 1830.

Edenton Gazette.
Vol. XXVI.....No. 14. Edenton, N. C. Saturday Morning, April 3, 1830. Whole No. 1214

[127] [p. 2] Edenton Academy. An abstract of a Report of the Instructors of Edenton Academy, read at the close of the recent Examination of the students of that Institution. FEMALE DEPARTMENT. The *First Class*, including nine persons, besides reading, writing, spelling and parsing, have reviewed Murray's Grammar to Prosody; and No. 1. of Woodbridge's Smaller Geography from the commencement, to Lakes in North America. All the members of this class entered the Institution when the session was half advanced, and all were present at the examination. ... The following persons however are more particularly worthy of commendation:

	Schol.	Behav.	Order.
Emeline **WAFF**,	3	1	1
Martha **HO[S]KINS**,	2	3	2
Elizabeth **LITTLEJOHN**,	1	4	2
Harriet **SKINNER**,	4	4	3

The *Second Class*, consisting of four persons, in addition to Reading, writing parsing, spelling & defining, have reviewed, from the beginning to Danish America, in Woodbridge's Smaller Geography; Murray's Grammar as far as irregular verbs; and nearly the whole of the first section in Colburn's Smaller Arithmetic_k_. This class also with one exception, entered the Academy when the session was half advanced, and have merited considerable credit for their industry and good behaviour. Geo. **THORP** and John **SMITH** are more particularly worthy of honorable notice.

	Schol.	Behav.	Order.
George **THORP**,	1	1	1
John **SMITH**,	3	2	2

The *Third Class*, composed of eight members, besides Reading, writing, parsing, spelling, defining and constructing Sentences, have reviewed Europe and Asia, in Woodbridge's Smaller Geography; Murray's Grammar, as far as Prosody; and the fifth, and part of the sixth sections of Colburn's Smaller Arithmetick. Of this class, the following persons are more particularly entitled to commendation.

	Schol.	Behav.	Order.
Mary **SMITH**,	2	1	1
Anna **BOND**,	2	2	2
Sarah **GRIMES**,	1	5	3

The *Fourth Class*, consisting of ten persons, in addition to the usual exercises of reading, writing, parsing, spelling, defining, grammar, & composition, have reviewed from Edward VI to George III, in Goldsmith's history of England, North America, South America, and part of Europe in Woodbridge's larger Geography; nearly half the rules and corresponding notes, in Murray's Exercises; and multiplication, subtraction, and division, in Colburne's large Arithmetick. The whole of the class have exhibited...a decided improvement, both in the excellence of their recitations and in the correctness of their behaviour. In these respects, those persons more particularly worthy of distinction are the following:

	Schol.	Behav.	Order.
Mary **MANNING**,	1	2	1
Ann **RIGHTON**	2	1	1

Edenton Gazette 3 April 1830

Penelope **CREECY**,	4	1	2
Ann **COX**,	3	5	3
Louisa **KNOX**,	5	3	3
Sarah **THORP**,	7	1	3

MALE DEPARTMENT. English Scholars The first & lowest class was composed of *two* small boys, in reading and defining the more difficult words, in writing, in spelling by rote, in committing arithmetical tables, and learning the questions on Woodbridge's smaller Atlas. Thomas B. **HOWETT** is the better scholar.

The *Second Class* was composed of *eight* boys, whose studies were reading in Murray's sequel with explaining the more difficult words; spelling by rote, arithmetical tables, Woodbridge's smaller Geography and Atlas; cyphering and writing. The behaviour of these boys has been quite creditable to their respective ages and progress in their studies. The three best scholars are Henry D. **NIXON**, Richard **PAXTON** and Frederick L. **ROBERTS**.

The *Third Class*, consisting of *seven* persons, were engaged in reading in prose and poetry, and defining the more difficult words; in Murray's English Grammar, in parsing, in Woodbridge's smaller Geography and Atlas, spelling by rote, arithmetical tables, cyphering and writing. The behaviour of the members of this class has been praiseworthy, they have made good progress in habits of regularity and application to their studies, and in a fondness for their books. The best scholar in the class is James W. **HOSKINS**, while Richard W. **BENBURY** and James W. **POPELSTON** rank next—Richard **HANDCOCK** and Thomas D. **MARTIN**, who have more recently joined the class, well deserve to be mentioned for the good beginning in study and behaviour which they have made and for the hopes of their improvement therein which they have excited.

The next scholar, Joseph B. **CHESHIRE**, was engaged in studying Woodbridge's large Geography and Atlas, in Gibson's surveying, in reviewing arithmetic, in writing, and in reading Robertson's History of America with maps. The past application of this young man has kept pace with his years. In several of his studies he has attained to a very considerable degree of accuracy, particularly in Arithmetic, maps and English Grammar.

Classical Students. William A. **LITTLEJOHN** and Casper W. **NORCOM** composed the first class, and were engaged in Latin Syntax, the Latin Reader, vols. I. and II. embracing 44 pages; the first 10 chapters in the Latin Tutor, ancient maps as far as required by their studies; and in writing and correct copies of the Chaps. of the Latin Tutor, and translations from the Latin Reader. Both of these boys have made considerable improvement during the session; W. A. **LITTLEJOHN** is the better scholar.

The studies of the next student, Robert H. **SMITH**, were the Syntax and observations in Adams' Latin Grammar; 61 pages of Latin Reader vol. II. and the first book of Caesar with a careful study of the map of ancient Gaul; ancient Geography, writing out the exercises of the Latin Tutor; Woodbridge's large Atlas and questions & arithmetic through compound Interest. The general behaviour and application of this student have been deserving of much praise, and his progress in his studies perfectly reward his exertions.

Thomas G. **HAUGHTON** studied and reviewed the Latin Grammar; 7th, 8th and 9th books of Virgil; 58 pages of the Greek Reader, Woodbridge's large Geography and Atlas with questions, and Bonycastles arithmetic to the Rule of Three. This student was absent a large portion of his time from school, mostly occasioned by sickness; in the latter part however, his application and progress considerably improved.

The Fourth Class was composed at the beginning of the session of Richard B. **CREECY** and Benjamin R. **NORCOM**; the latter was prevented from attending nearly the whole session by the state of his eyes. The studies of the former, R. B. **CREECY**, were the Philipics of Cicero and a part of his de Senectute; the Gospels of St. Matthew, Mark and John, Valpy's Greek Grammar; Woodbridge's large Geography, Atlas and questions, and Bonycastle's arithmetic trough [sic] practice. The behaviour and application of this student during the present session, have fully deserved the commendation bestowed on him and his class-mate, at the last examination; and he is exhorted to persevere, with renewed diligence, in the course in which it is believed that he has made a good beginning.

[128] Summary. The editor of the Tarborough Free Press says that he is authorised to state that the Hon. T. H. **HALL** will not be a candidate for re-election to the next Congress. ...

A public dinner was given to the Hon. Langdon **CHEVES**, on the 5th ult. by the citizens of Charleston. During which, he intimated his intention of returning to reside again in South Carolina. He has since

Edenton Gazette 3 April 1830

passed on north, to his residence near Philadelphia.

The North American Review has been sold by its late editor and proprietor, Mr. **SPARKS**, to Alexander H. **EVERETT**, late minister to Spain, under whose editorial management the work is to be conducted in future.

James W. **RIPELY** has resigned his seat in Congress, as a Representative from the State of Maine. We regret to state that the causes of his resignation are his own delicate health and that of his family.

Sam PATCH Found.—The body of this bold but unfortunate adventurer was found on the 17th in the river about six miles below Rochester. It was known to be his by the black handkerchief about his waist and other marks.

[129] [p. 3] Edenton: Saturday, April 3, 1830. ... The Court-House at *Winton*, Hertford County, together with all the records and papers of the County and Superior Court Clerks Offices, were consumed by Fire on Sunday night last—the work of an incendiary. It is said that an individual charged with the crime of forgery, procured a negro to set fire to the building, in the hope of destroying the evidence of his guilt. As the subject will undergo judicial investigation, we forbear all comment. The loss to the public and the confusion that must necessarily ensue, from the destruction of the papers of a Court of record, is incalculable.

[130] *Roanoke Inlet.*—Our worthy representative (the Hon. W. B. **SHEPARD**, from the select Committee to whom was referred the subject of re-opening Roanoke Inlet, on the 19th ult. reported the following resolution, which was referred to the Committee on Commerce, and ordered to be printed: *Resolved*, That the Secretary of War is directed to lay before this House at the commencement of the next session of Congress, an exact estimate of the cost of improving Roanoke Inlet, in the State of North Carolina, by means of an embankment across Roanoke and Croatan Sounds—that he inform this House as to the sufficency of said embankment when made of earth and wood after the plan of Hamilton **FULTON**; and that should the surveys on file in his office, together with that of Hamilton **FULTON**, not furnish sufficient data for these purposes, a re survey [sic] of said Inlet be again made.

[131] We learn with deep regret, (says the Philadelphia National Gazette) that William **MILLER**, Jr. Esq. a young lawyer of this city who enjoyed a valuable reputation in every respect, was killed on Sunday, at **NAUMAN**'s Creek, on the borders of the Delaware, in a duel with Lieut Charles G. **HUNTER**, of the U. S. Navy. It is said that Mr. **MILLER** died on the spot, the ball of his adversary having perforated his lungs. This melancholy catastrophe has excited great sensation.

[132] List of Letters Remaining in the Post Office at Edenton, the 1st day of April, 1830, which if not taken out by the 1st of July, will be sent to the General Post Office: **B.**—Thos. M. **BLOUNT**, Mary A. **BISSELL**, Thos. **BARNSWELL**, Richard **BEASLEY**, Charles C. **BISHOP**, 3, Rich'd **BROWNRIGG**, 2, **BROWNRIGG & REID**, Thomas **BROWNRIGG**, Sam'l **BROWN**. Thos. W. **BAKER**, 4. **F.**—Thomas D. **FLURY**. **G.**—John **GRANTHOM**, Jos. **GRANBERRY**, Mackey **GREGORY**. **H.**—Charles **HAUGHTON**, Thos. S. **HOSKINS**, Capt. Step. **HOLMES**. **J.**—Chas. E. **JOHNSON**, Daniel **JOY** or **TOY**. **K.**—Alfred W. **KNIGHT**, 2. **M.**—George **M'INTYRE**, Daniel **M'DOWELL**. **N.**—Mrs. Margaret **NEIL**. **P.**—Mrs. Elizabeth **PETTIJOHN**, Seth **PARKER**, **PARKER & GRANBERRY**, Capt. Isaac O. **PECK**. **R.**—William **RIGHTON**. **S.**—Philip **SIMPSON**, Jas. **SHERWOOD**, Miss Mary **SMALL**, Jos. C. **SKINNER**, Wm. R. **SURRY** or **LURRY**. Capt. Isaiah **SAVERN**, Dr. Wm. R. **SMITH**, Mrs. L. A. **SAWYER**, Lem'l **SAWYER**. **W.**—Capt. H. **WHITING**, Rich'd **WILDER**, Capt. James **WIXEN**, Wm. **WALTON**, Rev. ____ **WAIT**.—52. N. **BRUER**, P. M. April 3.

[133] This is to give Notice, that in *twenty days* from this date, I shall sell about 70 or 80 Likely Negroes, The Plantation whereon I now reside, all my Farming Utensils, Stock of Mules, Horses, Cattle, &c. Any credit required by purchasers can be had. Jona. **HAUGHTON**. Chowan Co. April 3.

[134] *NOTICE*. The Subscriber at March Term of Chowan County Court, qualified as administrator on the estate of *John CHESHIRE*, deceased, and hereby requests all persons indebted to the estate to come forward and make payment without delay. Those to whom the estate is indebted, are requested to present

Edenton Gazette 3 April 1830

their claims duly authenticated, for payment, within the time prescribed by law, or this notice will be plead in bar of a recovery. John COX, *Adm'r*. March, 25th 1830.

[135] Trust Sale. By virtue of a Deed of Trust executed by *John CHESHIRE*, dec'd, for certain purposes therein mentioned, the subscriber will proceed to sell on the 27th inst. at the late residence of the deceased, all of his Household and Kitchen Furniture—And on the same day in front of the Court-House, Twenty-Three Likely NEGROES, and a House near ANDERSON's creek; Also the following real estate lying and being in the Town of Edenton, to wit: a Dwelling HOUSE, out-houses and improvements, and the lots of Land situated in the new plan of said Town, distinguished and known by the letters A, B, C, D, E, F, G, H, I, K, L, M, N, O & P—Two Hundred and Fifty Acres of Land, adjoining the Lands of John POPELSTON and D. M'DONALD, Esquires, and one other Tract, containing 100 Acres more or less, adjoining the Lands of John POPELSTON or the lands of Thomas CHAMBERS and others.—Or as much of the above mentioned property as will satisfy the Trust. Terms made known on the day of sale. Jas. REED *Trustee*. By John COX. April 1, 1830.

[136] *FLOUR*. A Few Barrels Howard Street (Baltimore) FLOUR, just received and for sale low by N. BRUER. April 3.

Edenton Gazette.
Vol. XXVI.....No. 15. Edenton, N. C. Saturday Morning, April 10, 1830. Whole No. 1215.

[137] [p. 3] Edenton: Saturday, April 10, 1830. ... John MOORE, Jr. was convicted of horse-stealing, at the recent term of Chatham Superior Court, Judge DONNELL presiding: The culprit was sentenced to be whipped and put in the pillory, at next term of Chatham county court.

[138] *Geneva College*.—At the meeting of the Trustees of this Institution on Wednesday, the Rev. Richard S. MASON, Rector of Trinity Church, Geneva, (recently Rector of Christ Church in Newbern) was chosen President.

[139] MARRIED, On Saturday, the 3rd inst. in Pasquotank County, by the Rev. Mr. BUXTON, Exum NEWBY, Esq. to Mrs. Elizabeth WILSON, widow of Wm. WILSON, Esq.

[140] The first Quarterly Meeting with the Methodists for this station, will be held on the 17th and 18th of the present month. Rev. Thomas CROWDER, P. E. of the Norfolk District will attend. Edenton, 10th Apl. 1830.

[141] *Fancy & Fashionable* GOODS!!! John M. JONES, Just returned from the great Theatre of high life and fashion, has the pleasure to offer to his friends and customers, a select and extensive assortment of English French and American Fancy Goods, together with a neat and miscellaneous collection of all those small and useful articles necessary to make an assortment general and complete. His Grocery is stored with liquors of the choicest kind and quality, and a judicious variety of articles of inferior value, in the same department... April 10th.

[142] New Goods. *The subscriber has just received from New York...the following articles*, viz: Super blk Levantine and sinchews Silk, silk Camblet, Black Circassian for gentlemen...Tortoise tuck, side & long Combs, Mock do., Parasols and Umbrellas, Letter and foolscap Paper, Ink Powder, Quills, Bobbinett Lace, Irish and Russia Diaper...safety chains for watches, feather Fans, Willow clothes Baskets... sulphate of Quinine, tooth Brushes, Hair do.... James WILLS. April 10.

[143] James GORHAM *Has received...direct from New York, the following articles*...London Pins, patent thread, Ladies superior cotton Hose, Common do., patent Suspenders, Plaid Hdkffs, Brittania Do. Shell curl Combs, Brazillian side do. ...Havanna Hats for summer. Black silk cord. Long Lawns, Fancy Calicos, mourning Ginghams Searsucker, plaid Ginghams...Marking Canvass, carpet Binding. Ladies stuff & spring heel Pumps... April 10.

Edenton Gazette 10 April 1830

[144] *Notice*. The Subscriber at June term, 1829, of Chowan county Court qualified as Administrator on the estate of Stephen **DAIL** dec'd. All persons indebted to said Estate are requested to make payment, and those having claims against the same, are hereby notified to present them for payment within the time prescribed by law, or this notice will be plead in bar of a recovery. Wm. **WALTON**. Chowan county, Apl. 10th

[145] Spring Goods. The Subscriber has just received the following articles...from New York, and is daily in expectation of receiving his general assortment of Spring and Summer Goods, which he will sell at his usual prices. Blk. sinchews Silk, blk. satin Levantine, fine mull Muslins, long Lawns, swiss Muslins plain and figured...corset Lacetts, black silk Braids, black silk Cord, hoskin Gloves, spool, ball and skane [sic] sewing Cotton, flat head London Pins, patent Thread, white sewing ditto, Sulpher, foolscap and letter paper, gun-powder Tea, &c. Wm. F. **BENNETT**. Edenton, Apl. 10th. 1830.

[146] Boot And Shoe *Manufactory*. The subscriber having established himself in this Town, and taken the Shop formerly occupied by Mr. Nathaniel **HOWCOTT**, opposite Dr. M. E. **SAWYER**'s, begs leave to offer his services to the citizens thereof and the surrounding country; and by assiduous attention to the duties of his vocation, he hopes, he shall not fail to please those, who may favor him with their custom.

He has now on hand and intends keeping constantly, an excellent assortment of BOOTS, BROGANS, SHOES & PUMPS, for Gentlemen, Ladies, Children and Servants, made of the best materials at his own Shop. He takes pleasure in stating that he has now in his employ, several first rate workmen, ready to execute all orders to measure, with neatness and despatch. Orders from the country, will be punctually attended to.—All rips mended gratis. Matthew **DENSON**. Edenton, April 10.

[147] List of Letters Remaining in the Post Office at Plymouth, N. C. on the 1st April 1830, and which if not taken out, will be sent on the 1st of July next, to the General Post Office as Dead Letters: Edmund **ANDREWS** 2, John **BAKEMAN**, Ezra **BROWN**, Robinson **CROCKETT**, Thomas **COX**, Richard **EVERITT**, Levi **FAGAN** 3, Edward **HOWES**, Welcome **HOELL** 2, Thos. **JOHNSON**, Frances **JONES**, John **LONG**, Allen **MOORE**, J. W. **M'REA**, John H. **PORTINGTON**, Josiah **SIMPSON** 2, Wm. M. **SCOLFIELD**, Francis **WARD**, Luke **WILKINSON**, Thos. **WILKINSON**, Taylor H. **WALKER**, Sam. **WESKETT**, **JONES & WATSON**—28. Wm. A. **TURNER**, P. M. April 1st.

Edenton Gazette.
Vol. XXVI.....No. 16. Edenton, N. C. Thursday Morning, April 15, 1830. Whole No. 1216.

[148] [p. 2] *The Cotton Cleaner*.—This is a machine invented by Mr. James **GILLIAM**, of Greenville, for removing the trash from Seed Cotton, and for which he has claimed a patent. The purposes of this invention are thus explained by the Patentee. "The Cleaner may be attached to the gearing of a Cotton gin, and run at the same time that the gin is at work, as it only requires about a half horse power to clean from 3000 to 6000 lbs. per day. It seperates the dirt and trash from the Cotton, and prepares it for the Gin; and it has been observed that the Gin does not cut the staple of the Cotton so much to pieces after passing through it as it does without it. Therefore this machine preserves the staple of the Cotton and brushes off the stain that collects on it from remaining in the field under heavy falls of rain—consequently it is restored to its natural state, and in market it will command a higher price. ..."

Mr. **GILLIAM** has disposed of the right of using the machine in the States of South Carolina and Georgia, to Mr. Nathan **BERRY**, of Reedy Fork, Greenville District, (S. C.) who offers the right to individuals, Districts, or Counties, at a price so low as to place it within the reach of almost every farmer. Information respecting the utility of the machine, &c. may be obtained by addressing Mr. **BERRY**, at Reed [sic] Fork.—*Chas. Courier.*

[149] *Melancholy occurrence*.—Mr. *Francis* **NEWBY**, of Perquimans County, received a kick on the head on the 22d ult. from a horse which fractured his scull so badly that he died in three days after, leaving a widow and many friends to lament his death. Mr. **N.** was a soldier of the revolution, and after having escaped the bullets of the enemy in our struggle for independence, & lived to the good old age of 73 years, was killed by a kick from his own horse. *Elizabeth City Star*.

Edenton Gazette 15 April 1830

[150] *Masonic.*—We understand that the installation of the Hon. *Edward* **LIVINGSTON**, as Grand High Priest of the General Grand Royal Arch Chapter of the United States, vice *De Witt* **CLINTON**, deceased; and of the Hon. *Joel B.* **POINSETT**, as Deputy Grand High Priest of the General Grand Chapter, will take place, by commission in the city of Washington, on Saturday, the 3d of April next. The circumstance is mentioned for the information of distant members who may desire to be present at a ceremony so interesting to the Fraternity.—*National Intelligencer.*

[151] [p. 3] Edenton: Thursday, April 15, 1830. In consequence of a new arrangement of the Mails, our paper will be issued on Thursday instead of Saturday mornings. By this arrangement, we shall be able to give later news, and nearly all of our subscribers will receive their papers, two days earlier.

[152] The following persons have been appointed by the Marshall of the District of North Carolina, assistant Marshalls, for the purpose of taking the Census of their several counties, viz: John **SMALLWOOD**, Bertie County. William **WALTON**, Chowan. George **FEREBEE**, Camden. Benj. T. **SIMMONS**, Currituck. Wm. W. **STEDMAN**, Gates. B. J. **MONTGOMERY**, Hertford. William **WARD**, Martin. Elisha N. **RIDDICK**, Perquimans. John **POOL**, Pasquotank. Samuel J. **LEIGH**, Tyrrell. A. **CHESSON**, Washington.

[153] *Quick Work.*—The following decision of the President in relation to those concerned with the late duel near Philadelphia, has met with the applause and sanction of the people. The precedent is a good one, and ought to be exercised in every instance.
Navy Department, March 30, 1830. Sir—It has been proved to my satisfaction that Lieutenants Edmund **BYRNE** and Hampton **WESCOTT**, passed Midshipman Charles H. **DURYEE**, and Midshipman Charles G. **HUNTER**, of the Navy of the United States, were recently concerned in a DUEL, which took place between the last named officer and William **MILLER**, Jr. of Philadelphia, which resulted fatally to the latter. I respectfully recommend to you that the names of the said officers, Edmund **BYRNE**, Hampton **WESCOTT**, Charles H. **DURYEE**, and Charles G. **HUNTER**, be erased from the list of officers of the Navy of the United States. I am, very respectfully, &c. John **BRANCH**. *To the President of the U. States.* Let the above named officers of the Navy be stricken from the Roll. Andrew **JACKSON**. March 31st, 1830.

[154] The N. Y. Mercantile Advertiser, of the 6th inst. says:--By the Horatio, arrived last night from Rio Janeiro, we learn that Emanuel J. **WEST**, Esq. our new Charge d' Affairs to Chili, who embarked in the ship Alfred, of this port, was landed at the former place on the 1st of Feb. and died there on the 12th.
Thomas P. **DEVEREAUX**, Esq. of Raleigh, by the advice of the Senate, has been re-appointed by the President, Attorney of the United States for the District of North-Carolina.
Stephen **ELLIOTT**, Esq. of Charleston, President of the Bank of the State of South Carolina, died suddenly on the 28th ult.

[155] MARRIED, In Currituck County, on the 31st ult. by the Rev. Jeremiah **ETHERIDGE**, Mr. Benjamin **LAND**, to Miss Ann W. **WILSON**, of Norfolk County.

[156] DIED, In this County, on the 10th inst. Mr. Reuben **SMALL**, after a lingering illness. At Newbern, on the 27th ultimo, in the 65th year of his age, Gen. Durant **HATCH**, a patriot of the Revolution.

[157] Removed. The subscribers have removed their Stock of GOODS, to the Store formerly occupied by Messrs. **SAWYER & CLEVELAND**, opposite the one formerly kept in; where they invite their friends and public, to call and buy cheap and fashionable GOODS, just received...carefully selected in Philadelphia and New York... R. H. & J. G. **SMITH**. Edenton, Apl. 15, 1830.

Edenton Gazette.
Vol. XXVI.....No. 17. Edenton, N. C. Thursday Morning, April 22, 1830. Whole No. 1217.

[158] [p. 2] *Spontaneous Combustion.*—An instance of spontaneous combustion of Cotton and Tanner's

Edenton Gazette 22 April 1830

Oil, (which had accidentally come in contact) occurred in the store of Messrs. Thos. **FULLER** & Co. on the 28th ult. in Fayetteville, which, but for its discovery a little after 10 o'clock, would in all probability have caused the destruction of one-fourth of the business part of the town.

[159] [p. 3] Edenton: Thursday, April 22, 1830. Extract from a letter dated *Washington City,* April 13. Congress have at last determined to do the work that is before them. ... The business on which the Senate were engaged, was the nominations of the president, of Isaac **HILL**, David **HENSHAW** and Dabney S. **CARR**. Mr. **HENSHAW**'s appointment as collector at Boston, was confirmed by a single vote, 24 to 23; Mr. **CARR**'s also was a close vote, and the nomination of Mr. *Isaac HILL*, as the 2d Comptroller of the Treasury, *was rejected* by a vote of 33 to 15; a powerful majority. ...

[160] The dwelling house of Mr. *Andrew KNOX* of this County, together with its contents, and about $300 in money, was consumed by fire on Monday last—supposed the act of a vile incendiary, as there had been no fire about the house for some time, and it happened about 2 P. M. when Mr. **K**. (a single man) with all his negroes were at work in his field, at some distance from the house.

On Saturday last, *Mal.* **HAUGHTON**, *Thos. J.* **CHARLTON** and *Nath'l* **BRUER**, Esq'res, were elected Commissioners of this town for one year.

[161] *Columbia, N. C. Mar. 30th* 1830. Mr. Editor, You will oblige many of your friends by inserting in your paper the following Communication. At a numerous meeting of the inhabitants of Tyrrell County, assembled at the Court House in Columbia on Saturday the 20th inst. after solemn prayer to Almighty God, the question was taken on the expediency of forming a Bible Society, auxiliary to the North American Society in New York, to be denominated the Tyrrell Bible Society; which was unanimously agreed to. A Constitution was formed and the following officers chosen viz:--*Ebenezer* **PETTIGREW**, Esq. President. *Jeremiah* **WYNNE**, *Ephraim* **MANN**, and *John B.* **BEASLEY**, Esqrs. Vice-Presidents. *John A.* **SHAW**, Senr. Secretary. *Joseph* **HALLSEY**, Treasurer. Together with fourteen Directors. ...

[162] Congressional. In the Senate on Wednesday, the 15th inst. the bill from the House of Representatives, entitled an act to amend an act for the benefit of the incorporated Kentucky Asylum, for the education of the Deaf and Dumb, was read and ordered to a second reading. Mr. **WEBSTER** presented a memorial remonstrating against the removal of the Southern Indians beyond the Mississippi, and the extension of the jurisdiction of the Southern States over them. The bill for the relief of Beverly **CHEW**, and the heirs of William **EMERSON**, and of Edward **LORANE**, deceased, was ordered to be engrossed and read a third time. ...

[163] TAXES! I have received the Tax List for the year 1829, and am now prepared to settle with those who may call for this purpose. As heretofore, for the better accommodation of all parties, I shall attend in each Captain's District, (of the time and place, due notice will be given,) where all those who are interested, are requested to come. It is hoped and expected, that the usual punctuality will be observed in discharging these little debts, and that no one will delay making a full payment of the same, beyond the 31st of August. To extend the time beyond that period, would be the means of preventing my making a settlement with the proper Officers appointed to settle with me, agreeable to law; the propriety of which, is so well known to the public at large, that it is thought no time will be lost in making a speedy settlement.

All Juror Tickets at present out, will be received in payment, without regard to numbers, and those who may have more than sufficient to satisfy their Taxes, will receive the money for the balance. Wm. D. **RASCOE**, *Sh'ff.* Edenton, April 22.

Edenton Gazette.
Vol. XXVI.....No. 18. Edenton, N. C. Thursday Morning, April 29, 1830. Whole No. 1218.

[164] [p. 2] From the Milton Gazette. Arrest The Murderer. It becomes our duty, for the first time, to record a murder of an aggravated nature. On Monday the 12th instant a dispute arose between *Charles* **WILSON**, of this town, and *John* **MORRIS**, living in Pittsylvania county, Va. After some abusive language had passed between them, **MORRIS** retreated to a neighboring house, wither **WILSON** pursued

Edenton Gazette 29 April 1830

him, and on his way picked up a stone, weighing from 4 to 6 pounds, and on coming up with **MORRIS**, siting in a chair and leaning against the house, hurled the stone at him, which struck **MORRIS** on the head, of which wound he lingered until Thursday morning last, and died. Every medical assistance was afforded for his relief, but was all in vain. **WILSON** has made his escape; and though exertions have been made to arrest him, he still eludes the officers of justice. He is about five feet eight inches high, thick set, dark hair, and rather dark complexion. He is very remarkable for having had his back broken, when young, and its forming a projection so large that no dress can conceal it. He is intelligent, speaks with some fluency, and appears to be about 40 years of age. Editors of newspapers will insert this, particularly those in seaport towns, as he no doubt will leave the United States as soon as possible, being so easily described that he cannot fail being taken if he remains.

[165] [p. 3] Edenton: Thursday, April 29, 1830. ... The Hartford Times of the 6th inst. states that the Administration ticket for Representatives has succeeded in that town. H. L. **ELLSWORTH** and Cyprian **NICHOLS** are elected by a majority of 99 votes.

The death of the Hon. Nicholas **RIDGELY**, Chancellor of the State of Deleware, is announced in the Wilmington papers. After holding his Court on the 1st inst. he retired to bed, apparently in good health, and in 30 minutes was found a corpse!

A writer in a Philadelphia paper nominates Samuel L. **SOUTHARD**, as a candidate for the Presidency.

[166] From the Western Carolinian. *Presentment of the Grand Jury of Rowan.* The Grand Jurors for the county of Rowan, at April term, 1830, of the Superior Court, believe that they are not travelling out of their duty, to present the practice which prevails among a certain grade of Lawyers, while pleading at the bar, of abusing the characters of witnesses, and parties to suits, in no wise called for or justified by the circumstances of the case. We look upon it as a great evil in our courts of justice, and one that ought to be put a stop to, by the authority of the court and the moral sense of the community. The character or good name of a plain country farmer, however poor he may be, is as dear to him, and his humble family, as that of the rich and the great, and ought to be as much respected. ... Jas. L. **LONG**, *Foreman.*

[167] *Counterfeits.*—A counterfeit note of the Bank of the United States, of the denomination of $100, was offered and detected on Tuesday at one of our banks. It is of the letter G. payable to C. J. **NICHOLAS**, of the Richmond Branch, dated August 1st 1825, and signed Thos. **WILSON** Cashier and N. **BIDDLE**, President. It is said by an astute officer of the Bank, to be well calculated to deceive.—*Balt. Gaz.*

[168] MARRIED, In Washington City, on the 19th inst Mr. John H. **WHEELER** of Murfreesborough, N. C. to Mary, only daughter of the Rev. O. B. **BROWN**, of that city.

[169] DIED, In Washington City on Saturday the 17th inst. Gen. Alex. **SMITH**, a representative in Congress from Virginia.

[170] New Goods. The subscriber has lately received...from New York, his spring supply of GOODS, among which are...Irish Linen, 4-4 & 6-4 Cambrics, Book Muslins, Mull do. Plain and figured Swiss do. Ladies white & mixed cotton Hose, Madrass Hdkfs, Bandannoes, Spool & ball Cotton...Hoes, Axes and Spades.—ALSO—the following Groceries, viz: Teas, Snuff, Soap, loaf, lump & brown Sugar, Coffee, Cheese, Tobacco, Powder and Shot, various kinds of Liquors &c. &c. which he will sell at his usual low prices. R. H. **MIDDLETON**. April 20th 1830.

[171] NOTICE. The sale of *Clement H. BLOUNT's* Negroes conveyed in Trust &c. advertised to take place on the 27th inst. is postponed until Monday the 21 June next. Wm. R. **NORCOM**, *Trustee.* April 20th 1830.

Edenton Gazette.
Vol. XXVI.....No. 19. Edenton, N. C. Thursday Morning, May 6, 1830. Whole No. 1219.

Edenton Gazette 6 May 1830

[172] [p. 2] *Masonic.*—The National Intelligencer of the 22d inst. contains the addresses delivered by Messrs. Edward **LIVINGSTON** and J. R. **POINSETT**, at the installation of the Grand officers of the R. A. Chapter of the U. States, at Washington, on the 2d inst. ... Mr. Benjamin C. **HOWARD** of Baltimore made some pertinent remarks...

[173] [p. 3] Thursday, May 6, 1830. ... Miss Frances **WRIGHT** has returned from Port au Prince, where she has been for the purpose of settling about 30 colored people; in which, she succeeded to her own satisfaction as well as theirs. The Philadelphia Gazette says, she was received in the most friendly manner possible, by the authorities and people.

[174] A sharper, named Erastus **CUTT**, recently stole a horse in Ohio, and sold him to the owner, disguised with a new tail, and painted face. This is the sharpest **CUTT** we ever heard of.

[175] MARRIED, In this Town on Thursday evening the 29th ult. by the Rev. Mr. **AVERY**, Augustus **MOORE**, Esq. Attorney at Law to Miss Susan M. only daughter of John **ARMISTEAD** dec'd.
 In this County on the same evening, Mr. Wm. **BAGLEY** of Perquimans County, to Miss Mary **NEWBORN**.
 In this County on the [blank] inst. Mr. Jordan **SIMONSON**, to Miss Martha Ann **MATHIAS**.

[176] DIED, On Friday the 30th ult. Mr. Elisha **PARKER**, in the 86th year of his age, after a long and tedious indisposition, a respectable and industrious farmer of this County. Mr. **P.** was one of the few remaining relics of the revolution.

[177] Wm. F. **BENNETT** Gives notice to his friends and customers, that he has just received his full supply of Spring and Summer GOODS, from New York...and will be glad to accommodate them with any article in his line, at prices by no means extravagant... May 6th.

Edenton Gazette.
Vol. XXVI.....No. 20. Edenton, N. C. Thursday Morning, May 13, 1830. Whole No. 1220.

[178] [p. 2] The Fredericksburg Arena says, that 'Major **EATON** will in a few days, retire from the Department of War, and be succeeded it is supposed, by Major **HAMILTON** of South Carolina'—We know not on what authority, this statement is made... It will be recollected that Major James **HAMILTON** was a distinguished member of the last congress—and has been recently announced for the Governor's Chair in South Carolina. He had by a published letter, consented to serve.—*Richmond Compiler.*

[179] [p. 3] Edenton: Thursday, May 13, 1830. ..*Defalcation.*—The public have long been apprised of the removal of Col. James **ROBERTSON** from the office of collector of the port of Petersburg and that *we* gave it as our opinion, that he owed his removal to his extreme political violence. We now learn with regret, that Col. **R.** is a defaulter to a considerable amount, process having been served upon him, some time last week, at the suit of the United States, for about twenty-five thousand dollars. We forbear commenting on this unpleasant subject. *Old Dominion.*

[180] CONGRESS. On Tuesday the 4th inst. the Senate of the United States resolved itself on motion of Mr. **TAZEWELL**, into a High Court of Impeachments, and Mr. **BUCHANAN** of Pennsylvania, Chairman of the managers appointed by the House of Representatives to conduct the trial, appeared at their bar, and in the name of all the people of the United States impeached James H. **PEEK** of Missouri, of high misdemeanors in office.

[181] MARRIED, In this county, on Tuesday evening last, by the Rev. Thomas **MEREDITH**, Mr. Alexander **SPENCE** to Miss Frances, daughter of James **SATTERFIELD**, deceased.

Edenton Gazette.
Vol. XXVI.....No. 21. Edenton, N. C. Thursday Morning, May 20, 1830. Whole No. 1221.

Edenton Gazette 20 May 1830

[182] [p. 2] Domestic News. ... *TUSKINA*.—The Mobile Register of the 20th ult. says: "The Creek Chief **TUSKINA** reached here yesterday, in charge of an officer of the U. S. Army, and was delivered over to the custody of the Marshal of this District. An examination was had before a magistrate last evening on a charge of his having stopped the U. S. Mail in February last. He was held to bail in the sum of one thousand dollars, for his appearance at the May term of the District Court to be held in this city.

[183] *Change in the Cabinet*.—A paragraph is going the rounds in the opposition papers, affirming that Mr. Secretary **EATON** is about to retire from the War Office, and that he will be succeeded by Major **HAMILTON**, of South Carolina. It is not customary for us to notice these reports, but for the information of those who may imagine it possible to *drive* Major **EATON** from the War Department, we say it is *false*. So long as General **JACKSON** consents to be President, Major **EATON** will be Secretary at War. *N. Y. Cour.*

[184] [p. 3] Edenton: Thursday, May 22 [sic] 1830. ... The United States Cutter Dallas (late the Vigilant) commanded by Capt. John A. **WEBSTER**, arrived in this harbour on Saturday morning last from Ocracock, and sailed again on Monday for Elizabeth City. The Dallas is intended to cruize in Pamptico and Albemarle Sounds for the better protection of the Revenue, and will consequently be a frequent visitor to our Port. ...

[185] The Senate was on the 10th inst. engaged in the consideration of Executive business. ... The nomination of Amos **KENDALL** to the office of fourth Auditor of the Treasury, was confirmed... The nomination of M. M. **NOAH** to the office of Surveyor of the Port of New York, was *rejected*, by a vote of 25 to 23. The nomination of Moses **DAWSON** to the office of Receiver of Public Moneys at Cincinnatti, in the State of Ohio, and of J. B. **GARDINER** to be Register of the Land Office at Tiflin, in the same State, were rejected by large majorities.—*Nat. Intel.*

[186] The Rev. Leonidas **POLK**, of Raleigh, has been unanimously appointed by the Vestry of the Monumental Church, in Richmond, Assistant Minister to Bishop **MOORE**.

[187] MARRIED, In Greensborough, N. C. William **SWAIM**, Esq. Editor of the Greensborough Patriot, to Miss Abigail **SHERLY**, late of Norfolk, Va.

[188] State of North Carolina, *Pasquotank County*. Superior Court of Law, Spring Term, 1830. Alfred A. **TURNER**, vs. Susan **TURNER**.} Petition for divorce. That whereas a Subpoena has been issued against the defendant in this case, and which was returned by the Sheriff of Pasquotank County, that the said defendant was not to be found, and proclamation having been made publicly at the Court-House door of said County by the Sheriff, for the defendant to appear and answer as commanded by said Subpoena, and she having failed to do so—It is ordered by the Court, that notice be given three months in the Elizabeth City Star and Edenton Gazette, for the defendant to appear at the next Superior Court of Law, to be held for the County of Pasquotank, at the Court House in Elizabeth City, on the fourth Monday after the fourth Monday in September next, then and there to appear and plead, answer or demur to the Plaintiff's petition, or judgment *pro confesso* will be taken and the allegations heard ex parte.
    Witness Lemuel C. **MOORE**, clerk of said Court, at Elizabeth City, the 4th Monday after the 4th Monday in March, 1830, and in the 54th year of the Independence. L. C. **MOORE**, C'l'k. May 20.

Edenton Gazette.
Vol. XXVI.....No. 22. Edenton, N. C. Thursday Morning, May 27, 1830. Whole No. 1222.

[189] [p. 2] To the Editor of the United States Telegraph. House of Representatives, May 5, 1830. Sir: A word or two in reply to the letter of Mr. Jessee **SPEIGHT**, published in your paper yesterday, and I hope to hear no more upon the subject. It had been stated, in a speech published by Mr. **SPEIGHT**, that this House had refused to hear a remonstrance from the Legislature of N. Carolina, against the duty on salt, and had indignantly laid it on the table; and the Ralegh Star, upon the faith of this speech, had asserted that a memorial of the Legislature of North Carolina, on the subject of the salt tax, had, by this House, been laid aside, unnoticed and unread.

Edenton Gazette 27 May 1830

Such a proceeding, if it had occurred, would have been an indignity indeed, to North Carolina, which other persons here, besides Mr. SPEIGHT, would not have failed to notice; and it was to acquit them of the neglect and timidity, of having silently submitted to such a proceeding, that I sent you the communication of the 27th ult. The answer of Mr. SPEIGHT substantiates *all the facts* set forth in my communication. I have no interest in noticing the *argument* by which he attempts to prove that these facts warranted the statement heretofore made by him. Respectfully, your ob't sev't. Robert POTTER.

[190] [p. 3] Edenton: Thursday, May 27, 1830. ... Culture Of Silk. We were presented last week with a beautiful skier [sic] of white sewing silk, raised and prepared in the family of Col. J. I. TREDWELL of this Town; which is pronounced by competent judges to be superior both in appearance and quality to the best Italian sewing. The worms were fed from the white mulberry, and this specimen of silk proves, that our climate is peculiarly adapted to its culture, and that our ladies would find both pleasure and profit, by devoting a portion of their time to the rearing of silk worms.

[191] Summary. John C. CALHOUN, has been elected President, and Wm. CRANCH, Vice President of the Columbian Institute for the year 1830. ... S. H. JENKS, editor of the Boston Bulletin, it is understood, has been appointed a clerk in the Department of State by Mr. VAN BUREN.

[192] Joseph MANNING Takes this method to inform his friends and customers, that he has just received from N. York...the following articles, viz: Super olive green Cloth...Cassimeres...5 4 French Bombazine a superior article for men's summer wear. A large and general assortment of Vestings of a superior quality viz: Black English Florantine, do. do. Marseilles, white and buff figured and plain: A general assortment of Buttons, sewing trimmings, Linings, &c. &c. &c. all of which he offers for sale at a very small advance on cost, for prompt pay. Edenton, May 21.

[193] SHOCCO SPRINGS, *Warren County, N. C.* On the 1st day of June next, the Houses at Shocco Springs, nine miles South of Warrenton, and sixteen miles North of Lewisburg, will be opened for the reception of visitors. The great advantages of this watering place in most cases of Dyspepsia, other diseases and debility, having been tested by those who have attended them, to such, it is only necessary to say, that all the Buildings are in excellent repair and condition. ... To those who have not visited Shocco, it may be necessary to say, that the buildings are sufficiently numerous and conveniently arranged for the accommodation of a large assemblage. The private apartments will afford ample retirement to those who prefer it, and the public Halls are abundantly spacious to receive all who may desire company, and where music and dancing can be enjoyed by all such as delight in it.

An arrangement will be made to have Divine Worship performed at the Springs on the Sabbath day, where such visitors as may choose, can attend preaching without inconvenience. In addition to the valuable Medical qualities of the Shocco waters, they are located in a most healthy part of the country, surrounded by a polished society, where the invalid can be restored to health, in an agreeable circle. The best of servants have been provided; the Bar will be found to contain the choicest Liquors, and no pains will be spared to render the time of visitors perfectly comfortable.

My terms for Board, &c. will be $1 per day, for each grown person—Children and Servants half price. For Horses $15 per month, or 60 cents per day. Ann JOHNSON.

NOTICE. There will be a BALL and Party furnished at Shocco Springs, on the evenings of the 6th and 7th July. The Music provided for the occasion will not be inferior, if not superior, to any that was ever heard in North Carolina. Shocco Springs, May 1.

[194] State of North Carolina, *Chowan Court of Equity*, Spring Term 1830. John H. SMALL & als. *vs.* Wm. HUBBLE & als.} Petition for sale of Land. It appearing to the satisfaction of the Court, that Daniel SMALL, one of the defendants in this case, resides beyond the limits of this State; it is therefore ordered, that publication be made in the Edenton Gazette for three months, that the said defendant appear at our next Superior Court of Law and Equity, to be held for said County at the Court House in Edenton, on the second Monday after the fourth Monday of September next, then and there to file his answer to said petition, or judgment pro confesso will be taken as to him, and the cause set for hearing ex parte. Jas. BOZMAN, C & M. E. C. C. Edenton, May 27.

Edenton Gazette 27 May 1830

[195] *Leghorn and Navarino* BONNETTS. The Subscriber has just received a few Leghorn and Navarino Bonnetts, which she will sell uncommonly cheap—also figured changeable Silks, Italianetts, barrage Handkerchiefs, and palmyrine and gauze Neck Scarfs and long Shawls. Ann **NORFLEET**. N. B. The above articles being a consignment will be sold at very reduced prices. A. N. Edenton, May 27, 1830.

Edenton Gazette.
Vol. XXVI.....No. 23. Edenton, N. C. Thursday Morning, June 3, 1830. Whole No. 1223.

[196] [p. 2] Political. *Extract of a letter from Thomas JEFFERSON, Esq. to William B. GILES, Esq. dated 26th December 1825. Dear Sir*—I see as you do, and with the deepest affliction, the rapid strides with which the Federal branch of our government is advancing towards the usurpation of all the rights reserved to the States, and the consolidation in itself, of all powers foreign and domestic, and that too, by constructions which, if legitimate, leave no limits to their power. Take together the decisions of the Federal Court, the doctrines of the President, and the misconstructions of the Constitutional compact acted on by the Federal branch, and it is but too evident that the three ruling branches of that department, are in combination to strip their colleagues the State authorities, of the powers reserved by them, and to exercise themselves, all functions foreign and domestic. Under the power to regulate commerce, they assume indefinitely that also, over agriculture and manufactures, and call it regulation too, to take the earnings of one of those branches of industry, & that too, the most depressed, and put them into the pockets of the other, the most flourishing of all. Under the authority to establish post roads, they claim that of cutting down mountains for the construction of roads, of digging canals, and, aided by a little sophistry on the words "general welfare," a right to do, not only the acts to effect that, which are specifically enumerated and permitted, but whatsoever they shall think or pretend, will be for the general welfare. And what is our resource for the preservation of the Constitution? Reason and argument! You might as well reason and argue with the marble columns encircling them. The representatives chosen by ourselves? They are joined in the combination, some from incorrect views of government, some from corrupt ones, sufficient voting together to outnumber the sound parts, and with majorities of only 1, 2, or 3, bold enough to go forward in defiance. Are we then to stand to our arms?

"No! that must be the last resource not to be thought of until much longer and greater sufferings. If every infraction of a compact of so many parties, is to be resisted at once as a dissolution of it, none can ever be found which would last one year. We must have patience and long endurance then, with our brethren, while under delusion. Give them time for reflection and experience of consequences; keep ourselves in a situation to profit by the chapter of accidents—and separate from our companions only where the sole alternatives left, are the dissolution of our union with them, or submission to a government without limitation of powers."

[197] The trial of the Indian Chief **TUSKINA**, for attempting to stop the United States Mail, about which so much has been said, came on before the District Court of Alabama on the 7th inst. A bill of indictment was prefered [?] containing two counts, one for feloniously attempting to stop the mail, and the other for knowingly, wilfully obstructing its passage. The Grand Jury ignored the first count and found a true bill on the second. On this a conviction was had, and the prisoner was fined by the Court in the sum of one hundred dollars.

[198] Summary. ... It is stated in the Charleston City Gazette, that Col. William **DRAYTON** is about to vacate his seat in Congress, and he is proposed as the next Governor for South Carolina.

John **DE LA RUA** has been appointed Postmaster at Pensacola, vice John **FITZGERALD**, removed.

The Legislature of Connecticut have elected Gideon **TOMLINSON** (the present, Governor) to represent that state in the Senate of the United States, from the 4th of March next.

Calvin **PEASE** has been appointed a Judge of the Supreme Court of Ohio, in the place of Judge **GOODENOW**, resigned.

[199] [p. 3] Edenton: Thursday, June 3, 1830. We are requested to announce the following gentlemen

Edenton Gazette 3 June 1830

as candidates for a seat in the next General Assembly of this State: For the Town of Edenton, Major Samuel T. **SAWYER**. For the County of Chowan, William **WALTON**, Esq. in the Senate. Wm. **BYRUM**, Esq. and Major George **BLAIR**, in the House of Commons.

[200] *Daring Villiany.*—On the 8th ult. Messrs. Wm. **M'KENNEY** & Co. of Portsmouth, Va. shipped on board the Sch. Efrica, Capt. **MEEKINS**, sundry bales and boxes of dry goods, in value about $2000, consigned to a merchant of this place, with an understanding that the vessel was to take the inland route, via the Dismal Swamp Canal. A much longer time than usual expired, and nothing could be heard of the schooner—when suspicion became very strong, that all was not right, and Messrs. **M'K** & Co. effected insurance with one of our citizens, to the amount of $1800.

By the last mail intelligence was received here, that a vessel of the name and answering the description of the Efrica, was on the Eastern shore of Virginia, retailing goods at such a price, as to induce a belief that the Captain was playing a Yankee trick on some one—he sold Irish Linens and Lawns from 1 to 200 per cent under Philadelphia cost, and other goods in proportion. On the receipt of this information at Norfolk, the Revenue Cutter proceeded immediately in search of the fugitive, and we hope he is ere this, safely lodged in a more permanent shop. ...

[201] From the Newbern Spectator. *Another editor rewarded.*—Wm. **SWAIM**, editor of the Greensboro' Patriot, was married to Miss Abigail **SHIRLEY**, on the –[blank]—instant. On this interesting occasion, we beg leave to offer our brother our hearty congratulations: This should have been done in our last, but the unexpected intelligence made us bounce full three feet from our editorial chair, and threw us into a consternation from which we did not so readily recover. ...

[202] MARRIED, In Perquimans county on Thursday evening last, by the Rev. Mr. **ESKRIDGE**, Mr. Rob't A. **SHANNONHOUSE**, to Miss Mary E. **JENNINGS**.

[203] DIED, In Pasquotank county on the 26th ultimo Joseph **MULLEN**, Esq.
In Perquimans, Mr. Uriah **HUDSON**, in the 75th year of his age.

[204] Prospectus Of The CAROLINA SENTINEL. I pledge myself to give my utmost support to the present Administration, while it shall continue to act as it has heretofore acted—for the good of the People; while it continues to deserve what it has hitherto deserved—the thanks of the People. I believe that any encroachment of the *delegated* powers of the General Government, upon the State Sovereignties, is destructive of Liberty. I care not by what pretence it may be adorned, by what names it may be supported, I believe it to be contrary to the tenor of the Constitution, contrary to the immutable principles upon which the Constitution is based, and I therefore will firmly and fearlessly oppose any such encroachment. I believe that Industry can protect itself, and that high pseudo protecting duties never can attain such a desirable end. I believe that the self styled American System is false and foolish in theory, and ruinous in practice. These are the principal articles of my political creed, and I will defend them as well as I can. I will not be the bigotted or knavish tool of any Party, but I will, to the best of my ability, tell the truth, and the whole truth, and nothing but the Truth, concerning Public Men and Public measures.

The Carolina Sentinel will be published every Saturday at $2 50 a year, if paid in advance, or $3, if paid at the end of the year. ... A. J. **MAURICE**. Newbern, May 22.

Edenton Gazette.
Vol. XXVI.....No. 24. Edenton, N. C. Thursday Morning, June 10, 1830. Whole No. 1224.

[205] [p. 2] Congressional. ... *Virgil MAXCY*, of Maryland, was nominated by the *President* of the U. States, on Saturday, to the office of Solicitor of the Treasury which has just been created; and the nomination was confirmed without opposition. *Nat. Int. May* 31.

Much business of an Executive nature was transacted on Saturday. A part of it was the ratification of a Treaty recently concluded with Denmark; and another part of it was the rejection of the nomination of *Wharton RECTOR* to the office of Indian Agent, for which he was nominated, unsuccessfully a few days before, and the confirmation of Mr. **BRODHEAD**...to be Navy Agent at Boston... *Ibid.*

Edenton Gazette 10 June 1830

[206] [p. 3] Edenton: Thursday, June 10, 1830. Congress. ... The Secretary of the Navy, in conformity to a resolution passed by the house of Representatives a short time since, has forwarded to the Speaker, the report of the fourth Auditor on the accounts of Mr. Myles KING, late Navy Agent at Norfolk. From that report, it appears that Mr. KING is a defaulter to the Government and the Bank at Norfolk, in the sum of $44,479.37. The Norfolk papers seem to insinuate that there is some mistake in the report, and that Mr. KING will make it appear quite different when he makes out his statement.

[207] The annual convention of the Protestant Episcopal Church for the diocese of this State convened at Wilmington on the 20th and adjourned on the 24th ult. The Rev. Mr. AVERY of this town, was chosen President. At the next Convention to be held in Raleigh, on the 19th May 1831, it is believed a Bishop will be elected in the place of Bishop RAVENSCROFT, deceased.

[208] James B. THORNTON, of New Hampshire, has been appointed Second Comptroller of the Treasury, in place of Isaac HILL, rejected; and the appointment has been confirmed by the Senate.

The Vice President having on Friday the 28th ult. retired from the Chair of the Senate, for the remainder of the Session, the Hon. Samuel SMITH, of Md., was elected President of the Senate, protem.

It is said that the new sloop of war Concord, Capt. PERRY, fitting out at Portsmouth, (N. H.) has been ordered to repair to Hampton Roads by the 15th inst. for the purpose of receiving on board the Hon. John RANDOLPH, Minister to Russia.

Lieut. H. W. OGDEN, of U. S. navy, bearer of despatches from Mr. WHEATON, Charge d' Affaires at Copenhagen, arrived at New York in the Canada.

Col. A. H. ROWAN, of Kentucky bearer of despatches, sailed from New York lately, in the ship Wm. Byrnes, for Liverpool.

[209] *Epitaph*—Next to the famous epitaph on the tomb of LEONIDAS at Thermophylae, that to be seen over the grave of PUSH-MA-TA-HA, the Indian Chief who died at Washington a few years ago, is to our taste, the most felicitously simple, characteristic and expressive. That of LEONIDAS, "Stop Stranger! You tread on the ashes of a Hero!" was the fruit of a philosopher's study: poor PUSH-MA-TA-HA, is simply the last words he ever spoke—"When I am gone, fire the big guns over me." Had learning and genuis [sic] been invoked to the task we question if they could have acquitted themselves so happily. *Richmond Whig.*

[210] We learn that, during last week, a rencontre occurred in the town of Greenville, Pitt County, between a Mr. CHERRY and a Mr. EASON, in which EASON was first wounded by a gun discharged at him by CHERRY, and CHERRY was wounded by a pistol discharged at him by EASON. This, however, did not terminate the quarrel, and EASON having reloaded his pistol, CHERRY was killed by a second fire from EASON. Mr. CHERRY was the assailant in the first instance.—*Newbern Spectator.*

[211] *FOURTH OF JULY!!* The approaching Anniversary of our Independence on the 4th July being Sunday, the subscriber's friends and the public are respectfully informed, that that memorable event will be celebrated at his house on Saturday the 3rd, the day preceding. The subscriber will spare no pains to spread before those who may favor him with their presence, *a fine dinner*—he also informs them, that his liquors shall not be inferior to any the country will afford, and to make it still better, his charges shall be very moderate. Hend: D. JONES.

The members of the Green hall District Militia, are notified to attend on the day above mentioned, at their regular parade ground. H. D. JONES, *Captain.* Chowan Co. June 10.

[212] $20 Reward Will be given for apprehending and delivering to me, or confining in jail so that I get them again, my negro men ABNER and PRIMER, who ran away from me a short time since. ABNER is about 22 years of age, dark complexion, about 5 feet 8 inches high, and is somewhat lame in his right leg. PRIMER is a brother of his, is about 20 years of age, black, about the same height, and is a very likely fellow. They are believed to be lurking in the neighborhood of the town of Edenton. I will give the above reward to any person, for the apprehension of both, or $10 for each, and pay all reasonable expenses. Chas. W. MIXSON. Chowan Co. June 10.

Edenton Gazette 17 June 1830

Edenton Gazette.
Vol. XXVI.....No. 25. Edenton, N. C. Thursday Morning, June 17, 1830. Whole No. 1225.

[213] [p. 3] Edenton: Thursday, June 17, 1830. We are requested to announce the following gentlemen as candidates for a seat in the next General Assembly of this State: For the Town of Edenton, Major Samuel T. SAWYER. For the County of Chowan, William WALTON, Esq. in the Senate Wm. BYRUM, Esq. and Major George BLAIR, in the House of Commons.

We have been requested to say, that if Charles E. JOHNSON, Esq. will consent to become a candidate to represent the County of Chowan in the Senate of the State, in the next General Assembly, he will receive the support of MANY VOTERS.

[214] *The Rhinoceros.*—The brig Mars from Calcutta, has just brought into Boston the first animal of this description which has ever been in this country. He excites great curiosity; is said to be 15 months old and weighs 2,000 lbs.—his food consists of vegetables, and he consumes about 15 gallons of water daily.

[215] Mr. D. L. THOMAS of Baltimore, extensively known as the owner of a steam sugar refinery, hung himself on the 1st inst.

[216] We learn that Mr. RANDOLPH, the new Minister to Russia, has recommended Mr. John Randolph CLAY of Philadelphia, as Secretary of Legation; and as it is the practice of the Executive, we believe, to consult the wishes of our Foreign Ministers, in the selection of the Secretaries of legation, we presume Mr. CLAY will receive the appointment. *Nat. Int.*

[217] *Virtue Rewarded.*—A most extraordinary public meeting has been held in Sumner county, Tennessee, and a Committee appointed to investigate the unpleasant difficulties, that were supposed to have separated Gov. HOUSTON and his wife. The committee have reported (and the report was unanimously accepted) that the cause of separation was jealousy on the part of Gov. H—that his wife was a young lady of excellent family, and exemplary virtue—that Gov. HOUSTON was a "deluded man," and that "there is no semblance of doubt" that his wife is an "innocent and injured woman."

The Committee also publish a letter from Gov. HOUSTON to Mr. ALLEN, father of the lady, in which the Governor expresses himself satisfied of the chastity of his wife. The whole is a strange proceeding, but will have a tendency to satisfy public curiosity and rescue the character of a respectable lady from the foulest suspicions. *Cin. Amer.*

[218] DIED, In this town on the 10th inst. Mrs. Michael ROSS, for many years a member of the Baptist Church.

[219] *John M. JONES Has just received from New York, per Sch'r Pigot,* Gro de Nap and gauze Ribbons, Cambric, French and American Ginghams, Navarino and straw Bonnetts, Flat-headed Pins, Floss Thread and Cotton, Parisian Artificial Flowers, Bottle Cider, &c. June 17.

[220] Rev. Thomas CROWDER, of the M. E. Church, Presiding Elder of the Norfolk District, will hold his next Quarterly Meeting for this station, on the 26th and 27th of the present month. June 17th.

[221] Unanimity Lodge, No. 54. The Members of this Lodge, will celebrate the approaching festival of St. John the Baptist, (Thursday the 24th) at their Hall in the C. H. at half past 4 o'clock in the afternoon, when an oration will be delivered by a Brother. Members of adjoining Lodges and transient brethren, the clergy and citizens of the Town and adjoining country, are respectfully invited to attend. The Lodge will meet at 4 o'clock. By order, Ja. I. TREDWELL, *Sec'y.* Edenton, June 17.

[222] [p. 4] "*If you whip me, you shall pay for it.*"—Orrin KENT has been fined $80 in Oneida County, N. Y. for whipping his wife. His counsel contended—the varlet! that he had a right to flog her in a rational manner, to keep her in trim. A rational manner forsooth! We should like to know when rationality

Edenton Gazette 17 June 1830

is predicable of this vilest and lowest and most cowardly of all possible acts. A man thresh his wife *rationally!* Well that *would* be a new thing under the sun. The New York lawyer deserves to have his eyes scratched out by old maids with the gout in each arm, for setting up such a defence. We thought the courtesy of our judicial tribunals had long since settled this matter in the U. States, too decidedly for the most hardened pettifogger to venture upon so obselete a barbarism. However, the Oneida jury made it all right in this case; and we fancy that **KENT** (if the wretch has any thing to pay with) would hardly have been let off so easily if it had not appeared on trial that the fair victim was herself a little slippery. She was **KENT**'s second wife, and had jilted a Mr. **GILBERT** whom she had promised to marry on a Sunday, by marrying **KENT** on the Thursday previous.

Edenton Gazette.
Vol. XXVI.....No. 26. Edenton, N. C. Thursday Morning, June 24, 1830. Whole No. 1226.

[223] [p. 2] *Sudden Death.*—We have just been informed that at about half past 12 o'clock this day, Lemuel **SMITH**, Esq. the Corporation Attorney, fell dead in the Court Room, while engaged in pleading. [*N. Y. Com. Adv. June* 12.

[224] *Tribute of Respect.*—A public dinner was given in Charleston on the 10th instant, to the Hon. Joel R. **POINSETT**, late Minister to Mexico, in testimony of the high respect entertained for his character and public services, and of the cordiality with which his fellow-citizens of that city greeted his return amongst them. The company, says the Mercury, was numerous and highly respectable.

[225] In the city of Charleston, on the 22nd ultimo, James **SMITH**, who had been convicted of circulating inflamatory and seditious Tracts, known by the title of **WALKER**'s Appeal, was sentenced, according to a law of South Carolina, to pay a fine of one thousand dollars, and be imprisoned for twelve months.

[226] [p. 3] Edenton: Thursday, June 17, [sic] 1830. ... John P. **VAN NESS** has been elected Mayor of the city of Washington, in the place of Joseph **GALES**, Esq. who declined re-election.

[227] MARRIED, In this County on the 15th inst. by Wm. **GREGORY** Esq. Mr. John **WELCH** to Miss Charlotte, daughter of Mr. Allen **LASSITER**.

[228] DIED, In this County on Monday evening last, Mr. Joseph **SUTTON**.

[229] *A Runaway.* In December last a Negro of mine called **JIM**, otherwise Jim **WOOD**, ran off from my Farm in Scotland Neck. He is about 5 feet 9 inches high, 25 or 26 years old, very black and with lips thicker than ordinary negroes. I bought him of the Executor of James **WOOD** of Tyrrel, and I understand he has numerous relations in Washington, Tyrrel and Perquimans counties. I will give Twenty Five Dollars to have him caught and lodged in either of the jails of Edenton or Plymouth. Thomas **COX**. June 24, 1830.

[230] For Sale, A Valuable set of Blacksmith's Tools, consisting of a pair of large Bellows, Anvil, Vice, Hammers, Tongs, Screw-plates, Punches, Chisels, &c. &c. For terms, apply to Wm. D. **RASCOE**, Esq. or to T. V. **HATHAWAY**. June 24.

[231] Hyde Park FEMALE ACADEMY. The semi-annual Examination of the above Institution will commence on the 25th inst. The exercises will be resumed again on the 29th. Eliza J. **HARVEY**. Halifax Co. June 2, 1830.

[232] Notice. The subscribers having qualified at June term of Chowan Co. Court, as Executors to the last will and testament of *Elisha* **PARKER**, deceased, late of the County of Chowan; gives notice to all persons having demands against the estate of the said Elisha **PARKER**, to present them for payment duly authenticated, within the time prescribed by law; otherwise they will be barred of recovery. Those indebted are requested to make payment forthwith. Chas: E. **JOHNSON**, Jacob **PARKER**, *Executors*. Chowan Co. June 24, 1830.

Edenton Gazette 1 July 1830

Edenton Gazette.
Vol. XXVI.....No. 27. Edenton, N. C. Thursday Morning, July 1, 1830. Whole No. 1227.

[233] [p. 2] *Mail Robbery—and Reform.*—The Wheeling Gazette states, that Mr. **WILSON** of that place; put a letter in the Post Office directed to Pittsburg, containing $1000—the letter reached its place of destination, but not the money. *Christian* **WEIRICH**, the Post Master at Claysville, laboring under a sort of suspicion, was seized, searched, and the cash found in his pocket. He is now in jail at Pittsburg. On examining the post office at Claysville, $200 more was found, supposed to be purloined from another letter.

[234] *Internal Improvements.*—On the 3rd inst. Governor **OWEN**, David L. **SWAIN**, a member of the Board of Internal Improvements, and Jas. **MEBANE**, Wm. **BOYLAN** and Nathan **MENDENHALL**, of the Cape Fear Navigation Company, together with several other gentlemen, arrived at Fayetteville in a boat from Haywood, having passed down the river, for the purpose of inspecting the works now going on under the superintendance of Mr. **MEBANE**.—The citizens, previous to their arrival, called a town meeting, appointed committees, &c. and finally, invited them to take a cold snack, and drink a few toasts at the Lafayette Hotel. The object of their visit to Fayetteville was certainly a laudable one, but we think it looks shabby for men, while employed in important business, either public or private, to idle away their time at such gormandizing foolery.

[235] [p. 3] Edenton: Thursday, July 1, 1830. ... Mr. Philo **WHITE**, editor of the Western Carolinian, having received an appointment from the general government, (a Pursership in the Navy we understand,) has disposed of his interest in that journal to Messrs. **JONES & CRAIGE**.

[236] From the Newbern Spectator. THE SCHOONER EFRICA. Our enterprising citizens, Jos. S. **FOWLER** Esq. and Mr. C. V. **SWAN**, having seen in the Edenton Gazette, an advertisement, wherein it appeared that the schr. Efrica, Capt. **MEEKINS**, had sailed from Portsmouth, Virginia, bound to Edenton, N. C. via the Dismal Swamp Canal, laden with merchandise, consigned to a merchant of the latter place, and, that from certain suspicious circumstances, was presumed to be selling off the cargo clandestinely, left here on Friday last, for Bay River, where they had understood a strange schooner, with dry goods, had arrived, and that the Captain of the same was retailing them at very reduced prices. They succeeded in securing a considerable quantity of the goods, supposed to amount in value from four to five hundred dollars. Upon the arrival of Mr. **FOWLER** at Bay river, he being an acting Justice of the Peace for this County, he had brought before him Thomas **BRICKELL**, a sailor, and Asa **ROBERTS**, cook of the said schooner, from whose personal examination it appeared, that the said schooner was the Efrica of Washington N. C., Daniel **MEEKINS**, alias Thomas **WILSON**, (by which latter name he passed at Bay River) master and that he had taken in the merchandise at Portsmouth, Virginia, on freight for Edenton, N. C.—that instead of proceeding to the place of destination, they went to Old Plantation and Great Wycomico, on the Eastern shore of Virginia, when the Captain commenced retailing the goods; but becoming alarmed, lest he should be discovered, he proceeded to sea, and came in at New Inlet. Having lain two days at the Roanoke Marshes, they then came up to Bay River, when having taken a house he landed the balance of the goods, and recommenced the sale of the same.

From the examination of the witnesses, it appeared, that Thomas **BRICKELL** was born in Dorchester County, State of Maryland, and Asa **ROBERTS** was born in Perquimans County, N. C. near Hertford. Previous to the arrival of these gentlemen at Bay River, the Captain of the schooner had taken a boat on Tuesday morning, and, with a box of goods, had gone into the Creeks in the neighbourhood of Bay River, for the purpose of vending them, but assigning as the ostensible reason for leaving them, a determination to carry them to Newbern—but on the return to Newbern of Messrs. **FOWLER** and **SWAN**, it was ascertained the Captain had stopped at **ADAMS**' Creek, about forty miles below Newbern, where he was selling the goods. A boat was immediately despatched in pursuit of him on Saturday night the 19th instant, which returned on Sunday afternoon, but he had left **ADAMS**' Creek on Saturday evening, his place of destination unknown, since which period he has not been heard from. The goods taken at Bay River, are now in the possession of Jos. S. **FOWLER**, Esq. in Newbern, subject to the order and control of the owners, of which fact he has duly informed them by mail. ...

Edenton Gazette 1 July 1830

[237] *Union of Church and State.*—Married, in Boston, on the 20th ult. Mr. George *STATE* to Miss Evelina *CHURCH*! Many have laboured to keep *civil* and *ecclesiastical* matters apart; but it's all over with us now!

General E. W. **RIPLEY**, late of the United States army, and a most efficient officer in the last war, is a candidate for Congress from one of the lower districts of Louisiana.

[238] MARRIED, In Hertford, on Teusday evening last, by the Rev. Thos. **MEREDITH**, Mr. John S. **WOOD**, merchant of Windsor, to Miss Mary Eliza, daughter of Thomas D. **MARTIN** dec'd.

[239] To the Public. Notwithstanding my unwillingness to obtrude myself or my affairs on the public; justice to my family and self, requires, that when my character is aspersed, and my conduct misrepresented by *malicious* and *designing* persons, I should make known the circumstances which give rise to the calumny. A report has been industriously circulated, "*that my treatment of an unfortunate man, who was taken ill at my house, was marked with great unkindness and inhumanity; and that I sent him to Edenton in a cart, and turned him out of it, in the public streets.*" My object is now, to give a fair and candid statement of the facts connected with that man's illness, and my conduct towards him; and leave it to the decision of an impartial public, whether my treatment of him, was as it has been maliciously said unkind or inhuman. Mr. **ROBERTS**, the young man alluded to, was employed by me as a laborer. After being with me some time, he was struck with the palsy, which deprived him of the power of speech, and rendered useless one side of his body. The disease was one, with the cause or nature of which, I was totally unacquainted, and I was consequently at a loss to know, what method to take to relieve him; I therefore proposed sending for a Physician, but to that he objected, in consequence of his poverty and inability to pay. I however thought medical assistance necessary, and accordingly sent for Dr. M. E. **SAWYER**, who is employed by the Wardens to attend the poor. The inclemency of the weather prevented him from coming, and he sent medicine with directions how it should be used. After doing for him all in my power, and finding that he got no better and that there was no prospect of his ever being restored to the use of his limbs and speech; I resolved to send him either to his Mother who resides at the distance of Twenty two miles from my house, or to Edenton where he would be near a Physician, and of course receive better attendance. I communicated to him my intentions, and left it to his choice, to which of the two places he would go, and he preferred being sent to Edenton. Mr. **SPENCER** who boards at my house, was going to Edenton at the time, and I requested him to inform Mr. Jas. **BOZMAN**, the Treasurer of the Wardens, of his (**ROBERTS**'s) situation and deliver him over to his care. Upon its arrival there the cart in which he was carried, stopped before the door of Mr. **BOZMAN**'s store, where it remained until he Mr. **B.** made the requisite arrangements for his reception, which necessarily consumed some time. After the cart stopped, Mr. **ROBERTS** expressed as well as he could, a desire to be taken out; but from his situation, it was thought impracticable, as he could make use of but one side of his body.—To the surprise of Mr. **SPENCER** as he avers, while he was standing in the store, the servant who went with the cart, came to the door and informed him that Mr. **ROBERTS** had got out of the cart, and was standing by it supporting himself, by holding on to the tail-board. Mr. **S.** and young Mr. **GRIMES**, (who doubtless recollects the circumstance) both went out to him, and as soon as they could obtain sufficient assistance had him replaced.

This is an exposition of all the facts relating to this transaction, to the truth of which, Mr. **SPENCER** who was a witness to the whole, will no doubt attest.

While sick at my house, which was for six or seven days, Mr. **R.** received every attention it was in the power of my family or self to bestow, and had there been any likelihood of his recovering the power of speech, and use of his limbs, I should have been perfectly willing for him to have remained; but Doctor M. E. **SAWYER** himself, declared it as his opinion, that he never would. What then remained for me to do, but to send him to the persons appointed by law, to take care of and provide for the poor and the afflicted? The author or authors of those slanderous and falacious [sic] charges, I have not been able to discover. They like all those who filch from the good name of others, with the vain hope of adding somewhat to their own, "*shun the light*;" but they may yet be traced out, and meet with that exposure, which all such *malevolent traducers* deserve. Miles **WRIGHT**. Chowan Co. June 30, 1830.

[240] To Journeymen *BOOT & SHOE-MAKERS*. The subscriber wishes to employ 3 or 4 steady and

Edenton Gazette 1 July 1830

industrious first-rate Journeymen Boot and Shoe Makers—also, a Foreman who can come well recommended as a steady and good workman, capable of taking charge of a Boot and Shoe Manufactory, to whom constant employment and liberal wages will be given. Matthew **DENSON**. Edenton, July 1, 1830.

Edenton Gazette.
Vol. XXVI.....No. 28. Edenton, N. C. Thursday Morning, July 8, 1830. Whole No. 1228.

[241] [p. 3] To The Voters Of The Town Of Edenton. *Gentlemen*, Impelled by the desire to subserve your best interests, allow me to offer myself as a candidate to represent you in the house of Commons in the next General Assembly of the State of North-Carolina... ... I will advocate Laws to sustain both rich and poor; but more particularly will I devote myself to effect the passage of such laws as shall prevent wealth from aggressions upon poverty—I will advocate a Law that each man shall have a Homestead; whereby the unfortunate will have a refuge in poverty, without being thrown upon cold handed charity—I will advocate a new Bank, not with privileges to the wealthy, or to exclude the poor; but one bottomed upon the available funds of the State, and under its immediate direction... Malachi **HAUGHTON**. Edenton, 8th July 1830.

[242] Edenton: Thursday, July 8, 1830. ... MASONIC.—The following officers were elected at the 8th Annual Convocation of the Grand Chapter of North Carolina, held in Tarboro' on the 24th ult. M. E. Robt. **STRANGE**, Fayetteville, G. H. P. E. Mason L. **WIGGINS**, Enfield, D. G. H. P. E. James G. **MHOON**, Windsor, G. K. E. William **KERR**, Greensboro', G. S. M. E. Jos. R. **LLOYD**, Tarboro, G. Treas. M. E. Ed. B. **FREEMAN**, Halifax, G. Sec. M. E. Thos. P. **HUNT**, Raleigh, G. C. E. George **BLAIR**, Edenton, G. M.

[243] The President of the U. States has changed the punishment of George **WILSON**, one of the mail robbers, from death to imprisonment at hard labor for life.

[244] MARRIED, In Perquimans County, on Thursday the 24th ult. Mr. Edmund **WHITE**, to Miss Louisa **TOMS**, eldest daughter of Col. Francis **TOMS**, all of that county.

[245] DIED, In this County on Sunday the 4th inst. Carolina Virginia aged 4 mos. daughter of Chas. E. **JOHNSON**, Esq.

In Tyrrell County on Thursday the 1st inst. after a short indisposition, Mrs. Ann **PETTIGREW**, consort of Ebenezer **PETTIGREW**, Esq.

OBITUARY. Departed this life, on Saturday 19th June, at his residence in North Hempstead, Long Island, Dr. Benjamin **TREDWELL**. The deceased had reached the advanced age of ninety-five years, and had been a practicing physician for nearly the period of seventy years.—Few individuals have ever enjoyed the respect, it might be said the affections, of an extended community in so eminent a degree, and so uninterruptedly through life, as did the subject of this brief and imperfect notice. He was the friend and adviser, as well as the ministering agent for dispensing the blessings of health, to the inhabitants of a wide expanse of country. His devotion to the medical profession was ardent, unremitted, and successful, and, until within a recent period, the summons to the chamber of disease, though it came, "in the still watches of the night," was never unanswered. Dr. **TREDWELL** was fortunate in all the relations of life; the companion of his youth, his manhood, and his age, a sister of the learned and pious Bishop **SEABURY**, preceeded him but a few years to the grave; and of a large number of immediate descendants, each attained a station in society calculated to awaken the pride, and gratify the affection of a parent. The deceased was charitable, kind and considerate; his friendship was the delight of the exalted, and the solace of the lowly. His approach to the tomb was calm and peaceful as the closing shadows of a tranquil eve.—[New-York Morn. Her.

[246] *LIST OF LETTERS* Remaining in the Post Office at Edenton, the 30th of June 1830. Wm. **BYRUM**, John **BRADBURY**, George **BLAIR**, Richard **BEASLEY**, Mrs. Martha **BENBURY**, Joseph C. **BENBURY**, To the Baptist Church, Edenton, Mrs. Mary A. **BISSELL**, Rich'd T. **BROWNRIGG**, Thomas R. **BARNSWELL**, Thomas **BARNSWELL**.

Edenton Gazette 8 July 1830

A. B. CALE, Cullen CAPEHART, Samuel C. CHAMBERS, Thomas M. CARTER. Rev. P. W. DOWD. Silas W. ELLIOTT. Miss Margaret FLURY. Thomas GRANGER, Nathan D. GREGORY, Capt. Nathan GORDON. Mrs. Milly HAUGHTON, Charles HAUGHTON, David C. HIGGASON, Silvey HARTHEY, Chs. W. HOSKINS, John G. HANKINS, Jos. HAUGHTON, R. R. HEATH. Thomas JORDAN, John H. JONES, Mrs. Mary JOHNSTON. Andrew KNOX. William R. LEARY, William D. LOWTHER.

Jacob MYDGETT, E. MILLER, Chas. W. MIXSON, Geo. M'INTYRE, Mrs. Mariam M'GUIRE, Jacob MEAD, Marthyann MATTHIAS. George NOLAND. David PICKARD, Job PARKER, Willis PARKER. William D. RASCOE, Sheriff. Sheriff of Chowan County, Benjamin SMALL, 2, Samuel T. SAWYER. Chas. W. SKINNER, Josiah SKINNER, John STACY, Exum SIMPSON, Dr. J. A. SKINNER, William SIMONS.

Mrs. Frances P. TREDWELL, Mary TUMNER. Wm. WALTON, Sally WARFF, 2, Rev. H. WOOD, Richard WHIDBEE, Mrs. Huldah G. WRIGHT, Turner WILSON, Mrs. D. S. WARNIER, Sarah WHIPPLE, Rich'd WILDER.

Those persons who receive newspapers through the Post Office, are requested to call and pay the advance postage for the quarter which commenced the 1st inst. N. BRUER, P. M. July 8th 1830.

[247] LIST OF LETTERS Remaining in the Post Office at Hertford, July 1 1830, which will be forwarded to the General Post Office, as dead, if not taken out before the 1st of October next: John H. BLOUNT, J. R. BURBAGE, N. K. BROWN, Jordan & Charles CLARY, Miss Susan CLARY, John CAIL, Sam'l EURE, Dr. J. P. FREEMAN, Zechariah FLETCHER, 2, John GARLINGTON, John HANKINS, Henry HOLLOWAY, Dr. E. B. HARVEY, Gen. Jonathan JACOCKS, Lewis KELLENBURGER, James LEIGH, John LAMB. Secretary of Albemarle Lodge, 2, Dr. Wm. MITCHELL, Benj. MULLEN, Lugar MITCHEL, Edwin MOORE, Cornelius MOORE, Tamar NIXON, Thos. NEWBY, James M'NIDER, William PUGH, Benjamin PHILLIPS, Elisha PERRY, Moses ROUNDTREE, Isaiah ROGERSON, Henry SKINNER, 2, Secretary of Bible Society, Addison WHIDBEE, Miles WILDER, Thomas WILSON, Foster WHITEHEAD. John E. WOOD, P. M. July 8th 1830.

[248] LIST OF LETTERS Remaining in the Post Office at Plymouth, on the 1st of July, 1830: Wm. ALFORD, Wm. BRYANT, 2, Stephen BURTT, John S. COOMBS, Josiah FLOWER, 2, Hardy HARDISON, Benjamin K. HALL, Welcome HOWELL, 2, Samuel M. HORNSBY, Capt. JARVIS of Schr. Splendid, Asa JOHNSTON, Thomas LASSITER, Abraham MEAD, Peter O. PICOT, Richard PEACOCK, Hardy S. PHELPS, Chas. H. PHELPS, Ashbee C. PRITCHET, Henry A. RAYNER, James SHAW, Henry TRUE, 2, Benjamin WYNNS, Benjamin WANER, Alden WILSON. Wm. A. TURNER, P. M. July 8th 1830.

[249] Hillsborough Female *SEMINARY*. The Summer Examination of this Institution closed on the 22d inst. The next Session will commence on Thursday, the 8th of July.—An early attendance of the Scholars is desired. Terms as heretofore, viz: For Ordinary Tuition. In the 1st Class $15 00 Sess. 2d & 3d Classes 12 50 4th Class 10 00 Contingent expences 50 Ornamental Branches. Instruction in Music $24 00 Sess. Drawing & Painting 10 Needle Work from $1 to 3 00. Board can be obtained in the most respectable families of the place, at from $9 to 10 per month, including Wood, Washing, Candles, &c. W. M. GREEN, *Superin't*. Hillsboro', June 4, 1830.

[250] Commission Business. The subscriber having taken that large and commodious fire proof warehouse formerly occupied by Messrs J. & W. SOUTHGATE, with one of the best and most convenient wharves in the Borough of Norfolk, for the purpose of establishing himself in the COMMISSION BUSINESS, begs leave most respectfully to inform his friends, and the public, that all business committed to his charge shall be attended to with fidelity and despatch... ... The House and Wharf will, in a very few weeks, be in first rate condition to recieve any thing. J. S. WORMELEY. Norfolk, July 6, 1830.

[251] Geo. W. GRONLUND, Professor of Music, Respectfully informs the Ladies and gentlemen of Plymouth, Washington, Newbern, Raleigh, Fayetteville, and other places in the route through North Carolina, that he is now on his tour visiting the above mentioned places, for the purpose of *Tuning and*

Edenton Gazette 8 July 1830

Stringing PIANO FORTES.
Mr. **G.** makes it for the present, expressly his business, travelling through this State, for the purpose above mentioned; not because he cares for how many persons have gone or intend going through that district *ignorant* of their business, but simply because he feels desirous of honorably earning a few Dollars. He will take care to procure recommendations from highly respectable persons in Edenton, where he is now employed in tuning PIANOS & ORGANS, so that those who in future may feel disposed to honor him with their patronage, may not be deterred from doing so, by the repeated malicious insinuations of a certain unworthy individual. Edenton, July 8th 1830 ...

Edenton Gazette and Farmer's Palladium.
Vol. XXVI.....No. 29. Edenton, N. C. Thursday, July 15, 1830. Whole No. 1229.

[252] [p. 2] MISCELLANEOUS. BANK ROBBERY. John **FULLER**, the second teller of the U. States Branch Bank in Boston, pocketed, on Monday the 28th ult. $40,000, and made his escape. A reward of $500 is offered for the pilferer, and $2000 for the money. ... **FULLER** is represented to be a thick set man, about 5 feet 8 or 9 inches high, of full face, light complexion, sandy hair and prominent bright light blue eyes. ... **FULLER** is of respectable conne*x*ions he has a wife and interesting family of children in this city. ...

[253] [p. 3] Edenton: Thursday, July 15, 1830. We are authorized to announce William D. **RASCOE**, Esq. (the present incumbent) as a candidate for the Sheriffalty of this county.
We learn that William **JACKSON**, Esq. is a candidate to represent this County in the House of Commons, at the approaching Legislature of this State.

[254] The Hon. John **BRANCH**, Secretary of the Navy, is now on a visit to his former residence in Halifax County in this State. Mr. Roscius **BORLAND**, of Murfreesborough, N. C. has been admitted to County Court practice.

[255] We understand from the New York Commercial, that **FULLER** the bank robber (of whom an account is given on the opposite page) on Monday the 7th inst. sent for Mr. **FROTHINGHAM**, the Cashier of the Bank, and delivered himself up at his own house, and gave into Mr. F's possession all but 2,000 of the $40,000. ... He has been committed to prison to await his trial.
Wm. **DANDRIDGE** Esq. Cashier of the Bank of Virginia at Richmond, has resigned his situation in that institution.

[256] MARRIED, In Hertford, on Sunday evening last by the Rev. Thos. **MEREDITH**, John **BLOUNT**, Esq. of this town, to Miss Rebecca **BATEMAN** of the former place.
At Fayetteville, on the 30th ultimo, John W. **SANDFORD**, Esq. Cashier of the Branch of the U. S. Bank in that town, to Miss Margaret **HOLLIDAY**, eldest daughter of the late Rob't. **HOLLIDAY**, Esq.

[257] DIED, In Hertford county, on the 5th ultimo, Godwin **COTTON**, Esq. in the 70th year of his age.

[258] HYGEIA HOTEL, Old Point Comfort, VA. The subscriber, grateful for past favors, returns his sincere thanks for the liberal encouragement afforded the Hygeia Hotel since it has been in his occupancy, and respectfully informs the public, that for the last twelve months he has been engaged in making alterations and improvements. His ICE HOUSE filled with clean northern Ice. His BAR well stocked with the choicest Liquors, purchased by friends (experienced judges) in New York and Philadelphia; and his BEDS are of the very first quality. ... Arrangements will be made for Cotillion Parties, and Steam Boats employed on Parties of Pleasure to the Capes, whenever a sufficient number justifies it, and timely notice is given. A new BATHING HOUSE has been put up for the accommodation of Ladies, and there being two separate buildings for that purpose, Ladies or Gentlemen can have a Bath at any time of day, either warm or cold. Marshall **PARKS**. Old Point Comfort, July 1.

Edenton Gazette and Farmer's Palladium.
Vol. XXVI.....No. 30. Edenton, N. C. Thursday, July 22, 1830. Whole No. 1230.

Edenton Gazette and Farmer's Palladium 22 July 1830

[259] [p. 2] *University of North Carolina.*—At the late Annual Commencement of this institution, the following degrees were conferred: BACHELOR OF ARTS. Nathaniel H. **M'CAIN**, *Rockingham.* James W. **OSBORNE**, *Mecklenburg.* Cicero S. **HAWKS**, *Newbern.* George G. **LEA**, *Caswell.* Richard K. **HILL**, *Iredell.* Rawley **GALLAWAY**, *Rockingham.* John H. **EDWARDS**, *Person.* Elish. B. **STEDMAN**, *Pittsborough.* Wm. W. L. **KENNEDY**, *Washington.* John M. **STEDMAN**, *Fayetteville.* Aaron J. **SPIVEY**, *Bertie.* Benj. F. **TERRY**, *Pittsylvania, Va.* William K. **RUFFIN**, *Orange.* John A. **BACKHOUSE**, *Newbern.*

MASTER OF ARTS. Dr. Jesse **CARTER**, *of Caswell.* John **WINSLOW**, William **WRIGHT**.} *Fayetteville.* Charles B. **SHEPHERD**, Richard **LEWIS**, *Tarborough.* Jas. **PHILIPS**, N. M. **HENTZ**.} Profs. in the college.

DOCTOR OF DIVINITY. Rev. Adam **EMPIE**, *of William and Mary College, Va.* Rev. Cornelius **VERMULE**, *Harlaem, New York.*

[260] At a political meeting recently held in Hardin county, Kentucky; the Rev. Thos. **CHILTON**, father of the notorious Member of Congress deserted his friends,--and who is at the present moment despised alike by all parties,--delivered a speech, in which he commented with considerable severity upon the recreant and suicidal course of his son. ...

[261] *Imprisonment for debt.*—A Providence (R. I.) paper of the 31th [sic] of May, says: "Saturday last being return day, upwards of twenty persons were committed to jail in this town for debt, on executions. Among the debtors are many of our most worthy fellow citizens. One of them, Capt. Samuel **GODFREY**, is now eighty-six years of age, with the loss of hearing, and nearly bent double by infirmities. He is committed too not for a debt of his own, but for having been an endorser. Many of those thus cut off from active employments, were just re-commencing business, after having given up all they possessed, with a fair prospect of supporting themselves and families."

[262] Summary. ... Duff **GREEN** proposes to publish a Quarterly Journal, to be devoted to the matter connected with the Military and Naval service of the United States.

[263] [p. 3] Edenton: Thursday, July 22, 1830. Rev. Ethelbert **DRAKE**, of the Methodist Episcopal Church, expects to preach in this place on next Sabbath.

We have been requested by several persons to say, that if George W. **BARNEY**, Esq. will consent to run as a candidate to represent this Town in the approaching Legislature of this State, he will be supported by many voters.

At the present session of the Supreme Court, Frederick S. **BLOUNT** of Newbern, and Benj. H. **ALSTON** of Warren, obtained licenses to practice Law in the Superior Courts of this State.

Hon. John **BRANCH**, Secretary of the Navy, arrived at his seat in Halifax County, on the 10th instant.

Anthony **ROBINSON**, first Teller, has been appointed Cashier of the Bank of Virginia, in place of Wm. **DANDRIDGE**, Esq. resigned—and Wm. Beverly **DABNEY**, Esq. first Teller, in Mr. **ROBINSON**'s place.

[264] The following is a List of Members of Congress who attended from this State from the 5th of November, 1774, to the 3d of March 1789. John B. **OSKE**, Thomas **BURKE**, William **BLOUNT**, Timothy **BLOODWORTH**, Robert **BARTON**, Richard **CASWELL**, William **HOOPER**, Joseph **HEWES**, Cornelius **FLANETT**, Whitmel **HILL**, Benjamin **HAWKINS**, Allen **JONES**, Willie **JONES**, Samuel **JOHNSTON**, Abner **NASH**, John **RIM**, William **SHARPE**, John **SITGRIOUR**, John **SWAN**, Mr. **WILLIAMS**, Hugh **WILLIAMSON**, James **WHITE**.

[265] *Administrator's Notice.* Notice is hereby given, that the undersigned qualified at last June Term of Chowan County Court, as administrator on the estate of Joseph **JORDAN**, deceased—All persons indebted to said estate, are requested to make payment, and those to whom the estate is indebted are requested to present their claims properly authenticated within the time prescribed by law, or this notice will be plead in bar of a recovery. Wm. **WALTON**. Chowan Co. July 20, 1830.

Edenton Gazette and Farmer's Palladium 29 July 1830

Edenton Gazette and Farmer's Palladium.
Vol. XXVI.....No. 31. Edenton, N. C. Thursday, July 29, 1830. Whole No. 1231.

[266] [p. 3] Edenton: Thursday, July 29, 1830. The following persons are the candidates for the Sheriffalty of this County: Wm. D. **RASCOE**, Esq. the present incumbent. Wm. **SPARKMAN** and Jacob **PARKER**, Esquires.

[267] A number of the patriotic citizens of Gates County, celebrated the anniversary of our Independence, at Gaston, alias Gates Court House on the 3rd. inst. According to previous arrangement the congregation assembled at Lebanon Church, at the proper hour, where a pithy and appropriate Oration was delivered by Wm. E. **PUGH**, Esq. The oration being concluded the citizens repaired to Mr. H. **GILLIAM**'s Tavern, and partook of an excellent collation, at which Dr. John B. **BAKER** presided, assisted by Wm. W. **STEDMAN**. From the number of toasts drank, we take the following:
  By H. **GILLIAM**. *Wm. B. SHEPHARD*: the able advocate for opening the Roanoke Inlet; the faithful Representative of this Congressional district, and the zealous friend of Internal Improvement.
  By Dr. Jeptha **FOWLKES**. Free Schools, Education to the mind, is what aliment is to the body.
  By Dr. John B. **BAKER**. *John BRANCH*, Secretary of the Navy; a true North Carolinian.
  By Mills **ROBERTS**. Roanoke Inlet: May its sands speedily give place to the ocean element.
  By Dr. John B. **BAKER**. The town of Gaston, long may it flourish.
  By Wm. W. **STEDMAN**. The politics of Gates must change before this village will be called Gaston.
  By David **PARKER**. The Valley of the Roanoke; may its citizens exert every energy to open Roanoke Inlet.

[268] ORIGINAL. To the Editor of the Edenton Gazette. Sir: In your last paper, I observe a paragraph referring to a request made to you by "several persons," that I should become a candidate to represent the town of Edenton in the approaching session of the Legislature of this State. Permit me, sir, through the medium of your paper, in declining the flattering invitation, to express my grateful sense of the honor done me by those gentlemen, whoever they are, in evincing a conviction that my efforts could be at all servicable to the citizens of Edenton. ... G. W. **BARNEY**.

[269] *To the Citizens of Hertford County*: You will in a few days vote for persons to represent you in the Legislature of our State. It is the privilege of freemen. The undersigned are among the candidates for your votes. ... A crisis has arrived in our country that demands from them a firm and decided course. If the next legislature be one of incalculable importance to the State at large, as our public journals tell us, how much more is it important to the county of Hertford, which has been by a mysterious Providence deprived of her Court-House; all her public records destroyed; and the titles of her citizens to their property if not entirely lost, are loose and confused! It requires the best talents she possesses to remedy these evils. ... We, the undersigned, wish to put down that contemptible system called *electioneering*, and we solemnly pledge ourselves *not to treat at any muster, election, or other public collection with ardent spirits or any other drink whatsoever.* ... (Signed,) John H. **WHEELER**. of Murfreesboro'. Candidate for the House of Commons. Jacob **HARE**. B. J. **MONTGOMERY**. Candidates for the Senate. Hertford County, July 18th 1830.

[270] NOTICE. On Thursday the 19th of August next, (or the first fair day thereafter,) will be let out to the lowest bidder, at the place formerly occupied by Thomas **SMALL**, on the Virginia Road, the Building of the HOUSES for the reception of the Poor of Chowan County—A description of the Building, &c. and the Terms of payment will be made known on the day. Bond with approved security, will be required from the Contractor, for his faithful performance. Any information respecting the size and number of the Buildings, with a Plan of the same, can be had by applying either to Wm. R. **NORCOM** or Jas. **BOZMAN**. By the Wardens of the Poor. *For the County of Chowan*. Edenton, 28t^h July 1830.

Edenton Gazette and Farmer's Palladium.
Vol. XXVI.....No. 32. Edenton, N. C. Thursday, August 5, 1830. Whole No. 1232.

Edenton Gazette and Farmer's Palladium 5 August 1830

[271] [p. 2] Edenton: Thursday, August 5, 1830. Wm. **SPARKMAN**, Esq. has declined being a candidate for the Sheriffalty of this County.

[272] HEAT! HEAT!—In almost every paper we have opened for the past week, from the North, east, South or West, the extreme heat and drought are mentioned as not having a precedent for a number of years.—The heat has been so great in the cities of Baltimore, Philadelphia and New York, that many persons have fallen victim to the effects while they were engaged in their daily business, and numbers have died from drinking draughts of cold water.

[273] ELECTION RETURNS. *Pitt County*. Senate—M. **DICKINSON**. Commons—W. **CLARK** and W. **CLEMENT**. Sheriff—J. S. **CLARK**.

[274] The Cashier of the U. States Branch Bank in Boston, has paid the $500 offered for the apprehension of the late second teller of the said bank, to Mr. Joel **SMITH**.

[275] [p. 3] MARRIED, In Bertie County on the 22d ult. by Edward **HARDY** Esq. Mr. John H. **JONES** of Chowan County, to Miss Freeza **HARRELL** of the former County.

In Gates County on the 27th ult. by the Rev. Mr. **KITTERELL**, Rev. William **REED** of Perquimans County, to Mrs. Elizabeth **LASSITER** of the former County.

[276] DIED, In this County on Friday last, Rev. John **JORDAN**, for many years a member and minister of the Baptist Church.

In this County on Tuesday last, after a lingering illness, Miss Patsey **REA**, daughter of Mr. Samuel **REA**.

In this town on Thursday last, Martha Henrietta, infant daughter of Mackey **GREGORY** Esq.

[277] *NOTICE*. The subscriber has just received on consignment and offers *FOR SALE*, 18 ps. 42 inch hemp Bagging at 22 cents for cash or cotton, 20 ps. Tow do. at 17 cents, *ALSO*, A few boxes of Imperial Tea, as low as can be bought in the city of New York. James **WILLS**. August 5th 1830.

[278] NEW GOODS. Just received by Schr. Rising Sun, from New York, Ladies' black H. S. Gloves, Clark's spool Cotton. Black silk Braid, Green Florence, Thread Edgings and Footing. Brown Linen... Wm. F. **BENNETT**. August 5th 1830.

Edenton Gazette and Farmer's Palladium.
Vol. XXVI.....No. 33. Edenton, N. C. Thursday, August 12, 1830. Whole No. 1233.

[279] [p. 2] *Gravel*.—Our townsman, Mr. Joseph C. **ADDINGTON**, with a view of contributing to the relief of suffering humanity, has requested us to give publicity to the case of his son, who was afflicted with that racking disease, the gravel. He describes the agonies of the poor little sufferer as beyond our utmost idea of human indurance, and such as to excite astonishment that nature could bear them through so long a period. About eight weeks ago he took the child with him to Philadelphia, for the purpose of having the stone extracted by a surgical operation, and applyed to Dr. **PHYSICK**. The operation was performed by Dr. J. **RANDOLPH**, son-in-law to Dr. **PHYSICK**, in the short space of a minute and a half, and we are happy to say that the patient has returned home in perfect health. The stone (which Mr. A. has preserved) is as large as a partridge egg. *Norfolk Herald.*

[280] [p. 3] Edenton: Thursday, August 12, 1830. ... ELECTION RETURNS. *Currituck.*—Jonathan **LINDSAY**, Senate, W. D. **BARNARD** and Benjamin T. **SIMMONS**, Commons. Isaac **BAXTER**, Sheriff. *Bertie.*—Geo. O. **ASKEW**, Senate without opposition. Wm. **MHOON** and Alexander **MEBANE**, Commons. Lewis **BOND**, Sheriff, without any regular opposition. ... *Beaufort.*—Joseph B. **HINTON**, Senate, without opposition. **WILLIAMS** and **SMALLWOOD**, Commons. *Craven.*—Rich. D. **SPAIGHT**, Senate, without opposition. John M. **BRYAN** and Alex'r F. **GASTON**, Commons. James C. **COLE**, Sheriff.

Edenton Gazette and Farmer's Palladium 12 August 1830

Town of Newbern.—Charles G. **SPAIGHT**, no opposition. *Edgecombe.*—Louis D. **WILSON**, Senate. Hardy **FLOWER** and Gray **LITTLE**, Commons. John **PARKER** Sheriff. *Franklin.*—W. P. **WILLIAMS**, Senate. William **BRANCH** and Gideon **GLENN**, Commons. H. G. **WILLIAMS**, Sheriff. *Nash.*—W. W. **BODDIE**, Senate. Col. J. **ARRINGTON** and R. C. **HILLARD**, Commons. S. W. W. **VICK**, Sheriff. *Warren.*—Jno. H. **HAWKINS**, Senate. Jno. **BRAGG** and Ranson **WALKER**, Commons. Wm. C. **CLANTON**, Sheriff. *Granville.*—Wm. M. **SNEED**, Senate. Jas. **WYCHE** and Spencer **O'BRIEN**, Commons. L. **GILLIAM**, Sheriff.

[281] DIED, In this County on Tuesday the 22d of July, Mr. Luke **HOLLOWEL**, aged 75 years.

[282] *THE SUBSCRIBER.* Within 10 days, has lost a Silver Patent WATCH. He thinks he dropped it in the street near Mrs. **CHAPMAN**'s, and that it has been picked up by some one ignorant of the owner. A generous reward will be given to the person who delivers it to Jas. **NORCOM**. August 10th, 1830.

[283] *A Teacher Wanted.* The subscriber wishes to engage some person as a private Teacher to his children, who is of moral habits, of gentlemanly deportment and well qualified to teach the Greek and Latin Languages, Mathematics, Geography, and all the branches necessary to a good English education. Any gentleman wishing the situation, will communicate with the subscriber, by directing his letters to **BALLARD**'s Bridge Post Office, Chowan County, N. C. which will be promptly attended to. Chas. E. **JOHNSON**. The Editors of the Raleigh Star, Norfolk Herald and Petersburg Intelligencer, will insert the above twice in their respective papers, and send their accounts to this office for payment. August, 8th 1830.

Edenton Gazette and Farmer's Palladium.
Vol. XXVI.....No. 34. Edenton, N. C. Thursday, August 19, 1830. Whole No. 1234.

[284] [p. 3] Edenton: Thursday, August 19, 1830. ... FURTHER ELECTION RETURNS. *Pasquotank.*—Lemuel **JENNINGS**, Senate; Thos. **BELL** and John M. **SKINNER**, Commons. Josh. A. **POOL**, Sheriff, without opposition. *State of the Poll.*—Senate, **JENNINGS** 143, John **POOL** 129.—Commons, **BELL** 466, **SKINNER** 434, Thos. **JORDAN** 338, Willis **CASEY** 75, *Friend* Thomas **OVERMAN** 24. *Camden.*—Caleb **PERKINS**, Senate. Thos. **DOZIER** and Abner H. **GRANDY**, Commons. Luke G. **LAMB**, Sheriff. *Perquimans.*—Henry **SKINNER**, Senate. Benj. **MULLEN** and Thos. **WILSON**, Commons. James **LONG**, Sheriff, with [sic] opposition. *Halifax.*—Isham **MATTHEWS**, Senate. A. **BYNUM** and Thos. **NICHOLSON**, Commons. James **SIMMONS**, Sheriff. *Town of Halifax.*—William L. **LONG**. *Hertford.*—Jacob **HARE**, Senate. John H. **WHEELER** and Isaac **CARTER**, Commons. Rich'd. M. **COOPER**, Sheriff, without opposition. ... *Northampton.*—C. W. **BARNES**, Senate.—R. B. **GARY** and James **HALEY**, Commons.—Jos. H. **WOOD**, Sheriff. *Johnson* [sic.]—Hillary **WILDER**, Senate. Josiah **HOLDEN** and Kedar **WHITLEY**, Commons. Allen S. **BALLENGER**, Sheriff. *Beaufort.*—Sheriff, Stephen **OWENS** 554 Allen **GRIST** 458. *Lenoir.*—Wm. D. **MOSELY**, Senate, without opposition. Allen W. **WOOTEN** and Councel **WOOTEN**, Commons. Walter **DAVENPORT**, Sheriff. *Jones.*—Risden M. **M'DANIEL**, Senate. Nathan B. **BOUSH** and Owen W. B. **COX**, Commons. Wm. **HUGGINS**, Sheriff. *Green.*—Wyatt **MOYE**, Senate. James **HARPER** and Elisha **UZZLE**, Commons. John W. **TAYLOR**, Sh'ff. *Wayne.*—Gabriel **SHERARD**, Senate. James **RHODES** and John W. **SASSER**, Commons. Calvin R. **BLACKMAN**, Sheriff. *Carteret.*—D. W. **BORDEN**, Senate. Thomas **MARSHALL** and John F. **JONES**, Commons. Absalom **FULFORD**, Sheriff.

[285] An awful and destructive fire took place in Wilmington on the 2d inst. occasioned by lightning.— The editor of the "Cape Fear Recorder' is one of the principal sufferers, having lost all his printing materials, as well as his books, papers, &c. The account of this calamity which follows, is taken from an extra, issued by Mr. **HOOPER**, with borrowed implements. "The 2nd of August was a day of excessive heat. At about 10 o'clock, at night, the atmosphere changed and we had heavy falls of rain, attended by brilliant trails of lightning and heavy claps of thunder. At about 11 o'clock, the electric fluid descended on the northern end of Mr. **LANGDON**'s large wooden building on Market and Second St. and in a few seconds more, struck the same building, near the partition, which separated it from the house in which was the

Edenton Gazette and Farmer's Palladium 19 August 1830

Office of the Cape Fear Recorder. In its course, it set fire to quantities of produce and merchandize, combustible in their nature, and ignited some casks of liquor which burst with a tremendous explosion. The flames then began to blaze forth and to spread through the contiguous buildings & soon reached those which were adjoining on the south and east, on Second street; and burned with prodigious fury, until the whole block of wooden houses, from Second St. to Mrs. **WRIGHT**'s alley, was consumed. During the whole of this awful and sublime spectacle, the fire companies of the town performed their duty with admirable spirit and firmness. One engine was stationed to protect the South side of the Town Hall; another, at the east end of the same; and another, in Second street near Mr. **HALL**'s Livery Stable. These engines were plied with an unflinching courage, amidst torrents of rain; and amidst flashes of lightning the most vivid and piercing; and such rending claps of thunder, that the stoutest heart might have quailed under the portentious display of warring elements. Twice the belfry of the Town Hall was taking fire. The houses on the west side of Second street sweated continually from the prodigious mass of fire on the opposite side; and large flakes of fire were falling on the roofs of adjacent and distant houses.—The progress of the fire, was arrested at Mrs. **WRIGHT**'s alley, by the activity of the firemen in blowing up and pulling to pieces a small two story house, belonging to Mrs. **WRIGHT**, on the east side of the alley.

The other sufferers were, Samuel **LANGDON**, Esq. Mr. **CHAMBERS**, Mr. John **BROWN**, E. P. **HALL**, Esq. Mrs. **SCOTT**, Wm. C. **LORD**, Esq. Ancrum **BERRY**, Esq. Mrs. **WRIGHT**, Gabriel **HOLMES**, Esq. Mr. **TIBBITTS**, Archibald M. **HOOPER**, and Henry **SAMPSON**, (a colored man.)

[286] *TAXES*. The storm occasioned by the late election, having settled down to its proper level, brings to mind the necessity of my taking proper steps to discharge the duties incumbent upon me as a public officer; and having, in such an eminent degree received the approbation of my fellow citizens, that I have heretofore discharged those duties in a becoming manner, I have now to call upon them for their aid to enable me to do it hereafter.—To this end, I beg leave to call their attention to my former advertisement; and particularly request those who are delinquent, to call and settle their taxes, on or before the day named therein, (the 31st Inst.) as indulgence cannot be extended beyond that time, and I hope it will not be expected. Wm. D. **RASCOE**, *Shff*. Edenton, 19th Aug. 1830.

[287] HOTEL FOR RENT. The Subscriber being otherwise engaged in business, wishes to rent for a term of years, the HYGEIA HOTEL, with the furniture and servants if required. This house being well known as the most fashionable place of resort in this part of the country, it is thought unnecessary to describe its advantages here, as it is presumed that any person wishing to rent will examine the premises. Possession given in December next. For particulars inquire of the subscriber at the Hygeia Hotel. Marshall **PARKS**. Old Point Comfort August 19.

[288] Wm. F. **BENNETT** *Has just received from New York...* Roll Sulpher, superior quality, Laguira Coffee, fine and coarse Orange Gun Powder, Shot, Pimento, race Ginger, superior Cider Vinegar, Starch...Soap, Rice, Writing Paper...Bottle Corks, Opodeldock, Preston Smelling Salts, Sweet Oil, and Durable Ink. Edenton, August 19th.

Edenton Gazette and Farmer's Palladium.
Vol. XXVI.....No. 35. Edenton, N. C. Thursday, August 26, 1830. Whole No. 1235.

[289] [p. 2] MISCELLANY. ... *Mississippi*.—There are six candidates for Congress in Mississippi, among whom the name of the present member, Gen. **HINDS** does not appear. The candidates announced are Wm. L. **SHARKEY**, Richard W. **WEBBER**, James C. **WILKINS**, Franklin E. **PLUMMER**, David **JACKSON**, John H. **NORTON**. The election in this State has also taken place, and results will reach us in a few weeks.

[290] [p. 3] Edenton: Thursday, August 26, 1830. HORRIBLE.—We learn from several gentlemen, of the highest respectability in the County of Perquimans, that a young girl about 9 years of age, named **GOODWIN**, the step daughter of Amariah B. **KAIL**, of that County, died and was buried on the 12th Inst: from the general inhuman treatment of **KAIL** to this child, and from other circumstances, it was suspected it did not die in the course of nature, and on Saturday last, the Coroner summoned a jury of in-

Edenton Gazette and Farmer's Palladium 26 August 1830

quest, and had the body disinterred, when they found it brutally mangled and the neck broken, and returned a verdict of wilful murder, by some person to the jury unknown. A warrant we understand was immediately issued by the Coroner for **KAIL**, but he had not been arrested, at the date of our account. We hope the vigilant Solicitor for this Circuit, will give all proper directions for bringing the guilty author of this inhuman act, to condign punishment. The cause which is supposed to have moved this monster in human shape, was the hope of inheriting the childs property, worth some three or four thousand dollars.

[291] The Hon. Willis **ALSTON**, the representative in congress from the Halifax District declines a re-election, and Messrs. Jesse A. **BYNUM** of Halifax, Joseph J. **WILLIAMS** of Martin, and James G. **MHOON** of Bertie, are already in the field to succeed him; the two former are members of the present General Assembly, from their respective Counties; we have heard some three or four other Gentlemen spoken of as candidates.

[292] Stephen T. **MITCHELL**, of Pasquotank, has obtained a license to practice in the County Courts.

[293] ELECTION RETURNS. *State of the Poll of Perquimans.* SENATE. Henry **SKINNER** 160. Willis **RIDDICK** 135. COMMONS. Thomas **WILSON** 431. Benj. **MULLEN** 331. Elisha **BURKE** 232. *Tyrrell.*—John **BEASLEY** Senate, without opposition. Dan'l. N. **BATEMAN** and Benj. **SIKES**, Commons. E. **MANN**, Sheriff. *State of the Poll.*—Commons, Daniel N. **BATEMAN** 310. Benjamin **SIKES** 197. Hezekiah G. **SPRUILL** 183. Frederick **DAVENPORT** 105. Sheriff, E. **MANN** 321, Sam'l **RODGERS** 99. *Orange.*—William **MONTGOMERY**, Senate. J. **STOCKARD** and ---- [blank] **ELLISON**, Commons. Thos. D. **WATTS**, Sheriff. *Town of Hillsborough.*—William **PHILLIPS**. *Cumberland.*—William **MURCHISON** Senate. Alexander **M'NEILL** and Alexander **BUIE**, Commons. John **BLACK**, Sheriff, without opposition. *State of the Poll.*—**MURCHISON** 532. Neill **M'NEILL** 125. **M'NEILL** 662. **BUIE** 641. Howard H. **MASSEY** 321. *Moore.*—Alex'r. **MC NEILL** Senate. Dickerson **DOWD** and William **WADSWORTH**, Commons. Daniel **M'NEILL**, Sheriff.

Onslow.—Gen. Edward **WARD** Senate. Frederick **FOY**, and James **ROWE**, Commons. Bryce **FONVIELLE**, (re-elected) Sheriff. *Caswell.*—James **KERR**, Senate. Littleton **GWYNN** and Stephen **DODSON**, Commons. George **WILLIAMSON**, re-elected Sheriff. *Martin.*—Joseph J. **WILLIAMS**, Senate. William **WATTS** and Jesse **COOPER**, Commons. Sam'l. S. **SHEPHERD**, Sheriff. *New Hanover.*—Wm. B. **MEARES**, Senate. Thomas **HILL** and William S. **LARKINS** Commons. G. **HOLMES**, Sheriff. *Person.*—Robert **VANHOOK**, Senate. Thomas **M'GHEE** and Thomas **LAWSON**, Commons. J. **BARNETT**, Sheriff. *Town of Fayetteville.*—Louis D. **HENRY**, by a majority of 46 votes over William **WADDEL**. *Town of Wilmington.*—Joseph A. **HILL**, by a majority of 36 votes, over W. **STANLY**. *Rowan.*—D. F. **CALDWELL**, Senate, without opposition. Thos. G. **POLK** and Richmond **PEARSON**, Commons. Fielding **SLATER**, Sheriff. *Town of Salisbury.*—C. **FISHER**, without opposition. *Mecklenburg.*—Senate, J. **BLACKWOOD**. W. J. **ALEXANDER**, Col. Evan **ALEXANDER**, Commons. Col. John **SLOAN**, Sheriff. *Davidson.*—R. **HARRIS**, Senate. Joseph **SPURGIN** and William W. **WISEMAN**, commons. William **KENNEDAY**, Sheriff. *Cabarrus.*—Christopher **MELCHOR**, Senate, without opposition. Daniel M. **BARRINGER**, John C. **BARNHARDT**, Commons. William H. **ARCHIBALD**, Sheriff, without opposition. *Iredell.*—Senate, Pinckney **CALDWELL**. Jos. **BOGLE**, Richard **ALLISON**, Commons. Hiram **CALDWELL**, Sheriff. *Surry.*—Wm. P. **DOBSON**, Senate. Mordecai **FLEMING** and Alfred C. **MOORE**, Commons. **WRIGHT**, [sic] Sheriff. *Chatham.*—Joseph **RAMSEY**, Senate, without opposition. Nathan'l. G. **SMITH** and Joseph J. **BROOKS**, Commons. H. D. **BRIDGES**, Sheriff. *Robeson.*—S. **HOWELL**, Senate. John **PURCELL** and John **BROWN**, Commons. *Randolph.*—Abraham **BROWER**, Senate. Jonathan **WORTH** and Abraham **BROWER**, Commons. Geo. **HOOVER**, Sheriff. *Guilford.*—John M. **DICK**, Senate. Allen **PEOPLES** and Amos **WEAVER**, [?] Commons. James W. **DOAK**, Sheriff. *Richmond.*—Tryam **M'FARLAND**, Senate. James **MURPHEY** and Isham A. **DUMAS**, Commons. Wm. **CRAWFORD**, Sheriff, without opposition. *Gates.*—Wm. W. **COWPER**, Senate. Wm. W. **STEDMAN** and John **WILLEY**, Commons. James R. **RIDDICK**, Sheriff.

[294] MARRIED, At the Lake Drummond Hotel, within a hairs breadth of the North Carolina and Virginia line, on Tuesday the 24th Inst. by Wiley **MC PHERSON**, Esq. Mr. Elisha **ELLIS**, to Miss Elizabeth

Edenton Gazette and Farmer's Palladium 26 August 1830

ALTER, both of Portsmouth, Va.

[295] Rev. Thos. **CROWDER** of the M. E. Church, Presiding Elder of the Norfolk District, will hold his next Quarterly Meeting for this station on the 5th and 6th of September next. Edenton, August 26th.

[296] Copartnership Dissolved. The Copartnership heretofore existing under the firm of **MORGAN & COWPER** was dissolved by mutual consent on the 2d June inst. The business of said concern will be settled by L. M. **COWPER** to whom application m_____e for settlement of outstandings &c. &c. J. **MORGAN**, L. M. **COWPER**. Murfreesboro August 14.

[297] The Copartnership of **MORGAN COWPER** & Co. closed on the 30th April last. The business of that concern will likewise be settled by L. M. **COWPER**. J. **MORGAN**, L. M. **COWPER**, J. A. **BROWN**. August 14th, 1830. The Subscriber continues the mercantile business at the old stand formerly occupied by **MORGAN & COWPER**. L. M. **COWPER**. Murfreesboro, August 14.

Edenton Gazette and Farmer's Palladium.
Vol. XXVI.....No. 36. Edenton, N. C. Thursday, September 2, 1830. Whole No. 1236.

[298] [p. 2] MISCELLANY. ... *Distressing Calamity.*—We recently announced the marriage of Samuel **KEEP**, Esq. a native of this city, to Miss Julia **LENOX**, in Washington City. He arrived at Baltimore on the 9th inst. with his family, and put up at **BARNUM**'s Hotel. In the forenoon he called for a glass of cider, and the servant, by mistake, gave him corrosive sublimate. He drank half of it before he discovered the mistake. Feeling unwell, he sent for a physician, who used the stomach pump but to little purpose, as he died next day. Mr. **BARNUM** was absent at the time. Mr. **KEEP** was U. S. Agent at Pensacola. His agonized wife to whom he had been united but eight days, was left without a friend or protector. *Boston Pat.*

[299] *Introduction of Rice into America.*—**MARTIN** states, in his history of N. Carolina, that the planting of Rice was commenced in this country, in the year 1693 as follows: A brig from Madagascar, on her way to England, came to anchor off **SULLIVAN**'s Island. Thomas **SMITH**, going on board, received from the Captain a bag of seed Rice, with information of its culture in the East, its suitableness for food, and its incredible increase. **SMITH** divided the seed among his friends and an experiment being made in different soils, the success surpassed the expectation the Captain had excited. Thus, from this small beginning, accidently occurring, arose the staple commodity of Carolina, which soon became the chief support of the colony and the great source of its opulence.—*Ral. Reg.*

[300] [p. 3] Edenton: Thursday, September 2, 1830. In our last paper we made some remarks relative to a horrid affair said to have been committed by Mr. Amariah **CAIL** of Perquimans County. It will be seen on reference to another column, that Mr. John **CAIL** the father of the person alluded to, has contradicted our statement *nolens volens*. We sincerely hope, for the sake of Mr. C. and the community we live in, that the statement we made, may be erroneous; we however had no reason at the time to doubt it, having received our information from several respectable citizens of the county, in which the transaction is said to have taken place: if we have been misinformed, we take pleasure in correcting our statement, assuring Mr. C. that it would at all times give us pain to be instrumental in wounding the feelings of an innocent person, or exciting prejudice in an enraged community, against an individual charged with such an outrage, as the one alluded to. We presume the case will undergo a legal investigation, which will give Mr. C. an opportunity of showing his innocence, which we hope he may do, to the satisfaction of the most incredulous.

[301] The Hon. William **DRAYTON** of S. C. has been nominated by a Virginia Farmer in the National Intelligencer, as a candidate for Vice President of the United States, to be placed on the ticket with Mr. **CLAY** as President. ...

Mr. J. F. **KNAPP**, the murderer of Capt. **WHITE**, of Salem, Mass. has at length been found *guilty*, after having been tried by three distinct juries.

Edenton Gazette and Farmer's Palladium 2 September 1830

The Editors of the "Western Carolinian" printed at Salisbury have, it appears, involved themselves in a State prosecution, for an alledged libel upon the Hon. James **MARTIN** jr. one of the Superior Court Judges of this State.

[302] To the editor of the Edenton Gazette. Sir: In your last paper, I observe a statement reflecting deeply on the character of my son, Amariah B. **CAIL**. I take this opportunity of summoning the accuser to the proof of his defamation, unprecedented in malignity and falsehood. I deny in all and every particular that my son has ever been guilty of inhuman treatment to his step daughter; or that there was any evidence before the jury of inquest, save what prejudice created and ignorance received, of the unnatural death of the child referred to. If a warrant has been issued, its object is still and has been at his residence in Perquimans County, ready to submit to any scrutiny that the laws of his country require. You will awaken a feeling of gratitude in the wounded bosom of a father, if you will give this piece an insertion in your paper. Your obedient serv't. John **CAIL**. Perquimans County, August 23.

[303] The Supreme Court of this State adjourned on the 21st ult. after a session of ten weeks. We subjoin a list of cases decided, wherein persons in this section are interested. EQUITY CAUSES. James **HILL** vs James S. **JONES**, executor, from Hertford. Decree for complainant.

David L. **RYAN** vs the executors of John **BEASLEY**, deceased, from Bertie. Decree of the court below reversed.

William **LEE** vs James **NORCOM**, from Chowan. Decree for complainant.

TREDWELL's executors vs John **LANSTON**, adm. from Chowan. Decree for complainants.

Rebecca **BAILEY** and others vs Thomas L. **SHANNONHOUSE**, ex'r. of Thomas **DAVIS**, dec'd. from Pasquotank. Decree of the Court below reversed, with costs in this Court. Plea overruled, and cause remanded for further proceedings.

COMMON LAW CAUSES. Den on demise of C. **BURGESS** and others vs Willis **WILSON**, representative, and others, appt. from Camden. Judgment affirmed.

Den on demise of George **BLAIR** vs Elisha P. **MILLER**, appt. from Burke. Judgment reversed, and new trial granted.

Samuel **DOWDY** vs Willis **GALLOP** and others, from Currituck. Judgment affirmed.

The chairman to the use of Nathan **SMITH**, ex'r. vs Levi **FAGAN** and Josiah **FLOWERS**, adm'rs, &c. from Washington. Judgment affirmed.

The Justices to the use of Anthony **ARMISTEAD**, appt. vs G. L. **STEWART** and others, from Washington. Judgment affirmed.

Isaac **PIPKIN** and wife, appt. vs William & James D. **WYNNS**, from Hertford. Judgment reversed.

State Bank vs John W. **LITTLEJOHN** and others, appt from Chowan. Judgment reversed, and new trial granted.

Den on demise of **M'PHERSON** & **LERRY** vs Fen and **M'COY**, appt. from Camden. Judgment reversed and new trial granted.

Amos **PALMER** & Co. appt. vs Elijah **CLARK**, sh'ff. &c. from Craven. Judgment affirmed.

Etheldred J. **PEEBLES**, exr. &c. appt. vs Littlebury **MASON**, from Northampton. Judgment affirmed.

E. and M. **DUNSTAN** vs Benjamin **HARDY**'s executor, from Washington. Judgment affirmed.

The Chairman of Bertie County Court, appt. vs William **WATFORD**'s heirs and Joshua **OUTLAW**'s heir, from Washington. Judgment affirmed.

Justices of Currituck, &c. appt. vs Dennis **DOZIER**'s admr. from Currituck. Judgment affirmed.

STATE CAUSES. State vs. Elijah W. **KIMBROUGH**, appt. from Wake. Judgment affirmed and judgment for the State.

State vs. Negro **MOSES**, appt. from Craven.—Judgment affirmed and judgment for the State.

[304] ELECTION RETURNS. *Duplin.* Stephen **MILLER**, S. Wm. **WRIGHT** and Wm. K. **FREDERICK**, C. James K. **HILL** sheriff. *Sampson.* Edward C. **GAVIN**, S. Archibald C. **MONK** and Dickson **SLOAN**, C. Thomas K. **MORISEY**, sheriff. *Rockingham.* Robert **MARTIN**, S. Philip **IRION** and William **DONNELL**, C. Martin **ROBERTS**, sheriff. *Stokes.* John **HILL**, S. without opposition. Leonard **ZEIGLAR** and Joseph W. **WINSTON**, C. Salathiel **STONE**, Sheriff, without opposition. *Burke.* David **NEWLAND**, S. Alney **BURGIN** and Elias A. **HOOPER**, C. William C. **BUTLER**, sheriff.

Edenton Gazette and Farmer's Palladium 2 September 1830

Wilkes. Edmund **JONES**, S. William **HORTON** and Montfort **STOKES**, C. William **HAMPTON**, sheriff. *Bladen.* James J. **M'KAY**, S, without opposition. John J. **M'MILLAN** and Saltar **LLOYD**, C. Samuel **CAIN**, sheriff, without opposition. *Columbus.* Luke R. **SIMMONS**, S. Caleb **STEPHEN** and Marmaduke **POWELL**, C. Joshua **WILLIAMSON**, sheriff. *Montgomery.* John **CRUMP**, S. James M. **LILLY** and Reuben **KENDALL**, C. John M. **ALLEN**, sheriff. *Hyde.*—William **SELBY**, Senate. Thomas S. **SINGLETON** and Foster **JARVIS**, Commons. H. S. **SPENCER**, sheriff, no opposition. *Anson.*—C. **MARSHALL**, S. without opposition. ---- [blank] **WHITE** and ---- [blank] **MORRIS**, C. J. **MEDLEY** Sheriff.

[305] *Appointment by the President. James W.* **RIPLEY** to be Collector of the Customs for the District and Inspector of the Revenue for the port of Passamaquoddy, in the State of Maine, vice Leonard **JARVIS**, resigned.—*U. S. Telegraph.*

[306] Another Revolutionary worthy has been struck from the roll of existence. Col. Marinus **WILLETT** died in New York on the 23d inst. at the advanced age of upwards of 90 years.

[307] *Longevity.*—Alex'r. **AVERY**, of Johnston county, is one of the two only surviving members of the Congress which framed the Constitution of North Carolina, in 1776. He is now about ninety-five years old.—*Raleigh Register.*

[308] MARRIED, In Newbern, on the 23d inst. by the Rev. Leroy M. **LEE**, Rev. Vernon **ESKRIDGE**, of the Methodist Episcopal Church, and stationed Minister of Elizabeth City, N. C. to Miss Mary Ann **MC LIN**, daughter of the late Mr. John J. **MC LIN**, of that place.

In Washington, N. C. on the 24th inst. by the Rev. Vernon **ESKRIDGE**, Rev. George N. **GREGORY**, of the Methodist Episcopal Church, and stationed Minister of said town, to Miss Jane W. **TYLER**, daughter of Capt. John **TYLER**.

[309] DIED, In this town, on the 18th ult. Mary T. eldest daughter of Nathaniel D. **WRIGHT**, dec'd.
On the 31st ult. in the 4th year of his age, James Iredell, only son of George **BLAIR**, Esq.
On the 19th ult. at the Bedford Springs, Pennsylvania, Mrs. Mary C. **GILLIAM**, aged 42 years, wife of Henry **GILLIAM**, Esq. of Gaston, Gates County, N. C.

[310] Twenty five Dollars Will be given for the apprehension and confinement of **DERRY**, who ran away from the subscriber about 5 months ago.—**DERRY**, generally known by the Carpenter, is a brown mulatto, of a small stature and thin visage, about 5 feet 8 or 9 inches high. He speaks quick and rather boastingly, and, I believe, has lost some of his foreteeth. He has been several times seen, by persons of colour, near Nixonton, in Pasquotank County, in the neighbourhood of which place he has relations, by whom he is probably harboured and kept out. The above reward will be given for his apprehension and confinement, or twenty Dollars and reasonable charges, for his delivery to Jas. **NORCOM**. Edenton, Sept. 2.

[311] NOTICE. Abraham **RIDDICK** entered on the book of Strays for Hertford County, one bay horse Mule, supposed to be two years old: scar on his right fore foot, valued by Wm. **BATTLE** and A. **RIDDICK** at thirty dollars. Also one bay horse Colt, supposed to be one year old, no marks, valued by the above men at fifteen dollars. Perry **CARTER**, *Ranger.* Murfreesboro, Aug. 25th.

[312] ADVERTISEMENT. Entertainment on the Virginia and North Carolina Canal as usual, equal if not superior to any on the Canal route to the Southward, and said to be the most pleasant and healthy situation on that road. Charges 25 per cent less than any other establishment. The Subscriber is obliged, in his own defence, to make it known to the Public, that in consequence of a mean, pitiful and false report circulated by Asa **ROGERSON**, before he took himself off, and since by his emissaries, which was unknown to me, until lately some of my friends were so kind as to inform me.—The report was, that I had declined entertaining any person whatever. This was in order to induce my friends and customers to the House on the line, otherwise called the *House of Refuge*, which never would have been any House, had it

Edenton Gazette and Farmer's Palladium 2 September 1830

not been for Government money and that of Individuals. Wm. **FARANGE**. 24 miles from Portsmouth, 19 do. from Elizabeth City, and 2½ south of the line of the States. September 1, 1830.

Edenton Gazette and Farmer's Palladium.
Vol. XXVI.....No. 37. Edenton, N. C. Thursday, September 9, 1830. Whole No. 1237.

[313] [p. 3] Edenton: Thursday, September 9, 1830. We learn that Mr. Amariah **CAIL**, of whom we have before spoken, has been bound in a bond of $3,000 for his appearance at the next superior Court, to be held for Perquimans County. We are in possession of the evidence taken down at the trial before the Magistrate, but as the matter is to go before the Superior Court, we deem a publication of it at this time improper.

[314] ELECTION RETURNS. *Lincoln.*—Daniel **HOKE**, Senate, without opposition. Bartlett **SHIPP** and Andrew H. **LORETZ**, Commons. Thomas **WARD**, Sheriff. *Ashe.*—John **RAY**, Senate, without opposition. James **HORTON** and James **CALLOWAY**, Commons. John C. **GAMBILL**, Sheriff. *Macon.*—James W. **GUIN**, Senate. Thomas **TATHEM** and James **WHITAKER**, Commons. B. W. **BELL**, Sheriff. *Rutherford.*—J. **M'ENTIRE**, Senate. Robert **M'AFEE** and James M. **WEBB**, Commons. William **CARSON**, Sheriff. *Buncombe.*—Jas. **GUDGER**, Senate. Wm. **ORR** and James **WEAVER**, Commons. Nathaniel **HARRISON**, Sheriff.

[315] EDENTON ACADEMY. *Abstract of the Report at the Examination of the students of Edenton Academy, August* 1830. Female Department. I. The first and lowest class in this department consisted of 9 scholars, and were engaged in reading, writing, spelling, tables, geography & Atlas, grammar and parsing. ... The following were most distinguished for their scholarship and good behaviour: *Emeline* **WAFF** was first in the Class, being No. 1, both in scholarship and behaviour: *Mary D.* **HOSKINS** was second, being No. 1 in schol. and No. 3 in behaviour: *Harriet* **SKINNER** was third, being No. 2 in schol. and No. 1 in behav. Mary M. **NORCOM** and Jane **POPELSTON** were fourth and equal; the former being No. 3 in schol. and No. 4 in behav. and the latter, No. 5 in schol. and No. 2 in behaviour.

II. The second class was composed of 7 students: their studies, during the session, were more advanced parts of all those belonging to the first class, together with correcting the false Syntax in Murray's Exercises and working out the sums in two sections of Colburn's smaller arithmetic. ... The following is the standing of those most deserving of commendation:

	Schol.	Behav.
Eliz. **LITTLEJOHN**	No. 1	No. 1
Martha **HOSKINS**	2.	2
George **THORP**	3	3
John **SMITH**	4	3
Mary **BLOUNT**	5	2

III. The third class contained 6 members, and were engaged in reading in the Sequel, spelling in Walker's Dictionary, Woodbridge's smaller Geography & Atlas, both the small print and large, Syntax in Grammar and correcting Murray's Exercises, parsing, scanning and defining the difficult words in the English Reader, and Colburn's smaller arithmetic. ... The following are the persons most deserving commendation:

	Schol.	Behav.
Elizabeth **STRONG**	No. 1	No. 1
Mary **SMITH**	1	2
Sarah **WAFF**	3	2

IV. The fourth and highest class comprised 9 young ladies. ... The class have showed themselves very desirous to improve, and their behaviour, composed with that of the other and younger classes of the School, was fully equal to their advanced standing, and superior age. The members more deserving distinction are the following:

	Schol.	Behav.
Mary **MANNING**	No. 1	No. 1
Ann **COX**	2	2
Ann **SINGLETON**	3	1
Sally **THORP**	5	1
Penelope **CREECY**	4	3
Sally **ELLIOTT**	6	1

Edenton Gazette and Farmer's Palladium 9 September 1830

Jane **BONNER**, a young member of this School, not connected with any of the regular classes, commenced her studies only during the present session; she deserves especial credit for her behaviour, and her progress was quite equal to her circumstances.

Male Department. *English Scholars.* The first class of English Scholars consisted of 8 boys... The improvement of these boys in their behaviour, in their application to their studies, and also in their knowledge of them, has been deserving of much credit. The Examination of the class was generally satisfactory. The best scholars are Richard **PAXTON**, John W. **ROBERTS** and Thomas **HOWETT**, who ranked about in the order named.

II. The second class was composed of 5 members; the size and age of most of whom, were those of young men. ... The progress and behaviour of most of this class have been very gratifying; while the following are more deserving of commendation: viz: Richard **HANDCOCK** and James **HOSKINS**, who rank first, and Richard **BENBURY**, who is next. Thos. W. **THATCH**, who joined the class only this session, deserves equal credit with any of the above, for his behaviour and improvement during the time, which he has belonged to it.

III. The only remaining English scholar is Joseph B. **CHESHIRE**, who during the last two sessions, has been prosecuting his studies principally by himself. ... The examination of this student on all his studies was very creditable to himself and satisfactory to his Instructor; particularly his performances in the different parts of surveying.

Classical Scholars. I. George B. **SATTERFIELD** and Thomas D. **MARTIN** were engaged in studying and repeatedly reviewing different portions of Etymology in Latin Grammar, writing out Exercises in Latin Grammar, parsing the corresponding Exercises in the Latin Reader. The former began his Grammar at the beginning of the session, and the latter at the middle; the quantity studied by them was different, but the progress of each has been satisfactory and encouraging, and their behaviour commendable.

II. William A. **LITTLEJOHN** and Caspar W. **NORCOM** composed the next class, and studied Syntax with the notes in Adam's Grammar, 91 pages of the second part of the Latin Reader, ancient Geography; they wrote out correctly 102 pages of false Syntax in the Latin Tutor, and corrected verbally 39 pages more, and wrote English compositions every other week. The progress of both these boys in their studies, and their improvement in the art of studying, have been equally evident and creditable to them. W. A. **LITTLEJOHN** was unfortunately detained from school almost one half of the last two months of the session by sickness; the difference in scholarship between the two at this time, is extremely slight.

III. Daniel E. **JOHNSON** and Robert H. **SMITH**, although not in the same class, were both engaged in studying Latin Grammar and Cæsar, the former 5 books and the latter 7 of his Gallic Wars; and ancient Geography illustrative of Cæsar. The progress of D. E. **JOHNSON** was quite respectable during the session, and his performances at his examination satisfactory to the examiners. ...

IV. The studies of the next student, Richard B. **CREECY**, have been...in the same manner as the last mentioned scholar, and English and Latin Compositions. His performances at the Examination, especially on his Latin and Greek studies, were highly creditable to him and satisfactory to his Instructor, and showed a very considerable acquaintance with the construction, principles and parsing of the two Languages. Thomas G. **HAUGHTON**, another member of this department, left the Academy in the last of July, for the University of the State. He continued to the end, the same amiable course of conduct and the same progress in his studies, which had, at former examinations, repeatedly obtained for him a large share of deserved commendation.

[316] MARRIED, In this County on the 26th ult. Mr. Alfred **SATTERFIELD** to Miss Catharine **ELLIOTT**, daughter of Henry **ELLIOTT**, dec'd.

In this Town, on Thursday evening inst. by the Rev. Thos. **BARNUM**, Mr. Richard H. **MIDDLETON**, to Miss Catharine, daughter of Thos. **VAIL**, dec'd.

In this County, on the same evening, Mr. Joshua **PRATT**, to Miss Pathenia **SIMPSON**.

Edenton Gazette and Farmer's Palladium.
Vol. XXVI.....No. 38. Edenton, N. C. Thursday, September 16, 1830. Whole No. 1238.

Edenton Gazette and Farmer's Palladium 16 September 1830

[317] [p. 2] Summary. ... *New Cotton.*—The Petersburg Times says, a bale of new cotton, raised by Capt. Wm. **MOODY**, of Northampton county, N. C. was sold in that market on the 30th ultimo, at 12 cts.—being the first of of [sic] the new crop that has been received.

[318] [p. 3] Edenton: Thursday, September 16, 1830. A colored woman belonging to the heirs of Joshua S. **CREECY**, dec'd. was shot a few days past on the farm of John H. **LEARY**, Esq. about five miles below this place, and survived but a short time after the wound was inflicted. It is not known to a certainty who committed the inhuman and unfeeling act, but our informant says "circumstances speak strongly against the overseer," whose name we do not now recollect. We hope the aggressor, whoever he is, may be found out, and made to pay dear for his conduct. It is high time that a stop should be put to such barbarous conduct, and owners of slaves should never employ persons to oversee them, who have no idea of justice or humanity. It has been truly remarkable that such acts are committed, nine times out of ten, by persons who never owned a slave, and of course cannot appreciate their value.

[319] James R. **PRINGLE** is elected Intendant of the city of Charleston, by a majority of 84 votes over H. L. **PINCKNEY**, the late incumbent.

[320] The American Farmer heretofore published by Mr. J. S. **SKINNER** of Baltimore, has been transferred into the hands of Messrs. J. Irvine **HITCHCOCK** & Co. It is under the editorial management of Mr. G. B. **SMITH**, a gentleman fully capable of sustaining the reputation of the paper.

[321] ELECTION RETURNS. *Haywood.*—Wm. **WELCH**. Senate, without opposition. Ninian **EDMONDSTON** and James R. **LOVE**, Commons, James M'KEE, Sheriff. ...

[322] DIED, In Hertford on Tuesday last, Mrs. Eliza **HARVEY**, consort of Dr. Edmund B. **HARVEY** of that place.

[323] NOTICE. The subscriber has just received and offers for sale... Molasses, Coffee, Tobacco, Loaf, lump and brown Sugar. Sperm Candles, Pearl Ash, Starch, Gunpowder and Black Tea, Castile and common Soap, Cheese of an excellent quality put up in boxes, Rice, Raisins in whole and ¼ boxes, Box Salt for table use, Powder and Shot, Castor and sweet Oil... N. **BRUER**. September 16th 1830.

[324] *Miss Jane YEOMANS* Informs her friends and the public, that she will commence her *SCHOOL* at the residence of her mother, on the 27th instant. Edenton, Sep. 16th 1830.

[325] NOTICE. The subscriber respectfully informs the gentlemen and ladies of Edenton and its vicinity, that he has taken the shop on Main street, next door below Mr. Thos. **WAFF**'s Saddler's Shop, where he is prepared to manufacture gentlemen's BOOTS and SHOES and ladies Leather and Prunelle Shoes, at a short notice and in a neat manner. He further adds, that his best efforts will be used to please all those who may favor him with their custom. John **COUNCILL**. Edenton, Sept. 16, 1830.

Edenton Gazette and Farmer's Palladium.
Vol. XXVI.....No. 39. Edenton, N. C. Thursday, September 23, 1830. Whole No. 1239.

[326] [p. 2] Summary. The New York Commercial advertiser proposes the Hon. Ambrose **SPENCER** of that State as a proper person to run for Vice-President, on the **CLAY** Ticket. The Alexandria Gazette nominates the Hon. James **BARBOUR** of Virginia for the same station.
  Rev. Wilbur **FISK** is chosen President of the Wesleyan College at Middletown, Conn.
  Col. Thomas L. **M'KENNEY** has been removed from the post of head of the Indian Bureau in the Department of War.
  On the 20th inst. Charles **CARROL**, of Carrolton, the only surviving signer of the Declaration of Independence, completed his ninety-fourth year.
  Rowland **STEPHENSON**, the fugitive London banker, is now living in great splendour, near Bristol, Pa.. He keeps many servants and hunting horses, and is building a new house. **LLOYD**, his clerk, who

Edenton Gazette and Farmer's Palladium 23 September 1830

came with him to Savannah, resides with him, as does Thomas **HORNER** [or **HOFNER**,] the founder of the Collisseum in London, to build which **STEPHENSON** furnished much money.

Geo. D. **PRENTICE**, Esq. who is now in the western country, collecting materials for a biography of Henry **CLAY**, is engaged to edit the "Louisville Daily Journal," to be commenced in November.

[327] [p. 3] Edenton: Thursday, September 23, 1830. ... On Friday last the Coroner of this County, T. V. **HATHAWAY**, Esq. called a jury to hold an inquest over the body of the negro woman alluded to in our last—the verdict was, "that she came to her death on Monday the 13th of September, by being shot in the left thigh," which wound was believed to have been inflicted by one Davis **HASKETT** who was accordingly arrested and committed for trial.—As the matter will of course come before a legal tribunal, we forbear making any remarks respecting the evidence.

[328] From the Fayetteville Journal. We call public attention to the extracts made from the Wilmington Recorder, on the subject of the designs of a paper printed in New-Jersey entitled the "*Rights of All.*" The people in the Southern States must act in self-defence. If Northern fanatics will jeopardize our lives and our properties, and scatter among us the fire-brands of rebellion and servile war, let the blow fall upon the heads of those who suffer themselves to become the dupes of the machinations of those fanatics. ... The approaching General Assembly will be obliged to pass some severe, though salutary laws. ...

We have read these numbers, with mingled emotions of surprise and detestation—surprise, at the audacity; and at the insolent tone which pervades the editorial observations—and detestation, at the principles which the editor aims to promulgate under the cloak of religion; and under the profession of philanthropic feelings. An admission of the free colored people of the United States, to a full participation of rights with the white citizens; and a general emancipation of the blacks from slavery, are the purposes to which this print is evidently devoted. There is now no doubt in our minds, that a conspiracy for exciting insurrection in the South is carrying on, by the free colored people of the North, under a sense of imaginary wrongs and privations; and that a part, a small part only, we hope, of the profligate white rabble of that section of the Union, are combined with them in this conspiracy; and that emissaries have been dispersed, *for some time*, throughout the Southern States, for the purpose of disseminating false principles and infusing the poison of discontent. ...

In the mischievous publication referred to, we find persons mentioned as agents, whose names, we deem it our duty to republish, expressing our hope, that those who live in our sister towns, from their standing as men of character, may have it in their power to exculpate themselves, from the imputation of knowingly and wilfully engaging as supporters of principles, which are subversive of law and order.

From the Rights of All. Authorised Agents in North-Carolina. Newbern, John C. **STANLEY**. Elizabeth-town, Lewis **SHERIDAN**. Boston. (Mass.) David **WALKER**. N. Orleans, Peter **HOWARD**. Fredericksburg, Va., M. D. **BATSH** and Arthur **WARING**.

[329] ELECTION RETURNS. *Washington.*—Sam'l **DAVENPORT**, Senate. James A. **CHESSON** and Uriah W. **SWANNER**, Commons. William M. **CHESSON**, Sheriff.

[330] MARRIED, In this County, on Thursday evening last, by William **GREGORY** Esq. Mr. Allen **LASSITER**, to Miss Rachel **BEASLEY**, eldest daughter of Robert **BEASLEY**, dec'd.

[331] DIED, At Auburn, N. Y. on the 12th inst. the Right Rev. Henry **HOBERT**, Bishop of the Protestant Episcopal Church of the State of New-York.

[332] FLOUR In whole and half barrels, just received from Baltimore, and for sale by N. **BRUER**. Sept. 23.

[333] CHOWAN MILITIA Regimental Order. The commanding officers and each of their respective Companies, will parade at Edenton on the 22d of October next, armed and equipped according to Law. The commissioned and non-commissioned officers will meet for drill the preceeding day at 10 o'clock in front of the Court House, by order of Col. *Josiah M'KIEL.* D. **M'DOWELL**, *Adjutant.* Edenton, Sept. 20.

Edenton Gazette and Farmer's Palladium 23 September 1830

[334] NOTICE. The subscriber has qualified as Administrator on the estate of *James WILLIAMS*, dec'd. and hereby requests all persons indebted to the same, to come forward and make payment without delay, and those to whom the estate is indebted, are requested to present their claims duly authenticated for payment within the time prescribed by law, or this notice will be plead in bar of a recovery. Paul BUNCH, *Adm'r*. Chowan Co. Sept. 21st 1830.

[335] Banner of the Constitution. This paper will be discontinued at Washington on the 4th of December next, as announced under the editorial head on the 11th of August, but it will after that date for reasons assigned on the 8th of September, be continued at Philadelphia or New York, provided that the increased patronage obtained prior to the first of November, shall warrant the undertaking. ... Condy RAGUET. Washington, Sept. 16th.

[336] NOTICE. The Subscriber returns his grateful acknowledgements to the citizens of Edenton and its vicinity, for the liberal encouragement he has received, and earnestly solicits a continuance of the same. He expects in a few days to receive a good stock of leather and materials of an excellent quality. He has in his employment several excellent workmen and will have work manufactured for his customers and the public generally, as good, and at a rate as low or lower than can be done in this place. Orders from the country will be punctually attended to. Matthew DENSON. Edenton, Sept. 23. [See Item #146.]

[337] *STRAYED* From the subscriber about the first of June last, a small dark bay horse MULE, about four years old. He has been much chafed on the thighs, and his mane has been roached, but may have grown out since he went astray. A suitable reward will be given to any person who will deliver him to Joseph UNDERHILL. Chowan Co. Sept. 23rd.

Edenton Gazette and Farmer's Palladium.
Vol. XXVI.....No. 40. Edenton, N. C. Thursday, September 30, 1830. Whole No. 1240.

[338] [p. 3] Edenton: Thursday, September 30, 1830. ELECTION RETURNS. Brunswick.—Wm. R. HALL, S: John P. GAUZE and Benjamin LEONARD, C. The above completes the election returns for 1830.
    William L. CHESSON, Esq. has been appointed Clerk of Washington Superior Court of Law, in the place of Thomas TURNER, resigned.

[339] ITEMS. *Resignation.*—The Rev'd. Francis L. HAWKS has resigned the Rectorship of St. James' Church, Philadelphia, and has accepted a Professorship in Washington College, Hartford, Conn.
    Thomas MUNROE (the reformed Postmaster of Washington City,) has been elected President of the Bank of Washington, in the place of *George CALVERT*, resigned. ...
    Indian Affairs.—Sam'l S. HAMILTON has been appointed Chief Clerk in the Bureau of Indian Affairs, in place of Col. T. L. MC KENNEY, removed.
    Execution.—The Governor and Council of Massachusetts, have appointed Tuesday 28th inst. for the execution of Jno. Francis KNAPP, at Salem. ...

[340] LIST OF LETTERS REMAINING in the Post Office at Edenton, the 30th September 1830, which if not taken out by the 1st January 1831, will be sent to the General Post Office as dead letters. A.—Stark ARMISTEAD, 3. B.—Hon. John BROWN, R. T. BROWNRIGG, N. BLOUNT, George BLAIR, Mary A. BISSELL, Mrs. Nancy BLOUNT, Robert BARTEE, Nathaniel BOURNE. C.—Mary CUTRELL, Joseph B. CHESHIRE. D.—Matthew DENSON. G.—Providence A. GREGORY, 3. H.—Eliza HARRIS, Martha B. HARVEY, John G. HANKINS. J.—Charles E. JOHNSON. L.—Hester K. LEE, Hester C. LEE, 2, Capt. John LAMBERT, Thos. LEARY. M.—E. MILLER. O.—Simon R. OLIVERA. P.—Mrs. PARSONS care of Wm. M'NIDER, Reuben PETTIFORD. S.—Wm. SPARKMAN, Nancy P. SKINNER, Willis SITTERSON, Captain Lemuel SAWYER. T.—Charles TABER, Mrs. Frances P. TREDWELL. W.—Richard WOOD, 2, D. S. WARNIER, Miss Mary WILDER, Frances WILDER, Mrs. Sarah WHIPPLE, Benjamin WHITE. Y.—J. P. YOUNG, M. D.—44 N. BRUER, P. M. September 30th.

Edenton Gazette and Farmer's Palladium 30 September 1830

[341] MARRIED, In Gates County, on the 15th inst. by Jos. **RIDDICK**, Esq. Mr. David **HARRELL** of Elizabeth City, to Mary D. **HARRELL**, of the former County.

[342] DIED, In this town on Sunday morning last, Ann Collins, aged 16 days, infant daughter of Dr. M. **PAGE**, of Richmond, Va.

Edenton Gazette and Farmer's Palladium.
Vol. XXVI.....No. 40. [sic] Edenton, N. C. Thursday, October 7, 1830. Whole No. 1240 [sic].

[343] [p. 2] *TO THE PUBLIC*. My character having of late been unjustly and wantonly impugned and grossly censured, I feel it a duty which I owe to the Public as well as to myself, to put a stop to, and correct the mis-statements which have been made concerning me. They have grown out of the following facts: Some time in the first of the summer, I received through the medium of the Post Office, two papers called the 'Rights of All,' published in Bellville, N. Jersey, by a colored man. By whom those papers were sent, (having never subscribed for the same) I was utterly ignorant, and it was with reluctance I took them from the Office; I however did so, and after reading them, loaned one of them to a friend of mine, not thinking that any thing of an unpleasant nature would grow out of it. In this I was however mistaken; and in a short time after, I understood, that reports were in circulation, questioning the purity of my motives, and censuring me in a high degree, with having a desire to influence the colored population to seek a redress of their *pretended* wrongs. These reports gave me (knowing my innocence of the charge) great uneasiness of mind, and I immediately wrote letters to several of my friends in different parts of the country, and one also to the editor of the paper, (which was submitted to the inspection of a respectable gentleman of this place) requesting them to inform me, if possible, who had sent me the aforesaid papers. I have since received the following letter, from the editor of the "Rights of All," which I hope will satisfy the public mind, in regard to this unpleasant affair. And I do hereby declare, that I have not, neither have I ever had in my possession, any pamphlet or newspaper of a malicious nature, excepting the above named papers, (both of which are now destroyed) nor do I intend to have or circulate any thing of the kind, believing as I do, that it would tend more to increase than to diminish the miseries of the colored population. Rigdon M. **GREEN**. Edenton, Oct. 7th 1830.

The letter is as follows: "Belleville, N. J. Sept. 23rd 1830. *"Dear Sir*—I received yours of the 14th inst. and hasten to meet the inquiries it contained. The two papers No. 9 & 10, and I think bearing dates, March and May, I sent at the suggestion of a friend of mine, merely with the view of extending the patronage of my paper. And I further certify, and will do it on oath if necessary, that you are not a subscriber to the "Rights of All." nor never was, nor did I ever receive a line from you nor direct one to you, until the present correspondence. Yours Respectfully, Sam'l. E. **CORNISH**." "Mr. Rigdon M. **GREEN**." The editor of the Newbern Spectator, will please give the above one insertion in his paper, and forward his account to R. M. **GREEN**.

[344] Thursday, October 7, 1830. ... MARRIED, In this county on the 23rd ult. by Josiah **SMALL**, Esq. Mr. Starky **BADHAM** to Miss Nancy **M'GUIRE**.

[345] DIED, In this town on Tuesday evening last, Ann C. infant daughter of Mr. Edwin **BOND**.

[346] *ATTENTION* EDENTON GUARDS! You are requested to attend at the Court-House this afternoon, at 4 o'clock precisely, on business of the Company. A full attendance is respectfully and earnestly solicited, as the importance of the meeting renders it necessary that a majority of the Company should be present. By order of the Captain, A. **SPENCE**, *Ord. Serg't.* October 7th 1830.

[347] LIST OF LETTERS REMAINING in the Post Office at Plymouth, N. C. Oct. 1st, and which, if not taken out, will be sent to the General Post Office 1st January next. **A.**—William A. **ADAMS**, **C.**—Thomas **COPELAND**, George W. **CLEMENTS**, **D.**—H. **DOWNING**, S. **DUDLEY**, **E.**—Horace **ELY**, Francis **ELY**, **F.**—Enoch **FAGAN**, Wm. B. **FESSENDEN**. **G.**—T. **GRANGER**, J. W. **GARRETT**. **H.**—Robert R. **HEATH**. Thomas B. **HAUGHTON** 2, Wm. L. **HUNT** 4, John L. **HOWETT** or **HOWCOTT**, Jas. **HAMILTON**, Welcome **HOEL**. **J.**—R. **JERNIGAN**, S. L. B. **JASPER**. **L.**—Harriet **LEARY**. **M.**—Demsey **MARRINER**. **N.**—John F. **NEIL**, Nelson **NIXON** 2. **P.**—Samuel **PETTERICK**, Abishai **PRITCHETT**. **R.**—Baker **ROBERTS**. **S.**—Henry **SWANNER**, Jas. **SHAW**.

Edenton Gazette and Farmer's Palladium 7 October 1830

T.—Henry **TRUE** 2. **W.**—John **WOODLEY**, Solomon B. **WHITE**, Taylor H. **WALKER**. Wm. A. **TURNER**, P. M. Plymouth, Oct. 7, 1830.

[348] LIST OF LETTERS Remaining in the Post Office at Hertford, 30th Sept. 1830, which if not taken out before the 1st January 1831, will be sent to the General Post Office: Benj. **BERRY**, E. **BRIGGS**, James **DELK**, Job S. **ELLIOTT**, Joseph **ELLIOTT**, Hugh **GODFREY**, Benj. **GREGORY**, Arail **HARRELL**, Miss Susan E. **HAMPORE** [?] Wm. **MITCHELL**, Elisha **PERRY**, William **REED**, Abram **RIDDICK**, David **SLOAN**, Nathan **TOMS**, Wm. **THOMAS**, Nathan **WINSLOW**, James P. **WHIDBEE** 2, John **WICKER**, David **WHITE**, Messrs. **MULLEN & WILSON** 2. John E. **WOOD**, P. M. Oct. 7th.

[349] NEW GOODS. The Subscriber has just received from New York...a well selected assortment of DRY GOODS, *Groceries, Crockery*, Hardware, Medecines, Oils and Paints of all kinds, which together with his former stock, he will sell remarkably low for cash, good notes in advance, country produce or on a reasonable credit to responsible persons. Wm. **BADHAM**. Edenton, Oct. 7, 1830.

Edenton Gazette and Farmer's Palladium.
Vol. XXVI.....No. 42. Edenton, N. C. Thursday, October 14, 1830. Whole No. 1242.

[350] [p. 2] MISCELLANY. ... The Hon. Philip P. **BARBOUR** has been appointed, by the President of the U. States, Judge of the U. S. District Court, for the District of Virginia, vice George **HAY**, deceased. We have not yet understood whether Mr. **BARBOUR** accepts the appointment.

[351] *Imprisonment For Debt.*—The Boston Manufacturer says that all the Judges of the Supreme Court of Massachusetts have expressed a decided belief that the law authorizing imprisonment for debt is unconstitutional. Daniel **WEBSTER** has offered his services gratuitously, to plead against its constitutionality, whenever any respectable body of citizens shall request them.

[352] *Execution.*—Another scene in the history of the Salem Murder has passed.—John Francis **KNAPP**, paid the forfeit of his life on the 28th ult. for the agency in the prepetration [sic] of the horrible crime.

[353] [p. 3] Edenton: Thursday, October 14, 1830. ... During the past week, the Fall Term of Superior Court for Gates County, was held at Gaston—Judge **NORWOOD** presided. Wright **ALLEN** from Hertford County, was convicted of forgery, and sentenced to stand in the pillory one hour, receive 39 lashes, and imprisoned 12 calendar months. Jethro **BRINKLEY** was also convicted of the same crime, and sentenced to stand in the pillory one hour, receive 39 lashes, and imprisoned 6 months.—The sentences were forthwith carried into execution.

[354] Mrs. **MONROE**, consort of Ex-President **MONROE**, died in Loudon County, Va. on the 23rd ult.

[355] MARRIED, In this county on the 1st inst. by Jacob N. **PARKER** Esq. Mr. Silas W. F. **ELLIOTT**, to Miss Nancy **HURDLE**.

In Hertford, by Henry **SKINNER** Esq. Mr. James **LONG**, Sheriff, to Miss Martha **NIXON**, all of Perquimans county.

In suffolk Va. Mr. William **JONES** to Miss Martha **WILDER**, both of this county.

[356] DIED, In this county on the 8th inst. Mr. William **SIMONS**. In this county on the 9th inst. Minton, infant son of Nathaniel **WRIGHT** dec'd.

[357] FALL GOODS. I have just received from Philadelphia and New York, an extensive and beautiful assortment of DRY GOODS, suitable to the present and approaching seasons—as it regards style, quality and prices, they will compete with any in market. ... John M. **JONES**. Edenton, Oct. 14, 1830.

Edenton Gazette and Farmer's Palladium 14 October 1830

[358] NEW GOODS. The Subscriber has just received from New York...a supply of Fall and Winter Goods... Jas. **WILLS**. Edenton, Oct. 14, 1830.

Edenton Gazette and Farmer's Palladium.
Vol. XXVI.....No. 43. Edenton, N. C. Thursday, October 21, 1830. Whole No. 1243.

[359] [p. 2] *Naval.*—We have been politely favored with the following list of the Officers of the U. S. Schr. *Porpoise*, expected to sail in a few days for the West Indies. J. **PERCIVAL**, Esq. Lieut. Com'r. *Lieutenants.*—Frank **ELLERY**, Jno. **MANNING**, Edw'd **BOUTWELL**. *Sailing Master.*—H. R. **THACHER**. *Purser.*—Edward **FITZGERALD**. *Midshipmen.*—Chas. S. **BOGGS**, Henry **BOORAUM**, Geo. R. **GRAY**, ---- [blank] **JENKINS**, A. R. **TALIAFERRO**, A. P. **BUCK**. *Comdt's Clerk*—L. **KENDALL**. *Gunner.*—W. S. **COWEN**. *Master's Mate.*—W. **JACKSON**. *Passengers to join the West India Squadron*—Lieuts. J. B. **MONTGOMERY**, J. M. **RINKER**, J. G. **VAN BRUNT**.—*Norfolk Beacon.*

[360] [p. 3] Edenton: Thursday, October 21, 1830. ... Rev. Benjamin F. **ONDERDONK**, has been elected Bishop of the Diocese of New York, as successor to the late Bishop **HOBART**.

George E. **BADGER**, Esq. was thrown from his sulkey, between Raleigh and Louisburg, on Tuesday the 12th inst., and had one of his legs badly fractured.

Mr. *George* **POINDEXTER**, formerly a Representative in Congress from the State of Mississippi, has been appointed by the Governor of that State a Senator in Congress in the place of R. **ADAMS**, deceased.

At the recent commencement of Dickinson College, the degree of Doctor of Divinity, was conferred on the Rev. Gregory T. **BEDELL** of Philadelphia, and formerly of this State.

[361] MARRIED, In this Town on Thursday evening last, by the Rev. Thomas **MEREDITH**, Mr. William G. H. **LAMB** to Miss Evelina **REA**.

[362] DIED, On the 2d inst. at Ocracoke, after a lingering indisposition of nearly 9 months, Mr. Horatio **WALLACE**, in the 23d year of his age.

[363] Valuable Trust Sale. By virtue of a Deed of Trust executed by Clement H. **BLOUNT**, for certain purposes therein mentioned, the subscriber will offer for sale, before the Court House door in the Town of Edenton, on the 20th day of December next: That valuable FARM, whereon the said C. H. **BLOUNT** at present resides, containing three hundred and fifty-six acres (more or less,) adjoining the lands of Thos. **BENBURY** and Jos. H. **SKINNER**, Esqrs. Also another tract or parcel of LAND, containing 213 acres, adjoining the lands of Thomas **BENBURY** and Zebulon **PRATT**, Esqrs. Also at the same time from 15 to 20 LIKELY NEGROES. Terms made known on the day of sale, by Wm. R. **NORCOM**, *Trustee.* Edenton, Oct. 20th 1830.

[364] NOTICE. The subscribers regret not having the pleasure of offering as yet to their friends and the public, Goods of the Fall importation, but have the following articles on hand in good order, equal in quality to those of recent importations; which they can and will sell at a much lower rate than those subject to the recent advances of from 10 to 15 per cent.—viz: English and a few domestic Print, do. Scotch & French Ginghams...Cambrics, Irish Linens and Lawns...Prunelle Shoes, seal-skin & morocco do Gent's calf skin Shoes...Stationary, Foolscap and letter paper...Looking Glasses, English Readers and small Grammars, and a variety of other useful and necessary articles too tedious to enumerate. R. H. & J. G. **SMITH**. October 14th 1830.

[365] NEW GOODS. *I have just received...from New York, the following articles,* viz: Fancy Prints, Furniture do., Paste-boards, Linen Diaper, Taper, Ladies and gentlemen's Hose...Gentlemen's colored Cravats... Also, N. E. Rum, Rye Gin, Butter and Cheese, Old Sherry Wine, Jamaica Rum...Sperm Candles, Coffee, Shot &c. All of which will be sold as low as can be bought in this market. Wm. F. **BENNETT**. Oct. 21st 1830.

Edenton Gazette and Farmer's Palladium 21 October 1830

[366] NOTICE. At September Term of Chowan County Court, the subscriber qualified as administrator on the estate of John JORDAN, dec'd, late of said County. All persons indebted to said estate, are requested to make immediate payment, and those who have claims against the same, are requested to present them whithin [sic] the time prescribed by law, or this notice will be plead in bar of a recovery. Wm. WALTON. Chowan Co. Oct. 16th 1830.

Edenton Gazette and Farmer's Palladium.
Vol. XXVI.....No. 44. Edenton, N. C. Thursday, October 28, 1830. Whole No. 1244.

[367] [p. 2] Domestic. ... *Pennsylvania.*—The general election in Pennsylvania took place on the 12th instant. In the 1st congressional district, Joel B. SUTHERLAND has been re-elected over Stephen SIMPSON (both JACKSON men) by a majority of 1051. In the 2d district, Henry HORN (JACKSON) has been elected by a majority of 572 over Daniel W. COXE, the anti-JACKSON candidate. In the 3d district, John G. WATMOUGH, whom the Nat. Intelligencer denominates anti-JACKSON, but who according to a correspondent of the U. S. Telegraph, was supported as a friend of the Administration as well as his competitor, has been elected by a majority, of 662 over the present member, D. H. MILLER.

[368] [p. 3] Edenton: Thursday, October 21, [sic] 1830. ... The Superior Court for Perquimans County was held in Hertford during the last week. There were two cases for murder on the docket. In one of them, the State vs. Amariah CAIL, for the murder of his daughter-in-law, there was no bill found by the Grand Jury, and the defendant has been released from his bond. The other was the State vs. negro FRED belonging to Nathan WINSLOW, for the murder of a boy. He was found guilty of manslaughter, and received 40 lashes.

[369] MARRIED, In Murfreesboro' N. C. on Thursday evening the 14th inst. by the Rev. James DEY, Mr. F. M. CAPEHART, to Miss Martha COWPER, both of that place.
    At the residence of Mr. Luke WHITE, in Bertie county, on Sunday 17th inst. by the Rev. Reuben LAWRENCE, Zachariah ELLYSON Esq. to Mrs. Ceney FOSTER all of that county.
    In Washington City, on the 18th inst. by the Rev. Mr. POST, Gen. S. DONELSON of Tennessee, to Miss Margaret, daughter of the Hon. John BRANCH, Secretary of the Navy.

[370] DIED, In this town on Friday last after a short illness, Mr. Henry B. SATTERFIELD.
    In Washington, on the 15th inst. at the house of the Secretary of the Navy, the Rev. Daniel SOUTHALL, of Murfreesborough, North Carolina.

[371] REMOVAL. The subscriber respectfully informs his customers and the public, that he has removed to his new Store on Main street, two doors above Mr. Jas. WILLS' where he will be glad to receive as heretofore their favors. ... Wm. F. BENNETT. Edenton, Oct. 28, 1830.

[372] RALEIGH REGISTER. *To the Patrons of the Register and the Public.* After an experiment of seven years duration, we find that the population of North Carolina is not sufficiently dense to support a semi-weekly newspaper. We commenced the publication of the Register twice a week, with an insufficient number of subscribers to warrant the increased expense attending it, confidently trusting that it would secure for itself additional patronage. Having been disappointed in this expectation, and having no reason, from the inconvenient arrangement of the Mails, to calculate on any material augmentation to our list of semi-weekly subscribers, we have determined to discontinue that paper on the 15th November next, which day will complete the seventh year of its publication.
    After that period, the Register will be published every Thursday morning, and in order that we may be enabled to give our readers, a full detail of foreign and domestic intelligence; a clear and satisfactory account of the proceedings of Congress, and of our own Legislature; a faithful record of passing events, as well as an agreeable variety of Literary and Miscellaneous Articles, we shall publish our paper on a large imperial sheet, with an elegant new type, procured for the purpose. We cherish the hope that the exertions thus made to improve the oldest and one of the most widely circulating papers in the State, will not only merit a continuance of its present numerous subscribers, but be the means of adding to their

Edenton Gazette and Farmer's Palladium 28 October 1830

number. J. **GALES** & SON. Raleigh, N. C. Sept. 30. The Weekly Register will, after the above date, be forwarded to the late subscribers of the semi-weekly paper.

[373] SHOES, SHOES, &c. I have just received in addition to my former stock, a handsome and cheap assortment, of Morroco, Prunelle and *LEATHER SHOES*, Also Vinegar, Alspice, Nails, pure Holland Gin, &c. &c. N. **BRUER**. Oct. 28, 1830.

[374] For Sale or Rent. The House and Lot, at present occupied by Messrs. **MASON** & **MASSIN**. Also the Store and Warehouse on the wharf, adjoining the Lot occupied by Mr. R. H. **MIDDLETON**—Possession of the former will be given on the 1st January next, and the latter immediately. Enquire at THIS OFFICE [sic.] October 28th, 1830.

Edenton Gazette and Farmer's Palladium.
Vol. XXVI.....No. 45. Edenton, N. C. Thursday, November 4, 1830. Whole No. 1245.

[375] [p. 3] Edenton: Thursday, November 4, 1830. ... *Census.*—Wm. **WALTON**, Esq. has completed the census of Chowan County, which amounts to 6697.—In 1820 it amounted to 6464. Increase 233.

[376] MARRIED, In this town on Thursday last, by the Rev. Mr. **MEREDITH**, Mr. Peter **MASSIN** to Mrs. Mary E. **SMITH**, widow of R. W. **SMITH**, dec'd.

[377] DIED, On Wednesday the 27th ult. in Perquimans County, Mr. Zechariah **WEBB**.

[378] Dr. M. E. **SAWYER**, Jr. Offers his professional services to the inhabitants of Edenton and the adjoining country, and hopes by his assiduity to the duties of his profession, to merit a share of the public patronage. He may be found at all times (when not professionally engaged) at the shop of his father, whose advice in consultation, will be afforded in all difficult cases without charge. He proposes to keep a good supply of genuine medicine which he shall be willing to sell at the customary apothecary prices. Edenton, Nov. 4, 1830.

[379] Town Property for sale. Pursuant to a decree of the Honourable Court of Equity for Chowan County, I shall expose to sale at public auction, on Tuesday the 21st day of December next, at the Court House door in the town of Edenton, the part of a LOT of Ground with the DWELLING HOUSE and improvements thereon, belonging to the heirs of Sarah **FALLAW** deceased, situated in the old plan of the town of Edenton, on the south side of Queen Street, near the Academy. Terms cash for so much as will pay the costs; upon the residue a credit will be given of 9 and 18 months, the purchaser to enter into bonds with approved security to Jas. **BOZMAN**, C. & M. E. C. C. Edenton, Nov. 4, 1830.

[380] The Establishment of the N. CAROLINA JOURNAL is For Sale. This Office is well found in all the materials and furniture necessary for conducting a newspaper. It has two good Presses; and besides the Type in common use, it has a quantity of Ornamental, Job and other type, entirely new. The patronage of the Journal is respectable, and might be much extended. To a competent person, who would devote a portion of his time and talents to the mangement [sic] of this establishment, it holds out fair prospects of handsome renumeration.

Persons disposed to purchase, will apply to the Editor for terms, which will be liberal and accommodating. Editors with whom we exchange, will confer an obligation upon us, by the insertion of this notice, in their respective papers, a few times. Fayetteville, N. C. Oct. 27th.

Edenton Gazette and Farmer's Palladium.
Vol. XXVI.....No. 46. Edenton, N. C. Thursday, November 11, 1830. Whole No. 1246.

[381] [p. 3] Edenton: Thursday, November 11, 1830. ... Mr. Rich'd W. **BENBURY** of this county, raised a Pumpkin on his farm the present year that measures 4 feet 2 inches in circumference, 2 feet 6½ inches in length, and weighs 76 pounds.

Edenton Gazette and Farmer's Palladium 11 November 1830

[382] *U. S. Bank.* The following gentleman compose the new Board of Directors of the U. S. Branch Bank at Fayetteville: Jno. **HUSKE**, (President) John D. **ECCLES**. Charles P. **MALLETTE**. Edward W. **WILKINGS**. Williamson **WHITEHEAD**. John H. **HALL**, Alex. **ANDERSON** (Wilmington) Beverly **DANIEL** (Raleigh.)

[383] Lieut. **SANDS**, Mid. K. E. V. **ROBINSON**, Dr. W. **JOHNSON**, and Mid. W. H. **PENDELTON**, have arrived at New York from Brazil, having been sent home in consequence of being concerned in the duel, in which Dr. H. W. **BASSETT** was killed.

Mr. Osborn **HENLEY** was robbed of $4,900 in United States Bank notes on the 15th ult. near Dinwiddie Court House, Virginia, by three persons, who had blacked their faces to prevent discovery.

[384] *Appointment by the President.* George W. **BUCHANAN**, of Pennsylvania, to be Attorney of the United States for the Western District of Pennsylvania, in place of Alexander **BRACKENBRIDGE**.

[385] MARRIED, In Perquimans County, on Tuesday evening last, by the Rev. Mr. **MEREDITH**, Dr. John R. **HERNDON**, of this town, to Miss Sarah **SKINNER** daughter of Charles W. **SKINNER** Esq. of that County.

[386] DIED, In this county on Saturday the 6th inst. Mrs. Nancy **WALTON**, wife of Wm. **WALTON** Esq.
In Plymouth on Friday the 15th inst. Mr. John L. **PICKARD**.
At Sha__etown, Ill. on the 14th ult Hon. John **MC LEAN** one of the Senators in Congress from that State.

[387] CHEAP GOODS. *James GORHAM* Informs his friends and the public, that he has just returned from New York, and now opening the following extensive and splendid assortment of Staple and Fancy Goods, Hardware and Cutlery, Earthen and China Ware, Hats, Shoes, Groceries and medicines. ... All kinds of country produce will be received in trade. ... November, 5th 1830.

Edenton Gazette and Farmer's Palladium.
Vol. XXVI.....No. 47. Edenton, N. C. Thursday, November 18, 1830. Whole No. 1247.

[388] [p. 2] DOMESTIC. ... It is stated in the Cincinnati American, that Arthur **TAPPAN**, Esq. of New York, has made a donation of $20,000 to the Lane Seminary, a Presbyterian Institution in Cincinnati.

Appointments by the President. Matthew **HARVEY**, of New-Hampshire to be Judge of the United States, for the District of New Hampshire, in place of John S. **SHERBURNE**, deceased. Frederick **LIST**, of Pennsylvania, to be Consul of the U. States, for the port of Hamburg, in place of John **CUTHBERT**, removed. Nathaniel **NILES**, of Vermont, (now in Paris,) to be Secretary of legation to France, vice Charles Carroll **HARPER** resigned.

Massachusetts.—John **REED** and George **GRENNEL** Jr. has been re-elected to Congress in their respective districts. ...

The General convention of the Associated Methodist Churches, is now in session in this city... Rev. Francis **WATERS**, D. C., was chosen President, and William S. **STOCKTON**, Esq. Secretary.— [*Balt. Gaz.*

[389] [p. 3] Edenton: Thursday, November 18, 1830. ... James **BARBOUR**, Esq. Ex-Minister to the Court of St. James has been returned as elected, by the Sheriff of Orange County, Va. a delegate to the next Legislature from that County.

[390] A most outrageous *Murder*, says the Milton Gazette was committed, on the 12th of October, on the body of *Henry POLLY*, of Halifax, Va. by *Phillip P. VASS*, with whom **POLLY** lived as overseer. It seems that **POLLY** was seized by **VASS'** negroes, acting under his direction, who held him, until **VASS** *cut his throat!* **POLLY** lived speechless a few days, but, fortunately just before his death, he uttered a few words, sufficient to disclose the particulars of the horrid deed. **VASS** is confined in Halifax Jail.

Edenton Gazette and Farmer's Palladium 18 November 1830

[391] *Elijah W. KIMBROUGH* and negro *CARY* were executed on Friday the 5th inst. in Raleigh agreeably to the sentence of the law. The multitude, which assembled to witness their execution was greater, says the Register, than was ever before gathered in that City, and, to the shame and disgrace of human nature, a large portion of the crowd were *females*. **KIMBROUGH** made no confessions.

[392] A Clerk in a Bookstore in Pittsburg, has been fined twenty dollars and costs of prosecution, for cowhiding Mrs. Anne **ROYAL**. It would seem that the *gentleman* was in earnest, and laid on with such a good will, that blood followed the blows.—[*Richmond Whig.*

[393] MARRIED, In Halifax County on the 2d inst. James **SIMMONS** of the town of Halifax, to Miss Martha A. **COOK**.

[394] DIED, In this town on Tuesday night last, after a long indisposition Mr. Phillip **SIMPSON**.
    In Perquimans County on the 4th inst at the residence of Wm: **JONES**, Esq. Miss Ann **AIRS**, in the 17th year of her age.

Edenton Gazette and Farmer's Palladium.
Vol. XXVI.....No. 48. Edenton, N. C. Thursday, November 25, 1830. Whole No. 1248.

[395] [p. 3] Edenton: Thursday, November 25, 1830. THE LEGISLATURE. This body convened at Raleigh, on Monday the 15th inst. and a quorum of both Houses being present, proceeded to organise, by the appointment of their officers. D. F. **CALDWELL**, Esq. of Rowan, was elected Speaker of the Senate, by a majority of 3 votes, over R. D. **SPAIGHT**, Esq. of Craven. Charles **FISHER**, Esq. of Salisbury, was elected Speaker of the House, by a majority of 9 votes, over Wm. J. **ALEXANDER**, Esq. of Mecklenburg. The old clerks and doorkeepers were re-elected in the Senate. Charles **MANLY**, Esq. was elected Clerk of the House, and Thos. G. **STONE**, as assistant Clerk. ...

[396] Beat This Wake!—We have now in our office, two Radishes raised in the garden of James H. **HARVEY**, Esq. of this county; one measuring 24 inches in circumference, and weighing 5¾ lbs., the other measuring 23½ inches and weighing 7¾ pounds.

Edenton Gazette and Farmer's Palladium.
Vol. XXVI.....No. 49. Edenton, N. C. Thursday, December 2, 1830. Whole No. 1249.

[397] [p. 2] STATE LEGISLATURE. SENATE. *Wednesday, Nov.* 17. On motion of Mr. **MONTGOMERY**, the Senate proceeded to the appointment of the Standing Committees, pursuant to the rules of the Senate, which resulted as follows: *Committee on Finance.* Wm. M. **SNEED** Louis D. **WILSON** J. **BLACKWOOD** Geo. O. **ASKEW** Jos. B. **HINTON** Tryan **M'FARLAND** Edmund **JONES** Edward **WARD**.
    Of Claims. Robert **MARTIN** Gabriel **SHERRARD** Robert **VANHOOK** Wm. R. **HALL** J. **M'INTYRE** John H. **HAWKINS** S. **DAVENPORT** Shadrach **HOWELL**.
    Of Propositions and Grievances. Jos. J. **WILLIAMS** Jos. A. **RAMSAY** L. R. **SIMMONS** John **HILL** M. **DICKINSON** John **BEASLEY** Daniel **HOKE** W. **MURCHINSON**.
    Of Privileges and Elections. Stephen **MILLER** Ransom **HARRIS** W. **MONTGOMERY** William **WELCH** Wells **COWPER** W. **MOYE** Alex. **MC'NEILL** Wm. P. **WILLIAMS**
    On the Judiciary. Wm. B. **MEARES** R. D. **SPAIGHT** Isham **MATTHEWS** David **NEWLAND** Clem't. **MARSHALL** John M. **DICK** Henry **SKINNER** Charles L. **HINTON**
    On Military Affairs. Edmund **JONES** Edward **WARD** Jno. H. **HAWKINS** Gabriel **SHERRARD** J. J. **WILLIAMS**.
    Friday, Nov. 19. Mr. **SKINNER** presented to the Senate, in the name of Gen. Jona. H. **JACOCKS** of Perquimans, a volume containing the "Reports of the Board of Managers of Prison Discipline Society," which was ordered to be deposited in the Public Library. ... Mr. **BEASLEY**, from the committee appointed to conduct the balloting for one Engrossing Clerk, reported that Daniel **COLEMAN**

Edenton Gazette and Farmer's Palladium 2 December 1830

was duly elected.

HOUSE OF COMMONS. *Wednesday, Nov. 17.* ... Mr. Amos **WEAVER** submitted a Resolution that a message be sent to the Senate, proposing to raise a joint select committee to enquire into the *possibility* and expediency of so altering the law with respect to the appointment of Clerks of County Courts, as to vest the right of electing them in the people. ...

[398] [p. 3] Edenton: Thursday, December 2, 1830. ... The U. S. Sch'r Dallas, Captain Thomas **PAINE**, arrived in our harbour on Sunday last, and made a handsome and novel display of flags, signals, &c. This vessel is intended to supply the place of one of the same name, that visited our waters some time since, commanded by Capt. Jno. A. **WEBSTER**, and from her easy draught of water, will suit our navigation much better than the one that preceded her. ...

[399] MARRIED, In this town on Thursday evening last by the Rev. Mr. **AVERY**, Mr. John B. **GOELET**, of Washington County, to Miss Jane, eldest daughter of R. H. **SMITH**, Esq. of this place.

In Newbern, on the 22d. ult. Mr. Wright **WILLIAMS** of Elizabeth City, to Mrs. Catharine **TORRANS**. [See Item #410.]

[400] DIED, On the 25th ult. Eliza L. [?] in her 12th year, eldest daughter of Josiah **SMALL**, Esquire, of this county.

In Perquimans County, on Wednesday the 24th ult. Col. Francis **TOMS** a highly respectable citizen of that county.

In Norfolk, on the 25th ult. Col. Andrew J. **M'CONNICO**, for the last ten years Post Master of that place.

[Communicated.] Died on Friday evening last in Elizabeth City, Mrs. Ann **BUXTON**, wife of the Rev. Jarvis B. **BUXTON**, minister of Christ's Church in that place. During the short period of her residence there, she had, in an uncommon degree, won the affection and esteem of her acquaintance. In amiableness of manners, cheerfulness of disposition, unaffected piety and the faithful discharge of the duties of her sphere, few of her sex have equalled her. The perfect patience and resignation with which she bore the severe and protracted sufferings of her last illness excited the admiration of all around her. Thus having exhibited in her conduct the exemplary virtues of a christian, she closed her life with a calmness and hope, comforting to her friends, and worthy of her faith in Jesus Christ, in whom alone she trusted for salvation.

On Saturday evening the funeral services were performed and a sermon preached in the Church by the Rev. Mr. **AVERY** in the presence of a numerous assembly, whose tears bore witness to their deep feeling and sincere regret.

[401] State Bank of N. Carolina, *Edenton Agency, Nov. 26th 1830.*} All Notes for renewal at the Edenton Agency, must hereafter be in Bank, by or before 1 o'clock P. M., on the day on which they become due, or they will not be received before the next discount day (Thursday.) All accommodation Debts payable by Instalments of 5 per cent, every 90 days, if not punctually attended to, will no longer be received on the same terms, but if renewed within the next succeeding 30 days, will be required to be paid up in three Instalments. D. W. **STONE**, *Agent*.

[402] Mrs. **HARVEY**'s School Will commence again at Hyde Park, on the 15th of January next. Terms of tuition.—For the higher branches of literature, $10 per session—lower $7. Boys from 7 to 12 years of age will be taken. Dec. 1.

Edenton Gazette and Farmer's Palladium.
Vol. XXVI.....No. 50. Edenton, N. C. Thursday, December 9, 1830. Whole No. 1250.

[403] [p. 2] LEGISLATURE. SENATE. *Wednesday, Nov. 24.* ... The resignation of Richard **HOWETT**, Col. Commandant of Tyrrell Regiment of Militia, was read and accepted. ... *Friday, Nov. 26.* ... Mr. **COWPER** presented a bill to authorize the County Courts of Gates to appoint Wardens of the Poor and to build a poor and work-house, and for other purposes, which passed its first reading.

Edenton Gazette and Farmer's Palladium 9 December 1830

HOUSE OF COMMONS. *Thursday, Nov. 25.* ... Mr. W. J. **ALEXANDER**, from the Judiciary Committee, to whom was referred a bill more effectually to punish persons guilty of burning Court-Houses, Clerk's Office, &c reported the same without amendment and it was read the second time. [The bill constitutes the crime a capital felony and punishes it with death, without benefit of clergy.] ...

[404] [p. 3] Edenton: Thursday, December 9, 1830. ... *Green Peas in December!*—We have received as a present and curiosity, from Mr. John M. **JONES**, several green peas, perfectly matured, grown in the garden of Baker **HOSKINS**, Esq. near this place, which were gathered one day last week. We learn from Mr. **J.** that the vines from which they were taken, came up as volunteers, after the spring crop was removed. This is a curious instance of the unusual mildness of the present season, and which is not confined to this section, but even extends much further north. ...

[405] Walter F. **JONES**, Esq. has been appointed Post Master of Norfolk in the place of Col. A. J. **M'CONNICO**, dec'd. The Norfolk papers say that the appointment will give general satisfaction.

[406] The Rev. John **LELAND**, recently a celebrated preacher of the Baptist denomination, the same who wrote a letter to Col. **JOHNSON**, in favor of running the mails on the Sabbath, has (says the Middlesex Gazette) renounced the christian faith and the sacrament of the Lord's Supper, and been excommunicated the Church.

[407] *Appointments by the President.* Col. Robert **LOVE** of this State, and Mr. **FINLAY** of Pennsylvania, Commissioners on the part of the United States, for running and designating the boundary between Louisiana, the Territory of Arkansas, Mexico and Texas.

[408] The Legislature of South Carolina, met on the 22d ult. Henry **DEAS**, Esq. was elected President of the Senate, and Henry L. **PINCKNEY**, Speaker of the House.

[409] SUMMARY. ... J. J. **KNAPP**, another of the abettors in the murder of Capt. **WHITE**, of Salem, Mass. has been found guilty and sentenced to be hung. Geo. **CROWNINSHIELD** has also had his trial, which resulted in his acquittal. He is however held to bail for misprison of felony. ...
 The Hon. John **ROWAN**, of Kentucky, has been considerably injured by the overturning of the Stage near Louisville. He was on his way to Washington City.
 Alexander **MOORE**, convicted in South Carolina, of the crime of Forgery, was hung on the 12th ult. pursuant to sentence. ...

[410] MARRIED, In this town on Thursday morning last, by the Rev. Thomas **BARNUM**, John **WEBB** Esq. Post Master at Merry Hill, Bertie County, to Mrs. Sarah M. **WILLS**, widow of Mr. James **WILLS**, dec'd.
 In Wilmington, on the 10th inst. Lieut. John H. **WINDER**, of the U. S. Army, to Mrs. Caroline **EAGLES**.
 Errata.—We were led into an error last week, in publishing the marriage of Mr. **WILLIAMS** of Elizabeth City, which we copied from the Newbern Spectator. It should have been Mr. Thomas P. instead of Mr. Wright **WILLIAMS**.

[411] LANDS FOR SALE. The subscribers, surviving executors of Josiah **HEWES** late of Philadelphia deceased, offer for sale, an undivided moiety of the following Tracts of LAND, to wit: One Tract called the Coffee House Land, containing about 130 acres adjoining the Town of Edenton. One Tract of about 48 Acres, situated about a mile west of the town of Edenton, adjoining the lands of Mr. John **POPELSTON** and others. Also one other Tract of about 225 acres, situated on the south side of Albemarle Sound, and about 3 miles east of Skinnersville, in the County of Washington.
 Persons inclined to purchase will be advised of the terms by applying to the subscribers at Philadelphia, or to Malachi **HAUGHTON** of Edenton: if the Lands are not disposed of at private sale before the 4th of February next, they will on that day be sold at public auction before the Court House door in the town of Edenton. W. **MEREDITH**, Isaac **HARVEY** ... Edenton, 4th Dec. 1830.

Edenton Gazette and Farmer's Palladium 9 December 1830

[412] NEW GOODS. Further supplies have been received from New York, per Schr. Delight & Hope, consisting of Staple and Fancy Dry Goods, Shoes, Groceries and Stationary... We think it unnecessary to mention every article as our assortment is now complete, and we only invite the calls of those who wish to purchase, that they may be convinced of the cheapness of the same. R. H. & J. G. **SMITH**. Dec. 1.

Edenton Gazette and Farmer's Palladium.
Vol. XXVI.....No. 51. Edenton, N. C. Thursday, December 16, 1830. Whole No. 1251.

[413] [p. 1] *A profitable tempest.*—When Isaiah **THOMAS**, printer of the Farmer's Almanack, was called upon by a printer's devil to know what he should put against the 13th July, Mr. **T.** replied, "any thing," upon which the boy set "rain, hail and snow," at which the country was amazed, but it so happened that it actually rained, hailed and snowed on that day, and proved a profitable storm to the proprietor of the Almanack for the future numbers.

[414] [p. 3] Edenton: Thursday, December 1, 1830. ... THE LEGISLATURE. ... On Monday the 6th inst. Willie P. **MANGUM** was elected U. S. Senator, for six years, from 4th March next, vice Gen. **IREDELL**, resigned. ... On Saturday the 4th, after three ballotings Robt. H. **BURTON**, of Lincoln, was elected Public Treasurer, for the ensuing year, vice Col. **ROBARDS** resigned, over his competitor, Wm. S. **MHOON**, of Bertie. ... On Tuesday the 7th. James **GRANT** was re-elected without opposition, Comptroller of the State, for the ensuing year. ...

[415] Distressing News. Our intelligence, (says the Newbern Spectator,) from the Bar, since the late Gale, is of a most distressing, disastrous character. We have seen a Pilot from below, who speaks of the blow as equalling in violence any he had ever witnessed. It commenced on Monday afternoon, from the North West, and continued to increase until 3 o'clock next morning, when it blew a hurricane: it began to abate about 11 o'clock. Among the losses we have ascertained the following: The schooner Ariel, of this place, Capt. **SCOTT**, after losing her masts, was driven among the breakers, and lost with her crew and pilot, Wm. **KILGO**, on board. The schr. Superb, also of this place, went on shore at Ocracock Point and bilged. We understand that the Ariel and Superb made every exertion, when drifting out, to strike on Ocracocke Point; this the Supurb, by the skill and address of her pilot, was enabled to effect. The Ariel, losing her masts, could not reach it, and passing the Superb, was shortly after seen to go down with her crew and pilot on the quarter deck; Schr. Prentiss Boy, from the upper Counties, dragged, both anchors ahead, among the breakers, and was lost with her crew. Schr. Experiment, of Portsmouth, was driven to sea and is considered lost with her crew. Sloop Eagle, of New York, ashore on Ocracock and bilged. A schooner from the North Counties, ashore at Ocracock. Sch: Emmeline, ashore on Portsmouth. Other loss was suffered by the shipping, but we have not heard the extent or the particulars.

[416] MARRIED, In Princess Ann County, Va. by the Rev. Mr. **SHERWOOD**, Dr. Wm. P. **MORGAN** of Murfreesboro' N. C. to Miss **Letitia CORNICK**.

[417] DIED, In Raleigh on the 3rd inst. Mrs. **HOGG**, wife of Gavin **HOGG**, Esq.

[418] Unanimity Lodge, No. 54 The Members of this Lodge will celebrate the approaching festival of St. John the Evangelist on Monday the 17th at their hall in the Court House at half past 10 o'clock A. M. when an oration will be delivered by a Brother. Members of adjacent Lodges and transcient bretheren [sic,] the clergy and citizens of the Town and country, are respectfully invited to attend. Suitable arrangements will be made for the accommodation of the Ladies. The Lodge will meet at 10 o'clock. By order J. H. **HAUGHTON**, *Sec'y.* Edenton, Dec. 16, 1830.

Edenton Gazette and Farmer's Palladium.
Vol. XXVI.....No. 52. Edenton, N. C. Thursday, December 23, 1830. Whole No. 1252.

[419] [p. 3] Edenton: Thursday, December 23, 1830. *Christmas.*—It being a general practice in this office, to give the persons engaged therein, a short time for re-creation during the Christmas holidays; the

Edenton Gazette and Farmer's Palladium 23 December 1830

Gazette will not be issued again until the 6th January next.

[420] *Destructive Fire!*—It is always painful to us to record...the ravages of this devouring element...and we believe it is the first time for many years, that a misfortune by fire has occurred in our Town... On Sunday morning last, at about ¾ past 4 o'clock, our citizens were aroused from their slumbers, by the awful cry of "Fire!" which proved to be too true. Our Town guard being out at the time and proceeding up Main street, heard a noise in the direction of Mr. John **COX**'s Store, and supposing it to be some one trying to enter it for the purpose of plunder, immediately repaired thereto, and to their astonishment and deep regret, found the Store on the inside in flames—no time was lost in communicating the intelligence to the citizens, but it was too late, the fire had advanced too far to be put out or any article to be saved, and the books, papers, goods, &c. to a large amount were all consumed. It is believed to be the work of an incendiary, and a fellow has been committed to jail suspected of being the perpetrator. ...

[421] *Disaster.*—We learn from the New York papers, that the schr. Olivia Cox, **PIKE**, from Murfreesboro, and bound for that port, was driven ashore a few miles north of Barnegat during the late storm. Capt. **PIKE** and one of the crew perished soon after landing.

[422] MARRIED, In Hertford on Tuesday last by the Rev. Mr. **MEREDITH**, Henry **GILLIAM**, Esq. of Gates County, to Mrs. Elizabeth **WOOD**, widow of Edward **WOOD**, dec'd.

[423] DIED, In this County on the 22d inst. Mrs. Mourning **BADHAM**, wife of Myles **BADHAM**, Esq.

[424] FOR RENT And possession given on the first of January next, the land and improvements thereon, situated at **NEWBY**'s Bridge, known by the name of Belvedier, consisting of a large and commodious DWELLING HOUSE, Store House and every other out house necessary for a Public House, or for a private family. The situation is a very desirable one for the former, and not surpassed by any country place for mercantile transactions in this section. A further description is deemed unnecessary, as it is thought that any person disposed to rent will view the premises. For terms apply to David **WHITE** near **NEWBY**'s Bridge or Exum **NEWBY**, Elizabeth City, Perquimans Co. Dec. 20.

[425] Almanacks for 1831, *and a few Lithographic Views of of* [sic] *the D. S. Canal, for sale by* T. J. **BLAND**.

1831

Edenton Gazette.
Vol. XXVII.....No. 1. Edenton, N. C. Thursday, January 6, 1831. Whole No. 1353. [Note: The second, third and fourth pages bear the head "Edenton Gazette and Farmer's Palladium," thereafter.]

[426] [p. 1] Published Weekly by Wm. E. **PELL**, For the Proprietor, Three Dollars per annum, in advance. Advertisements inserted on the usual terms. Letters to the Editor, must be post paid.

[427] [p. 2] Summary. ... The annual meeting of the State Bible Society was held in Raleigh on the 13th ult., the President (Doct. **CALDWELL**) being absent, Fred. **NASH**, Esq. one of the Vice Presidents, presided.
 Rumor says that the Hon. Mr. **LIVINGSTON**, Senator in Congress from Louisiana has expressed an intention of resigning his seat. Hon. Jas. **BROWN**, late Minister to France is spoken of as a candidate to succeed him. ...
 H. G. **OTIS**, Esq. has been re-elected Mayor of the city of Boston, for the ensuing year. ...
 Hon. John Q. **ADAMS** and lady have arrived at Washington City. It is rumoured that the Anti-Masons will nominate him for the Presidency. ...
 The President has nominated to the Senate the following gentlemen as commissioners for the adjustment

Edenton Gazette and Farmer's Palladium 6 January 1831

of claims provided for under the Danish treaty, viz: Geo. WINCHESTER of Baltimore, Stephen SIMPSON, of Philadelphia, and Jesse HOYT of N. Y. ...

A new paper under the title of the "Daily Journal," has made its appearance in Louisville, Ky. under the charge of Geo. D. PRENTICE, Esq. Mr. CLAY's Biographer—of course it is a CLAY paper. ...

A new paper entitled "The Globe" has made its appearance in Washington City and supports the present administration. It is conducted by F. P. BLAIR, Esq. late of Kentucky. ...

Major Jas. HAMILTON of S. C. was on the 9th ult. elected Governor of that State, by a majority of 26 votes over R. J. MANNING. Gen. E. B. DUDLEY, member of Congress from the Wilmington District in this State declines a re-election. ...

At an election held in Guilford County on 13th ult. for choice of representative in the House of Commons of this State in place of Amos WEAVER, whose seat was vacated in consequence of his ineligibility—G. C. MENDENHALL was elected. ...

Hon. Cadwallader D. COLDEN, who was nominated by the Anti-Masons positively declines being considered a candidate for Congress at the ensuing election in New-Jersey.

[428] Edenton: Thursday, January 6, 1831. ... We very much regret the loss sustained by Mrs. Martha BLOUNT, in having a valuable negro man named ABRAM, a carpenter, drowned on Saturday night last, while he was attempting to cross in a canoe, the creek which separates this place from Hayes. We learn that ABRAM had been drinking freely, and was so much intoxicated, that he was incapable of holding on to the canoe after she had upset, until assistance could be afforded. He was not found until the next day. The coroner held an inquest over the body on Monday.

[429] [p. 3] *Legislature.*—This body after having nine ballotings for Governor of the State, elected Gen. Montfort STOKES, of Wilkes county, on the 17th ult. to that office for the ensuing year. ... R. H. BURTON, the Treasurer elect having resigned, the Legislature on the 20th, went into an election to supply the vacancy, when (what a wonder!) on the 1st balloting, Wm. S. MHOON, of Bertie County was elected. ...

[430] [p. 3] The following are the officers of the Grand Lodge recently appointed at the meeting held in Raleigh for the ensuing year. Richard D. SPAIGHT, of Craven, Grand Master; George BLAIR, of Chowan, Grand Senior Warden; John H. WHEELER, of Hertford, Grand Junior Warden; B. A. BARHAM, of Raleigh, Grand Treasurer; & John C. STEDMAN, of Raleigh, Grand Secretary.

[431] The following gentlemen have been elected Councillors of this State for the ensuing year. Alfred JONES, Daniel M. FORNEY, George W. JEFFREYS, John G. BLOUNT, David NEWLAND, Gideon ALSTON and Nathan B. WHITFIELD, Esquires.

[432] MARRIED, In Newbern, on Monday the 27th ult. by the Rev. J. R. GOODMAN, Charles B. SHEPARD, Esq. to Miss Lydia G. JONES, daughter of the late Frederick JONES, Esq.

[433] DIED, In this town very suddenly on the 24th ult Mr. R. H. MIDDLETON, merchant.
In Elizabeth City, on Sunday morning last, very suddenly, Isaac N. LAMB, Esq. Attorney at Law.

[434] The members of the Edenton Missionary Society, and all others friendly to the institution, are respectfully requested to attend an annual meeting to be held on Wednesday evening the 12th inst. at 7 o'clock in the Methodist Church; on or before which time, it is expected that those who are in arrears to the Society, will hand in the amount to Mr. Richard HOWETT, the Treasurer. By order of the President, Wm. E. PELL, *Sec'y* Jan. 6.

[435] Edenton Academy. The Superintending Committee of Edenton Academy, respectfully inform the public, that this Institution is now opened, under the care of teachers, who, for character, learning, skill in teaching, and gentlemanly deportment, merit the patronage of the community. Mr. BOGART has charge of the Female Department, and Mr. BRIGGS, that of the Male Department. ... Board in good families may be obtained, we are authorized to say, lower than formerly. John AVERY, R. H. SMITH, Jos. MANNING, D. M'DONALD, John COX. Jan. 6.

Edenton Gazette and Farmer's Palladium 6 January 1831

[436] List of Letters Remaining in the Post Office in Edenton, on the 31st Dec. 1830, which, if not taken out by the 1st April, will be sent to the General Post Office. John AVERY, (Chowan) Reading B. ALEXANDER, Nath'l BEASLEY, BAGLEY & ELLIOTT, Hon. Bedford BROWN, Thos. BEELY, Cullin BUNCH, Wm. BRATTEN, Emily BRICKHOUSE, Thos. BARNSWELL, 2, John BLOUNT, 2 W. W. BENNETT, The heirs of Major Charles CHURCHILL, Thos. COCKRAN, Caleb W. COTTLE, Capt. John B. CARR, 2, Charles CREECY, Stephen ELLIOTT, Sr., Zecheriah EVANS, Polly FLOYD, Whitmel FELTON, Thomas GREGORY, Wm. GREGORY, Everard GARRETT, Nathan GREGORY, Myles HALSEY, Dr. Fred. HOSKINS, Thos. HEDRICK, Thomas B. HAUGHTON, Hend. JONES, Eliza J. JONES, Richard JORDAN, Morris W. KENNEDY Hester K. LEE, Grace LITTLEJOHN, Jane LADLING, Lavina M'GUIRE, Misses Ann & Eliza NORFLEET, John NIXON Sr., Robert NIXON, S. R. OLIVERA, Job PARKER, Sr., 2, Peter & Willis PARKER, John PAINE, 2, John PETTIJOHN, Phillip POINTER, Samuel ROOT, Wm. B. ROBERTS, Mary SKINNER, Alfred SATTERFIELD, Willis SITTERSON, Lemuel SKINNER, Wm. SPARKMAN, Exum SIMPSON, Philip SIMPSON, Rebecca SMALL, John SPENCER, Jas. I. TREDWELL, G. M. THOMPSON, Joseph M. VADIN, Benjamin WYNNE, Cap. Benj. WYNNS, Isaac WILLIAMS, Rich'd H. WHIDBEE, Humphrey WRIGHT.—70 N. BRUER, P. M. Jan. 6.

[437] List of Letters Remaining in the Post Office at Plymouth, N. C., Jan. 1st 1831, and which if not taken out before, will be sent to the General Post Office, on the 1st of April next: Charles BLOUNT, John D. BARBER, 2, John CORNELL, William CURRELL, Thos. CURRELL, Nath'l EVERITT, Josiah J. EVERITT, 2, Josiah FLOWER, John GOELET, Ezekiel HARDISON, Henry HARDY, Thos. B. HAUGHTON, R. R. HEATH, Silvery JAMES, Andrew JAMES, Johannah KEYS, Hardy S. PHELPS, Ransom RIDPASS, Tho. SOUTHERLAND, Uriah W. SWANNER, Silas SNELL, Thos. H. TURNER, Abner N. VAIL, Solomon B. WHITE, Reddick WATSON.—27. Wm. A. TURNER, P. M. Jan. 6.

[438] NOTICE THIS! The subscriber has just received from New York, a supply of Cut-Nails, from 6d to 20d, which will be sold low, also a supply of Family Flour, Goshen Butter, Loaf & Lump Sugar, Brown ditto...Sperm and Tallow Candles, Sperm Oil, Plug Tobacco, 8 by 10 Window Glass, Guns, Castings, and a beautiful assortment of Plain and figured Bonnet Ribbons. As he is disposed to sell as cheap as possible, those who may wish any of the articles above named, or any article in the staple and fancy way, will do well to give him a call at the corner store formerly occupied by Mr. Henry WILLS, where will be found an assortment of Goods, not inferior to any in the place. James GORHAM. Jan. 6.

[439] *Hillsboro' Female* SEMINARY. The Winter Examination ended on the 7th inst. The next session will commence on Thursday, the 20th January, 1831. This Institution has now been in successful operation five years, and continues, notwithstanding the pecuniary straitness of the times, to receive a full share of public patronage. ... A neat and well-selected Apparatus, together with a handsome Cabinet of Minerals, facilitate the task of instruction in the several studies of Chemistry, Natural Philosophy, Mineralogy. Two Teachers are always present in the School, and it is their constant aim to ensure obedience and promote improvement: not by blows, but by arguments of affection and self-respect. Rewards and punishments are administered with a parental hand.

The Superintendant deems it proper to state, that his health is so far restored, as to enable him, as formerly, to give his personal attention to the School. Any pupils that may come recommended to his care, will either be taken into his own family, or else placed in eligible boarding houses, and receive from him a paternal oversight. The moderate terms of Board and Tuition, together with the deservedly high reputation of Hillsboro' for health, good society, and religious privileges, justly demand the attention of Parents and Guardians. ... Board can be had in the best families of the place at $9 per month, including wood, candles, washing, &c. Wm. M. GREEN, Sup'dt. Dec. 8th 1830.

Edenton Gazette.
Vol. XXVII.....No. 2. Edenton, N. C. Thursday, January 13, 1831. Whole No. 1354.

[440] [p. 1] *William H. HORAH*, Esq. of Salisbury, has been appointed Cashier of the Branch of the

Edenton Gazette and Farmer's Palladium 13 January 1831

State Bank at that place, vice Col. John **BELL**, resigned: and Mr. *Wm. E. TROY*, has received the appointment of Clerk, in the place of Mr. **HORAH**.

[441] [p. 3] Edenton: Thursday, January 13, 1831. ... James **BOZMAN**, Esq. of this town, has been appointed one of the Councillors of State in the place of John G. **BLOUNT**, Councillor elect, who declined the appointment.

[442] DIED, In Perquimans County on Wednesday 5th inst. Mrs. Elizabeth **ROGERSON**, widow of Isaiah **ROGERSON**, dec'd.

[443] The Planter's Inn. The Proprietor of this establishment in returning to his friends and patrons his sincere thanks, for the kind patronage they have heretofore bestowed upon him; takes this opportunity of informing them that he has quit his former residence, and taken the commodious house on Main street, lately in the occupancy of Mr. Jeremiah P. **DORSEY**, where he intends keeping a Public House, under the above title. ... The situation is airy, healthy and pleasant; and its proximity to the business part of the Town, renders it highly eligible to the weary traveller and permanent boarder. ... His table will at all times be furnished with the best the country affords—his bar room well stocked with the choicest wines and liquors—his stables, carriage house and shelters are spacious, and the former well ventilated, and supplied with the best of provender, and attended by experienced and steady Ostlers... Relishes, beefsteak and oyster suppers (when the latter can be had) will be furnished at the shortest notice. Wm. **M'NIDER**. Edenton, Jan. 13th 1831. N. B. Those of my friends and customers who have been in the habit of calling on Mr. **PROCTOR** as my agent in the Market, will please hereafter call on Mr. George W. **M'NIDER**, who will serve them punctually, and on the usual good terms. W. **M'N**.

[444] Dr. **HERNDON** Respectfully but earnestly requests those persons who are indebted to him, to come forward and make payment. As he has heretofore been unusually indulgent, and as this is a season when money is comparatively plenty, he hopes that this call will not be in vain. P. S. Dr. H. has removed to the office which recently belonged to Dr. **SKINNER**, where he holds himself in readiness to attend to professional business. Edenton, Jan. 13t^h 1831.

[445] List of Letters Remaining in the Post Office at Hertford, on the 31st Dec. 1830, which, if not taken out before the 1st of April next, will be sent to the General Post Office: Wm. S. **BRYANT**, John **WHITE**, Miss Matilda **BRUSH**, Charles Archibald **WINTHRAWP**, Wm. **PORTER**, Dr. Charles M. **FORD**, Allen **MONDREYER**, Lemuel **GREGORY**, William **BURNHAM**, Mrs. Martha W. **JONES**, Jesse **STALLINS**, Mrs. Fanny **FORBES**, Messrs. **BAGLEY & ELLIOTT**, E. P. **AKERMAN**, Joseph **NEWBY**, James **BUNCH**, Robert F. **PAINE**, Nathan **TOMS**, **BRYAN & MULLEN**, J. **WILSON**. J. R. **BURBAGE**, P. M. Jan. 1, 1831.

[446] CAUTION! Some time in the month of March last, a man calling himself *Alexander J. MAURICE*, came to this place, professing to be a Universalist Preacher, and as such, was cordially received by the friends of Universalism. Some short time after his arrival, his friends becoming his sureties, he was enabled to purchase one half of the Printing Press, Types, and other materials used in the Office of the Carolina Sentinel, together with some other articles, amounting in all to about Eighteen Hundred Dollars. Scarcely have six months elapsed, when this same unprincipled scoundrel has shamefully absconded, and left his friends to pay his debts. Since his departure from this place, we have heard of his having carried away a gold watch entrusted to his care by a lady in the country, for the purpose of having it repaired in this place; of his endeavouring to pass a note forged by himself to the amount of $300; of his purchasing several watches on the eve of his departure, for which he gave his notes; of his borrowing several sums of money, and finally leaving his tavern bill unpaid.

This notice is therefore to caution the public, (particularly, in Philadelphia and New York, where he has been seen) to discountenance such a villian. Said Alexander J. **MAURICE** is about five feet five inches high, dark complexion, black hair and grey eyes, with a very prominent forehead. Editors throughout the States would confer a favour on the community by giving the above one or more insertions. C. R. **GREENE**, Edw'd S. **JONES**. Newbern, Dec. 21st 1830

Edenton Gazette and Farmer's Palladium 20 January 1831

Edenton Gazette.
Vol. XXVII.....No. 3. Edenton, N. C. Thursday, January 20, 1831. Whole No. 1355.

[447] [p. 2] An accident occurred on Thursday afternoon, which threatened to bring the business of the Legislature to a melancholy close. The roof of the Capitol was discovered about 5 o'clock to be on fire, doubtless communicated by a spark from a chimney. The fact was speedily made known to both Houses, and the members waited for no formal adjournment. By the spirited exertions of some of our citizens who were about the Capitol, assisted by the members and a number of colored persons, the fire was extinguished with but a little damage to the building. ... The thanks of the Legislature have been voted to John B. MUSE, the Governor's Private Secretary, and to Richard ROBERTS, one of the Door-Keepers, for the intrepid and active conduct on the occasion. A law has also passed for covering the Capitol with copper, tin, or some approved composition. *Raleigh Reg.*

[448] [p. 3] Edenton: Thursday, January 20, 1831. ... *A Large Hog.*—We never saw so large a Hog before, as was exhibited in our Market on Tuesday morning last. He was raised by Joseph N. HOSKINS, Esq. of this town, was three years old, and weighed 550 pounds. ...

[449] *Supreme Court.*—The following gentlemen have obtained licenses to practice law in the Superior Courts of this State: John B. MUSE, of Pasquotank; and Chas. H. SHEPARD, of Newbern.

[450] At a meeting of the Board of Agriculture for the State, held on the 1st inst. his Excellency Montfort STOKES was appointed President, and Charles FISHER, Esq. Vice-President of the Board, for the ensuing year.

[451] A pumpkin weighing 134 pounds has been raised this season, by Mr. Benjamin BELL, of Greenville, Pitt County.

[452] On the 29th ult. Thos. EWING, the opposition candidate, was elected U. S. Senator from Ohio, on the 7th balloting, by a majority of three votes over Mr. WILLIAMS, the Administration candidate.

It is stated in the U. S. Telegraph, on the authority of a letter from Frankfort, Ky. dated the 28th ultimo, that Mr. CLAY was then in that place, and was a candidate for the Senate of the U. States. It is also stated, that Gen. John ADAIR would be run by the friends of the Administration. ...

[453] MARRIED, In this county on the 6th inst. by Charles W. MIXSON, Esq. Mr. Willis SITTERSON to Miss Mary BROUGHTON.

[454] DIED, In Gates county on the 10th inst. Mr. James W. RIDDICK in the 29th year of his age.

[455] The Wardens of this County are particularly requested to meet at the place where the Houses are located, intended for the reception of the Poor, on Monday next, in the early part of the day, if fair, if not the next fair day. By order, Edwin BOND, *Sec'y.* Edenton, 20th Jan. 1831.

[456] Williamsboro' FEMALE ACADEMY. Mrs. O'BRIEN proposes to resume her school at this place on the 4th Monday of the present month. The aid which she will have will be adequate to the calls of the seminary. The subscriber, when not on his circuit, will feel it his duty, as it shall be his pleasure, to devote his leisure hours to the promotion of the best interests of the pupils, entrusted to our care and protection. Terms—For board and tuition in the higher branches of polite literature and science, $60 per session of five months. Do. do. for the elementary branches or first rudiments, $50. Music, per session $25. Spencer O'BRIEN. Williamsboro', Granville County. Jan. 8th 1831.

Edenton Gazette.
Vol. XXVII.....No. 4. Edenton, N. C. Thursday, January 27, 1831. Whole No. 1356.

[457] [p. 1] CAPTIONS *Of the Laws passed at the Legislature of* 1830-31. Public Acts. ... 8. To pre-

Edenton Gazette and Farmer's Palladium 27 January 1831

vent all persons from teaching Slaves to read or write, the use of figures excepted. [Any white person teaching a slave to read or write, to be subjected to fine or imprisonment; any free person of color convicted of the same, to be whipped, not exceeding thirty-nine lashes.] ... 31. To prevent the circulation of seditious publications and for other purposes. [Provides that any person who shall knowingly bring into the State, with an intent to circulate, or knowingly circulate or publish such publications, or endeavor to excite insurrection, shall, for the first offence, be imprisoned not less than one year, be put in the pillory, and whipped, at the discretion of the court; and for the second offence shall suffer death without the benefit of clergy.]

[458] [p. 3] Edenton: Thursday, January 27, 1831. ... Appointments by the President, by and with the advice and consent of the Senate. *Edward PESCUD*, to be Surveyor and Inspector of the Revenue for the Port of Petersburgh and City Point, in the State of Virginia, vice John H. **PETERSON**, deceased. *William LINN*, to be Receiver of Public Moneys, for the District of Lands subject to sale at Vandalia, in the State of Illinois, vice Wm. L. D. **EWING**, removed. *John Randolph CLAY* of Pennsylvania, to be Secretary of Legation of the United States, at St. Petersburgh. *Thomas FINLEY*, of Maryland, to be Marshal of the United States for the District of Maryland, whose commission has expired.

[459] MARRIED, In Northampton County, on the 30th ult. by the Rev. Mr. **REED**, Mr. Levi **BEEMAN** of Gates, to Miss Louisia **LUTON** of the former county.

[460] DIED, In this County on Wednesday, the 19th Mr. Starke **BADHAM**.

[461] Prospectus Of A New Weekly Paper. *To be published in Washington, North Carolina.* Entitled THE UNION. *"The Union—it must be preserved."* By George **HOUSTON**, Jun. The public have repeatedly witnessed the instability attending the various periodicals which, for many successive years, have appeared in this town. ... No pains have been spared, however, to ascertain the causes which led to the failure of our predecessors; and we trust the evils they encountered are so far discovered, that we may not only avoid a similar fate, but be enabled to awaken that confidence in the press which it was once permitted to enjoy. ... Confiding in the wisdom, integrity, and patriotism of our present Chief Magistrate, whose most ardent desire we believe to be to maintain the Union in harmony and the Constitution in its purity, we shall give a firm, decided, and unwavering support to the measures of his Administration. ...

[462] *CO-PARTNERSHIP.* E. P. **NASH** & Co. *Booksellers & Stationers*, Norfolk, VA. By the association of the subscriber, the BOOK, *Stationary & Fancy Business* will be carried on under the above firm. E. P. **NASH**, *of Norfolk, Va.* Miles **NASH**, *of N. Carolina.* They will feel grateful for any order that their friends or the public generally, may be kind enough to favour them with, and assure them, that no pains will be spared in giving general satisfaction. Jan. 22, 1831.

Edenton Gazette.
Vol. XXVII.....No. 5. Edenton, N. C. Thursday, February 3, 1831. Whole No. 1357.

[463] [p. 1] CAPTIONS *Of the Laws passed at the Legislature of* 1830-31. Private Acts. ... 11. To authorise Major John **CLARK**, or him and his associates, to build a toll bridge across Pungo river. ... 27. To establish the town of Gatesville, in the county of Gates, and to incorporate the same, and for other purposes. ... 46. To make valid certain official acts of Ezekie [sic] **BROWN**, Surveyor for the county of Davidson, and of Joshua **WILSON**, Entry taker of said county. ... 59. To authorise James H. **MARTIN** and William **HOUGH** to build a gate across the road leading from Wadesboro' in the county of Anson, to **DUNMAS**' Ferry on great Pedee river. ... 64. To authorise the County Court of Gates to appoint Wardens of the Poor, and to build a Poor and Work house, and for other purposes. ... 70. To authorise Daniel **GRAHAM** to erect a gate across the road leading from Fayetteville to Tarborough. ... 87. To authorize Aquilla **DAY**, otherwise called Aquilla **WILSON** a free person of colour to reside in this State.

Resolutions. 1. Resolution in favor of Solomon **GREEN**. 2. In favour of Samuel **REED**. 3. In favour of Duncan **BLACK**. 4. In favour of John **BALMORE**. ... 6. In favour of George **WATSON**, and Wm. **KENNON**. 7. In favour of Bridger J. **MONTGOMERY**. 8. In favor of John **COULTER**. 9.

Edenton Gazette and Farmer's Palladium 3 February 1831

In favor of William CARSON. 10. In favor of John BROWN. 11. In favor of Thomas BELL. 12. In favour of the legal representatives of the late Chief Justice TAYLOR. 13. Authorising a loan of Arms to Danl. H. BINGHAM. 14. In favor of the securities of James EASTWOOD. [15 and 16 were skipped by the editor.] 17. In favor of John MAC RAE. 18. In favor of David ROGERS. ... 20. In favour of David GRAYBEAL. ... 25. Returning thanks to John B. MUSE and Richard ROBERTS for their spirited and active conduct in extinguishing the fire which threatened to destroy the Capitol: also compensating the latter for his services.

[464] [p. 3] Edenton: Thursday, February 3, 1831. A man by the name of Joseph PLUMSTEAD, for some time a resident of this County, died on the road, about a mile from this place, on Saturday Last. An inquest was held over him—verdict of the jury, that he came to his death by a constant habit of intoxication.

Josiah S. JOHNSON, at present a Senator in Congress from Louisiana, was on the 10th ult. re-elected for six years.

Rev. Francis L. HAWKES, of Washington College, Hartford, has been elected rector of St. Stephen's Church in New York.

[465] *House of* Entertainment. The subscriber respectfully informs his friends and the public in general, that he has taken that large and commodious house in the town of Hertford, Perquimans County, recently and for a long time past occupied by Mrs. WOOD, and known as WOOD's Tavern, which he intends keeping open as a Public House for the accommodation of travellers and others who may favor him with their custom. The well known character of the House, he will exert all his powers to sustain, and pledges himself, that every department shall be so managed as to give entire satisfaction to those who may call upon him. Charges moderate. John GATLIN. Hertford, Feb. 1, 1831.

[466] Seine Twine *For Sale*. The subscribers have on hand about 500 pounds London SEINE TWINE, which they will sell low for Cash, or payable 1st June next. J. C. & W. R. NORCOM. Plymouth, Feb. 1, 1831. P. S. Any order will be attended to by applying to John COX, Esq. at Edenton.

Edenton Gazette.
Vol. XXVII.....No. 6. Edenton, N. C. Thursday, February 10, 1831. Whole No. 1358.

[467] [p. 2] Domestic. *Most distressing occurence.* About a month since, Mr. Abraham RIDDICK of Nansemond County Va. with his wife and child, were returning from Mrs. RIDDICK's father's, after spending the Sabbath, and in attempting to cross a Bridge a short distance from home the sleeper gave way; the driver being quite a small boy and unable to check the horses, they were plunged together with the carriage and persons into the stream below, which in consequence of the enormous quantity of rain was very rapid.—They sustained no injury from the fall, nor did the carriage immediately fill with water; the mother was several times heard to say "*save the child,*" but before they could extricate themselves from that miserable situation the carriage filled. Mr. RIDDICK made his escape by forcing through the window, which was shut, and with great difficulty gained the shore; discovering his child, but 3 months old, floating down the stream, he proceeded to and saved it, but the mother having no assistance, remained in the carriage some 20 or 30 minutes, till assistance was obtained, when alas! her spirit had fled. All the assistance that could be given she had, but no effort would answer. She has left an affectionate husband and fond father and mother, with a large circle of friends and acquaintance to lament her untimely death. *Norfolk Beacon.*

[468] [p. 3] Edenton: Thursday, February 10, 1831. *Snow Storm.*—We experienced on Monday last, a genuine old fashioned snow storm. The snow commenced falling, with the wind about North, at 9 o'clock, A. M., and continued without intermission until about the same hour P. M., when, after falling to the average depth of 4 inches, it abated. Several sleighs were put in requisition during the afternoon of Monday, and on Tuesday our streets made a lively appearance; as by this time, a goodly number of goods-boxes, were hunted up by some of our citizens, and were seen gliding along, apparently much to the gratification of those who occupied them.

Edenton Gazette and Farmer's Palladium 10 February 1831

[469] *Small Pox.*—As exaggerated reports may be circulated in the country and at a distance, of a case of Small Pox in this Town; we deem it our duty as public journalists, and to prevent any unnecessary alarm, to state all the facts, and leave the community to judge for themselves.

The schr. Gen. Jackson, Capt. Durant **TILLETT**, arrived at this port one day last week from Charleston, S. C.; the Captain in a day or two became indisposed and took lodgings at Mrs. **GARDNER**'s Tavern, and called in one of our most respectable physicians, who on the second or third day pronounced it a decided case of Small Pox. Measures were immediately taken by the Commissioners of the Town to prevent any intercourse with the House, and on Monday night last, Capt. **TILLETT** died and was buried the following day. Every precaution was used that experience could suggest, and with such effect, as in our opinion to prevent the possibility of a spread of the disease; and in this opinion we are sustained by the attending physician.

[470] Silvester **BROWN**, Esq. of Newbern, has been appointed British Consular Agent for that port.

The Legislature of Kentucky has adjourned without electing a U. S. Senator in the place of John **ROWAN**, Esq. whose term of service expires on the 3rd March next.

The Legislature of Alabama adjourned on the 15th January, having passed 127 laws, public and private. John **GAYLE** and Sam'l B. **MOORE**, Esqrs. are before the people of that State as candidates for Governor.

[471] DIED, In this town on Monday night last, Capt. Durant **TILLETT** of Currituck county.

[472] NOTICE. The subscriber having qualified at the last December term of Chowan County Court, as administrator to the estate of Henry B. **SATTERFIELD**, dec'd. late of this town, hereby requests all persons indebted to said estate, to make immediate payment; and those to whom the estate is indebted, are also requested to present their claims duly authenticated, within the time prescribed by law, or this notice will be plead in bar of a recovery. Wm. F. **BENNETT**, *Adm'r*. Edenton, Feb. 10th 1831.

Edenton Gazette
Vol. XXVII.....No. 7. Edenton, N. C. Thursday, February 17, 1831. Whole No. 1359.

[473] [p. 3] Edenton: Thursday, February 17, 1831. ... Gen. John **FLOYD** has been re-elected Governor of Virginia, under the new constitution.

The following gentlemen, in addition to those already announced, have been admitted into the practice of Law in this State. *In the Superior Courts.*—W. E. **PUGH**, of Bertie; Thomas S. **HOSKINS**, of Edenton, Samuel SPRUILL, of Tyrrel.

[474] [Communicated.] OBITUARY. Died on the 5th inst., at his late residence in Washington County, N. C., of a sub-acute inflammation of the Liver, Thomas **WALKER**, Esq., aged 56 years. Mr. **WALKER** had suffered for six months previous to his death, the effects of this formidable disease, during which time, at various periods, the symptoms exhibited such an amelioration, as to induce in himself and his friends a delusive hope of his recovery. Five or six weeks, however, before his decease, his malady increasing confined him to his bed; and although often yielding to the means adopted for his relief, it at length bid defiance to all opposition, destroying its victim, and bereaving his family of a sure friend and a firm protector. Well-known and justly esteemed in the community of which he was a member, by all who are morally capable of forming a correct estimate of character, Mr. **WALKER** lived in the faithful and conscientious discharge of all the duties appertaining to his station. He was an industrious, thriving and highly respectable farmer: He was a good neighbor, always mindful of the rights and feelings of others. He was a tender husband, an indulgent and affectionate father, and a master who governed entirely by the attachment inspired by his uniform mildness and lenity to his slaves! He was a forbearing creditor, and always exercised a scrupulous promptitude in the performance of his pecuniary obligations. His sympathy and benevolence were universal: ... He helped the poor, relieved the distressed and assisted the embarrassed. ...

[475] MARRIED, In this County on Thursday last, by Charles W. **MIXSON** Esq. Mr. John **TAYLOR** to Mrs. Polly **REA**, widow of Mr. James **REA**, deceased.

Edenton Gazette and Farmer's Palladium 17 February 1831

In Winton, (N. C.) on Thursday evening 10th inst. by John **VANN**, Esq. Mr. James **COSTIN**, of Gates, to Miss Mary **JORDON**, of Hertford County.

On Saturday evening, the 22th [sic] inst. at the same place, by James D. **WYNN**, Esq. Mr. Joseph J. **BARNES**, of Gatesville to Miss Louisa R. **CROSS**, of Winton.

[476] DIED, In this Town on the 3d inst. Charlotte Catharine, infant daughter of Wm. **M'NIDER** Esq..

[477] NOTICE, That on Thursday the 24th of February 1831, the sale of the perishable estate of *Francis TOMS*, dec'd, will commence at his late residence in Perquimans County—Consisting of Household and Kitchen FURNITURE, Implements of Husbandry, a wheat Machine, several valuable Horses, two prime Mules, work-oxen, carts, Hogs, Cattle, Sheep, and a large quantity of Fodder, Peas, Oats, 4,500 pounds of Bacon, a large quantity of Lard, and a great variety of other valuable property, will be sold on Thursday and Friday: And on Saturday the 26th. at the aforesaid place, will be sold *Twenty very valuable* NEGROES, Men, women, boys and girls. Also about 400 Barrels of Corn. At the same time and place will be hired for the present year, several valuable Negroes, men, women, boys and girls. Six months credit will be given to the purchasers, they giving bond with approved security to the ADMINISTRATOR. Perquimans Co. Feb. 14th.

[478] The Rising Sun TAVERN, Windsor, N. C. The subscriber takes this method to inform his friends and the public generally, that he has recently purchased that well established House, for many years known to some, by the above name, and better known to others as ***BRICKELL's TAVERN***, where he intends to keep a house of Entertainment, for those who may favour him with their company.—He flatters himself, that it is unnecessary to enter into detail and say what he will do, as it is his determination, to endeavour by all means, to support the good character which has been so long meted (not unjustly) to this establishment; and let those who may favour him with a call, judge for themselves, whether the proprietor is not worthy of the encouragement he solicits. Wm. **WATSON**. Windsor, N. C. Feb. 17th.

[479] TO TRAVELLERS. Persons wishing a private conveyance (either in a Gig or Carriage) to Hertford, Eliz. City, Norfolk, Suffolk, Gates Co. Ho., or elsewhere, can at all times be accommodated, on making application to Wm. **M'NIDER**. Feb. 17th 1831.

Edenton Gazette.
Vol. XXVII.....No. 8. Edenton, N. C. Thursday, February 24, 1831. Whole No. 1360.

[480] [p. 3] Edenton: Thursday, February 24, 1831. ... MARRIED, In Plymouth, on Thursday evening last by Alfred **WINCHELL**, Esq. Mr. Anthony **ARMISTEAD**, to Miss Ann Louisa, eldest daughter of Horace **ELY**, Esq. all of that place.

[481] DIED, In the State of Kentucky, on the 17th ult. of a lingering disease, in the 26th year of his age, Mr. Silvanus **HOWETT**, formerly of this town. Mr. H. was for several years a worthy and active member of the Methodist Episcopal Church, and it may be truly said of him, that his walk corresponded with his profession. In the various relations which he stood to society, he discharged his obligations with becoming fidelity, and clearly evinced in all his transactions with men, that his religion consisted not in the flimsy texture of a mere name. He was a firm friend and a comfortable associate. Notwithstanding his path through life's dreary waste, seemed checkered with disappointments and dangers, yet he was never neglectful to "look aloft" to that Friend in whom he trusted, for succour and protection. He bore his afflictions with astonishing fortitude and resignation; being sensible of the fact, that his "afflictions which were but for a moment, should work out for him a far more exceeding and eternal weight of glory." He was ever careful to be able at all times, to give a "reason of the hope that was in him." and in this particular he was evidently successful. And such were the consolations of religion, afforded him in the hour of death, that he looked upon the "grim monster" with a smile, and bade him welcome—and in the triumphs of faith, his cumbrous clay fell sweetly asleep in the arms of Jesus, and his happy spirit returned to that God who gave it. He has left many relatives and friends who had been endeared to him by the ties of consanguinity and years of friendship, to lament their loss—but they sorrow not as those without hope;

Edenton Gazette and Farmer's Palladium 24 February 1831

believing that their loss is his gain. The writer of this small tribute of respect, was well acquainted with the deceased, and can bear testimony to the truth of the foregoing remarks—and he in conclusion, is lead to exclaim with the prophet, "Let me die the death of the righteous, and let my last end be like his."

At Tallahassee, in Florida, on the 29th of December, 1830, after a few days of painful illness, Mr. Horatio MORGAN, formerly of Murfreesborough (N. C.)

[482] Thos. S. HOSKINS, Attorney At Law, Begs leave to inform his friends and the public, that he has removed his Office to the East room of the building in which Dr. HERNDON's office is at present located, near the Court-House, where he holds himself in readiness to attend to any business within the scope of his profession. Edenton, Feb. 24th 1831.

[483] Just Received...from New York: Stationary. Foolscap paper different qualities (some ruled,) Letter do. do. white and pink; 1, 2, 3 & 4 quire blank Books, Bank Memorandum do.; Quills, cut and blown Glass Inkstands; Sand Boxes (very neat.) School Books, and a few scrap tables for 1831: Hardware. Weeding Hoes...Cut Nails...Trace Chains, Axes, Spades, Shoe Knives. Tooth Brushes, &c: Groceries, &c. ... Expected Daily, A general Assortment of Cutlery and Fancy Hardware, Jewellery, Medecines, &c. John M. JONES. Feb. 24th 1831.

[484] NOTICE. *The subscriber has just received from New York, the following articles:* Weeding Hoes, Bradley's Axes; Trace Chains, Shovels, Bed Cords; Shoe Knives, (long bladed,) Ruled Paper, Gilt edge Letter do.; Webster's Spelling Books. Memorandum do., Sulphate Quinine...Opium...Floor Brooms, Cloth do., &c. ALSO, A general assortment of Iron, Wm. F. BENNETT. Feb. 24th 1831.

[485] $10 REWARD. Ranaway on the 15th inst. without any provocation whatever, my negro man **JERRY**. He is about 24 years of age, 5 feet 7 or 8 inches high, of a dark complexion, sharp face, and stoops a little when walking. I will give the above reward for his apprehension and delivery to me, or his confinement in jail. Baker **HOSKINS**. Edenton, Feb. 24th.

Edenton Gazette.
Vol. XXVII.....No. 9. Edenton, N. C. Thursday, March 3, 1831. Whole No. 1361.

[486] [p. 2] MISCELLANY. ... The Governor of South Carolina offers a reward of Three Hundred Dollars for the apprehension of James CUSAC, who is charged with the murder of John LUKE, in Darlington District, on the 7th inst. The said CUSAC is represented to be 22 years of age, about 5 feet 9 or 10 inches high, with black hair and eyes, ordinarily fair in complexion, usually dressed in broadcloth, is neat in his appearance, and retiring and reserved in society.

[487] [p. 3] Edenton: Thursday, March 3, 1831. ... Samuel ALPHEUS, formerly of this place, a hand belonging on board one of the Light Boats, while on his passage from Winton to Norfolk a short time since, in the canal-boat Experiment, was knocked overboard by the main-boom and drowned.

[488] *State Bank.*—Our readers will recollect, that some time since Duncan CAMERON, Esq. gave notice to the Directors of this institution his intention of resigning his place as President; but was induced by the wishes of the stockholders to continue in that station some months longer. He accordingly resigned the office on the 22d ult., when Peter BROWN, Esq., of Raleigh, was unanimously chosen by a full board of Directors in his place.

[489] At a meeting of the citizens of Murfreesboro', held on Friday evening the 18th ult., for the purpose of inviting the President to visit that place, Mr. John W. SOUTHALL was called to the chair, and John A. BROWN, Esq. was appointed Secretary. The object of the meeting having been explained, Wm. J. RANSOM, Esq. submitted the following resolutions, which were unanimously adopted: Whereas the administration of Andrew JACKSON, President of the United States, elicits our highest approbation: and whereas we entertain an unshaken belief in the sincerity of his patriotism, and the purity of his political integrity...and desirous of manifesting the same: *Therefore be it resolved*, We approve of that line of

Edenton Gazette and Farmer's Palladium 3 March 1831

conduct he has pursued since his election to the Presidency—That our most zealous hopes and sanguine expectations have been fully realised in the wisdom of his measures, and we return our unfeigned thanks for his endeavours, to restore "the constitution" to its pristine beauty and excellence... ... *Therefore, be it resolved*, A committee be appointed to represent to him the good feelings the inhabitants of this place entertain towards him, and request him, to visit it, when he shall pass through our State. Whereupon a committee was appointed consisting of the following gentlemen Lewis M. **COWPER**, Col. John H. **WHEELER**, Col. Chas. **SPIERS**, Col. Moses **CLEMENTS**, Dr. Thos. V. **ROBERTS**, Richard W. **JOHNSON**, Wm. **TRADER**, Thomas **SHAW**, Wm. S. **RANSOM**, Hardy M. **BANKS**, Jas. J. **PHILIPS**.

[490] MARRIED, In Perquimans county (N. C.) on Thursday evening last, by the Rev. Mr. **OWEN**, Gen. Jonathan H. **JACOCKS** to Mrs. Grizelle P. **FLETCHER**, all of that county.

In Bertie county (N. C.) on the 27th ult. by John **WEBB**, Esq. Mr. James **RAYNER** to Miss Francis **LAWRENCE**, daughter of Rev. Reuben **LAWRENCE**.

[491] DIED, In this town on Tuesday morning last, after a lingering illness, Mr. William **GRIMES** a native of the county of Bertie, but for many years past a resident of this town. Mr. **GRIMES** had for a long time, held the office of County Jailor and Town Constable, and although in these situations, calculated as, they naturally are, to produce enmity and ill-will, and considered by all as subordinate, such has been the line of his conduct, and such the promptness of his action, as to challenge the approbation of every good citizen, and induce them all to ask, "where shall we find a successor?" Many in the discharge of higher public duties, might learn a valuable lesson from the example of our decased [sic] friend.

In the midst of life, we are in death. It was but ten days ago we noticed the marriage of Mr. Anthony **ARMISTEAD** of Plymouth—to-day, he is no more. He departed this life on Saturday morning last, verifying in an eminent degree, the old proverb, which says "the House of easting [sic] shall be turned into the House of mourning." A young and interesting wife, with a large circle of acquaintances are left to mourn their irreparable loss.

Edenton Gazette.
Vol. XXVII.....No. 10. Edenton, N. C. Thursday, March 10, 1831. Whole No. 1362.

[492] [p. 3] Edenton: Thursday, March 10, 1831. ... Hon. James **NOBLE**, a Senator in Congress from the State of Indiana, died in Washington City, on the 26th ult.

[493] John A. **CAMERON**, Esq. has sold the establishment of the North Carolina Journal to Messrs. Thos. L. **HYBART** and Wm. F. **STRANGE**, by whom that paper will in future be conducted.

[494] The following appointments have been confirmed by the Senate: *George W. IRVING*, (several years ago American Minister to Spain) to be Charge des Affairs to Constantinople. *Wm. J. DUANE*, to be Commissioner (with Messrs. **WINCHESTER** and **HOYT**) to adjust the claims under the Danish Treaty, in the place of Stephen **SIMPSON**, rejected. The nomination of *S. C. STAMBAUGH*, as Indian Agent to the Menominee tribe, was rejected by the Senate.

[495] DIED, On the 9th inst. after a severe illness of a few days continuance, James **BOZMAN**, Esq., son of Mr. Joseph **BOZMAN**, of this Town. In the death of this gentleman, society has to deplore the loss of a useful and respectable member. His relations to the community in which he lived, were so numerous and so various, that his loss will be seriously and severely felt. To his family the stroke is peculiarly severe and afflicting; for in his social and domestic character he was amiable and exemplary. He was a tender, affectionate and provident husband, a dutiful and obedient son, and a kind and indulgent father. In the discharge of his duties as a magistrate, he was vigilant, zealous and faithful; and in every civil and political station in which he was called upon to act, he manifested a sincere desire to promote the cause of virtue and the public prosperity. By all who knew him, he will be long remembered as the firm friend of liberty and equal rights, and an enemy to every sort of injustice, tyranny and oppression!—[*Communicated.*

Departed this life, on Monday morning last, at his residence near **BALLARD**'s Bridge, Ephraim

Edenton Gazette and Farmer's Palladium 16 March 1831

ELLIOTT, Esq., aged 52 years. Mr. E. has been Post Master at that place for several years, which duties he fulfilled with the utmost exactness. He was also a Justice of the Peace in this County. In the death of this gentleman, the county is bereaved of one of its most active officers, and the neighborhood in which he lived, of one of its best neighbors. It may be truly said of him, that he was "an honest man, the noblest work of God."—[*Communicated.*

[496] State Bank of N. Carolina, *Edenton Agency, Mar.* 4th 1831.} The Bank at this place will after the first day of May next, be kept open only two days in the week; (Fridays and Saturdays,) when Notes that are falling due can be attended to. The day of discount having been changed from Thursdays to Saturdays; notes that will hereafter become due on Thursdays, will be in time for renewal if handed in by the Saturday next succeeding. D. W. **STONE**, *Agent*. March 10th.

[497] Furniture *FOR SALE.* The subscriber will offer for sale at public Auction, on Tuesday the 22d inst., the second day of Chowan County Court, before Mr. Jos. N. **HOSKINS'** Tavern, a quantity of FURNITURE of excellent workmanship and finish, consisting of Beaureaus, Work Tables, &c. The terms of sale will be made known on that day. Thos. D. **FLURY**. March 10th 1831.

[498] NOTICE. On Friday the 11th March at the late residence of Thomas **WALKER**, in Washington County, will be sold on a credit of six months, a number of HORSES, MULES, *HOGS, CATTLE AND* Sheep, a quantity of Pork, Wheat, Peas, Fodder, &c. and a great variety of Farming Utensils—and at the same time and place there will be hired out for the remainder of this year a number of Likely Negroes. B. **MAITLAND**, Jordan **WALKER**, *Executors*. Plymouth, Feb. 21, 1831.

Edenton Gazette.
Vol. XXVII.....No. 11. Edenton, N. C. Wednesday, March 16, 1831. Whole No. 1363.

[499] [p. 2] MISCELLANY. *A prolific family.*—"Go forth and multiply" was a command, and in the following case, the particulars of which have been handed to us for publication, the mandate has been well obeyed. John H. **SMITH** and Elizabeth **IRELAND**, both of Suffolk county, L. I. were married in the year 1765—the husband then in his 20th year, and the wife in her 16th. They are still living in the enjoyment of health, at a ripe old age; the former being in his 87th, and the latter in her 83d year. Their descendants are as follows, viz: 17 children, 97 grand children, 135 great grand children, 1 great, great grandchild—Total 250 of whom 210 are now living. As a proof of the good example, and the sage councils of the aged pair, in all the 210 descendants yet living, not one of them is dissipated or intemperate. How seldom in a family so numerous can as much be said—in this case, the old adage is not verified—"there is a black sheep in every flock." May their descendants yet to come, be as virtuous as those of whom we speak! N. Y. Mer.

[500] [p. 3] Edenton: Wednesday, March 16, 1831. In consequence of a new arrangement of the Northern Mail, (which leaves this place for Somerton on Wednesday evening at 3 o'clock, instead of Thursday morning,) our paper will be issued hereafter on Wednesdays instead of Thursdays. We hope to be able by this arrangement, to furnish the most of our readers with the Gazette much earlier.

[501] We are indebted to the politeness of Capt. **R. S. HALSEY**, of the Schr. Ocean, last from Turks Island, for the perusal of several numbers of the Royal Gazette, published at Nassau, Barbadoes [sic.] From the Gazette of Feb. 5th, we make the following extract, which will be found to be important: *Nassau, House of Assembly, Jan.* 28th 1831. Ordered, That the Address of the House to the Governor, of the 26th inst. His Excellency's answer thereto, and the report of this day, of the Committee on the subject of the American Slaves, lately seized for a breach of the abolition Laws, be published in the Royal Gazette, and that the Clerk do furnish copies thereof for that purpose. The Committee appointed to investigate the circumstances attending and consequent upon the late loss near Abaco of the American brig Comet with a cargo of Slaves, report as follows—

Mr. Isaac **STAPLES**, late the master of the American Brig Comet, of New York, Mr. Stephen **FOXWELL**, late the mate of the same, Mr. Joseph **CORRY**, master of the Island Sloop Sarah, William

Edenton Gazette and Farmer's Palladium 16 March 1831

FOX, Esq. Searcher of the Customs at Nassau, and John STORR, Esq. the Commercial Agent of the United States for this Colony, having been examined by the committee, in this case, it appears that the Brig had sailed from Alexandria in the District of Columbia, bound to New Orleans with 164 American born slaves on board (which with one afterwards born on the voyage, made 165.) and that having encountered very severe weather on her passage, very rarely seeing the sun, or other of the heavenly bodies, to govern her course, the vessel was considered to be much farther to windward than she really was, and at about ten o'clock of the night of the second instant, steering due south, she unexpectedly grounded on an insulated [sic] reef, between eight and ten miles to windward of the mainland of the Island of Abaco, and was there totally lost;--before day light the next morning however, an Island Sloop and some sail boats coming to the Brig's assistance, the lives of the officers and crew, and passengers, and of all the slaves, were saved, with a quantity of provisions and some water, by landing the whole on a small Key, called Spanish key, situated between the reef and the main land, at the distance of about three or four miles from the former, and five or six from the latter. This Key, though so denominated, is in fact a bare, desert and uninhabited rock, furnishing neither vegetation or fresh water for the use of man or beast, not a quarter of a mile in width, though much more in length, and separated from the main land by a channel of sufficient depth to admit of the passage of the largest of our common Island vessels. From thence the master of the Comet, with his people and the passengers, and slaves, were conveyed to the harbour of Nassau, in three small Island vessels, employed for the purpose, and a Brig of 126 Tons, was then immediately purchased, to forward those slaves to their port of destination, when William FOX, Esquire, as Searcher of the Customs, detained the said Island vessels with the slaves, then still on board, eleven of them having previously made their escape to the shore by night, and been by the proper authorities lodged in the Nassau Work-house; and on that detention being reported to the principal officers of the Customs, by the Searcher, he by their orders, proceeded to seize those slaves, and releasing the Island vessels from detention, instituted proceedings in the Court of Vice Admiralty against the Slaves (those in the work house excepted) with a view to their condemnation for an alledged breach of the abolition Laws. The slaves on board the Island vessels were then landed on Hog Island, immediately opposite to the Town of Nassau, and quartered in Barracks there, where they still remain under the charge of the officers of the Customs. ...

[502] Obadiah HOOPER was hung on the 10th ult. in Pendleton District, S. C. for passing a counterfeit note.

[503] Circuit Court of the U. States, for the Southern District of New-York—Judge BETTS; presiding.—The Grand Jury having found true bills of indictment against Charles GIBBS, Thomas WALMSLEY, and Robert DAWES, three of the crew of the late brig Vineyard, they were yesterday morning arraigned, and counsel having been assigned to them, they were remanded to prison, to await their trial, which we understand is set down for Monday next.—*Mer. Adv.*

[504] The General Naval Court Martial, assembled at the Navy Yard at Philadelphia, for the trial of Com. John O. CREIGHTON, having completed the same, adjourned on Thursday, the 17th ult. *sine die*. The decision of the Court is not known, and will not be until it shall have undergone the consideration of the Executive.

[505] Rev. Thomas CROWDER will hold his next Quarterly Meeting for this station at the M. E. Church, on the 26th and 27th inst.

[506] Turks Island SALT. For sale, afloat Three thousand Bushels heavy Turks Island Salt. Jas. GORHAM. Edenton, March 15th 1831.

Edenton Gazette.
Vol. XXVII.....No. 12. Edenton, N. C. Wednesday, March 23, 1831. Whole No. 1364.

[507] [p. 3] Edenton: Wednesday, March 23, 1831. We learn from good authority that Col. *John H. WHEELER*, of Murfreesboro' will be a candidate to represent this District (composed of the counties of

Edenton Gazette and Farmer's Palladium 23 March 1831

Chowan, Currituck, Camden, Perquimans, Pasquotank, Gates and Hertford) in the next Congress of the United States.

We have today published on our first page, the Circular of Wm. B. **SHEPARD**, Esq. to his constituents in this district—he is a candidate for re-election.

John A. **CAMERON**, Esq. of Fayetteville, N. C. has been appointed by the President, Vice consul of the United States at La Vera Cruz, in Mexico, in the place of Wm. **TAYLOR**, resigned.

[508] TO THE HEIRS *Of Abraham HARMAN, dec'd; late of Hertford County, and others concerned in the will of said HARMAN:* Whereas Abraham **HARMAN** did make, publish and declare his will and testament; and since his death the said will was proved and recorded in Hertford County, and the records of said County were destroyed by fire in the month of March 1830, among which records the said will of Abraham **HARMAN**, dec'd, was also destroyed; this therefore is to give notice to all whom it may concern that at the May Term of Court of Pleas and Quarter Sessions for Hertford County, I shall file a petition to establish said will, according to the act of Assembly of North Carolina in such case made and provided. Parker **HARMAN**, *Executor of Abraham HARMAN*. Hertford Co. Mar. 15th 1831.

[509] NOTICE. The subscriber qualified as administrator to the estate of Henry **NEWBERN**, at the September Term 1830, of Chowan County Court. All persons indebted to said estate are requested to make immediate payment, and those to whom the same is indebted are requested to present their claims within the time prescribed by law, or this notice will be plead in bar of a recovery. Willis **PARKER**. Chowan Co. Mar. 21st 1831.

Edenton Gazette.
Vol. XXVII.....No. 13. Edenton, N. C. Wednesday, March 30, 1831. Whole No. 1365.

[510] [p. 3] Edenton: Wednesday, March 30, 1831. ... To The Freemen *Of the counties of Perquimans, Pasquotank, Camden, Chowan, Currituck, Gates and Hertford*: Fellow-Citizens:--I am a candidate to represent you in the next Congress of the United States. In presenting myself for this high and responsible station, it is no less your privilege to require, than it is a pleasure for me to state the principles which I advocate, and which will regulate me should I be so fortunate as to receive your confidence and support. It has been a maxim, which I early learned from the wise and experienced, that the legitimate end of all government, is the welfare and happiness of the people. ... During the last four years that I have had the honour to represent a large and respectable portion of our district in our State Legislature, I can confidently appeal to those familiar with its proceedings, for evidence of the sincerity with which I have constantly kept this great principle in view. ... I have been always a warm supporter of the present Administration. ... I am gentlemen, Your obedient servant. John H. **WHEELER**. *Murfreesboro' N. C., Mar.* 21st 1831.

[511] DENTISTRY. L. **PARMLY** Will remain in Edenton a few days; and can be consulted at Mr. **HOSKINS**' Tavern. Ladies will be attended at their dwellings if preferred. March 30th 1831.

[512] NOTICE. The subscriber qualified as Administrator to the estate of *James BOZMAN*, dec'd, at the late term of March Court for the County of Chowan. All persons indebted to said estate are requested to make immediate payment; and those to whom the same is indebted are requested to present their claims within the time prescribed by law, or this notice will be plead in bar of a recovery. John **COX**, *Adm'r*. March 30th 1831.

[513] NOTICE. On Wednesday the 13th day of April next, I shall proceed to sell at the late residence of *James BOZMAN*, dec'd, all of his Household and Kitchen FURNITURE, Bacon, Lard, Pork, &c. &c. And on the following day shall commence at the store on Main Street, and sell the entire Stock of DRY GOODS, Hardware, Crockery and GROCERIES, which comprise a well selected and general assortment. Also the furniture of the store, and at the same time several valuable House servants, and Ten Shares of State Bank Stock subject to a lien of six hundred dollars. Six months credit will be given on all sums of ten dollars and upwards—under Cash. John **COX**, *Adm'r*. March 30th 1831.

Edenton Gazette and Farmer's Palladium 30 March 1831

[514] State of North Carolina, Gates County. *Court of Pleas and Quarter Sessions February Term*, 1831. Peter B. MINTON, vs. Thomas POWELL.} Original Attachment Levied on Land. Miles WELCH, vs. the same.} Original Attachment Levied on Land. Wm. D. TAYLOR, vs. the same.} Original Attachment Levied on Land. It appearing to the satisfaction of the Court that the defendant Thomas POWELL is not a resident of this State—It is therefore ordered, that publication be made in the Edenton Gazette for six weeks, that unless the said Thomas POWELL do appear at our next Court to be held for the said County at the Court House in Gatesville, on the third Monday in May next, and replevy, final judgment will be entered against him. Teste, J. SUMNER, Cl'k. March 30th 1831.

[515] Piano Forte For Sale. The subscribers have received on consignment a splendid Piano Forte, with Harp and Piano Pedal of great beauty and superior tone, which they offer for sale for Cash or on time. Any person desirous of seeing it, can do so, and also have an opportunity of trying it, by applying at the Counting Room of R. H. & J. G. SMITH. March 30th 1831.

Edenton Gazette.
Vol. XXVII.....No. 14. Edenton, N. C. Wednesday, April 6, 1831. Whole No. 1366.

[516] [p. 3] Edenton: Wednesday, April 6, 1831. ... A Fine Ox. My friends and customers, and the public generally, are respectfully informed, that that noble animal, fatted on the farm of Col. Josiah M'KIEL, of this county, and which was exhibited in our streets on Friday last, will be slaughtered and carried into market on Monday the 10th inst.; where any person who may desire it, can be furnished with a *choice cut*—no mistake. Wm. M'NIDER. Edenton, April 6th 1831.

[517] List of Letters remaining in the Post Office at Hertford, 1st April 1831: Albemarle Lodge, No. 77, Shadrach WALLIS, Jesse CHAPPEL, Dempsy HARRELL, Jas. BUNCH, Willis LAMB, William HASKIFT, Lemuel BARROW, Silas W. ELLIOTT, Jas. PRUDEN, Jas. P. WHIDBEE, Alfred M. GATLIN, John STAWNSON, William P. DRINKWATER, Richard SUTTON, James WESSON, Mrs. Fanny FORBES, Jas., Caleb & Isaac SAWYER, John M. WOODWARD, James M. GOODWIN, Wm. P. GOODWIN, James MULLIN, Jesse MUNDAY, Dr. Wm. MITCHELL, James MOORE.—25. J. R. BURBAGE, P. M. April 1st 1831.

[518] List of Letters Remaining in the Post Office at Edenton, 31st March 1831. **A**—John AVERY (Chowan,) 2. John & Jesse ASBELL. **B**—Wm. BENBURY, John W. & Julian BUNCH, Richard BEASLEY, Lewis & Nath'l BOND, jr. Edmund BRINKLEY, 2, Wm. R. H. BOZMAN, Cullin BUNCH, John M. BATEMAN, Nath'l J. BEASLEY, George BLAIR, R. T. BROWNRIGG, 2, John BONNER & Benj. BOYCE, Thos. BROWNRIGG, Baker & Jacob BAKER, Wm. BENBURY, John BLOUNT, Nathan E. BRICKHOUSE, Jos. C. BENBURY, R. W. BENBURY. **C**—Capt. Thos. CHAMBERS, Samuel CASWELL, Samuel G. CHESTER, 2, Thomas COCKRAN, 2, Chas. & Wm. CITIZEN, Henry & Bennett COFFIELD, James, Joel & G. CHAPEL, Carrier Edenton Gazette, Charles CREECY. **D**—John DOUGLASS, 2, S. DOLBY & John COFFIELD, Matthew DENSON. **E**—Wm. & Willis ELLIS, Stephen ELLIOTT, 2, Stephen EEOTT [sic,] Willis ELLIOTT & Wm. CLEMENTS, Jacob & Zech. EVANS. **F**—Wm. FOREHAND & Jno. DEVERSON, Wm. FLOYD & Wm. FORD, Henry FLURY, Wm. & Jesse FLOYD. **G**—Catharine GARDNER, Winneyfred GREGORY, Thomas GREGORY. **H**—Benj. HICKERMAN, James HARRELL, Charles HAUGHTON, Thos. V. HATHAWAY, Nathaniel HOWCOTT, Jos. HORNIBLOW, John G. HANKINS, Charles HOSKINS. **J**—Cela JORDAN, Wm. JONES. **K**—Sarah P. KNOX, Robert KEATING. **L**—Geo. LAMB, Wm. G. H. LAMB, Lewis LATHLEY. **M**—Joseph MERRYMAN, Daniel M'DOWELL, 3, John B. MISKELL, Wm. & Rich'd MIDDLETON, Lavina M'GUIRE. **N**—Jos. & Jno. NORCOM, Thos. NEWBY. **P**—Henry S. PARKMAN, Zeb., Jos. & Nathan PRATT, Jno. PAINE, 2, Job. PETTIJOHN. **R**—Tho. B. RUSSEL, James REED, 2, Wm. RIGHTON, Mrs. Martha REA, Wm. B. ROBERTS, Wm. & Willie REA. **S**—Sheriff of Chowan Co., Chas. W. SKINNER, Louisa A. SAWYER, Samuel T. SAWYER, Joshua SKINNER, Lemuel SKINNER, 2, John G. & Benj. SMALL, Josiah & Sam'l SKINNER, Thos. & Alfred SATTERFIELD, John STANLEY. **T**—James I. TREDWELL, Legal representatives of Sam'l TREDWELL. **W**—Thomas WESTON, George WHITE, Wm.

Edenton Gazette and Farmer's Palladium 6 April 1831

WALTON, Sarah L. **WAFF**, Benj. **WYNNE**, Rich'd **WOOD**, Wm. W. **WILKERSON**—108. N. **BRUER**, P. M. April 1st 1831.

[519] List of Letters Remaining in the Post Office at Plymouth, N. C. on the 1st April 1831. These letters if not taken out before, will be sent to the General Post Office, on the 1st July next: Clarkey **AIRS**, William **ALLEN**, Jos. **BATEMAN**, Benjamin **BARNES**, John **BATEMAN**, Albert **BEAL**, Joshua S. **CLARKE**, Thomas **CURRELL**, Remark **CHASE**, 3, James **COBB**, Hardy **EVERITT**, Enoch **FAGAN**, Maria **HILL**, Zechariah **HOWES**, 4, Samuel **HAWTHORN**, John D. **HALSTEAD**, James **HAMILTON**, Seldon **JASPER**, Hetty **JAMES**, Silvery **JAMES**, Andrew **JAMES**, Johannah **KEYS**, John **LONG**, Nehemiah **MANSON**, 2, John **MANSON**, Abishui **PRITCHETT**, Daniel **RICH**, Daniel **SMALL**, 2, Uriah W. **SWANNER**, Wm. A. **TARKINTON**, Joseph **TOXEY**, Lewis **VERAL**, Asa **VOLAVER**, Abner N. **VAIL**, 2, John **WILLIAMS**, Jordan **WALKER**.—44. W. A. **TURNER**, P. M. April 1st 1831.

Edenton Gazette.
Vol. XXVII.....No. 15. Edenton, N. C. Wednesday, April 13, 1831. Whole No. 1367.

[520] [p. 3] Edenton: Wednesday, April 13, 1831. *Dreadful Accident.*—We learn that a ferry-boat belonging to John **COX**, Esq. of this town, sunk on Friday night last, during a severe wind, while on her passage from a fishery on Chowan river, with stores for another fishery on the Sound, and it is supposed that the two negroes who were on board of her have perished. The boat was seen on Friday evening anchored off against the fishery of C. E. **JOHNSON**, Esq., and it is believed that the heavy wind from the north, threw the stores on board, on one side, and she immediately filled with water and sunk, and the negroes being asleep in the cabin, not aware of their danger, have no doubt perished.

[521] On the 3d instant, *Gabriel MOORE*, Governor of the State of Alabama and United States' Senator elect, resigned his office as Governor into the hands of Samuel D. **MOORE**, of Jackson county, President of the Senate, who will constitutionally exercise the functions of Executive officer until his successor is qualified at the next session of the General Assembly.

[522] DIED, In this County, on Thursday last, Mr. Jacob **BOYCE**. On Friday last, Capt. Samuel **HEDRICKS**.

[523] NOTICE. The subscribers having determined to close their business in Edenton, will sell any article in their line, (Stationary excepted) at 10 per cent. advance on New York cost for *Cash*. R. H. & J. G. **SMITH**. April 10th 1831.

[524] NOTICE. The subscriber has just received from Norfolk, the following articles which he offers for sale on the most reasonable terms for *Cash only:* 20 Bbls Fresh Family and Mountain Flour, 5 Hhds prime quality N. O. Sugar, which he will sell by the barrel if required. 20 bbls New E. Rum, 20 sacks Liverpool blown Salt. 15 boxes No. 1. Soap. 2 Bags Alspice, 2 do. Pepper. ALSO, A quantity of Turk's Island Salt, which he will sell to Fishermen on the usual credit. S. R. **OLIVEIRA**. Edenton, April 13th 1831.

[525] LOOK AT THIS! The subscriber has just received...from New York, a considerable quantity of Rope, Nails, Iron, Oils and Paints of divers kinds, all of which he will sell remarkably low for Cash, or at a reasonable profit on a short credit to solvent persons. Wm. **BADHAM**. April 13th 1831.

[526] FOR SALE. The subscribers offer by the hogshead, Barrel, Box and Bag, Whiskey, N. E. Rum, Super Holland Gin, Sugar, Soap and Coffee, for Cash. R. H. & J. G. **SMITH**. April 13th 1831.

[527] Seasonable Goods. I am now opening the following articles of seasonable Goods: Large size green Veils, crape Hdkfs, Fancy silk and gauze ditto, Angola Hose...Heavy silk Bandannoes, Super black Sinchews... James **GORHAM**. April 9th 1831.

Edenton Gazette and Farmer's Palladium 13 April 1831

[528] PUBLIC HOUSE. The subscriber takes this method to inform his friends and the public generally, that he has taken the Tavern lately occupied by Mrs. Elizabeth **WOOD**, in this place, and intends keeping a decent House of Entertainment, for all who may favor him with their company; and respectfully solicits the patronage of all such and particularly those gentlemen who have heretofore been in the habit of resorting the house. He deems it unnecessary to enter into a long detail and say what he will do, as it is his determination to endeavour by all means to give general satisfaction, and invites all persons to call and judge for themselves, whether or not the proprietor is worthy of the encouragement he solicits. John **GATLING**. Hertford, April 13t^h 1831.

Edenton Gazette.
Vol. XXVII.....No. 16. Edenton, N. C. Wednesday, April 20, 1831. Whole No. 1368.

[529] [p. 3] Edenton: Wednesday, April 20, 1831. ... **JACKSON** Meeting. A large and respectable portion of the citizens of Wake county, N. Carolina, having met at the court house in Raleigh, in pursuance of notice heretofore given, to express their views of the administration of President **JACKSON**, and take such measures as would promote his re-election. The meeting was organized by appointing *Romulus M. SAUNDERS*, Esquire, Chairman, and *Henry M. MILLER*, as Secretary. The Chairman very briefly and eloquently stated the object of the meeting. James **GRANT**, Esquire, submitted the following preamble and resolutions, which were read and unanimously adopted, viz: Whereas the citizens of this county, in common with the freemen of North Carolina, repose undiminished confidence in the integrity and talents of Andrew **JACKSON**, President of the United States...it is the opinion of this meeting that the preservation of the great interest and civil quiet of our beloved country require the re-election of Andrew **JACKSON** to the Presidency of the United States: *Therefore, Resolved*, That his moral energy, characteristic firmness and patriotic devotion to the principles of the Constitution...merit our approbation and gratitude, and eminently qualify him for the important and responsible station to which he has been called by the voice of the nation. Mr. William H. **HAYWOOD** offered the following resolution, which was unanimously adopted: *Resolved*, That for the purpose of promoting concert and union among the friends of the present administration in this State, it is recommended to our fellow citizens in the different counties of the State to hold meetings for the expression of their will, and to advance the re-election of Andrew **JACKSON**.

Alexander J. **LAWRENCE**, Esq. offered the following resolution which was unanimously adopted, viz: *Resolved*, That the Chairman appoint a corresponding committee of seven, and a committee of Vigilance of 22. H. M. **MILLER** offered the following resolutions, which were unanimously adopted, viz: *Resolved*, that these proceedings be signed by the Chairman and Secretary, and a copy be forwarded to the President. *Resolved therefore*, that the Editors of this city be requested to published [sic] these proceedings in their newspapers. R. M. **SAUNDERS**, Chairman. H. M. **MILLER**, Secretary.

Committee of Correspondence.—Alex. J. **LAWRENCE**, Wm. H. **HAYWOOD**, Jr. Wm. **HILL**, James **GRANT**, Wm. S. **MHOON**, John C. **STEDMAN** and Henry M. **MILLER**.

Committee of Vigilance.—Col. Allen **ROGERS**, William B. **DUNN**, Charles L. **HINTON**, Newton **WOOD**, Anderson **WILKINS**, Johnston **BUSBEE**, Willis **WHITAKER**, Nathaniel G. **RAND**, Woodson **CLEMENTS**, Wesley **JONES**, Kimbrough **JONES**, William R. **HINTON**, Dr. Thomas **COTTRELL**, Henry **JONES**, Henry **M'GEHEE**, Thomas **ROYCROFT**, Henry **WARREN**, James M. **MANGUM**, Absalom P. **WOODALL**, James D. **NEWSOM**, Darrell **ROGERS** and David **HOLLAND**.

[530] MARRIED, In Little Rock, Arkansas Territory, by the Hon. P. T. **CRUTCHFIELD**, Mr. William T. **YEOMANS**, junior Editor of the Arkansas Advocate, to Miss Martha A. W. **NASH**, late of Missouri.

[531] DIED, In Hertford, on Thursday the 7th inst. Mrs. Eliza **ELLIOTT** consort of Mr. Exum **ELLIOTT** of that place.

[532] NOTICE. The subscribers having been appointed at March Term of Chowan County Court, Commissioners to superintend the building of a new bridge across Machimacomic Creek, at the place where **BOULTON**'s Bridge now stands, give notice that on the 21st day of May next, they will let out the building of said Bridge to the lowest bidder, before Mr. Jos. N. **HOSKINS**' Tavern in the town of

Edenton Gazette and Farmer's Palladium 20 April 1831

Edenton; at which time and place, the terms, plan and manner of building will be made known. Baker **HOSKINS**, Wm. **BULLOCK**, *Com'rs.* Chowan Co., April 20th 1831.

Edenton Gazette.
Vol. XXVII.....No. 17. Edenton, N. C. Wednesday, April 27, 1831. Whole No. 1369.

[533] [p. 2] Domestic. *Mournful casualty!*—We announce, with deep sympathy to the affliction which the event visits on her fond parents, and in the hope that it will operate as a solemn warning to young persons, the fact, that Sarah, the interesting little daughter of Mr. John D. **GORDAN**, aged about 4 years, was poisoned yesterday from eating *yellow Jessamine flowers*. The child, we learn, was in good health at the breakfast table, went out and came home an hour or two after, to breathe her last in the arms of her parents who are overwhelmed with grief by the sudden and heart rending event. *Norfolk Beacon.*

[534] *University of Pennsylvania.*—At a Medical Commencement of this institution, held on the 24th ultimo, the degree of Doctor of Medicine was conferred on the following gentlemen from North Carolina: Geo. **BLACKNALL**, Lawson F. **HENDERSON**, Robert H. **DALTON**, Thos. D. **PARKE**, Algernon S. **PERRY**, G. W. **CALDWELL**, James K. **MISHET**, William L. **HOGAN**, John **ALLISON**, Calvin C. **COVINGTON**, Joseph H. **CHEAIRS**.

South Carolina Medical College.—At the Commencement of this College, held on the 18th ult. the following gentlemen from this State also received the degree of Doctor of Medicine: James F. **HARDY**, Walter A. **NORWOOD**, William C. **TATE** and William H. **TRENT**.

Transylvania University, Ky.—At a late commencement of this University, the same degree was conferred on the following gentlemen from this State: Chas. W. A. **ALEXANDER**, S. P. **BURNETT**, N. E. **M'LELLAND** and Rufus A. **WALLACE**.

[535] [p. 3] Edenton: Wednesday, April 27, 1831. ... *Mammoth Grape Vine.*—We are informed by a friend, that there is now growing on Chowan river, near Mr. James **COFFIELD**'s fishery, a bunch Grape Vine, measuring 41¼ inches in circumference at its base and nearly as large at its first branch (forty feet from the ground,) and reaching to the tops of the loftiest trees near it.

John **HAYWOOD**, Esq. of Windsor, N. C. has been appointed by the President, Surveyor and Inspector of the revenue for that port, vice James **PALMER**, dec'd.

Gen. Robert B. **TAYLOR**, of Norfolk, has been elected, by the Legislature of Virginia, under the new Constitution, Judge of the first Judicial District, by one vote over the late incumbent R. E. **PARKER**, Esq.

[536] DIED, In Baltimore, on Friday, 15th inst. in the 47th year of his age, the Hon. Rollin C. **MALLARY**, for several years past a member of the House of Representatives of the U. States from Vermont and for the last five or six years Chairman of the Committee on Manufactures.

[537] FOR SALE. The subscriber has on hand and offers for sale the following articles, very low for Cash or Country produce: 30 Casks Stone Lime, 30 barrels New England Rum, 25 do. Whiskey, 4 Hhds Do. Hogsheads Molasses, 3 do. Sugar, 40 coils Cordage assorted sizes, 300 bushels Cadiz Salt...7 Kegs prime Tobacco, 100 lbs. best chewing do., Soap and Candles by the box, Coffee by the Bag. J. H. **HAUGHTON**. April 27th 1831.

Edenton Gazette.
Vol. XXVII.....No. 18. Edenton, N. C. Wednesday, May 4, 1831. Whole No. 1370.

[538] [p. 2] Mr. A. E. **MILLER** of Charleston, and John B. **IRVING** have undertaken the publication of the Southern Review, for the next three years, and H. S. **LEGARE** will be associated with the editor Stephen **ELLIOTT**, in the Literary Department. ...

[539] *Joseph A.* **HILL**, Esq. of Wilmington, declines accepting the nomination of his friends in Brunswick, as a candidate for Congress, in the place of Gen. **DUDLEY**; and Gen. **M'KAY** has been solicited to offer his services.

Edenton Gazette and Farmer's Palladium 4 May 1831

[540] [p. 3] Edenton: Wednesday, May 4, 1831. *Gale.*—We rarely witness at this season of the year, as severe a storm as was experienced here last week. It commenced raining on Tuesday evening, and about 10 o'clock, P. M., the wind blew with considerable violence and continued until Thursday morning, when it subsided, it however continued to rain until the evening of the same day. A number of fences and an old wind-mill in this town were prostrated by it, and we apprehend that the growing crops of corn and cotton were much injured. ...

[541] DIED, In Gates County, last week, Mr. Decatur **PERRY** of the North Banks, Currituck County, North Carolina.

Edenton Gazette.
Vol. XXVII.....No. 19. Edenton, N. C. Wednesday, May 11, 1831. Whole No. 1371.

[542] [p. 3] Edenton: Wednesday, May 11, 1831. ... OBITUARY. Died on Friday night last, after a lingering indisposition, Henry **FLURY**, Esq. in the 68th year of his age, a respectable inhabitant of this town. In discharging the various duties both in civil and religious life, which devolved upon him, Mr. F. had for many years, won the esteem and friendship of the community in which he lived, in no small degree. As a representative in the State Legislature from this town and Magistrate of the County, he deserved and commanded the confidence of his constituents and fellow citizens; and such was his devotedness to business while he held the latter station, that he was in almost every instance resorted to for the adjustment of difficulties, &c. which transpired under his jurisdiction, and he was universally respected for his righteous decisions. He was withal a good man and a faithful friend. His friendship was extended alike to all, nor did he look upon any man as his enemy—his deeds of charity and benevolence so far as he was capable, were bestowed indiscriminately on his fellow-beings, with a willing hand and cheerful heart. He obeyed that divine injunction to the letter, which says "Visit the sick, &c." and the helpless and distressed always found in him a sympathising benefactor. From the infirmities of old age and exposure, his mind as well as his body had been for some time much impaired, yet, notwithstanding this, he was not unmindful of the relations in which he stood to his God and his fellow men. It is worthy of remark, that so far as his capabilities extended, no man deserved in a more eminent degree the respect and good will of his fellow citizens, and few men possessed a larger portion of those qualities requisite to the character of a christian and philanthropist—As he drew near to the tomb, his usefulness in society was necessarily diminished, but this was the time when his virtues and piety exhibited themselves most conspicuous. Although his bodily afflictions were of the severest kind, he found consolation and support in One who had been the object of his attachment for nearly two score years. It was about the time of his dissolution that he needed help, and that help was afforded. He conversed of death with the greatest composure for months before his exit, nor did the monster alarm him as he approached nearer the tomb; he could look up with confidence and claim Jesus as his friend and heaven his home,--and such were the exercises of his mind at this time, that he frequently broke out in strains of triumph, "Glory be to God," "the best of all God is with me." He has left fond friends to lament their loss, but their tears are wiped away by the recollection that they shall see him again in another state of existence. May those of his friends whom he has left behind (and they are not few) imitate his example and aspire after that wisdom which is the result of an acquaintance with God.

[543] Spring Goods. *New Stock Entire!* The subscriber has just returned from New York with a general assortment of Spring and Summer GOODS, which, for Cash, will be sold as low as they can be bought in the place; and he flatters himself that his assortment is as well selected as any other, and begs leave, respectfully, to invite a call from those persons who have to purchase articles in his line... N. **BRUER**. May 11th 1831.

[544] $70 Reward. Runaway from the subscriber on the nights of the 4th and 6th instant, two negro men, (slaves) **ISAAC** and **TOM**. ISAAC is about five feet 10 or 11 inches high, erect in stature, about 30 years of age, young look, likely, slim built, speaks quick, little lighter color than a negro, commonly called Isaac **TREDWELL**. He has travelled much, and driven a carriage, is therefore generally known on the main post roads. He has been almost constantly travelling for 12 months past, and may have

Edenton Gazette and Farmer's Palladium 11 May 1831

forged free papers, as I believe he has been designing some time to get away.

Tom **HASSELL** is about 20 or 21 years old, very likely, about 5½ feet high, eyes redish, speaks quick and loud, has a scar over one of his eyes, I think his right one, a shade lighter in his color than usual, stout built. I will give Fifty Dollars for **ISAAC** if taken out of the state and delivered to me, or so that I get him, or Forty Dollars for the same if taken within the state. I will give Twenty Dollars to any one who will deliver Tom **HASSELL** to me. Jona. **HAUGHTON**. The editor of the Norfolk Herald will please insert this three times in his paper, and forward the account to this office. May 11th 1831.

[545] To Travellers. Persons wishing a private conveyance to Elizabeth City, Norfolk, Gates, Winton, or any other place, can be accomodated with a commodious Carriage and good Horses or with a good gig and horse, on application to the subscriber—who still continues to keep a House of Entertainment at his old stand on Main street.—His charges are as follows: For Breakfast or Supper 30 cts. Dinner 40 Man & Horse per day $1 50 Over 6 days 1 25 Man per day 87½ Wm. **M'NIDER**. Edenton, May 11, 1831.

Edenton Gazette.
Vol. XXVII.....No. 20. Edenton, N. C. Wednesday, May 18, 1831. Whole No. 1372.

[546] [p. 3] Edenton: Wednesday, May 18, 1831. ... Mr. Whitmell **STALLINGS**, jr. of Gates County, killed a Bear a few days past which weighed 486 lbs.

[547] The Rev. Jarvis B. **BUXTON**, for the last three years Rector of Christ's Church, in this place, having been elected the second time to the Rectorship of St. John's Church, Fayetteville, has accepted the invitation, and left for that place. He will first go to Richmond, where he intends to take Priest's orders. The Vestry of Christ's Church have invited the Rev. Philip B. **WILEY** to the charge of this congregation—Eliz. City Star.

[548] The family of the Hon. John **BRANCH**, late Secretary of the Navy, passed through this place on Sunday last, on the way to their former residence at Enfield. We understand that Mr. **BRANCH** will probably leave Washington City in eight or ten days.—Tarboro' F. Press.

[549] *Wilmington District.*—At an adjourned meeting of the citizens of Wilmington, to nominate a suitable person to represent that district, the following Resolution was offered and concurred in: *Resolved*, That this meeting, reposing full confidence in the ability, integrity and sound republican principles of *Gov. John OWEN*, of Bladen, do recommend him as a suitable person to be supported at the approaching election, as Representative of this district in the next Congress of the United States. And that C. **DUDLEY** and J. A. **HILL**, Esqrs. compose a committee to communicate to Gov. **OWEN** the sense of this meeting.

And on motion of Joseph A. **HILL**, Esq. the annexed Resolution was unanimously adopted: *Resolved*, That we approve the independent, upright and honest course pursued by Gen. *Edward B. DUDLEY*, while acting as the Representative in Congress of this District.

[550] NOTICE. The subscriber having qualified at last March Term of Chowan County Court, as Administrator to the estate of Ephraim **ELLIOTT**, dec'd, requests all those persons who are indebted to said estate, to come forward and make payment without delay; and those to whom the same is indebted are also requested to present their claims duly authenticated, within the time prescribed by law, or this notice will be plead in bar of a recovery. Wm. **ELLIOTT**, *Adm'r*. Chowan Co. May 17th 1831.

[551] FLOUR! FLOUR!! A Fresh supply of FLOUR, of a superior brand, in whole and half Barrels, just received from Baltimore. ALSO, Rye Gin, Whiskey, N. Rum, &c. On hand, a few dozen of Champaign of an excellent quality, and for sale by N. **BRUER**. Edenton. May 18th 1831.

Edenton Gazette.
Vol. XXVII.....No. 21. Edenton, N. C. Wednesday, May 25, 1831. Whole No. 1373.

Edenton Gazette and Farmer's Palladium 25 May 1831

[552] [p. 2] Domestic. ... *Caution to Parents.*—We learn from the Frederick, (Md.) Examiner, that a child of L. P. W. **BALCH**, of that city, aged about three years, was very near dying a few days since, in consequence of eating a quantity of the kernels of apricots. These are of a poisonous nature, as they contain the prussic acid. The child was rescued from approaching death by the timely application of an emetic, and speedily recovered.

The Rt. Rev. Nathaniel **BOWEN**, Bishop of the Protestant Episcopal Church of the Diocese of South Carolina sailed from Charleston on the 27th ult. in the ship Lady Rowena, for Liverpool; he is accompanied by the Rev. Paul **TRAPIER**; and visits Europe for the benefit of his health, impaired by his assiduous attention to the duties of his sacred office.

Another explosion took place at the powder works of Mr. Daniel **ROGERS**, near Newburgh, on Monday last, and one of the workmen, Elihu **TUDOR**, was killed.

[553] [p. 3] Edenton: Wednesday, May 25, 1831. ... MARRIED, In this county on Thursday evening last, by Thos. I. **CHARLTON**, Esq. Mr. John **PROCTOR** to Miss Mary, daughter of Mr. Allen **LASSITER**.

In Newbern, N. C. on Friday the 13th inst. by Rev. Dr. **LEACH**, Rev. Philip **ANDERSON**, Minister of the M. E. Church at Washington, N. C. to Miss Susan Jane **SPARROW**.

[554] TAXES DUE. The Taxes for 1830 are now due, and those persons who are liable to pay the same in Chowan County, are requested to do so, by the last day of August next, as that is the longest time that can be given for the payment thereof. For the better accommodation of persons residing in the country, I shall sit at stated times, in the different Captains' Districts in the County, of which I shall hereafter give notice. Juror Tickets, without regard to number, will be received in payment. Wm. D. **RASCOE**, *Sh'ff*. Edenton, May 24, 1831.

Edenton Gazette.
Vol. XXVII.....No. 22. Edenton, N. C. Wednesday, June 1, 1831. Whole No. 1374.

[555] [p. 3] Edenton: Wednesday, June 1, 1831. The following act for the better regulation of our town, was passed at the last session of our Legislature. We publish it for the benefit of all concerned:
Be it enacted by the General Assembly of the State of North Carolina, and it is hereby enacted by the authority of the same, That the commissioners of the town of Edenton, are hereby authorised to class the free white male taxable inhabitants of said town into companies of five or more for the purpose of watching said town at night; and it shall be the duty of the said commissioners to appoint some individual of each company captain of the watch for the night, and duly to notify the said captain and company of the place of meeting and the time at which they shall commence the performance of their duties; and if any person duly notified shall fail to attend at the hour and place appointed, and duly to watch during the night, such delinquent, without sufficient excuse, to be judged of by the said commissioners, shall forfeit the sum of not more than twenty shillings, not less than ten shillings, to be recovered before any justice of the peace living in said town, who is hereby authorised to give judgment and issue executions for the penalties mentioned in this act, with costs.

[556] Jesse **EASON** of Camden, the man who killed a Mr. **GREGORY** some time since, was tried at the last Superior County [sic] and found guilty! Judge **DONNELL** presided—EASON is to be hung on Friday, 3d. inst.

[557] The noted Governor **DESLA**'s son, who fled from the United States, died in Texas about the middle of March. On his death-bed he made confession of the murder of **BAKER**, and one other individual living in Texas, "besides being guilty of crimes equally criminal as murder."

[558] Thos. **CHILTON**, of retrenchment memory, a representative in the last Congress from Kentucky, lately died in that place.

[559] Unanimity Lodge, No. 54. The members of Unanimity Lodge, No. 54, are requested to meet at the Lodge Room, on Saturday next at 5 o'clock, P. M., instead of the usual hour. A full meeting is desired, as

Edenton Gazette and Farmer's Palladium 1 June 1831

business of importance is to be transacted. By order, J. H. **HAUGHTON**, *Sec'y*. June 1st 1831.

[560] FOURTH OF JULY! This memorable day—a day long to be remembered by every true-hearted American, will be celebrated at my House, (as has been customary for several years past,) and my friends and the public generally are informed that no pains on my part will be spared, to provide a sumptuous repast for their accommodation. The members of the Green Hall District, Militia Company, and others liable to military duty in the said District, are notified to attend on the above day on the usual Parade ground, armed and equipped according to law. H. D. **JONES**, *Capt.* June 1st 1831.

[561] Plymouth Railways. The subscribers are prepared to haul up vessels of every description for the purpose of graving and repairing, and promise to do the work cheap and well with despatch. They also hold themselves responsible for all damages done by reason of hauling up, &c. Terms of hauling up 20 cents per Ton; and $1 50 per day, for every day the vessel lies on the ways after the first 24 hours. P. **CORNELL** & Bros. Plymouth, June 1, 1831.

Edenton Gazette.
Vol. XXVII.....No. 23. Edenton, N. C. Wednesday, June 8, 1831. Whole No. 1375.

[562] [p. 3] Edenton: Wednesday, June 8, 1831. ... *Dreadful Fire.*—With feelings of deep regret and heartfelt sorrow, we present to our readers the intelligence of the destructive conflagration of the flourishing town of Fayetteville in this State. ... The newspaper establishments having been destroyed, we have received no papers from that place—we are indebted to the Norfolk Beacon and Newbern Spectator, for the following particulars, which they received verbally from stage passengers.

It seems the fire originated in a kitchen in the business part of the town on Sunday noon, the 29th ult. from a negro woman putting too much light-wood on the fire. It is said that the wind blew violently at first, but died away, and such was the rapidity with which the flames spread, it was impossible to arrest their progress. The number of houses destroyed are computed to be between 3 and 500. Among them were the Presbyterian and Episcopal Churches, Cape Fear and U. S. Banks, Printing Offices, Hotels, and nearly every store in the town. The Engine House caught fire and the heat was so great that the Engines could not be gotten out and of course were consumed. The Court-House, Methodist Church, and Post Office, were the only principal buildings saved. Some of the merchants it is said, removed their goods several times but it was of no avail. The Banks saved their books and most of the money. The produce in the town was destroyed, of which a large quantity was cotton. The desolation produced is represented as being inconceivable.

[563] *Gates county, N. C. May* 25th 1831. Mr. Editor, At a meeting of the Gates Circuit Missionary Society, held at Philadelphia Meeting House in the county of Gates, the 14th inst., the subject of intemperance was considered, when the following preamble and resolutions were unanimously adopted: Whereas, we have long witnessed with deep regret, the demoralizing effects of candidates and their friends treating at elections: *Therefore resolved*, That we will not vote for any candidate who treats, or who may give his consent for his friends to do so. *Resolved*, That the preacher in charge of Gates Circuit be requested, together with the local preachers in the bounds of said circuit to use their influence to get the male members of the church, with all others who are friendly to the cause of temperance to adopt a similar resolution. *Resolved*, That the above resolutions be published in the Edenton Gazette, and the Christian Advocate and Journal and Zion's Herald. Geo. **KITERELL**, *Pres't.* E. **SMITH**, *Sec'y.*

[564] *Episcopal Convention.*—The annual Convention of the Protestant Episcopal Church in the Diocese of North Carolina convened at Christ Church, in Raleigh, on Thursday, 19th ult. and adjourned on Saturday. The Rev. Levi S. **IVES**, present Rector of St. Luke's Church, in the city of New York, was elected Bishop of the Diocese, in the place of the Right Reverend John S. **RAVENSCROFT**, deceased. ...

[565] Unanimity Lodge, No. 54. The Officers and Members of Unanimity Lodge, No. 54 Edenton, are requested to wear the usual badge of mourning for the space of thirty days, from the 4th inst. as a token of respect for their dec'd brother, Henry **FLURY**. By order of the Lodge, J. H. **HAUGHTON**, *Sec'y.*

Edenton Gazette and Farmer's Palladium 8 June 1831

[566] NOTICE. *To Rebecca **FORGERSON** and son Hardy, Caswell **FORGERSON** and wife Martha of the State of Virginia, and others who may be concerned, in the will of Hardy **BRITT**, late of the County of Hertford:* Take notice that at the August Term 1831 of the Worshipful Court of Pleas and Quarter Sessions held in and for the county of Hertford, I shall produce and endeavour to establish, as true and correct, a copy of the last will and testament of Hardy **BRITT** dec'd., the original of which was destroyed among the records by the burning of the Court House of said County of Hertford. Richard T. **CROSS** *for himself and wife.* Hertford Co. May 27, 1831.

Edenton Gazette.
Vol. XXVII.....No. 24. Edenton, N. C. Wednesday June 15, 1831. Whole No. 1376.

[567] [p. 3] Edenton: Wednesday, June 15, 1831. Through the solicitations of many voters, *Joseph H. **SKINNER***, Esq. has consented to become a candidate to represent this County in the House of Commons, at the approaching Legislature of this State.

Many voters request the privilege of announcing *Chas. E. **JOHNSON***, Esq., as a candidate to represent this County in the Senate, in the approaching General Assembly of this State.

The Jubilee. In pursuance of the notice contained in our last paper, the citizens of the Town and its vicinity, convened in the Court-House on Friday the 10th ult., for the purpose of making suitable arrangements for the celebration of the approaching 4th. The meeting was organized by appointing Dr. James **NORCOM** to the chair, and D. W. **STONE**, Esq. secretary. When on motion it was ordered, that a committee be appointed consisting of Gen. R. T. **BROWNRIGG**, Col. Wm. **BULLOCK**, N. **BRUER**, S. T. **SAWYER**, Jos. N. **HOSKINS**, Chas. W. **MIXSON** and Augustus **MOORE**, Esqrs. to make all necessary and suitable arrangements, and to request some gentleman of the town to deliver an oration adapted to the occasion. It was on motion further ordered, that the name of the Chairman be added to the above committee, when on motion the meeting adjourned *sine die*. On the succeeding day the committee appointed for the purpose, waited upon *Thomas S. **HOSKINS***, Esq. who politely consented to become the orator of the day.

We have been requested by *H. D. **JONES***, Esq., to say to his friends and the public, that the celebration of the anniversary of American Independence, will be held at his house on Saturday the 2d of July, instead of Monday the 4th, as published in this paper; at which time and place those persons subject to militia duty in the district are notified to attend.

We feel much gratification in being able to state, that contributions (by individual subscription from our citizens,) to the amount of $438 have been made and transmitted to Fayetteville, for the relief of our fellow-citizens of that place, who suffered so severely by the late fire. ...

[568] *Lightning!*—During the rain yesterday, which was accompanied with some severe thunder and lightning, a warehouse on the wharf belonging to Jon. H. **HAUGHTON**, Esq. was struck and set fire, which was soon extinguished by the rain.—There were several persons in the house at the time, and one of them John W. **STANDLEY**, son of Mr. John **STANDLEY** of this town, was considerably stunned by the shock, and remained insensible for some time.—It is supposed that the lightning was attracted by some *lime* in the house.

Edenton Gazette.
Vol. XXVII.....No. 25. Edenton, N. C. Wednesday June 22, 1831. Whole No. 1377.

[569] [p. 2] Domestic. ... Farnifold **GREEN**, Esq. of the U. S. Navy, has been appointed to the command of the Revenue Cutter, Dallas, vice Captain **PAINE**, resigned.

[570] North-Carolina CONSTITUTIONALIST, And State Rights' Advocate. *"The Liberty of the Press—the shield of Freedom—the scourge of Tyrants."* Wm. S. **RANSOM** & Wm. **POTTER**, Propose to publish in the City of Raleigh, N. C. a political newspaper, under the above title. They promise to give to the public an independent and consistent Republican State Rights' paper; one that will always support its principles and regard truth; that will labor to further the views of the true friends to liberty and democracy. They will contend for the "Union" to the last—support General **JACKSON** for a re-election to the

Edenton Gazette and Farmer's Palladium 22 June 1831

Presidency, and oppose H. **CLAY** and the political promotion of those who would advance his pretensions. ... Mr. **RANSOM** (intending to retire from the Bar as soon as the necessary number of subscribers is procured) will devote his time exclusively to the editorial department.

The first number of the 'Constitutionalist' will appear as soon as one thousand subscribers shall have been obtained. Persons holding Subscription Lists, will please return them, addressed to the Editors at Raleigh by the first of August next. CONDITIONS. The North-Carolina Constitutionalist, will appear weekly on an imperial sheet in new type, and on good paper (except during the session of the legislature, when it will be isued [sic] semi-weekly) at three dollars per annum, payable on receipt of the first number, or four dollars at the end of six months. ... Raleigh, May 14, 1831.

[571] [p. 3] Edenton: Wednesday, June 22, 1831. We are authorised to announce Wm. **WALTON**, Esq. as a candidate to represent this County in the Senate, in the next Legislature of this State.

We are and have been authorised to announce Joseph H. **SKINNER** and John T. **BENTON**, Esqrs. as candidates to represent this County in the Commons, in our next Legislature. We learn that Wm. **JACKSON** and Wm. **BYRUM**, Esqrs. are candidates also for a seat in the Commons.

[572] At a meeting of a number of the citizens of Chowan County, held at **EVANS'** Meeting House, on Wednesday the 15th of June, to agree upon measures for raising a contribution for the relief of the sufferers by the late awful and destructive fire which has overwhelmed Fayetteville: Josiah **COFFIELD**, being called to the chair, and Jacob N. **PARKER** appointed Secretary.—the following resolutions were adopted.

Resolved, That the citizens of Chowan County, deeply and sincerely sympathise with their fellow citizens of Fayetteville, in the awful visitation of Providence, which has desolated their Town, and reduced to poverty so many families. Resolved, that a subscription be immediately opened for their relief. Resolved, that subscription papers be presented to such of the citizens of Chowan as have not attended this meeting, and that C. E. **JOHNSON**, Job **PARKER**, Exum **SIMPSON**, Wm. **WALTON**, William **BULLOCK**, Rev. Z. **EVANS**, Rev. B. **NIXON**, Rev. Miles **WELCH**, Josiah **COFFIELD**, Jacob N. **PARKER**, William **BYRUM**, R. T. **BROWNRIGG**, H. D. **JONES**, Josiah **SMALL**, Baker **HOSKINS**, William **JACKSON**, Dr. John **BROWNRIGG**, John T. **BENTON**, John **PAINE**, Thomas **SATTERFIELD**, Everard **GARRETT**, Miles **BADHAM**, Jas. **COFFIELD** and Jos. B. **SKINNER**, be appointed for that purpose. Resolved, that the persons appointed for receiving subscriptions, meet at **EVANS'** Meeting House on the 14th day of July next, to ascertain the aggregate sum collected, and that they severally pay over the several sums to Jos. B. **SKINNER**, who is hereby appointed Agent in behalf of this meeting, to transmit the amount to the proper authorities of Fayetteville, to be appropriated to the relief of the destitute and suffering families of said Town. Resolved, that the Secretary be requested to prepare and hand subscription papers to such persons as have been appointed by this meeting to receive subscriptions. Resolved, that the proceedings of this meeting be published in the Edenton Gazette. Josiah **COFFIELD**, *Ch'm.* J. N. **PARKER**, *Sec'y.*

[573] DIED, In this Town on Wednesday morning last, at the residence of Edmund **HOSKINS**, Esq. Miss Ann, daughter of Mr. Joseph **NORCOM** of this County.

[574] State of North Carolina, *Washington County.* Court of pleas & Quarter-Sessions, May Term, 1831. In obedience to an order of the said Court, notice is hereby given to owners of lands through which the Plymouth Turnpike Road runs; that the Plymouth Turnpike Company having filed their petitions in the said Court, in order to have the Land on which the road is made, assessed and condemned for the use and benefit of said road, and that unless the owners of said Lands come forward at the next Court of Pleas and Quarter Sessions of said county to be held in the Court House in Plymouth on the third Monday of August, 1831, and make themselves parties Defendants to said petition, the petition will be heard *ex parte* and a decision had: Witness, Joseph C. **NORCOM**, Clerk of our said court, the third Monday of May 1831. Jos. C. **NORCOM**, *Cl'k.* Plymouth, June 22, 1831.

Edenton Gazette.
Vol. XXVII.....No. 26. Edenton, N. C. Wednesday June 29, 1831. Whole No. 1378.

Edenton Gazette and Farmer's Palladium 29 June 1831

[575] [p. 3] Edenton: Wednesday, June 29, 1831. We are authorised to announce *Samuel T. SAWYER*, Esq., as a candidate for re-election, to represent this town in the next General Assembly of this State.

[576] *Festival of St. John the Baptist.* Agreeable to previous notice the members of Unanimity Lodge, No. 54, assembled at their Hall in this place, at 10 o'clock A. M. on the 24th inst., when a procession was formed, which moved to the Baptist Church. The ceremonies were commenced by an appropriate and impressive prayer from the Rev. Mr. **ATKINSON** of the Methodist E. Church, (who was invited to officiate on the occasion,) after which Major Samuel T. **SAWYER**, (the Master of the Lodge) delivered an eloquent, feeling and appropriate Oration... The throne of grace being again supplicated by the Rev. Mr. A., the procession was again formed and the members returned to their Hall, where they partook of some refreshments provided for the occasion.

[577] We are authorized to state that the Rev. Levi Silliman **IVES**, elected Bishop of the Protestant Episcopal Church in this State, has accepted the office; and that it is expected his consecration will take place in Philadelphia, some time during the month of September next, of which due notice will be given.

[578] We had not recovered from the shock produced by the news of the Fayetteville fire, before our ears were saluted with the unwelcome news of another, not so appalling in its consequences, but of considerable injury to the State. By the arrival of a gentleman from Tarborough last week, we learned that the State House at Raleigh had been consumed and the elegant statue of **WASHINGTON** mutilated and destroyed. The mail on Saturday night confirmed the dreadful tidings. The following letter received at Newbern from Raleigh contains the particulars, so far as we have been able to learn them.
Raleigh, 21st June, 1831. Our State House is in ashes!! About 7 o'clock this morning, the alarm was given, and upon hurrying to the spot, it was discovered that the whole of the inside of the roof of the Capitol was in flames, utterly beyond the reach of human effort to extinguish them. The outer walls are all that is now left to tell where once stood this magnificent building. Some of the furniture of the two Halls is saved, also the records of the Comptroller, Supreme Court, and Clerk's Offices. Great efforts were made to save the Statue, but in vain. It is horribly mutilated by the falling timbers, and of course destroyed—the head and arms, and I believe one of the legs are entirely off. The Executive, Treasury, and Secretary's offices, were at an early period covered with wet blankets, and each house manned with half a dozen negroes, with tubs of water, by which means the buildings were saved.—There was most fortunately for the town, a stiff breeze from the South West. The Episcopal Church, State Bank, and old Bank House, were in great danger. Notwithstanding the thick foliage of the intervening grove, and the fire proof state of the *top* of the Capitol, still large flakes of burning coals and timber fell profusely on them. And all this was the work, not of an *incendiary* to be sure, but of the most reckless and unpardonable carelessness. One of the workmen who had been employed in the covering of the building, has brought upon the State this catastrophe. It seems they used fire in soldering on the plates of zinc, and had an iron vessel or kettle in which they kept it. When the hands went to work this morning, this fellow, instead of getting the proper vessel to carry up the fire in, carried a coal betwen [sic] two blazing shingles, and as it is supposed, dropt [sic] some of this match into the combustible materials of the garret.

[579] The Washington Globe says the War Department has never been offered to any other individual than the Hon. *Hugh L. WHITE*. The Richmond Enquirer thinks that Judge **W.** will agree to serve. The Enquirer also states that *Phillip P. BARBOUR*, Esq. has declined the office of Attorney General of the United States.

[580] The trial of James W. **MARSHALL** for the unlawful shooting of William **GALT**, at Richmond, Va. has eventuated in the acquittal of the former.

[581] PRIVATE BOARDING. Mrs. **GARDINER** takes this method of informing her friends and the public generally, that, hereafter, it is her intention to keep a Private *BOARDING HOUSE*; where parents and guardians, can get board for their children and wards, at the moderate price of $60 per year, and the strictest attention paid to their morals. Mrs. G. flatters herself, that with assiduity and attention, her long experience in keeping a public House, with addition of moderate charges, she will receive a liberal share

Edenton Gazette and Farmer's Palladium 29 June 1831

of patronage. N. B. Her charge for man and Horse per day, will be $1, and all other charges in proportion. Edenton, June 30th, [sic] 1831.

[582] NOTICE. Whereas Messrs. R. H. & J. G. SMITH have sued out an original attachment against one Washington W. BENNETT, returnable before T. I. CHARLTON, Esq. one of the Justices of the peace of Chowan County: The said W. W. BENNETT is hereby notified to appear at the counting room of the said T. I. CHARLTON in the town of Edenton on Friday the 20th day of July next and replevy the property levied upon and plead to the said attachment; otherwise final judgment will be rendered against him. Edenton, June 29th 1831.

[583] State of North-Carolina. *Washington County.* Court of Pleas and Quarter-Sessions, May Term, 1831. Ezekiel BONNER, vs. Chas. H. SILKMAN} Attachment. It appearing to the satisfaction of the Court that Charles H. SILKMAN is not an inhabitant of this State: It is therefore ordered that publication be made in the Edenton Gazette for six weeks, that unless the said SILKMAN doth appear at the next Court of Pleas and Quarter-Sessions of said county, to be held in the Court-House in Plymouth, on the third Monday in August next, and then and there plead answer or demur, Judgment final will be entered against him and the money in the hands of P. O. PICOT, garnishee, will be condemned to satisfy the said Judgment. Test, J. C. NORCOM, *Cl'k.* Plymouth, June 20th 1831.

Edenton Gazette.
Vol. XXVII.....No. 27. Edenton, N. C. Wednesday July 6, 1831. Whole No. 1379.

[584] [p. 3] Edenton: Wednesday, July 6, 1831. ... FOURTH OF JULY. Agreeable to previous arrangements, this day was celebrated in this place, by the citizens of the town and its vicinity, in a suitable manner. The day was ushered in by the firing of cannon and the ringing of all the bells. At 11 o'clock, a procession of the citizens was formed at the Court-House and marched to the Baptist Church, when the throne of grace was supplicated by Rev. Mr. MEREDITH, followed by an appropriate hymn. The Declaration of Independence was read in a clear and distinct manner by Dr. John R. HERNDON; and the choir then sung the patriotic song, "Freedom's Jubilee," with much spirit and animation. After which, the Orator of the day, Thomas S. HOSKINS, Esq. delivered an oration, neat, chaste, and appropriate for the occasion, and from which we hope hereafter, we shall be furnished with extracts for publication. The company then retired, and at 2 o'clock about 60 persons sat down to an elegant dinner, prepared by Jos. N. HOSKINS, Esq. On motion, Baker HOSKINS, Esq. was chosen President of the day, and Joseph H. SKINNER, Vice President. After the cloth was removed, a number of patriotic toasts was drunk accompanied with enthusiastic cheering, and interspersed with spirited songs, suitable to the occasion. ...
    VOLUNTEER TOASTS. By the President of the Day, Gen. A. JACKSON: May he at the ensuing election be proclaimed president of the United States for another constitutional term. By the Vice President. The sages and soldiers of our Revolution: Pioneers of liberty and independence we hallow their memories while enjoying the blessings they achieved. By Dr. Jas. NORCOM. Our Union and our Government... By Dr. John R. HERNDON. The United States: Perpetuity to their Union, the assured source of their happiness, and infallible guarantee of their safety. By Thos. S. HOSKINS. The fifty fifth anniversary of the National independence. ... By A. SPENCE. John MARSHALL, Chief Justice of the United States. By G. W. BARNEY. The citizens of the County of Chowan. By Chas. HAUGHTON. Pleasant feeling to the friends of Gen. JACKSON; but may his enemies be thorned in imagination. By H. W. COLLINS, Gen. LA FAYETTE: The friend of WASHINGTON and illustrious benefactor of our country. By James NORCOM, jr. The Orator of the day. By James COFFIELD. May the opening of Roanoke Inlet be speedily accomplished. By John E. WOOD. The ladies of Chowan: As lovely as though they had looked into Paradise and caught its earliest and freshest bloom By Josiah COFFIELD. Better crops and better times.

[585] Married in Bath, Steuben Co. N. Y. on the 11th ult. Mr. Moses ALEXANDER, aged 98, to Mrs. Frances TOMKINS aged 105! They were taken out of bed dead the following morning.!!

[586] MARRIED, In Newbern on the 30th ult. by the Rev. Mr. ARMSTRONG, John M. JONES, Esq. merchant of this town, to Miss Sally J. daughter of Wm. HANDCOCK, Esq. of the former place.

Edenton Gazette and Farmer's Palladium 6 July 1831

[587] DIED, In this County last week, Mr. Ashley **FLEETWOOD**. Also on Monday last, Mr. Chas. **SITTERSON**.

[588] List of Letters Remaining in the Post Office at Edenton, 30th June, 1831: **B**.—Jas. R. **BENT**, Hon. John **BROWN**, Hester **BROWNRIGG**, Capt. **BRICKHOUSE**, Capt. Marco D. **BUSANCH**, 2, Mrs. Ann D. **BOZMAN**, Capt. Wm. A. **BOZMAN**, Rich'd T. **BROWNRIGG**, 2, John **BLOUNT**. **C**.—Richard B. **CREECY**, John **COX**, 2, Burrel **CARLISLE**. **D**.—Samuel **DAMERON**. **G**.—Frances Ann **GRAY**, Thomas **GREGORY**, Edward H. **GOELET**. **H**.—J. **HAUGHTON**, George W. **HOLMES**. **J**.—Thomas **JORDAN**, Jona. H. **JACOCKS**, R. A. **JOYCE**, Thomas **JOHNSON**. **K**.—John **KING**, Rob't **KEATING**. **L**.—Capt. **LAMBERT**. **M**.—James **MARKS**, Daniel **M'DOWELL**, Abram **MORGAN**, John **MACKENZY**, Samuel V. **MITCHELL**. **O**.—S. R. **OLIVEIRA**, 4. **P**.—Chas. L. **PHELPS**, 2, John **POPELSTON**. **S**.—Nath'l **SHERWOOD**, Louisa A. **SAWYER**, Merriam **SAWYER**. **T**.—Sarah A. **THORP**. **V**.—Capt. Wm. **VAN SCHAYCH**. **W**.—Alexander W. **WHITE**, J. **WISEMAN**, Messrs. John **WHITE** & Co. and Richard **TEASDALE**, Margaret **WELCH**, George **WHITE**, 2, D. **WARNIER**, William **WILLIAMS**, Edward **WINGATE**, Benjamin **WYNNE**. N. **BRUER**, P. M. Edenton, July 1, 1831.

[589] List of Letters Remaining in the Post Office at Plymouth, N. C. July 1st. 1831: James **ADAMS**, Jno. M. **BATEMAN**, Wm. M. **CHESSON**, 2, C. **CORNELL**, Charles **COOK**, Alexander **CAMERON**, Moses R. **COLMAN**, George W. **CLEMENTS**, Joseph **CHRISTOPHER**, Jas. **DAMON**, Richard **EVERETT**, Joseph **GARRETT**, John W. **GARRETT**, Wm. **GARDNER**, Aaron **HARRISON**, James **HAMILTON**, Freeman **KINGSMAN**, John **LONG**, Ephraim A. **LAMBERT**, Mebzas **LITCHFIELD**, George **M'INTYER**, Miss Sally Jane **MARLEY**, Hardy J. **PHELPS**, Abeishai **PRICHETT**, Mr. ___[blank]___ **PARKMAN**, Martin T. **PEAKS**, Joshua **SLAVIS**, Kennith **SALINGER**, A. N. **VAIL**, Lewis **VINAL**, Levi **VINAL**, Sally **WATERS**, Samuel **VERNELSON**, Cornelia **WHITE**, John M. **WILLIAMS**, Solomon B. **WHITE**, Anthony **WATCHMAN**, Miss Mary **YOUNGE** or **LOUNGE**. Wm. A. **TURNER**, P. M. Plymouth, July 1, 1831.

[590] NOTICE. The following articles have just been received from New York and are offered for sale on my usual terms: Dunstables of the latest fashion, and corded Muslin. ALSO Copal and bright Varnish, Glue, Seidlitz and Soda Powders, fresh Lemon Syrup, Quinine, Jujube Paste, and excellent article for coughs—Pocket Lights, Tonkay Beans, ground Sulphur, rolled Sulpher, Allum and Crome Yellow. N. **BRUER**. Edenton, July 6, 1831.

Edenton Gazette.
Vol. XXVII.....No. 28. Edenton, N. C. Wednesday July 13, 1831. Whole No. 1380.

[591] [p. 3] Edenton: Wednesday, July 13, 1831. The following are the candidates to represent this County, in the next Legislature of our State. *Senate.* Wm. **WALTON**, Esq. and Col. William **BULLOCK**. *Commons.* Joseph H. **SKINNER**, William **BYRUM**, William **JACKSON**, and John T. **BENTON**, Esqrs. *Town of Edenton.* Major Samuel T. **SAWYER**.

[592] The Weather. The weather in this quarter at this time, is and has been almost of an unprecedented character. We have had more or less rain every day for 24 or 25 days past, and we now find fire, and the common winter garments, quite comfortable. The cotton crop is very unpromising... The reverse may be said of the corn crop...

[593] The following letter confirming the mournful intelligence of the death of the venerable *MONROE*, is from a friend in New York, dated the 5th inst: "Yesterday the fifty-fifth anniversary of our Independence, was ushered in by the merry ringing of bells and the rapid and deafening roar of Artillery. ... The venerable *James MONROE* breathed his last yesterday, (the 4th inst.!!) about three o'clock P. M. ...

[594] MARRIED, In Elizabeth City (N. C.) on Thursday June 30th. by the Rev. Philip B. **WILEY**, Benjamin **ALBERTSON**, Esq. Editor of the Elizabeth City Star, to Miss Louisa **MOORE**, daughter of Col. Henry **MOORE**, of Newton (R. I.)

Edenton Gazette and Farmer's Palladium 13 July 1831

In Caswell county, N. C. Mr. William **BEAN** to Miss Sarah **GREENFIELD**.

[595] $10 Reward. Runaway from the subscriber on the night of the 10th inst., without the smallest provocation whatever, my negro woman **AZZY**. She is so well known that a description is deemed unnecessary. I will give the above sum to any person who will confine her in jail, or deliver her to me, and pay all reasonable expenses. All persons are forwarned harboring or employing her, at their peril, as I will prosecute any who may offend to the extent of the law. It is more than probable, she may be found in the neighborhood of Col. Wm. **BULLOCK**'s, where she has a husband. Wm. B. **ROBERTS**. Chowan Co. June [sic]13.

[596] Notice to Fishermen. The subscriber takes this method to inform his old friends and customers, that he will be able to furnish them in October next at Edenton, with the article of *Cotton Twine*, of such quality and on such terms as cannot fail to suit. The article now offered is made of superior New Orleans Cotton, of No. 12 yarn—and will be found of *nearly or quite double the strength* of the best Cotton Twine now in use by the fishermen near Edenton. Sam'l. **FOWLER**. Hartford, Conn. 1st July 1831.

Edenton Gazette.
Vol. XXVII.....No. 29. Edenton, N. C. Wednesday July 20, 1831. Whole No. 1380 [sic.]

[597] [p. 2] *New York*, July 5. *West Point.*—By a regulation of the Department of War, it is directed that the five cadets of each class who shall graduate with the highest honours, shall be attached to the next Army Register and published. The following is the list of Cadets to whom this honor was awarded at the late examination. *First Class.*—Roswell **PARK**, N. York, Henry **CLAY**, Kentucky, Jas. **ALLEN**, N. Carolina, Henry E. **PRENTISS**, Maine, Albert M. **LEE**, Tennessee. *Second Class.*—Robert V. **SMITH**, Mississippi, Geo. W. **WARD**, Mas. Jacob W. **BAILEY**, R. Island, Benjamin S. **EWELL**, Va. George W. **CASS**, Ohio. *Third Class.*—Fred'k A. **SMITH**, Mass. Wm. H. **SIDELL**, New York, Jona. G. **BARNARD**, Mass. Roswel W. **LEE**, Mass. Rufus **KING**, New York. *Fourth Class.*—William **SMITH**, New York, H. **LAUGHBOROUGH**, Ky. John F. **LEE**, Dist. Columbia, Jas. **SANDERS**, Florida, Curran **POPE**, Kentucky.

[598] *John N. TAZEWELL*, Esq. has been appointed by the Governor of N. Carolina, a Commissioner to take the acknowledgement or proof of Deeds or other Conveyances of Lands, lying in North Carolina; or any other writing under seal to be used in the State; with power to administer oaths, take depositions, and examine witnesses under any commission emanating from any of the Courts of the said state relative to causes depending or to be brought in those Courts.

[599] We learn (says a late Lynchburg Virginian) that *John RANDOLPH*, of Roanoke, has certainly declined being a candidate for Congress.

[600] [p. 3] Edenton: Wednesday, July 20, 1831. Wm. **WALTON**, Esq. has declined being a candidate to represent this County in the Senate, in the next Legislature, and Gen. R. T. **BROWNRIGG** is a candidate in his stead. Col. **BULLOCK**, whom we announced last week, and Gen. B. are consequently in the field for that station.

[601] *Legislature.*—The next session of this body will no doubt be an important one, and the reason is obvious, that the greatest care should be taken by the eastern counties, to send their best men to represent them. Carelessness in this respect has grown into a crime, which will never be atoned for until the people look more to their interests than they have heretofore done.—The people of the West begin to agitate the question of calling a Convention in this State, with a view, among other objects, of removing the Capitol farther West. It is to the interest of the Eastern part of the State, that no convention be called, and every exertion should be made to prevent it. The removing of the Capitol is not the paramount object of the West, in getting up a convention, but if they can accomplish this, they have other and more injurious purposes to the interests of the East, in view. For the purpose of checking such a step, the citizens of Wake County, have nominated Messrs. George E. **BADGER** and T. P. **DEVEREAUX**, Esqrs. to represent

Edenton Gazette and Farmer's Palladium 20 July 1831

them, and Messrs. Wm. GASTON and John H. BRYAN, Esqrs. are spoken of in Craven County. Are *we not* interested? The following is an extract of a letter from a friend in Raleigh, on the subject: he says "If ever there was a time when the East required strong men in the Legislature, now is the time—their political existence depends upon it. In the West they are putting forth their strongest men, and are agitating the question of a removal of the seat of Government. It is not the Capitol they want, but they know that the Capitol cannot be moved but by *Convention*, and *that* is what they want. If they get a Convention, they may deprive some of our small counties of some of their members and disfranchise our boroughs—having full power to do any thing they please. We ought by all means to do every thing placed within our power, to keep them from calling a convention."

[602] Treating At Elections. At a meeting of a number of the citizens of the County of Chowan, at EVAN's Meeting House, on the 14th inst. C. E. JOHNSON, Esq. was called to the Chair, and Stephen SKINNER, Esq. appointed Secretary. The subject of treating at elections being under consideration, the following resolutions were proposed and unanimously adopted: *Resolved*, That the right of electing public agents, is the most important right of Freemen—the only sure guarantee of liberty, and should therefore be exercised with deliberation and soberness. *Resolved*, That the practice of treating with intoxicating drink at public meetings and at elections, by candidates for public appointments, or their friends, with a view of influencing votes, is designed as a bribe the most debasing and demoralizing; and that this meeting do most solemnly recommend to the electors and the candidates to desist from the iniquitous practice. *Resolved*, That the above resolutions be published in the Edenton Gazette, and that copies of them be set up at public places in the County. ... On motion the meeting then adjourned *sine die*. Chas. E. JOHNSON, *Ch'm*. S. SKINNER, *Sec'y*.

[603] We are gratified in being able to state, that our waters are soon to be occupied by a Steamboat, to ply between this place and Plymouth, and thereby make the passage from Norfolk via Eliz. City, &c. to Charleston, the most desirable of any now in operation on the Southern route, as the only impediment heretofore existing, was the want of a safe and expeditious conveyance across the Sound. A sufficiency of stock has already been subscribed, and a contract entered into for the building of a boat of suitable dimensions, &c.: and we learn, that the enterprising gentlemen who have taken the contract (the Messrs. CORNELL's of Plymouth,) have already commenced operations, and will in all probability complete the Boat by the first of October.

A meeting of the stockholders was held on Monday last, and the following persons appointed Directors, viz: Dr. M. E. SAWYER and Jonathan H. HAUGHTON, Esq. of this place, and Josiah COLLINS, jr. and Wm. R. NORCOM, Esqrs. of Washington County. Josiah COLLINS, Esq. was elected President, and Wm. D. RASCOE, Esq. Treasurer of the Company for the ensuing year.

[604] A Post Office has recently been established at Old Neck, Perquimans county—Matthew JORDAN, Post Master.

[605] Hon. Lewis CASS of Ohio, Governor of the Michigan Territory, has been appointed by the President Secretary of the Department of War.

[606] NOTICE. The subscribers will offer for Sale at PUBLIC AUCTION, on the 2d of August next, their entire Stock of Goods in Edenton... Terms of sale, 4 months for all sums over Five dollars, and all sums under Five dollars, Cash. R. H. & J. G. SMITH. July 20th 1831.

[607] State of North Carolina, *Pasquotank County*. Superior Court of Law, Spring Term, 1831. Alfred A. TURNER, vs. Susan TURNER. Whereas a subpoena has been issued against the defendant in this case, which was returned by the Sheriff of Pasquotank County "not to be found," and proclamation having been publicly made at the Court House door of said County by the Sheriff, for the defendant to appear and answer as commanded by said subpoena, and she having failed to do so: It is ordered by the Court that notice be given three months in the Elizabeth City Star and Edenton Gazette, for the defendant to appear at the next Superior Court of Law, to be held for the County of Pasquotank at the Court-House in Elizabeth City on the fourth Monday after the fourth Monday in September next, then and there to appear

Edenton Gazette and Farmer's Palladium 20 July 1831

and plead answer or demur to the plaintiff's petition, or judgment pro confesso, will be taken and the allegations heard ex parte. Witness Lemuel C. MOORE, Clerk of the said Court at Elizabeth City the 4th Monday after the 4th Monday in March, in the year of our Lord 1831, and 55th year of the Independence of said State. Lem. C. MOORE, Cl'k. Eliz. City, July 18th 1831.

[608] List of Letters Remaining in the Post Office at Hertford, the 30th June 1831, which if not taken out by 30th Sept. next, will be sent to the General Post Office: E. P. AKERMAN, John H. BLOUNT, Joseph BOGUE, Mrs. Priscilla BANK, Mrs. Mary CARTER, George CURTIS, Sarah ELLIOTT, Jas. L. FORD, Jos. T. GRANBURY, Gen. Jon. H. JACOCKS, Albemarle Lodge, Hugh LARY, Hoff LARY, Jacob LAMB, John MING, Robert M'CAULEY, Seth SUMNER, Abraham SANDERS, Peter SCARBOROUGH, Benj. THOMAS, Jas. P. WHIDBEE.—21. J. R. BURBAGE, P. M. July 1st 1831.

Edenton Gazette.
Vol. XXVII.....No. 30. Edenton, N. C. Wednesday July 27, 1831. Whole No. 1381.

[609] [p. 2] The New York Mercantile says, "We understand that a short time before his death, Col. *MONROE* placed the whole management of his affairs in the hands of his son in-law [sic] *Samuel L. GOVERNOUR*, Esq. to whose disposition he also has entrusted all his valuable papers—among which are many of the most interesting character."

[610] [p. 3] Edenton: Wednesday, July 27, 1831. *Malachi HAUGHTON*, Esq. is announced as a candidate to represent this Town in the next Legislature.

[611] DIED, In this town on Friday last, at the residence of T. I. CHARLTON, Esq., Mrs. Sarah LEARY, widow of John LEARY, dec'd. of this County.

Edenton Gazette.
Vol. XXVII.....No. 31. Edenton, N. C. Wednesday August 3, 1831. Whole No. 1382.

[612] [p. 3] Edenton: Wednesday, Aug. 3, 1831. *Horrible.*—We learn that a man by the name of COMBS, has been committed to jail in Windsor, Bertie County, charged with having murdered his wife and child, by beating and drowning them. Some of the particulars have come to our knowledge, but as this unnatural and unfeeling wretch, will shortly be arraigned before the bar of his country to answer to the charge, we forbear mentioning them.

[613] We have received the prospectus of a newspaper about to be published in the town of Murfreesborough, N. C. by Mr. John CAMPBELL. It proposes to support the re-election of Gen. JACKSON to the Presidency, and also his Republican principles. We wish the editor much success. Subscriptions will be received at this office.

[614] CONGRESSIONAL CANDIDATES. The following gentlemen are candidates to represent the several districts in North Carolina, in the next U. S. Congress. 1st district, William B. SHEPHARD is opposed by John H. WHEELER. 2d. John BRANCH, without opposition. 3d. Thomas H. HALL, opposed by Joseph R. LLOYD. 4th. Jesse SPEIGHT, no opposition. 5th. James J. M'KAY—Edward B. DUDLEY having declined. 6th. Robert POTTER, no opposition. 7th. Edmund DEBERRY, opposed by Lauchlin BETHUNE. 8th. Daniel L. BARRINGER, no opposition. 9th. Augustin H. SHEPPERD. do. 10th. Abraham RENCHER, do. 11th. Henry W. CONNOR, opposed by Bartlett SHIPP. 12th. Samuel P. CARSON, opposed by Anthony CASEY. 13TH. Lewis WILLIAMS, no opposition.—[*Tarborough Free Press.*

[615] *Return Jonathan MEIGS—New version.*—We know not the writer of the following communication, but as he tells rather a plausible story we admit him.—*Port. Courier.* Mr. SMITH:--In your paper of yesterday, I saw copied a foolish story which went the rounds of the papers some eight or ten years since, respecting the origin of the name of the former Post Master General. It is a matter of no conse-

Edenton Gazette and Farmer's Palladium 3 August 1831

quence except so far as it is connected with the early history of the country. The facts are these. The grandfather of Mr. **MEIGS** resided in Connecticut in the infancy of that colony, at which time it is well known that hostile Indians were no curiosity. His oldest son, named Jonathan, was carried off when young by the Indians, and after an absence of several years, his father despairing of his return, named another son Jonathan. In a few years the first Jonathan was unexpectedly recovered from the Indians, and to distinguish him from the younger he was called Return Jonathan. He was a Colonel in the Connecticut line during the Revolutionary war, and was esteemed a valuable officer. When the emigration to the North Western Territory commenced he removed there and was one of the first settlers of Marietta, Ohio.—He was living a few years since, and was employed as Agent in one of the Western Territories. The former Post Master General was his son, and was called after him. These particulars were received directly from R. J. **MEIGS**, jr. by a friend of the writer of this article.

Edenton Gazette.
Vol. XXVII.....No. 32. Edenton, N. C. Wednesday August 10, 1831. Whole No. 1383.

[616] [p. 3] Edenton: Wednesday, Aug. 10, 1831. *Congressional Election*. We have heard from the Currituck and Hertford elections in this district, which according to the statements, leave Mr. **SHEPARD** 300 ahead of Mr. **WHEELER**. In Currituck, the poll stood, for **SHEPARD** 518, for **WHEELER** 211—334 majority. In Hertford Mr. **WHEELER** obtained 34 votes majority over Mr. **SHEPARD**. *For the Legislature.*—In Currituck, for the Senate Jonathan **LINDSAY**—Commons, Jno. B. **JONES** and Benj. **SIMMONS**. We have not heard the particulars from the Hertford election. *Bertie County.*—For Congress, John **BRANCH**. Senate, George O. **ASKEW**. Commons, Lewis **THOMPSON** and David **OUTLAW**. There was no opposition.

[617] *Appointments by the President.* Louis **M'LANE**, of Deleware, to be Secretary of the Treasury of the United States. Martin **VAN BUREN**, of New York, to be Minister Plenipotentiary and Envoy Extraordinary of the United States, to the King of the United Kingdom of Great Britain and Ireland. Aaron **VAIL**, of New York, to be Secretary of the legation to the United Kingdom of Great Britain and Ireland, in the place of Washington **IRVING**, Esq., who has signified his wish to retire from that station. Robert B. **GILCHRIST**, of Charleston, to be Attorney of the United States, for the District of South Carolina, in the place of Edw. **FROST**, resigned.

[618] *Treating.*—We have pleasure in learning from the best authority, that the Hon. Edmund **DEBERRY** has determined not to treat in the present electioneering campaign. His opponent, Mr. **BETHUNE**, has pledged himself in his circular to pursue the same course. This is gratifying to the friends of temperance.—*Fayetteville Journal.*

[619] MARRIED, On Thursday night last, by the Rev. Vernon **ESKRIDGE**, the Rev. Irvine **ATKINSON**, stationed minister of the Methodist Episcopal Church in this place to Mrs. Mary **ROBERTS**, relict of the late Wm. C. **ROBERTS**.

[620] DIED, At her residence near this place, on Sunday night, the 7th inst. after a short confinement, Mrs. Mary **HOLMES**, relict of the late Rev. Henry **HOLMES**. In recording the death of this truly good woman, we do so with the strongest emotions of grief, which however becomes merged in the consolation and full assurance that she has gone to the "bosom of her Father and her God." Mrs. H. was for many years a member of the Baptist Church, and in her pious walk, godly conversation, gentle and unassuming deportment and placid disposition, told to the world that she had resolved to make religion her study for life. In all situations, up to the time of dissolution, she evinced the greatest composure and resignation, and portrayed in an eminent degree, the character of the true christian, in her yielding submission to the will of the Almighty. To her friends and connexions her loss is irreparable—but let it be their consolation, that their loss is her gain. Among her associates a void is left—let them walk in her footsteps, imitate her virtues and prepare to meet her in Heaven.

In Gates County, at the residence of her father, on Saturday the 6th inst. Mrs. Mary Ann **EURE**, wife of Hillory H. **EURE** Esq. of Hertford.

Edenton Gazette and Farmer's Palladium 10 August 1831

[621] STRAY HORSE. The Subscriber has taken up, and has now in his possession a likely bay Horse, about 15 hands high; he was found in my corn field with a line bridle on, one day last week. The owner can have him by coming forward, proving property and paying charges. Wm. B. **ROBERTS**. Chowan Co. Aug. 10, 1831.

Edenton Gazette.
Vol. XXVII.....No. 33. Edenton, N. C. Wednesday August 17, 1831. Whole No. 1385.

[622] [p. 3] Edenton: Wednesday, Aug. 17, 1831. ELECTION RETURNS. ... *Camden.*—Senate, Hayw'd **BELL**. Commons, **GRANDY** and **DOZIER**. *Pasquotank.*—Senate, John **POOL**. Commons, T. **BELL** and John M. **SKINNER**. *Perquimans.*—Senate, H. **SKINNER**, Commons, **TOWNSEND** and **WILSON**. *Gates.*—Senate, **COOPER**. Commons. W. **STALLINGS** and ___[blank]___ **RIDDICK**. *Hertford.*—Senate, B. J. **MONTGOMERY**. Commons E. A. **CHAMBLEE** and G. C. **MOORE**.

[623] TO MARINERS. *Collector's Office, Edenton 15th August* 1831. The Light House at the South entrance of Roanoke Marshes, will be lighted up on the 20th inst. D. **M'DONALD**, *Coll'r.*

[624] Anti-Tariff Meeting. In accordance with public notice a meeting of the citizens of Bertie County was held in the Court House at Windsor on Tuesday, 9th August, 1831, which being organized by the appointment of Robert C. **WATSON** to the chair, and Joseph B. G. **ROULHAC**, Secretary, the following resolutions were moved and unanimously adopted: *Resolved,* That this meeting deeply lament the unhappy state of excitement which has been created throughout the United States by the passage of the Tariff laws. *Resolved,* That all imposts except those for the purposes of revenue, are contrary to the spirit of the constitution, highly inexpedient, and unequal in their operation on different sections of the union. *Resolved,* That we think the proposed convention to be held in the city of Philadelphia on the 30th Sept. next, is well calculated to unite the energies of those opposed to those laws, and that we will cheerfully join our fellow citizens of the United States in that convention, for the purpose of using all constitutional means to effect their repeal. *Resolved,* That Jos. D. **WHITE**, David **OUTLAW** and Joseph B. G. **ROULHAC** be requested to attend said convention, in behalf of this county. *Resolved,* That we respectfully solicit and request the concurrence of other parts of the State in our solicitations to James **IREDELL**, late Senator in Congress, and Thomas **RUFFIN**, Judge of the Supreme court, that they attend as delegates of the State of North Carolina in said convention. *Resolved,* That the proceedings of this meeting be signed by the chairman and secretary, and forwarded for publication, to such Editors as are believed to be favorable to its object. R. C. **WATSON**, *Chairman.* J. B. G. **ROULHAC**, *Sec'y.*

[625] DIED, In this Town on Wednesday morning last, Mary Matilda, infant daughter of Wm. **MC'NIDER**, Esq.

In Perquimans County, a short time since, Jane Caroline, daughter of Capt. John **LANSTON** of that county.

Edenton Gazette.
Vol. XXVII.....No. 34. Edenton, N. C. Wednesday August 24, 1831. Whole No. 1386.

[626] [p. 3] Edenton: Wednesday, Aug. 24, 1831. ... The following will show the state of the poll in the counties of Tyrrell, Gates, Perquimans and Hertford: TYRRELL—Senate, Geo. D. N. **BATEMAN**. State of the Poll—**BATEMAN** 190, **HASSELL** 125. Commons—H. G. **SPRUILL** and Charles **M'CLEESE**. State of the Poll.—H. G. **SPRUILL** 241. Chas. **M'CLEESE** 233; S. B. **SPRUILL** 22; Frederick **DAVENPORT** 66. Congress.—J. R. **LLOYD**, the inlet man, 383 [?]. T. H. **HALL**, opposite 69. GATES—State of the poll—Senate, W. W. **COOPER** 231; John C. **GORDON** 133. Commons.—Whitmel **STALLINGS** 424; Lem'l. **RIDDICK** 265; John **WILLIE** 263. D. S. **GOODMAN** 151; Isaac R. **HUNTER** 150. PERQUIMANS.—Senate, Hen. **SKINNER** 111; W. **RIDDICK** 107; John H. **BLOUNT** 63. Commons. Thos. **WILSON** 401; Jos. W. **TOWNSEND** 351; Benj. **MULLEN** 287. HERTFORD.—Senate, **MONTGOMERY** 181; **SHARP** 137. Commons, **CHAMBLEE** 313; G. C. **MOORE** 307.

Edenton Gazette and Farmer's Palladium 24 August 1831

[627] Pursuant to public notice, a meeting of the citizens of Edenton and its vicinity, was held in the Court-House on Saturday afternoon, the 20th inst. for the purpose of taking into consideration the propriety of appointing Delegates to represent our County and State, in an Anti-Tariff Convention, proposed to be held in Philadelphia, on the 30th day of September next. The meeting was organized by calling Augustus MOORE, Esq. to the Chair, and appointing Thomas S. HOSKINS Esq. Secretary. The objects of the meeting were briefly stated by the Chairman; after which Major S. T. SAWYER made a few appropriate remarks, and offered for the consideration of the meeting the following resolution:

Resolved, That a committee be appointed to draw up a report and suitable resolutions to be submitted to the consideration of an adjourned meeting: and that the Chairman nominate the persons of whom said committee shall consist; which was adopted. The chairman subsequently proposed the following persons to compose the committee, viz: N. BRUER, D. W. STONE, Chas. E. JOHNSON, Esqrs. and Maj. Sam'l T. SAWYER. It was then moved that the name of the Chairman be added to the committee; which was adopted. Whereupon it was on motion agreed, that this meeting adjourn till next Saturday the 27th inst., and at 4 o'clock, precisely, in the afternoon of that day, it is particularly requested that the citizens of the Town and County generally, will give their punctual attendance. Aug. MOORE, *Ch'm.* T. S. HOSKINS, *Sec'y.*

[628] At a meeting of a respectable number of the citizens of Perquimans county at the Court House in Hertford on the 18th day of August 1831, Thomas LONG, Esq. was called to the chair, and Joseph W. TOWNSEND appointed Secretary. The object of the meeting being explained by a citizen, the meeting proceeded to elect delegates to attend the Anti-Tariff Convention to be held in the city of Philadelphia, on the 30th of September next. The names of Jonathan H. JACOCKS, Charles W. SKINNER, Miles ELLIOTT, Edmund WHITE, Joseph T. GRANBERY, and John E. WOOD, Esquires, were put in nomination and unanimously elected. On motion it was ordered, that the proceedings of the meeting be reduced to writing, signed by the Chairman and Secretary, and a copy thereof be handed to each of the delegates. Thos. LONG, *Chairman.* J. W. TOWNSEND, *Sec'y.*

[629] Hon. Andrew STEVENSON has been re-elected a member of Congress in Virginia, without opposition.

[630] *Congressional.*—In the second, fourth, fifth, sixth, eighth, ninth, tenth, twelfth and thirteenth congressional Districts of this State, there being no opposition, the following gentlemen are respectively elected, viz: *John BRANCH, Jesse SPEIGHT, Robert POTTER, James MC KAY, Daniel L. BARRINGER, Augustin H. SHEPPERD, Abraham RENCHER, Samuel CARSON, and Lewis WILLIAMS.* Of these, Messrs. *BRANCH* and *MC KAY* are new members. In the third District, Doct. *HALL* is doubtless elected over his competitor *Jos. R. LOYD.*—[Raleigh Register.

[631] MARRIED, In this County on Tuesday night last by Rev. Jacob D. RASCOE, Mr. Charles TABER of this town, to Miss Mary, daughter of Mr. Nathaniel WILDER.

In DURANTs Neck, Perquimans County, on the 11th inst. by Rev. Wm. REED, Mr. Daniel H. GOODMAN to Miss Clarissa Louisa Ryan JORDAN.

[632] DIED, In this County, on the 20th inst. Mary Elizabeth, youngest daughter, of Wm. RIGHTON, Esq.

Edenton Gazette.
Vol. XXVII.....No. 35. Edenton, N. C. Wednesday August 31, 1831. Whole No. 1387.

[633] [p. 2] Domestic. From the Norfolk Beacon. INSURRECTION IN SOUTHAMPTON. We have purposely refrained from noticing this unwelcome occurrence, until proper and effective measures should be concerted for its suppression, and until we should be in possession of some authentic information to counteract the many exaggerated statements with which gossip rumour, with her hundred tongues, has hourly abused the public confidence, since Tuesday last. We now proceed to give such particulars of the tragical event as have come to our knowledge.

Edenton Gazette and Farmer's Palladium 31 August 1831

On Tuesday last, about noon, it was rumored here, that verbal intelligence had reached Portsmouth by that day's stage, that an insurrection had broken out among some deluded Slaves near the *Cross Keys*, in the County of *Southampton*, on Sunday night 21st inst. and that forty individuals of all ages and sexes had fallen victims to their murderous designs. Upon tracing this report we learned, that the sad reality had been announced to the citizens of Suffolk that morning by express from Jerusalem, and had filled all classes in that town with horror and apprehension. The intelligence was so awful and unexpected, that it was received with much hesitation and could by all to whom it was communicated, until the afternoon, when the arrival of Col. **CHARLTON**, express from Suffolk, left no room for conjecture or uncertainty as to the facts before stated. He left there after the departure of the stage, and added confirmation strong, by letters giving the names of the unhappy victims.

The members of our Court were speedily convened, and Judge R. B. **TAYLOR** being invited to the conference, measures were immediately concerted of safety for our own community, and for affording the most prompt and efficient aid to to [sic] the citizens of Southampton in their calamitous circumstances. Application being made to Com. **WARRINGTON**, at the Navy Yard, he very promptly replied that arms and ammunition to any required amount would be furnished at a moment's warning from that depot. The *Mayor* was also directed to communicate the intelligence to Col. **HOUSE**, commanding officer at Fortress Monroe, and request that he would furnish as many of the troops of the garrison as could be spared, and that he (the Mayor) would apply to the U. S. ships *Natchez* and *Warren*, lying in the Roads, for such of the Marine force and Seamen as could be dispensed for the occasion.—The Mayor was further directed to employ the Steam Boat Hampton to convey them with all expedition to Suffolk. It is due to Col. **WAINWRIGHT**, Commandant of the Marine Corps here, to notice the alacrity with which he attended the invitation of the Court to aid their deliberations, and his prompt offer of co-operation in any way in which his personal services, and those of his command, would be acceptable.

To Capt. **CAPRON**, of the Independent Volunteers, was confided the communications for Col. **HOUSE**, Com. **ELLIOT**, of the *Natchez*, and Capt. **COOPER** of the *Warren*. ... The Col. gave immediate orders for three Companies, with a piece of artillery, to embark on board the Hampton, under the orders of Col. **WORTH** and Maj. **KILBY**, and at 6 o'clock, the boat left the Point, and proceeding for the *Natchez* and *Warren*, delivered the despatches to Com. **ELLIOT** and Captain **COOPER**, who cheerfully acquiesced in the request of the Mayor, and in addition, the Commodore handsomely volunteered a choice body of *Seamen* under the orders of his flag captain, **NEWTON**, and went himself in command of the detachments from the two ships. The Military and Naval expedition arrived at Suffolk between 10 and 11 o'clock on the same morning, and greatly contributed to relieve the apprehension so powerfully excited among the citizens. They took up the line of march a short time after their arrival, for the scene of slaughter, and we since learn, had proceeded 22 miles that night towards Jerusalem—they had not however yet come in contact with any of the miscreants, who being closely pressed by the militia of Southampton and a large body of mounted men sent from Murfreesboro', Winton and the neighboring Counties, were directing their force towards South Quay, probably with the intention of taking to the Dismal Swamp. ... A friend...arrived here yesterday from Suffolk, states their number to be variously computed from 40 to 100, but as he thinks not exceeding the latter. ... They are said to have had several smart skirmishes with detachments of the militia in the vicinity of the Cross Keys, in which several of the deluded wretches have been killed, and some taken prisoners.

The militia of the Counties of Virginia and North Carolina proximate to the scene of insurrection, are generally under arms; but all accounts concur in stating that they are very deficient in proper arms, accoutrements and ammunition—and that *Cavalry* (of which unhappily all our former fine corps are disbanded) are perhaps the only species of troops that could ensure the capture of the Insurgents. Upon such intelligence reaching here on Wednesday, about thirty citizens of Norfolk and Portsmouth formed themselves into a company under the orders of Capt. J. S. **GARRISON**, and Lt. Charles **JOHNSON**, mounted and well equipped, and proceeded the same evening for Southampton, taking under their convoy an abundant supply of pistols, cutlasses and cartridges—furnished by Com. **WARRINGTON**, from the Navy Yard depot. ...

An express which arrived at Suffolk from Jerusalem, yesterday morning, reported, that 64 whites had been killed and several others were missing; the blacks in a state of confusion; were closely pursued by the Militia, and when overtaken shown no quarters. Among the killed are Mrs. Catharine **WHITEHEAD** and 5 daughters, 1 son and 1 grand son; Mr. Levi **WALTERS** (or **WALLER**'s) [sic] family, 14

Edenton Gazette and Farmer's Palladium 31 August 1831

in number, himself the only one that escaped; Mr. **TRAVIS** and family 5; Mr. **WILLIAMS** and family, 5; Mr. Jacob **WILLIAMS** and family, 4; Mr. **VAUGHAN**, sister and family, 5; Mr. **BARTON** and wife, 2; Mr. **REISSE** and family, 5—together with others not recollected, making the above number 64. The *Norfolk Junior Volunteers*, Lt. Com. **NEWTON**, left here yesterday morning for Southampton, via Suffolk, in the Steam Boat Constitution.

[634] [p. 3] Edenton: Wednesday, Aug. 31, 1831. ... THE INSURRECTION! ... It seems that the insurrection was entirely local in its character, and originated with a few misguided and desperate slaves, who commenced an indiscriminate and savage slaughter, and in their progress through the country, either from coercion, threats, or allurements, were enabled to increase the strength of their forces to about the number of forty, and not two hundred as was represented. It commenced without any general previous concert or matured design.—Their object appeared to be that of revenge, rapine and plunder, while in their hurried and disorderly march, old age and helpless infancy—robust manhood and feminine weakness, all alike, fell victims to their merciless and diabolical fury. Nearly sixty persons without regard to age, sex or size, were cruelly and brutally murdered. But their career was almost as short as it was wicked and bloody. The militia from the adjoining Counties with the most laudable promptitude, repaired to the relief of their suffering neighbors, and soon caused the insurgents to feel that weight of vengeance which they had so cruelly inflicted upon the whites. In two *short days*, they were nearly all killed to a man, and the insurrection completely suppressed! An awful warning to that class of our population, of the folly and madness of ever engaging in similar hopeless attempts.

With us we have detected no signs nor symptoms of an insurrectionary spirit; the slaves appear quiet, peaceable and unoffending, and while we recommend *vigilance* to our citizens, we would likewise respectfully suggest, that they should not suffer the present excitement, to cause them to deviate from their accustomed mild and moderate treatment to the slaves. The innocent should not suffer on account of the wicked—nor the just be confounded with the unjust.

[635] In pursuance of the resolution published in the last Gazette, an adjourned meeting of the citizens of the Town of Edenton and County of Chowan, assembled in the Court House, on the afternoon of the 27th inst. for the purpose of appointing delegates to represent the County and State, in the Anti-Tariff Convention proposed to be held in Philadelphia, on the 30th September next. Major Samuel T. **SAWYER** was called to the chair, and Thomas S. **HOSKINS**, Esq. requested to act as Secretary. The object of the meeting was then explained at considerable length by the chairman, when D. W. **STONE**, Esq. on the part of the committee appointed for that purpose, presented the following resolutions: Whereas it is a right which belongs to the people, peaceably to assemble together at any time to remonstrate and protest against the passage or continuance in operation of any unjust and oppressive Laws; and whereas it is proposed that a convention of Delegates from those parts of the Union oppressed by the Tariff Laws, be held...for the purpose of devising measures for their modification; and whereas it is an object as much to be desired by North Carolina as by any of her sister States: ... *Resolved*, That all duties are partial in their operation and that their imposition for any other purposes than those of revenue are unjust and oppressive and if not to the letter, are contrary to the spirit of the Constitution. *Resolved*, That ___[blank]___ be requested to attend said convention in behalf of this meeting. *Resolved*, That we will cheerfully co-operate with our fellow-citizens of the United States in using all constitutional means so to modify the Tariff Laws as to make them as little oppressive as the nature of the case will admit. *Resolved*, That we cordially unite with our fellow citizens of Bertie in respectfully soliciting the Hon. James **IREDELL**, late Senator in Congress and Hon. Thomas **RUFFIN**, Judge of the Supreme Court, to attend said convention as Representatives of the State of North Carolina. ...

On motion, it was resolved, that the blank in the fourth resolution be filled with the names of three persons; whereupon Major S. T. **SAWYER**, Jos. B. **SKINNER** and Nathaniel **BRUER**, Esq'rs. were severally nominated and elected to attend the convention to be held in Philadelphia in behalf of the citizens of the County of Chowan. On motion, it was further resolved, that the Hon. Willie P. **MANGUM**, be respectfully requested to attend in company with the Hon. Jas. **IREDELL** and the Hon. Thomas **RUFFIN**, in behalf of the State, and that a copy of these proceedings be forwarded to him. ... S. T. **SAWYER**, *Ch'm*. T. S. **HOSKINS**, *Sec'y*.

Edenton Gazette and Farmer's Palladium 31 August 1831

[636] *Another Revolutionary Patriot gone.*—David **WILLIAMS**, the last of the captors of Major **ANDRE**, died at Rensselaerville, on Tuesday last, in the 79th year of his age. His remains were on Thursday, interred with military honors, at Livingstonville, Schoharie county.

[637] The Virginia papers notice the melancholy death of one of their most talented men, Alfred H. **POWELL**, Esq. who while engaged in arguing a cause before the County Court of Fredrick, was seized with an apoplectic fit and almost immediately expired. He had just been elected a member of the Legislature of that State.

[638] MARRIED, In Washington County, on Wednesday evening last by Rev. Irvine **ATKINSON**, Mr. John G. **HANKINS**, of this place, to Miss Permelia, daughter of Mr. Joseph **CHRISTOPHER** of that county.

[639] DIED, In this town, last evening, Mrs. Catharine **GARDNER**, after a severe illness.

In Newbern, on Wednesday evening last, Charles G. **SPAIGHT**, Esq. Attorney at Law, and Representative elect of that town in the next General Assembly of this State.

Edenton Gazette.
Vol. XXVII.....No. 36. Edenton, N. C. Wednesday September 7, 1831. Whole No. 1388.

[640] [p. 3] Edenton: Wednesday, September 7, 1831. *Insurrection!*—It is believed that this dreadful affair has been put an end to in Southampton County. ... Unremitted exertions are making, however, to bring to justice all the offenders, who evaded apprehension, and all those who seem to be in any manner connected with the transaction, are forthwith remanded to jail to await their trial. Since our last 19 negroes in this County have been taken up and committed to jail in this place. We understand a large number of citizens from the several counties bordering on the Dismal Swamp, commenced yesterday to scout this great rendezvous for runaway slaves &c. It is hoped their efforts will not be in vain. P. S. Since writing the above, we learn from an undoubted source, that there have been killed in South Hampton [sic] County upwards of one hundred negroes, consequent upon the late insurrection in that county. We also learn that fourteen of the thoughtless, savage wretches have been tried, of whom, thirteen were convicted, and are to be hung during the present week—there are thirty more now in the jail at Jerusalem yet to be tried, besides others in jail at Bellfield.

[641] SUPREME COURT. We extract the following from the list of Causes decided by the Supreme Court of North Carolina, at its Summer term of 1831. *Equity Causes.* William **KEATON** and wife vs. Enoch **COBBS** and wife. Decree according to report. John **PIKE** and others vs. Starke **ARMISTEAD** and others, from Chowan. Decree reversed. W. H. **PUGH**, vs. William **BRITTON**, from Bertie. Injunction perpetuated at the costs of defendant. Wm. **JOHNSTON**, vs. Trustees of the University from Anson. Appeal dismissed and cause remanded to the court below. Henry **STEPHENS** vs. Horace **ELY**, from Beaufort. Report confirmed, and decree according. Sampson **WILDER** vs. Charles W. **MIXSON** and wife, from Bertie. Bill sustained. Decree. Thomas **COX** and wife, and Nancy **HALL** vs. Executors of David **CLARK** and others from Halifax. Decree for defendants.

Law Causes. Samuel **SIMPSON** vs. James S. **BLOUNT** from Beaufort. Judgment affirmed. Thomas **SANDERSON** vs. James S. **BLOUNT** from Beaufort. Judgment affirmed. Thomas **SANDERSON** vs. Nehemiah **ROGERS** and Son, Horace **ELY**, garnishee, from Washington. Judgment affirmed. Governor, to the use of the President and Directors & Co of the Bank of Cape Fear, appt. vs. Alex. **ELLIOTT**, ex'r of Robert **CAMPBELL** and others, from Cumberland. Judgment affirmed. Seth **SUMMER**, ex'r of James **SUMMER**, dec'd, vs. James **WHEDBEE**, from Perquimans. Judgment reversed and new trial. John **COX** and others vs. Benj. **DELANO**, from Chowan. Judgment affirmed. James I. **TREDWELL** vs. Wm. D. **RASCOE**, from Washington. Judgment affirmed. Jacques **LEGARDE** and wife vs. Wm. M. **CHESSON**, Sheriff of Washington county. Dismissed at the cost of the defendant.

[642] *Prize Tragedy.*—The premium of five hundred dollars, offered by Mr. **PELBY**, of Philadelphia for

Edenton Gazette and Farmer's Palladium 7 September 1831

the best original Tragedy, has been awarded to Mrs. *Caroline L. HENTZ*, formerly of Chapel Hill, N. C. and now resident at Covington, Kentucky. The committee was composed of Messrs. D. P. **BROWN**, R. P. **SMITH**, and J. B. **BOOTH**, who were unanimous in their decision.

[643] MARRIED, In this town, on the 25th ult. by Nathaniel **BRUER** Esq. Mr. Nathan D. **REED** to Miss Margaret **SHERWOOD**. ...

[644] NOTICE. The Subscriber, desirous of removing to the South, will sell at private sale at very reduced prices, his Town property, consisting of DWELLING HOUSES, Store Houses, Wharf and Dock with a large & commodious Warehouse, Cooper's and Blacksmith's shop connected—also, two Vessels, one of 77, the other 76 54-95 Tons burthen. Great bargains can be had if application be made within three months. J. H. **HAUGHTON**. Edenton, Sept. 7, 1821. [sic]

[645] NOTICE. The Subscriber has just received from New York...the following articles, which he will sell on his usual terms: Children's col'd prunelle Boots, Men's lined and bound Shoes, Women's leather welted Shoes, Gentlemen's Morocco Pumps, Maccaboy Snuff, X cut Saws, German Steel 7 feet long. Soap. ... Wm. F. **BENNETT**. Edenton, Sept. 7, 1831.

[646] *CASH IN MARKET.* The subscriber wishes to purchase negroes of both sexes from 12 to 25 years of age, for which he will give the highest cash prices. For further information apply at Joseph N. **HOSKINS'** tavern. Oliver **LUND**. Edenton, Sept. 7, 1831.

Edenton Gazette.
Vol. XXVII.....No. 37. Edenton, N. C. Wednesday September 14, 1831. Whole No. 1389.

[647] [p. 1] From the Richmond Whig of Saturday Evening, September 3d. We have been astonished since our return from Southampton, (whither we went in Capt. **HARRISON**'s Troop of Horse,) in looking over the mass of exchange papers accumulated in our absence, to the number of false, absurd and idle rumors, circulated by the Press, touching the insurrection in that county. Editors seem to have applied themselves to the task of alarming the public mind as much as possible, and of persuading the slaves to entertain a high opinion of their strength and consequence. ...

    The universal opinion in that part of the country is that **NAT**, a slave, a preacher, and a pretended Prophet, was the first contriver, the actual leader, and the most remorseless of the executioners. According to the evidence of a negro boy whom they carried along to hold their horses, **NAT** commenced the scene of murder at the first house (**TRAVIS'**) with his own hand. Having called upon two others, to make good their valiant boastings so often repeated, of what they would do, and these shrinking from the requisition: **NAT** proceeded to despatch one of the family with his own hand. Animated by the example and exhortations of their leader, having a taste of blood, and convinced that they had now gone too far to recede, his followers dismissed their qualms and became as ferocious as their leader wished them. To follow the bloody dogs from the capture of **TRAVIS'** house, before day, to their dispersion at **PARKER**'s cornfield early in the afternoon, where they had traversed near 20 miles, murdered 63 whites, and approached within 3 or 4 miles of the village of Jerusalem, the immediate object of their movement—to describe the scenes at each house, the circumstances of the murders, the hair breadth escapes of the few who were lucky enough to escape—would prove as interesting as heart rending. Many of the details have reached us, but not in so authentic a shape as to justify their publication, nor have we the time or space. Let a few suffice. Of the events at Dr. **BLOUNT**'s we had a narrative from himself, and his son, a lad about 15, distinguished for his gallantry and modesty, and whom we take the leave to recommend to Gen. **JACKSON**, for a warrant in the Navy or at West Point. The Doctor had received information of the insurrection, and that his house would be attacked, a short time before the attack was made. Crippled with the gout, and indisposed to fly, he resolved to defend his house. His force was his son, overseer and three other white men. Luckily there were six guns, and plenty of powder and shot in the house. These were barely loaded, his force posted, and the instructions given, when the negroes from 15 to 30 strong; rode up about day break. The Doctor's orders were that each man should be particular in his aim, and that one should fire at a time; he himself reserved one gun, resolved if the house was forced, to sell his life as

Edenton Gazette and Farmer's Palladium 14 September 1831

dearly as he could. The remaining five fired in succession upon the assailants, at the distance of fifteen or twenty steps. The blacks upon the fifth fire, retreated, leaving one killed (we believe) and one wounded, (a fellow called **HARK**,) and were pursued by the Doctor's negroes with shouts and execrations. Had the shot been larger, more execution would doubtless have been done.

Mrs. **VAUGHAN**'s was among the last houses attacked. A venerable negro woman described the scene with great emphasis. It was near noon, and her mistress had been making some preparation in the porch for dinner, when happening to look towards the road, she descried a dust and wondered what it could mean. In a second, the negroes mounted and armed, rushed into view, and making an exclamation indicative of her horror and agony, Mrs. **VAUGHAN** ran into the house.—The negroes dismounted and ran around the house, pointing their guns at the doors and windows. Mrs. **VAUGHAN** appeared at a window, and begged for her life, inviting them to take every thing she had. The prayer was answered by one of them firing at her, which was instantly followed by another, and a fatal shot. In the meantime, Miss **VAUGHAN**, who was up stairs, and unapprised of the terrible event until she heard the noise of the attack, rushed down and begging for life, was shot as she ran a few steps from the door. A son of Mrs. **VAUGHAN**, about 15, was at the still house, when hearing a gun, and conjecturing, it is supposed, that his brother had come from Jerusalem, approached his house, and was shot as he got over the fence. ...

It is with pain we speak of another feature of the Southampton Rebellion; for we have been most unwilling to have our sympathies for the sufferers, diminished or affected by their misconduct. We allude to the slaughter of many blacks, without trial, and under circumstances of great barbarity. How many have thus been put to death (generally by decapitation or shooting) reports vary; probably however some five and twenty and from that to 40; probably a yet larger number. To the great honor of General **EPPES**, he used every precaution in his power, and we hope and believe with success, to put a stop to the disgraceful procedure.—We met with an individual of intelligence, who stated that he himself had killed between 10 and 15. He justified himself on the ground of the barbarities committed on the whites; and that he thought himself right, is certain from the fact of his having narrowly escaped losing his own life in an attempt to save a negro woman whom he tho't innocent, but who was shot by the multitude in despite of his exertions. ... Let the fact not be doubted by those whom it most concerns, that another such insurrection will be the signal for the extirpation of the whole black population in the quarter of the state where it occurs. ... The presence of the troops from Norfolk and Richmond, alone prevented the retaliation from being carried much farther.

At the date of Capt. **HARRISON**'s departure from Jerusalem, Gen. **NAT** had not been taken. On that morning however, **DRED**, another insurgent chief, was brought prisoner to Jerusalem, having surrendered himself to his master, in the apprehension no doubt of starving in the swamps, or being shot by the numerous parties of local militia, who were in pursuit. **NAT** had not been certainly heard of since the skirmish in **PARKER**'s cornfield which was in the termination of the insurrection, the negroes after that dispersing themselves, and making no farther attempt. He is represented as a shrewd fellow, reads, writes, and preaches; and by various artifices had acquired great influence over the minds of the wretched beings whom he has led into destruction. It is supposed that he induced them to believe there were only 80,000 whites in the country, who being exterminated, the blacks might take possession. ... If there was any ulterior purpose, he probably alone knows it. For our own part, we still believe there was none; & if he be the intelligent man represented, we are incapable of conceiving the arguments by which he persuaded his own mind of the feasibility of his attempt, or how it could possibly end but in certain destruction. We therefore incline to the belief that he acted upon no higher principle than the impulse of revenge against the whites, as the enslavers of himself and his race; that being a fanatic he possibly persuaded himself that Heaven would interfere; and that he may have convinced himself, as he certainly did his deluded followers to some extent, that the appearance of the sun some weeks ago, prognosticated something favorable to their cause. ...

A more important inquiry remains—whether the conspiracy was circumscribed to the neighborhood in which it broke out, or had its ramifiations [sic] through other counties. We at first, adopted the first opinion; but there are several circumstances which favor the latter. We understand that the confessions of all the prisoners, go to shew that the insurrection broke out too soon, as it is supposed, in consequence of the last day of July being a Sunday, and not as the negroes in Southampton believed the Saturday before. The report is that the rising was fixed for the fourth Sunday in August, and that they supposing Sunday, the 31st July, to be the first Sunday in August, they were betrayed into the error of

Edenton Gazette and Farmer's Palladium 14 September 1831

considering the 3d Sunday as the 4th.—This is the popular impression, founded upon confessions, upon the indications of an intention of the negroes in Nansemond and other places to unite, and upon the allegation that Gen. **NAT** extended his preaching excursions to Petersburg and this city; allegations which we however, disbelieve. It is more than probable nevertheless that the mischief was concerned and concerted under the cloak of religion. The trials which are now proceeding or impending in Southampton, Nansemond, Sussex and else where will develope all the truth.

We regret to be under the necessity of adverting to any disagreeable circumstance connected with the expedition of the Richmond Troop of Cavalry to Southampton; but the conduct of one individual, deserves and shall receive at our hands, the exposure and the chastisement, which in the opinion of all who have heard it, it most richly deserves.—On Thursday morning the 25th, we arrived at Jerusalem, and took up our quarters at the tavern of Mr. Henry B. **VAUGHAN**. This individual was the brother-in-law of Mrs. **VAUGHAN**, whose melancholy fate and that of her family is noticed above. He had no family, and is wealthy. Under these circumstances, good feeling would have suggested the propriety of his charging no more than would indemnify him, a base and sordid love of pelf, could alone have prompted the idea of speculating upon men in our situation. We tended our own horses, with little aid from his servants; did not sleep in his house; were furnished with the coarsest and sometimes, stinking fare; many neither ate nor drank at his table, but were entertained by the hospitality of the inhabitants; detachments were absent on several occasions; and the troop left on Wednesday, making the times less than five days. It will excite astonishment to learn that for this time, with this accomodation, and under all the circumstances of the case, the Landlord produced a bill of $800! To state the fact, is to inflict on him, the severest punishment—the indignation of the public.

[648] [p. 2] The Richmond Enquirer, of Friday, says, "Gen. **EPPS** writes to the Governor on the 30th (Tuesday,) that every thing was quiet in Southampton, and he thought was likely to continue so—but in comsequence of the dispatches received from Nansemond and the Isle of Wight, a Council of War had been held, at which it was determined that as a precautionary measure, a strong patrol in these counties ought to be kept up—and accordingly instructions had been despatched to the commanding officers of the Regiment to put out such patrols. ... The P. S. of Gen. **E**'s. letter states, that a negro man had just been brought in as a prisoner by the same of **SAM** the slave of a Mr. **FRANCIS**. He had been concerned in the massacre, and had been one of the active leaders—but he denied that there had been anything like a general concert among the slaves. It was confined to the immediate neighborhood of the scene. ...It is reported that a map was found and said to have been drawn by Nat **TURNER**, with poke berry juice, which was descriptive of the county of Southampton! ..."

[649] A four days meeting will be held at the **BALLAD**s Bridge church, commencing on Thursday before the 2d Sunday in November next. The brethren in the ministry and all others are respectfully invited to attend. Myles **WELCH**. Chowan, Sept. 14, 1831.

[650] [p. 3] Edenton: Wednesday, September 14, 1831. ... We have before us a paper "**BADGER**'s Weekly Messenger" containing an engraving and an essay on the safety of the steam engine, invented by our neighbour, Wm. A. **TURNER** Esq. of Plymouth. We learn from the same paper that Mr. **T**. has already secured the patent...

[651] Edward **STANLEY** Esq. is a candidate in opposition to Charles **SHEPARD** Esq. to represent the town of Newbern.

[652] Storm At New Orleans. We learn from extracts taken from New Orleans papers, that a violent storm was experienced at that place on the 16th ult. ... A paper of the 20th August says: The Levee is injured to an immense amount, and at this moment Lake Ponchartrain has so swollen as to inundate the whole of the rear of the city up to Rampart street; the temporary huts at Milneburg (the end of the Rail Road,) and much property has been blown and washed away. ... [We fear the inundation and the rains will be productive of a great deal of sickness.] Below the city considerable damage has been sustained in the orchards and gardens. A crevasse broke out near Mr. **DE ENDE**'s warehouse. The chasm is nearly filled up—Another broke through the levee opposite Mr. **BUREAU**'s property; but that also is repaired.

Edenton Gazette and Farmer's Palladium 14 September 1831

The amount of losses accrued by the mere destruction of rafts, which have floated away, is rising 20,000 dollars. It is confidently asserted that the violence of the Mississippi waters, together with the long duration of previous rains, has burst the levees in several places below the city; the river being naturally at a low stage, and the waters having already receded, the crevices cannot be very dangerous, and must be easily repaired. At Terre-aux-Boeuf the ground lies under four feet water; all the inhabitants, from the interior, have taken refuge in their garrets, and have before their eyes the gloomy certainty of their irremediable ruin.—Their misfortune is so much the more to be deprecated as they depend exclusively upon their manual industry, and look upon their scanty crops as almost the only means of maintaining their families. Serious damages have also been sustained by planters generally...

The water which flowed the marshes bordering on lake Ponchartrain, has reached the back part of the city as far as Rampart street, and intercepted all land communication with the streets beyond; there are three feet of water in Treme street, and four feet have been measured somewhat farther. Every thorough fare in the direction of the city is navigated in boats. ...

[653] DIED, In Pasquotank County on Sunday night last in the 60th year of her age, while on a visit to her daughters in that county, Mrs. Mary **BOND**, for many years an inhabitant of Chowan county, but more recently a resident of this Town.

In Perquimans county, on Thursday last, very suddenly, Joshua, aged about 3 years, son of Benjamin S. **SKINNER** Esq.

In Newbern, on Saturday the 3d inst. Mrs. Margaret **DONNELL**, consort of the Hon. John R. **DONNELL** of that place.

[654] THE OLD STAND. Received per Sch. Maria from New York a general assortment of Medicines, Paints, &c. Fancy Soaps, Cologne and Lavender Water... John M. **JONES**. Edenton, Sept. 14, 1831.

[655] NEW FLOUR. By the Sch. Atlas I have just received new wheat FLOUR, which is offered for sale. N. **BRUER**. Sept. 14, 1831.

Edenton Gazette.
Vol. XXVII.....No. 38. Edenton, N. C. Wednesday September 21, 1831. Whole No. 1389 [sic.]

[656] [p. 1] ANTI-TARIFF MEETING. At a meeting of the citizens of Wake County, N. C. opposed to the present restrictive system, held at the Court-House in the city of Raleigh, on Monday the 15th ult. for the purpose of taking into consideration of the propriety of appointing delegates to the Anti-Tariff Convention proposed to be held in Philadelphia on the 30th September next: Hon. James **IREDELL** was called to the Chair, and John B. **MUSE** appointed Secretary. ... Gen. Romulus M. **SAUNDERS** also addressed the meeting... *Resolved,* That whilst we rejoice in the success of every honest pursuit of the American citizen, and in the prosperous investments of his capital, whether in commerce, agriculture, or manufactures, we deprecate as unjust and impolitic every attempt to regulate, by legislation, the industry of the country; thus controlling the operations of society, in giving an undue advantage to one pursuit over another. *Resolved,* That whilst we recognize the power of Congress to pass all needful laws for the regulation of commerce, and for raising revenue, we deny its constitutional competency to impose and continue a Tariff of duties with the sole view of protecting manufactures, to the injury of commerce and agriculture. ... *Resolved,* That Charles L. **HINTON**, Willis **WHITAKER** and Alfred **JONES**, Esquires, be appointed as a committee to confer with such committee or committees, as may be appointed by the counties of Orange and Person, and that they have the power of selecting not exceeding three persons as delegates for representing this Congressional district in the aforesaid Convention. ... The meeting then adjourned. Ja. **IREDELL**, Ch'm. Jno. B. **MUSE**, Sec'y.

[657] [p. 3] *Insurrection!*—During the last week a report was current in town, obtained from papers and a letter received from Newbern, that an *insurrection* had broken out among the negroes in Jones and Duplin counties, and that they had murdered *seventeen* white families!—This turns out to be a base fabrication. From information received since, by the editor of the Newbern Spectator, from a respectable citizen of Duplin, we gather the following facts. It seems a short time since, a disclosure was made to the white

Edenton Gazette and Farmer's Palladium 21 September 1831

citizens of Duplin by a *free person of color*, that a conspiracy existed among the negroes, to revolt and murder the white population. He mentioned the principal actors in the game, who were immediately taken up and examined, and sufficient evidence adduced against *two* of them to satisfy the citizens of the existence of such a plot—they were immediately made to feel the weight of that punishment they so richly merited, by being *shot*. ... We have been furnished with the following facts in a proof slip by our friends of the Raleigh Star: *Observer Office, Fayetteville, Sept.* 14, 3 *P. M.* Two of the gentlemen who went from this place to Clinton on Monday night; have this moment returned... We have procured from one of them the following statement, drawn up by himself at Clinton. It is worthy of entire reliance. "On Sunday the 4th inst. the first information of the contemplated rising of the Blacks, was sent from South Washington. The disclosure was made by a free mulatto man to Mr. **USHER** of Washington, who sent the information to Mr. **KELLY** of Duplin. It appears from the mulatto's testimony, that **DAVE**, a slave belonging to Mr. **MORISSEY** of Sampson, applied to him to join the conspirators, stated that the negroes in Sampson, Duplin, and New Hanover, were regularly organized and prepared to rise on the 4th October.

DAVE was taken up, and on this testimony convicted.—After his conviction, he made confession of the above to his master, and in addition gave the names of the four principal ringleaders in Sampson and Duplin, and several in Wilmington, named several families that they intended to murder.—Their object was to march by two routes to Wilmington, spreading destruction and murder on their way. At Wilmington they expected to be reinforced by 2000, to supply themselves with arms and ammunition and then return. Three of the ringleaders in Duplin have been taken, and **DAVE** and **JIM** executed. There are 23 negroes in jail in Duplin county, all of them no doubt concerned in the conspiracy. Several have been whipped and some released. In Sampson 25 are in jail, all concerned directly or indirectly in the plot.

The excitement among the people in Sampson is very great, and increasing; they are taking effectual measures to arrest all suspected persons. A very intelligent Negro Preacher named **DAVID**, was put on his trial to day and clearly convicted by the testimony of another negro. The people were so much enraged, that they scarcely could be prevented from shooting him on his passage from the Court House to the jail. All the confession [sic] made induce the belief that the conspirators were well organized, and their plans well understood in Duplin, Sampson, Wayne, New Hanover, and Lenoir. Nothing had transpired to raise even a suspicion that they extended into Cumberland or Bladen, except that **JIM** confessed that **NAT**, Col. **WRIGHT**'s negro, (who has been missing since the discovery of the plot,) had gone to Bryant **WRIGHT**'s, in the neighborhood of Fayetteville, to raise a company to join the conspirators. ..."

[658] Lieut. Frederick **NORCOM**, of this place, during the late session of the Supreme Court in Raleigh, obtained license to practice law in the County Courts of this State.

[659] Dr. Samuel L. **MITCHELL**, of New York, a distinguished physician and citizen, died a short time since, in that city.

Hon. A. M. **SCOTT** has been chosen Governor of the State of Mississippi, from among five candidates.

Davy **CROCKETT**, of Tennessee, has been elected to stay at home, and Mr. **FITZGERALD**, a **JACKSON** man has been chosen to fill his place in Congress.

[660] From the Baltimore American, Sept. 12. *Destructive Hurricane at Aux Cayes, Jacmel, Jeremie and St. Jago De Cuba.* The schr. Cicero, **WATTS**, arrived here yesterday from Port au Prince, whence she sailed on 30th August. From the report of Capt. **WATTS**, and a passenger in the Cicero, we learn that on the night of the 12th and morning of the 13th Aug. a violent hurricane passed over the town of Aux Cayes, and nearly destroyed it; leaving only eight houses standing. The loss of lives was immense, supposed to be not less than eight hundred to one thousand; the bodies of seven hundred persons were found after the storm had subsided. The vessels in the harbor were all destroyed. The town of Jeremie was almost in ruins, only ten or twelve houses standing. ... The town of Jacmel was nearly destroyed, and all the vessels in the harbour totally lost. ... Passengers in the Cicero, Capt. John **FLETCHER**, of the brig Evergreen, of Wilmington, N. C. lost at Jacmel on the night of the 12th of August; crew saved with the exception of one man; Capt. Thomas S. **HAYES**, of schr. Henry Clay, of Baltimore, also lost at Jacmel; crew saved with the exception of one seaman, named George **BEAN**, of St. Mary's, Md; Josiah **STO-**

Edenton Gazette and Farmer's Palladium 21 September 1831

VER, of schr. Columbia, of Portsmouth, N. H. lost at Jacmel at the same time.

[661] *Fatal Duel.*—We learn from the St. Louis times of Aug. 27, that the differences which had for some time existed between the Hon. Spencer **PETTIS**, (member of Congress elect) and Major **BIDDLE**, were terminated on the afternoon of the 26th, by an appeal to arms. The challenge was given by Mr. **PETTIS**, and accepted by Major **BIDDLE**, who being near-sighted, fixed the distance at five feet. At that distance (with pistols) the parties fought. Mr. **PETTIS** was shot through the side, just below the chest—the ball passing entirely through the body; and Major **BIDDLE** was shot through the abdomen—the ball lodging within. Mr. **PETTIS** died at three o'clock next morning. Major **BIDDLE**'s wound was considered very dangerous, though some hopes were entertained that it might not prove mortal.

Since preparing the above paragraph, we have seen a letter from St. Louis…under date of August 28, which states that Maj. **BIDDLE** died that morning. Thus closes this bloody and tragic "affair of *honor.*" *Baltimore Patriot.*

[662] MARRIED, In Hertford County on Thursday the 11th inst. by William **WYNN** Esq. William **WALTON** Esq. of this county, to Miss Sarah C. **JONES** daughter of the late James **JONES** Esq. of the former county.

[663] DIED. Died at the residence of his father on Wednesday the 14th inst. Mr. Isaiah **BUNCH**, son of Mr. Elijah **BUNCH** of this county in the 22nd year of his age.

On Saturday the 17th inst. Edward Douglas aged about 22 months son of Capt. John C. **SPENCER** of this county.

Edenton Gazette.
Vol. XXVII.....No. 39. Edenton, N. C. Wednesday September 28, 1831. Whole No. 1391.

[664] [p. 2] From the Oxford Examiner. State of North Carolina. County of Granville. *Superior Court of Law, begun and held on the first Monday of September, A. D.* 1831. The Jurors for the State, upon their Oath, present, that Robert **POTTER**, late of the County of Granville aforesaid, (Attorney at Law.) being a person of a wicked and malicious disposition, and contriving and wickedly intending one Lewis K. **WILLIE**, a youth of tender age, to maim and disfigure, on the twenty-eighth day of August in the year of our Lord, one thousand eight hundred and thirty one, at and in the said County of Granville, with force and arms, in and upon the said Lewis K. **WILLIE**, in the peace of God and the State, then and there being, on purpose, unlawfully did make an assault; and that he the said Robert **POTTER**, with a certain knife, which he the said Robert **POTTER**, in his right hand, then and there, had and held, both the testicles of him the said Lewis K. **WILLIE**, on purpose, unlawfully did cut out, with intent, him the said Lewis K. **WILLIE**, in so doing to maim and disfigure, against the form of the Act of the General Assembly, in such case made and provided, and against the peace and dignity of the State.

And the Jurors aforesaid, upon their Oath aforesaid, do further present, that the said Robert **POTTER**, afterwards, to wit, on the same day and year aforesaid, at and in the County of Granville aforesaid with force and arms, in and upon the said Lewis K. **WILLIE**…unlawfully and of his malice aforethought did make an assault… John **SCOTT**, Sol'r. Gen'l. The Indictment having been read from the Clerk's Table, the defendant was desired to plead; when he stated, that he could not plead *unqualifiedly* guilty—but being informed from the bench that he must say one or the other, he said, to waive all formality, he would say GUILTY. The Court, then proceeded to try him upon the submission.

Lewis K. **WILLIE** was called on the part of the State. The witness was brought before the Court in a litter—his appearance was pale, and apparently very feeble. Having been sworn, he proceeded to give testimony, as follows, as near as may be. … Witness proceeded.—That until the time of committing the violence charged in the indictment, he had never seen or suspected any thing unfriendly on the part of Mr. P. but the reverse. That on Sunday the 28th of August, the prisoner came to his father's house, and requested witness to aid him in getting a dog home, which was at his father's—that defendant procured his rifle, and dog and they proceeded together about half a mile, when defendant desired witness to help him tie the dog—witness said it was unnecessary, but the defendant insisted, when witness dismounted and caught the dog to hold him until defendant could tie him.—The defendant approached and threw a leather strap over witness' neck, and drew it so tight as to choke him—then requested him to cross his hands, which being done they were tied. Mr. **POTTER** then led witness out of the road, and told him that he had made his cousin Isabella (**POTTER**'s wife) a W__[blank]__ then bound his legs—witness swore to Mr. **P.** that he was innocent of the charge—defendant proceeded to perform the operation charged in indictment. Having unbound him, defendant asked if they should part as friends—witness gave his hand. Defendant told witness, that Dr. **TAYLOR** must know of the deed, and no one else, not even witness' father—Mr. **P.** stated that if he heard any thing more of the matter he would send that strumpet home to her father.

Examined by **NASH**.—Had seen Mr. **POTTER** at the Camp Meeting on the preceeding sabbath—witness was at Robt. **TAYLOR**'s from Friday until Sunday morning—never measured strength or scuffled with the prisoner—coming to Oxford, met R. **POTTER**—went back with him to get the rifle and dog—at prisoner's request, witness changed his horse for prisoner's gig, as it might make a difference in the dog's following—about half a mile from his father's house, stopped to tie the dog as before stated—prisoner appeared very friendly, and the witness supposed him to be sporting with him after he was tied. Prisoner then made the charge against witness—and threatened to cut his throat if he resisted—does not recollect any threat for divulging the affair—went home and sent for the Doctor.

Cross-examined by **POTTER**—Do not recollect the charge of guilt with Mrs. **P.** before his hands were bound, did not apprehend personal violence—after witness was released he said—"Mr. **POTTER**, how did you find it out?" and being told that she had confessed, he said it was true. The defendant demanded of the witness, upon his solemn oath, to say whether he was guilty or not of intercourse with Mrs. **POTTER**? the witness emphatically denied his guilt or having ever made any advances. Witness stated that Mr. **POTTER** held a knife in his hand, and he acknowledged that he was guilty through fear of personal danger, &c.

By **NASH**—Perfectly innocent of improper conduct with Mrs. **POTTER**—his confession of guilt made through fear, inspired by the expression of the prisoner's countenance. Dont [sic] recollect expressing a willingnes [sic] to keep the matter secret, nor to part as friends but gave his hand. The witness stated, that after he got home he sent for the Doctor, and then pursued **POTTER** with his gun, but becoming very weak from loss of blood, he was compelled to return home. Mr. **POTTER** now addressed the Court at considerable length, at the close of which he briefly stated the testimony upon which he relied for his justification.—This testimony consisted in a confession of guilt on the part of Mrs. **POTTER**, to himself and to sundry persons afterwards. The judge declared that no such testimony would be received, as it was illegal. ...

S. **PHILPOT** was sworn in behalf of Mr. **POTTER**—Was at school near Mr. Robert **TAYLOR**'s—once or twice at Mr. Robert **TAYLOR**'s—saw young **WILLIE** there—never saw any thing amiss between the parties—saw no actions or gestures, which indicated any thing improper. Dr. W. V. **TAYLOR** was sworn, and gave evidence as to the nature of the wound which we deem unnecessary to detail. ... Several gentlemen testified to the moral and correct conduct of the young man. The defendant was then ordered to jail, to await the sentence of the Court.

On Friday the prisoner was bro't into Court to receive his sentence. An argument now arose upon a point of law... **SEAWELL** for the prosecution, took the following distinctions: "In this indictment there are two counts, the one charges the Defendant under the Statute, the other as at Common Law. In this case it is clear, that the statuary [sic] provision of the State, in relation to maiming, has not specified the offence of which the defendant is charged; nor was it intended that such provision should result by implication. The terms of the statute are...for the first offence, stand in the pillory for two hours, have both his ears nailed to the pillory and cut off, and receive 39 lashes on the bare back. The second section of the same statute enacts, "That if any person or persons, shall on purpose, unlawfully, cut or slit the nose, bite or cut off a nose or lip, bite or cut off an ear, or *disable any limb or member*, of any other persons, with intent," &c.—All persons so offending are subject to six months' imprisonment, and to be fined at the discretion of the Court. ... His honor sentenced Rob't **POTTER** to pay a fine of One Thousand Dollars, and costs of prosecution, and be imprisoned for six Calendar months, and thereafter until the said fine costs be paid.

In conclusion, we will state that Mr. **POTTER** is indicted for maiming in the same manner, on the same day, the Rev. Lewis **TAYLOR** of this county and also stabbing him in the head and thigh. As this indictment will be tried at the spring Term of the Superior Court, we will not remark upon it, further

Edenton Gazette and Farmer's Palladium 28 September 1831

than to say, that immediately after the commission of the offence for which he was tried as above, he proceeded to the meeting house where Mr. **TAYLOR** performed divine worship on that day, and prevailed upon the Rev. Gentleman to accompany him home, he on the way haltered him and maimed and stabbed him as stated. He then carried Mr. **TAYLOR** to his house and sent for a physician. Mr. **TAYLOR** is now we learn in a fair way to recover, although he has been considered very dangerous. We are done with this matter at least until the trial on the other indictment shall be over.

[665] [p. 3] Edenton: Wednesday, September 27, 1831. We learn that at the late Term of Bertie Superior Court, the notorious Jesse **COMBS**, who we some time since stated had drowned his wife and child in that County, was tried and sentenced to be hung on the 4th November next.

[666] The Governor of Virginia has issued a proclamation, offering a reward of Five Hundred Dollars for the apprehension of Gen. **NAT**, (as he is called) the contriver of the Southampton insurrection. The following is the description given of the fellow: **NAT** is between 30 and 35 years old, 5 feet 6 or 8 inches high, weighs between 150 and 160 lbs. rather bright complexion, but not a mulatto, broad shoulders, large flat nose, large eyes, broad flat feet, rather knock-kneed, walks brisk and active, hair on the top of the head very thin, no beard, except on the upper lip, and the top of the chin, a scar on one of his temples, also one on the back of his neck, a large knot on one of the bones of his right arm, near the wrist, produced by a blow.

[667] MARRIED, In this town on [?] last evening, by the Rev. Mr. **ADDISON** Mr. Thomas J. **MILLER**, to Miss Priscilla, daughter of Mr. Simon **STALLINGS** of Gates County.

[668] DIED, Near this place on Sunday morning last, of her lingering indisposition, Mrs. Margaret **SATTERFIED** [sic,] widow of Henry B. **SATTERFIELD** dec'd.

[669] State of North Carolina, *Washington County*. Court of Pleas and Quarter-Sessions, August Term, 1831. Wm. **DOUGLASS**, & Co. vs. Alpheus **FORBES**, jr.} Attachm't. It appearing to the Court in this case, that the defendant is not a resident of this State: It is therefore ordered that publication be made in the Edenton Gazette for six weeks, for Alpheus **FORBES**, to come forward replevy and plead answer or demur: or judgment final will be entered up against him and the property so attached will be condemned to satisfy the same.—Witness Joseph C. **NORCOM**, Clerk of our said Court, the third Monday of August 1831. J. C. **NORCOM**, *Cl'k.* Sept. 27th, 1831.

Edenton Gazette.
Vol. XXVII.....No. 40. Edenton, N. C. Wednesday October 5, 1831. Whole No. 1392.

[670] [p. 3] Edenton: Wednesday, October 5, 1831. ... List of Letters Remaining in the Post Office at Edenton on the 30th September 1831. B—Thomas M. **BLOUNT**, James **BOZMAN**, 2, R. T. **BROWNRIGG**, 2. Mary A. **BISSELL**, Jos. C. **BENBURY**. C—Burrel **CARLISLE**. D—Wm. F. **DUTTON**, Mary **DANIEL**. G—Edward H. **GOELET**, 2, Catharine **GARDINER**, Jno. B. **GOELET**. H—Chas. **HAUGHTON**, Henderson **HARRIS**, Jas. H. **HARVEY**, 2, John A. **HAMMETT**, James **HARRELL**, Henry **HOMER**. J—Sely **JORDAN**, Wm. **JACKSON**. I—James **IREDELL**, 2. K—Phillis Dominick **KING**, Elizabeth **KING**. M—Hon. James **MARTIN**. N—John **NIXON**. O—S. R. **OLIVERA**. R—**ROSE** (a colored midwife.) S—To the Sheriff of Chowan County, 2, M. E. **SAWYER**, Charles **SANDERLIN**, Wm. **SHEPARD**, Robert **SPENCE**, Mr. **SUTTON**, Mrs. Louisa **SAWYER**, Lemuel **SAWYER**, Thos. P. **SMITH**. W—Miss Catharine **WHITE**, Jordan M. **WOOD**, Wm. **WELCH**, Benj. **WYNNE**, Abagail **WOOD**, George **WHITE**, Sr., Thomas **WESTON**, Elizabeth **YOUNG**.—49 N. **BRUER**, P. M. Oct. 5th 1831.

[671] *To all whom it may concern.* The subscriber has determined to remove in a few weeks to the West. He believes that he has settled all his just debts; but if there be any person or persons yet having claims against him, either by bond, note, or open account, he takes this method to request them to come forward immediately for settlement. And all persons indebted to him are hereby requested to make immediate

Edenton Gazette and Farmer's Palladium 5 October 1831

payment, as no longer indulgence will be given. Joshua **MEWBORN**. N. B. He particularly notifies those with whom he is bound as security or endorser to come forward and take new securities, &c. as he is determined to be bound no longer, and wishes to have all his affairs properly adjusted, before he takes his departure. J. M. Chowan Co. Oct. 5th 1831.

[672] List of Letters Remaining in the Post Office at Plymouth, N. C. Oct. 1st 1831. Joseph **ASKO**, Sally Ann **BRITT**, John M. **BATEMAN**, Mrs. Maria **CHESSON**, Andrew L. **CHESSON**, Hezekiah **CHESSON**, Joseph **CHRISTOPHER**, William L. **HUNT**, Richard **LEARY**, Joshua **LONG**, William W. **SKILES**, Swain **SWIFT**, John **THOMPSON**. Wm. A. **TURNER**, P. M. Oct. 1st 1831.

[673] Wm. H. **REDWOOD**, *Commission Merchant*, Norfolk, VA. Offers his services to Farmers and Planters, Merchants Lumber Getters and others, in the sale of all kinds of Produce and Lumber, the purchase of Goods, and in the transaction of business as a *General Commission Merchant*. ... Oct. 1, 1831.

Edenton Gazette.
Vol. XXVII.....No. 41. Edenton, N. C. Wednesday October 12, 1831. Whole No. 1393.

[674] [p. 2] *The Missionaries.*—The Federal Union says that on the 22d ultimo. eleven white men, convicted in Gwinnett Superior Court, of illegal residence in the Cherokee country, were brought to Milledgeville under sentence of four years imprisonment in the penitentiary. Their names are Samuel A. **WORCESTER**, Elizur **BUTLER**, James **TROTT**, Samuel **MAYO**, Edward **DELOSIER**, Surcy **EATON**, Thomas **GANN**, A. **COPELAND**, Benjamin F. **THOMPSON**, James A. **THOMPSON**, and John F. **WHEELER**. **WORCESTER** and **BUTLER** are Presbyterian missionaries; **TROTT** is a Methodist missionary, and **WHEELER** was one of the printers of the Phœnix. All but **WORCESTER** and **BUTLER** were pardoned by the Governor on their promise not again to violate the law of the state, regulating the residence of white men in the Cherokee nation, and were not carried within the walls of the Penetentiary. When **WORCESTER** and **BUTLER** were informed that the Governor would pardon them on their making a similar promise, **WORCESTER** replied he had taken the course he had pursued, from a firm conviction of duty—if he had been disposed to submit, he would not have proceeded so far—he had applied to the supreme court, and expects to hear from his application: **BUTLER** stated, that according to his views, he could not take the oath of allegiance to the State, without perjuring himself—he could not consent to a change of residence with his present feelings. These two are now enduring the sentence of the law in the Penitentiary.

[675] *Gen. NAT.*—Extract of a letter from a gentleman in Fincastle, Va. to his friend in Richmond:--Gen. Nat. **TURNER** of Southampton passed through **PRINCE**'s Toll gate about 18 miles from Fincastle a few days ago. Mr. **PRICE** and **SCOTT** stopt him on the road thinking he was a runaway, but he escaped from them leaving his coat in their possession, and a powder horn full of powder, and a book with his name in it, which led to the information. They were still in pursuit of him.

[676] [p. 3] Edenton: Wednesday, October 12, 1831. ... NEW STORE. The Subscriber has just returned from New York, with an excellent stock of seasonable and Cheap Goods, just opened at the store recently occupied by R. H. & J. G. **SMITH**, consisting of *Dry Goods*, Groceries, Crockery, Hardware, &c. which he is determined to dispose of to customers at a very small advance on *prime cost*, for Cash. ... Wm. H. **GRIMES**. Edenton, Oct. 12, 1831.

[677] Call at the Old Stand for BARGAINS. Just received from New York, first chop buckskin Gloves, cotton, silk, angola, worsted, and lamb's wool Hoisery [sic]...Cravats... Suspenders...Groceries, Hats, Stationary, and a general assortment of School Books &c. &c. ... John M. **JONES**. October 12,1831.

[678] List of Letters Remaining in the Post Office at Hertford, September 30th 1831. Jeremiah **ASHLEY**, Dr. A. **BURDRALL**, Miss Pherebee E. **BAGLEY**, John **BROCK**, James **BANKS**, Robert **GILASTER**, Gen. Jonathan H. **JACOCKS**, Robert C. **JENNINGS**, Wm. **MITCHELL**, Job **PERKINS**, Robert C. **PRITCHARD**, Henry **SKINNER**, Sheriff of Perquimans County, Abraham **SANDERS**,

Edenton Gazette and Farmer's Palladium 12 October 1831

Charles W. SKINNER, Jno. E. WOOD, Isaac WILLIAMS, Thomas WARD. J. R. BURBAGE, P. M. Oct. 12, 1831.

Edenton Gazette.
Vol. XXVII.....No. 42. Edenton, N. C. Wednesday October 19, 1831. Whole No. 1394.

[679] [p. 1] From the Philadelphia Gazette. Free Trade Convention. *Philadelphia, Friday, September 30, 1831.* At twelve o'clock, Mr. Joseph R. EVANS, of Philadelphia, called the meeting to order, and moved that Col. Burwell BASSETT, of Virginia, should take the Chair, as Chairman *pro tempore*. The motion was unanimously adopted. Mr. Theodore SEDGWICK, of Massachusetts, then moved that the Delegation from *each* State appoint two of their number as a Committee to nominate a President and other Officers, to be afterwards ballotted for by the Convention. ... Mr. RAGUET, of Philadelphia, was appointed Secretary, *pro tempore*. The Secretary stated, that one hundred and fifty-one Delegates had inscribed their names in the book. *Saturday, Oct. 1, 1831.* ... At ten o'clock the meeting was called to order, by the Hon. Burwell BASSETT, the Chairman pro tem. ... There was one individual present, whose nomination would unite all votes. He, [Mr. GALLATIN] therefore, nominated Mr. P. P. BARBOUR of Virginia, for the office of President. ...

When the President had resumed the Chair, the different Delegations reported that they had elected the following gentlemen, members of the GENERAL COMMITTEE. *Maine.*—Josh. CARPENTER, Chas. Q. CLAPP. *Massachusetts.*—Theodore SEDGWICK, Henry LEE. *Rhode Island.*—William HUNTER. *New York.*—Albert GALLATIN, John Aug. SMITH. *New Jersey.*—Cornelius L. HARDENBURG, Henry VETHAKE. *Pennsylvania.*—Thomas P. COPE, Clement C. BIDDLE. *Maryland.*—Wm. W. HANDY, A. D. JONES. *Virginia.*—James M. GARNETT, John W. JONES. *North Carolina.*—James IREDELL, Wm. A. BLOUNT. *South Carolina.*—William HARPER, Daniel E. HUGER. *Georgia.*—John M. BERRIEN, Eli S. SHORTER. *Alabama.*—Enoch PARSONS, H. GOLDTHWAITE. *Mississippi.*—Geo. POINDEXTER. *Tennessee.*—William E. BUTLER, Alexander PATTON.

Mr. BERRIEN, of Georgia, stated that it was desirable to ascertain the operations of the duties in various parts of the Union, and, as some parts were not represented on this floor, he would offer a resolution to invest the president with discretionary power to invite persons capable of giving information, to a seat within the bar. The resolution was unanimously adopted, and the Convention adjourned to 12 o'clock, on Monday. *Monday, Oct. 3, 1831.* At twelve o'clock the Convention met according to adjournment. ... The President announced the names of several gentlemen, whom, he had invited to take seats within the bar. [Among the gentlemen...was Mr. Henry D. SEDGWICK, a native of Massachusetts, but, we believe, for some time a resident of New York. He was the proposer of the Convention, through the medium of the New York Evening Post. A few weeks ago he was struck with paralysis. The disease does not affect his mind, and, his interest in the objects of the Convention being undiminished, he was conducted to his seat by the assistance of his servants and his friends.] A letter was received from John I. MUMFORD, Esq. of N. York, stating that he had deposited in the Hall, for the use of the Members of the Convention, several hundred copies of the Report of the Committee on Commerce, of the year 1829.

Mr. GALLATIN, Chairman of the Federative Committee, by direction of that Committee, reported two resolutions, one directing an Address to the People of the United States, the other a Memorial to Congress, to be prepared, to promote the objects of the convention. These resolutions were adopted without a dissenting vote.. ...

[680] [p. 3] Edenton: Wednesday, October 19, 1831. ... Hon. John RANDOLPH, late Minister to Russia, returned to the United States the other day in the ship Hannibal from London. It is stated in the Globe, that the Hon. James BUCHANAN, has been recently appointed Minister to Russia. Gen. Micajah T. HAWKINS, of Warren County, is a candidate to represent the districts composed of the Counties of Granville, Franklin, Warren and Nash, in the Congress of the United States, to supply the place of Robt. POTTER. ... Mr. ADAMS, it is said, has declined being the candidate of the Anti-Masons for Governor, and the Hon. Samuel LATHROP of West Springfield has been nominated.

Edenton Gazette and Farmer's Palladium 19 October 1831

[681] CHOWAN GUARDS! ATTENTION! You are hereby notified to attend at the parade ground before the Court House, on Saturday afternoon next, at half past 3 o'clock precisely, armed and equipped according to law. Punctual attendance must be observed. By order of the Captain, A. SPENCE, O. S. Oct. 19th 1831.

Edenton Gazette.
Vol. XXVII.....No. 43. Edenton, N. C. Wednesday October 26, 1831. Whole No. 1395.

[682] [p. 1] From the Philadelphia Gazette. FREE TRADE CONVENTION. *Wednesday, Oct.* 5, 1831. At twelve o'clock the meeting was called to order. ... The following letter from James RONALDSON, Esq. of Philadelphia, was received... *To the President and Members of the Free Trade Convention at Philadelphia. Cedar Street,* Sept. 11, 1831. ... What would be the effect, on the price of iron, of perfect confidence on the part of the public and iron manufacturers—that the present system is not uncertain and vacillating, but a permanent one? ...

[683] [p. 3] Edenton: Wednesday, October 26, 1831. ... The Grand Jury of Wake County in this State, during the last session of the Superior Court in Raleigh, found a "True Bill," on the submission of an indictment by the Attorney General, against Wm. Lloyd GARRISON and Isaac KNAPP for the circulation in that county, contrary to the laws of the State, a "seditious publication," called "the Liberator" published in Boston by the aforesaid persons. It remains for the Executive of this State to demand them from the Commonwealth of Massachusetts to appear for trial. There may be some difficulty in getting them.

[684] DIED, In Perquimans County on the 12th inst. Mr. James WHIDBEE, an old and respectable farmer in that county.

[685] Splendid Goods THE OLD STAND. Just received from New York, the latest *London* and *Parisian* Style of Fancy Goods, viz: Printed cotton Hose for ladies, Very rich belt Ribbons, Furniture Dimity, 6-4 Crape Hdkfs... Long & Short Brooms, Gum Arabic, &c... John M. JONES. Oct. 26th 1831.

[686] Fall and Winter Goods. The Subscriber has just received the following Goods from New York...Scarlet and straw belt Ribbons, Taffita do, mixed Sattinett... ALSO, Cheese, Butter, N. O. Sugar, Loaf and Lump do. N. E. Rum, Rye Gin, buck and duck Shot. Wm. F. BENNETT. October, 16, 1831.

[687] Twenty Cents Reward. Ranaway from the Subscriber about the 1st inst. a white boy about 18 years of age by the name of John M. JONES, an indented apprentice to the shoe making business. I hereby forwarn any person or persons harboring or employing him in any manner whatever, as I shall prosecute every such offender to the extremity of the law. Silas SNELL. Washington Co. 25, 1831. [sic]

Edenton Gazette.
Vol. XXVII.....No. 44. Edenton, N. C. Wednesday November 2, 1831. Whole No. 1396.

[688] [p. 1] From the Philadelphia Gazette. FREE TRADE CONVENTION. *Thursday, Oct.* 6, 1831. ... It being then stated that the printer had not ready the copies of Address to the People, which had been ordered to be printed for the use of Members, the Convention took a recess till one o'clock. ... *Friday, Oct.* 7, 1831. ... Mr. GALLATIN...intended simply to move that all the argumentative part of the Address, on the question of constitutionality, shall be struck out.

The ayes and noes were then taken, and it appeared that there were 35 for striking out, and 159 against striking out, as follows: YEAS: *Massachusetts.*—Theodore SEDGWICK, Joseph ROPES. *Rhode Island.*—Wm. HUNTER. *New York.*—Jonathan GOODHUE, Thos. R. MERCEIN, Jno. A. STEVENS, Isaac CAROW, Jno. CONSTABLE, Jas. BOORMAN, Geo. GRISWOLD, Benj. L. SWAN, Geo. T. TRIMBLE, Zebedee RING, Albert GALLATIN, Jacob LORILLARD, Jas. G. KING, Chas. H. RUSSELL, Isaac BRONSON, James HEARD, Silas M. STILWELL. *New Jersey.*—C. L. HARDENBURG, J. C. VAN DYCK, J. Bayard KIRKPATRICK, Miles C. SMITH, Henry CLOW, Henry VETHAKE, John R. THOMSON, R. F. STOCKTON.

Edenton Gazette and Farmer's Palladium 2 November 1831

Pennsylvania.—Edw. D. INGRAHAM, Sam'l. SPACKMAN, Thos. P. COPE. *Maryland.*—Geo. HOFFMAN, Jno. J. DONALDSON. *N. Carolina.*—Edw. B. DUDLEY. *S. Carolina.*—Henry MIDDLETON.

NAYS: *Maine.*—Josh. CARPENTER, Chas. Q. CLAPP, S. H. MUDGE. *Massachusetts.*—Henry LEE, T. S. POMEROY, Sam'l. SWETT, Gideon TUCKER, Jno. L. GARDNER, George PEABODY, Pickering DODGE, Isaac NEWHALL, Henry WILLIAMS, Edw'd. CRUFT, William GODDARD, Ebenezer BREED, Thomas P. BANCROFT, John PICKENS. *New York.*—Preserved FISH, J. LEONARD, Edwin BERGH, H. KNEELAND. *New Jersey.*—John POTTER. *Pennsylvania.*—Jos. R. EVANS, Geo. EMLEN, Clement C. BIDDLE, J. M. BARCLAY, E. LITTELL, Sam'l. F. SMITH, Isaac W. NORRIS, Richard PRICE, Henry R. WATSON, John A. BROWN, Philip H. NICKLIN, Coudy RAGUET, William MC ILHENNY. *Maryland.*—William W. HANDY, Arnold D. JONES. *Virginia.*—Philip P. BARBOUR, Henry E. WATKINS, Richard BOOKER, Jas. M. GARNETT, Sam'l. L. VENABLE, Thos. R. DEW, Wm. MAXWELL, Benj. F. DABNEY, R. O. GRAYSON, S. A. STORROW, Charles COKE, John W. JONES, Walker HAWES, Phil. A. DEW, J. BROCKENBROUGH, Thos. MILLER, Wm. G. OVERTON, Geo. C. DROMGOOLE, Randolph HARRISON, Charles YANCEY, Robert BURT, Ferdinand W. RISQUE, Malcolm MACFARLAND, Thos. W. GILMER, Burwell BASSETT, R. H. ANDERSON, Josiah ELLIS, Charles EVERETT, Alex. Gordon KNOX, Geo. M. PAYNE, James S. BRANDER, William O. GOODE, Wm. TOWNES, John DICKINSON, Wm. B. ROGERS, Wm. P. TAYLOR, John H. BERNARD, Linn BANKS, Wm. H. ROANE, Jas. LYONS, John TABB, Jas. JONES, Thos. T. GILES, Archibald BRYCE, Jr. James MAGRUDER, Wm. DANIEL, Jr. S. H. DAVIS, Littleton UPSHER. *N. Carolina.*—Joseph B. SKINNER, Louis D. WILSON, Jas. IREDELL, Wm. R. HOLT, Jos. B. G. ROULHAC, Wm. A. BLOUNT, Jos. D. WHITE, S. T. SAWYER, David OUTLAW, Thomas S. HOSKINS, John E. WOOD, J. W. COCHRAN, Nathaniel BRUER. *S. Carolina.*—Zach P. HERNDON, Jas. G. SPANN, F. W. DAVIE, Jas. CUTHBERT, Thos. PINCKNEY, T. D. SINGLETON, Wm. BUTLER, Jos. W. ALLSTON, Henry N. CRUGER, Charles MACBETH, Henry C. YOUNG, A. P. BUTLER, H. A. MIDDLETON, Thos. R. MITCHELL, W. WILKINSON, Philip TIDYMAN, Stephen D. MILLER, Wm. POPE, John FRASER, Job JOHNSON, John D. EDWARDS, John CARTER, Langdon CHEVES, Joseph F. JENKINS, Hugh WILSON, J. H. GLOVER, T. Pinckney ALSTON, Edw. RICHARDSON, Wm. HARPER, Wm. C. PRESTON, Henry MIDDLETON, Daniel E. HUGER, Hugh S. LEGARE, Jno. TAYLOR, Thomson T. PLAYER, J. Berkley GRIMHALL, James ROSE, William SMITH, Thos. WILLIAMS, Jr., Thos. FLEMMING. *Georgia.*—Eli S. SHORTER, Rob't. HABERSHAM, Alex'r. TELFAIR, John CUMMING, Seaborn JONES, J. Macpherson BERRIEN. *Alabama.*—John A. ELMORE, B. S. BIBB, Enoch PARSONS, Alfred V. SCOTT, John W. MOORE, Howell ROSE, P. WATERS, H. GOLDTHWAITE, Ward TAYLOR, Archibald P. BALDWIN, William J. MASON. *Mississippi.*—Geo. POINDEXTER. *Tennessee.*—William E. BUTLER, Alexander PATTON.—159. ...

[689] [p. 3] Edenton: Wednesday, November 2, 1831. ... At a recent election in Charleston, S. C. for a representative to supply the place of Wm. AIKEN, deceased, the nullification candidate M. J. KEITH, succeeded, against the Union candidate, John ROBINSON, by a majority of only eight! out of 2,700 votes.

Appointments by the President.—Auguste DAVEZAC, of Louisiana, to be Charge d'Affairs of the U. States near His Majesty the King of the Netherlands. James A. DUNLAP, of Florida, to be Attorney of the United States for the Middle District of Florida, vice James G. RINGGOLD deceased.

[690] The following gentlemen compose the new Board of Directors of the Branch of the United States Bank in Fayetteville, N. C. John HUSKE, C. P. MALLETT, John H. HALL, Elisha STEDMAN, Duncan MC RAE, Wm. MC INTYRE, John KELLY, Rev. DANIEL, Raleigh, Aaron LAZARUS, Wilmington. And at a meeting of the new Board on Tuesday last, John HUSKE, Esq. was unanimously re-elected President.

[691] MARRIED, In this County on Tuesday night last, by Wm. GREGORY, Esq. Mr. Dow GASKINS of Bertie, to Miss Deborah LASSITER.

Edenton Gazette and Farmer's Palladium 2 November 1831

[692] DIED, In this County yesterday morning Mr. Allen **LASSITER**.

[693] Unanimity Lodge, No. 54. The members of Unanimity Lodge No. 54, are requested to meet at their Hall in the Court House, on Saturday next, at half past 2 o'clock P. M., for the transaction of business of importance. Punctual attendance is solicited. By order of the Master, J. H. **HAUGHTON**, *Sec'y*. Nov. 1st 1831.

[694] NEW GOODS. The subscriber has just returned from New York, and is now opening at his old stand, a handsome and general assortment of GOODS, suitable for the season, which he will sell *low*. N. **BRUER**. Nov. 1st 1831.

[695] Real Estate For Sale. State of North Carolina, *Chowan County—In Equity*. Pursuant to a decree in Equity of October Term last, the Master will sell at the Court House in Edenton, at Public Auction, on Thursday the 24th inst. four half Lots of ground with the Dwelling House and other improvements thereto belonging, situated in the town of Edenton and County aforesaid, bounded on the north by George **WAFF**'s lots, on the east by Broad Street, on the south by Gale street, and on the west by Thomas **MEREDITH**'s lots, in the new plan of said Town; belonging to the heirs of Charles **ROBERTS**, dec'd. Also; the one undivided half of a small tract of Land, lying in the County aforesaid, adjoining the lands of Jos. B. **SKINNER**, Wm. **BULLOCK** and others, containing about twenty five acres, belonging to the aforesaid heirs. The terms of sale are six and twelve months credit, the purchaser to enter into bond with approved security, to R. T. **HOSKINS**, C. & M. E. Novem. 1st 1831.

Edenton Gazette.
Vol. XXVII.....No. 45. Edenton, N. C. Wednesday November 9, 1831. Whole No. 1397.

[696] [p. 3] Members Of The Legislature, For 1831. *Anson*. Clement **MARSHALL**, S. Wm. A. **MORRIS** and Alexander **LITTLE**, C. *Ashe*. Jno. **RAY**, S. James **CALLOWAY** and Toliver **WITCHER**, C. *Brunswick*. William R. **HALL**, S. J. P. **GAUSE** and Samuel A. **LASPEYRE**, C. *Buncombe*. James **ALLEN**, S. J. **BREVARD** and J. **CLAYTON**, C. *Beaufort*. William S. **ROWLAND**, S. Richard H. **BONNER** and David C. **FREEMAN**, C. *Burke*. Mark **BRITTAIN**, S. Alney **BURGEN** and E. P. **GLASS**, C. *Bladen*. John T. **GILMORE**, S. John J. **MC MILAN** and Robert **LYON**, C. *Bertie*. George O. **ASKEW**, S. Lewis **THOMPSON** and David **OUTLAW**, C. *Craven*. Rich'd. D. **SPAIGHT**, S. Abner **HARTLY** and Wilie M. **NELSON**, C. *Carteret*. Thomas **MARSHAL**, S. Jas. W. **HUNT** and Jno. F. **JONES**, C. *Currituck*. Jonathan J. **LINDSAY**, S. John B. **JONES** and Benjamin T. **SIMMONS**, C. *Camden*. Haywood **BELL**, S. Thomas **DOZIER** and A. **GRANDY**, C. *Caswell*. James **KERR**, S. Littleton A. **GWYNN** and John T. **GARLAND**, C. *Chowan*. Richard T. **BROWNRIGG**, S. Joseph H. **SKINNER** and William **JACKSON**, C. *Chatham*. William **RENCHER**, S. Hugh **MC QUEEN** and J. **BROOKS**, C. *Cumberland*. John D. **TOOMER**, S. David **MC NEILL** and John **BARCLAY**, C. *Cabarrus*. Christopher **MELCHOR**, S. D. M. **BARRINGER** and William **M'LEAN**, C. *Columbus*. Luke R. **SIMMONS**, S. Marmaduke **POWELL** and Caleb **STEPHENS**, C. *Davidson*. Charles **HOOVER**, S. John **HOGAN** and J. M. **THOMAS**, C. *Duplin*. Stephen **MILLER**, S. W. **WRIGHT** and Jos. **GILLESPIE**, C. *Edgecombe*. Louis D. **WILSON**, S. Redding J. **PITTMAN** and Hardy **FLOWERS**, C. *Franklin*. Wm. P. **WILLIAMS**, S. Gideon **GLENN** and Jas. **DAVIS**, C. *Guilford*. John M. **DICK**, S. Amos **WEAVER** and Allen **PEOPLES**, C. *Gates*. William W. **COWPER**, S. W. **STALLINGS** and Lemuel **REDDICK**, C. *Granville*. William M. **SNEED**, S. Spencer **O'BRIEN** and James **WYCHE**, C. *Greene*. Wyatt **MOYE**, S. Arthur **SPEIGHT** and Jas. **HARPER**, C. *Halifax*. Isham **MATTHEWS**, S. Thos. **NICHOLSON** and John R. J. **DANIEL**, C. *Hertford*. Bridger J. **MONTGOMERY**, S. Elisha A. **CHAMBLEE** and Godwin C. **MOORE**, C. *Hyde*. William **SELBY**, S. Thos. S. **SINGLETON** and Foster **JARVIS**. C. *Haywood*. L. W. **PARHAM**, S. N. **EDMONSTON** and J. L. **SMITH**, C. *Iredell*. Pinckney **CALDWELL**, S. Geo. F. **DAVIDSON** and Joseph M. **BOGLE**, C. *Jones*. Risden **M'DANIEL**, S. Jas. **HOWARD** and Owen B. **COX**, C. *Johnston*. David **THOMSON**, S. Josiah **HOLDER** and A. **SANDERS**, C. *Lincoln*. Daniel **HOKE**, S. Jacob **ABERNATHY** and Henry **CAUSLER**, C. *Lenoir*. William D. **MOSELY**, S. Allen W. **WOOTEN** and Shadrac **WOOTEN**, C. *Moore*. Josiah **TYSON**, S. Wm. **WADSWORTH** and Gideon **SEAWELL**, C.

Edenton Gazette and Farmer's Palladium 9 November 1831

Montgomery. Reuben **KENDALL**, S. Pleasant M. **MASK** and Geo. W. **M'CAIN**, C. *Mecklenburg.* H. **MASSEY**, Sen., S. John **HART** and James **DAUGHERTY**, C. *Martin.* Jesse **COOPER**, S. Jos. **ROBERTSON** and John **CLOMAN**, C. *Macon.* Jas. W. **GUINN**, S. Jas. **WHITAKER**, Sen. and Thomas **TATHAM**, C. *New Hanover.* M. W. **CAMPBELL**, S. William S. **LARKINS** and Wm. J. **WRIGHT**, C. *Nash.* Willis W. **BODDIE**, S. Joseph **ARRINGTON** and George **BODDIE**, C. *Northampton.* James T. **HAYLEY**, S. Richard **CRUMP**, jr. and John M. **MOODY**, C. *Onslow.* L. **DESHONG**, S. J. P. **THOMPSON**, G. A. **THOMPSON**, C. *Orange.* William **MONTGOMERY**, S. James **MEBANE** and Joseph **ELLISON**, C. *Person.* Robert **VANHOOK**, S. Benjamin A. **SUMNOR** and Thomas **MC GEHEE**, C. *Pasquotank.* John **POOL**, S. T. **BELL** and John M. **SKINNER**, C. *Pitt.* Alfred **MOYE**, S. Roderick **CHURRY** [?] and Henry **TOOLE**, C. *Perquimans.* Henry **SKINNER**, S. T. **WILSON** and J. **TOWNSEND**, C. *Rowan.* David F. **CALDWELL**, S. Thomas G. **POLK** and Richmond M. **PEARSON**, C. *Randolph.* Benjamin **ELLIOTT**, S. Jonathan **WORTH** and A. **CUNNINGHAM**, C. *Rockingham.* Robert **MARTIN**, S. Benjamin **SETTLE** and Wilson **HILL**, C. *Robeson.* Shadrac **HOWELL**, S. William L. **MILLER** and Alexander **WATSON**, C. *Richmond.* Tryam **MC FARLAND**, S. Walter E. **LEAK** and Duncan **MC LAURIN**, C. *Rutherford.* John **MC ENTIRE**, S. James M. **WEBB** and J. **GREEN**, C. *Sampson.* David **UNDERWOOD**, S. Archibald **MONK** and D. **SLOAN**, C. *Surry.* Wm. P. **DOBSON**, S. D. W. **COURTS** and Mordecai **FLEMMING**, C. *Stokes.* John **HILL**, S. Joseph **WINSTON** and Leonard **ZIGLAR**, C. *Tyrrell.* D. N. **BATEMAN**, S. H. G. **SPRUILL** and Chas. **M'CLEESE**, C. *Washington.* Samuel **DAVENPORT**, S. Waters **BECKWITH** and Uriah W. **SWANNER**, C. *Wilkes.* John **MARTIN**, S. Eli **PETTY** and W. C. **EMMIT**, C. *Warren.* John H. **HAWKINS**, S. John **BRAGG** and Thomas J. **JUDKINS**, C. *Wayne.* Gabriel **SHERARD**, S. John W. **SASSER** and John **BROADHURST**, C. *Wake.* Henry **SEAWELL**, S. Wm. H. **HAYWOOD**, jr. and Nathaniel G. **RAND**, C.

Borough Members. *Edenton* Samuel T. **SAWYER**. *Wilmington* Daniel **SHERWOOD**. *Fayetteville* Louis D. **HENRY**. *Salisbury* Charles **FISHER**. *Halifax* William L. **LONG**. *Hillsborough* Thomas J. **FADDIS**. *Newbern* Charles G. **SPAIGHT**. Since deceased. Place to be supplied.

[697] Edenton: Wednesday, November 9, 1831. ... *Accident.*—We learn with regret, that on Friday morning last, the Cotton-Gin of Josiah **COFFIELD**, Esq. of this County, was entirely by [sic] fire, with the cotton and other articles which were within. ...

[698] *Match Race.*—We understand that a Match Race is to be run on Thursday the 17th inst. in this County, on the road leading from Baker **HOSKINS**' to Jos. B. **SKINNER**'s, between Thos. B. **HAUGHTON**'s bay horse, a Sir Archie colt, and Benj. **WHITE**'s bay gelding—1 mile heat—Purse $100. It is probable there will be other horses on the track to run, and those who are fond of this kind of sporting, may calculate on some *fun*.

[699] Capt. Benj. **WYNNS**, lately from Turk's Island in the Schr. Thos. Wynns, has furnished us with the following statement for publication... Mr. Editor, You may serve persons bound to Turk's Island, by making public, that by an Act of the Bahama Legislature, the same duties are exacted now on all articles from the United States, as were formerly payable, although some have been remitted wholly or in part, by the British Government; and vessels from the British West Indies with parts of their outward cargo, are obliged to pay the duties again at Turk's Island, on *all they enter for sale there, notwithstanding they may have already paid them at the Port from whence they came.* ... Benj. **WYNNS**.

[700] *Gen. NAT certainly taken.* It is no longer a matter of doubt that this villain is at length taken. ... NAT was apprehended within a mile and a half of the place where he commenced his bloody deed. He made no resistance when Mr. **PHIPPS**, the gentleman, who took him came upon him, but surrendered immediately. He was taken in a cave, and is now confined in Jerusalem jail to await we suppose, the infliction of that punishment which is due to the perpetration of a crime of the blackest hue.

[701] MARRIED, In this County on Thursday evening last, by Rev. Mr. **MEREDITH**, Mr. Wm. S. **BLOUNT**, of Perquimans County, to Miss Eliza A. eldest daughter of Mr. Chas. **HAUGHTON**, of this County.

Edenton Gazette and Farmer's Palladium 9 November 1831

[702] DIED, On Friday morning last, after a severe illness, Mrs. Elizabeth **BOND**, wife of Mr. Edwin **BOND**, of this town, in the 30th year of her age. Though the disease which terminated her life was severe and protracted, yet she bore it with that fortitude, and resignation to the Divine will, which had so repeatedly exhibited itself in her conduct, in times of trial and difficulty, while sojourning among us. It was not the lot of Mrs. **B.** to walk in the higher circles of society—to be courted and applauded by the rich and the great, yet, nevertheless, her virtues in the humbler walks of life were easily discovered by all those who had formed an acquaintance with her. She was by no means a stranger to the consolations which flow from a hope in Christ, but for many years had made the religion of Jesus the choice object of her life, and the word of truth, the man of her council. She, however, had never attached herself to any branch of the Christian Church, the cause of which we are unacquainted: but the beauties of Christianity shone brightly in her course through life, were her consolation in the hour of death, and we trust her crown of rejoicing in the kingdom of Heaven. She has left a husband and four small children to mourn their loss.

[703] *Dry-Goods*, SHOES, GROCERIES, Crockery, Hardware, Blacksmith's Tools, Drugs and Medicines. all of which he will sell remarkably cheap, either for *Cash, good notes, Staves, Cotton, Corn and Peas*, or on the usual credit to responsible dealers. ... Wm. **BADHAM**. Nov. 8th 1831.

[704] Valuable Fishery *FOR SALE*. By virtue of a Deed of Trust executed to me by Horace **ELY**, I shall on the 10th day of December next, offer for sale in the Town of Plymouth, that well known Fishery on the Roanoke River, formerly owned by Jeremiah **SLADE**, dec'd, but more recently owned and occupied by the said Horace **ELY**. The terms will be made known on the day of sale. Benj. **MAITLAND**, *Trustee*. Plymouth, Nov. 4, 1831.

[705] Five Dollars Reward. Runaway from the subscriber on the 24th ult. a free colored boy named Josiah **PRICE**, an indented apprentice. He is about 14 years of age, very dark mulatto, and about 5 feet 2 or 3 inches high. It is believed he is lurking in the neighborhood of Gates Court House, where he has a grandmother, and two brothers named Jim and Peter **PRICE**, who will no doubt make exertions to conceal him. I will give the above reward and pay all necessary expenses to any person who will deliver him to me or so confine him that I get him again. Lem'l **SKINNER**. Chowan Co. Nov. 9th 1831.

Edenton Gazette.
Vol. XXVII.....No. 46. Edenton, N. C. Wednesday November 16, 1831. Whole No. 1398.

[706] [p. 3] Edenton: Wednesday, November 16, 1831. ... We understand that 'Gen. **NAT**.' was tried by the Court on last Saturday week at Jerusalem, and sentenced to be hung on Friday last. ... There were three other negroes tried on the testimony of **NAT**, who were condemned to be hung on the same day.

[707] It is proposed by the Milton Spectator, that a public meeting of the citizens of Caswell Co. be held for the purpose of paying respect to their late distinguished fellow-citizen, Bartlett **YANCEY**, by adopting a resolution to alter the name of the village in which the Court House of that county is situated, to that of "Yancey."

[708] *Randolph Macon College.*—We are gratified in being able to state that this Institution will shortly commence its preparatory operations, under very flattering prospects. The Institution is located at Boydton, in Mecklenburg Co., Va., under the superintendence and patronage of the Methodist E. Church. The board of Trustees met at Boydton on the 13th ult. for the purpose of appointing a President and Professors, and we learn, says the Lynchburg Virginian, conferred those appointments on the following gentlemen: John **EMORY**, D. D. of N. York, President and Professor of Moral Science. Rev. M. P. **PARKS**, Professor of Mathematics. Landon C. **GARLAND**, (now of Washington College, in Lexington, Professor of Natural Science. Robert **EMORY**, A. B. of N. York, Professor of Languages. The Preparatory School will go into immediate operation, under the superintendence of Mr. R. **EMORY**. ...

[709] Wm. **BELLANGEE**, Dentist, Very respectfully informs the Ladies and Gentlemen of Edenton and its vicinity, that he will attend to his professional duties at Jos. N. **HOSKINS'** Tavern, or at the residence

Edenton Gazette and Farmer's Palladium 16 November 1831

of those who may desire his services. Edenton, Nov. 16, 1831.

Edenton Gazette.
Vol. XXVII.....No. 47. Edenton, N. C. Wednesday November 23, 1831. Whole No. 1399.

[710] [p. 3] Edenton: Wednesday, November 23, 1831. ... Hamilton C. JONES, Esq. has recently issued proposals to establish a new paper in Salisbury, N. C. to be called "The Carolina Watchman," devoted to Politics, Literature, Criticism, and the present Administration. If Mr. JONES gets up the Watchman, there will be three newspapers published in that town.

Mr. John CAMPBELL has issued proposals to publish in the town of Windsor, Bertie county, a newspaper, entitled the 'Windsor Herald.' It will advocate the re-election of Gen. JACKSON.

We have received several numbers of the Milton Spectator, edited by N. J. PALMER, Esq., and published in Milton, in this State. We wish them all success.

[711] Proposals have been issued by Mrs. Ann ROYALL, for publishing in the city of Washington, a weekly paper, to be called the 'Paul Pry.'

[712] The N. Y. Journal of Commerce contains the following notice of a singular suicide:--Mr. S. C. BENJAMIN, of New York, from Philadelphia, left his berth and plunged into the sea, sometime during Monday night. A letter was found in the pocket of a coat left behind, addressed to Mr. Isaac PRICE, 308 Market-street, Philadelphia, in which he says:--"The loss of one whose absence is insupportable, has led my spirit to the resolution of bidding farewell to time. My body I must of course leave behind; and that I may not occasion any one trouble respecting the disposal, I give it for its grave the deep Atlantic. And let not Turk, Christian nor Pagan have the foolish assurance to pronounce my doom, until their spiritual law-givers and doctors of theology know more of our Creator, and the mystery of life and death than I do."

[713] Unanimity Lodge, No. 54. A Punctual meeting of the Officers and members of Unanimity Lodge, No. 54, is requested at their Hall in the Court-House on the first Saturday in December next;--at which time an election of Officers will take place, and other business of importance brought before the Lodge. By order, J. H. HAUGHTON, *Sec'y*. Edenton, Nov. 23, 1831.

Edenton Gazette.
Vol. XXVII.....No. 48. Edenton, N. C. Wednesday November 30, 1831. Whole No. 1400.

[714] [p. 3] Edenton: Wednesday, November 30, 1831. *Distressing.*--Much anxiety has prevailed in our community for several days past, to know the fate of Thos. B. HAUGHTON, Esq. one of our most worthy and enterprising citizens; and we are sorry to say, that the circumstances of the case, leave little or no doubt on our mind that he, with three of his valuable negroes have found a watery grave. Mr. H. we understand, left his residence in this County, on last Monday week, in a row-boat with two negroes for Plymouth, with the intention of returning home on the next day. He visited Plymouth, and on Tuesday left that place and on his return homeward, called at his farm in Washington County with the view of getting some articles which were wanting on his farm in this County; this being done he resumed his journey homewards, taking with him his three negroes before mentioned, although his overseer strongly remonstrated against it, in consequence of the boat being too deeply loaded and the wind blowing very rapidly. In consideration of the continuance of the high winds, which began on Monday evening and lasted until Wednesday, Mr. H's. absence did not create much uneasiness in his family until Thursday, as they no doubt hoped he had not continued his journey under such unfavorable weather, but alas! delusive hope. On enquiry being made, it was ascertained that he had left his farm in Washington, as above stated, and the conclusion was and is up to this time that he with the negroes have perished. Search being made, on Sunday last, the boat, his trunk, and some other articles were found upset in the bay. Neither of the bodies so far as we know, have as yet been found.

[715] In conformity to the wishes of the citizens of Newbern, Wm. GASTON, Esq. has consented to represent them in the Legislature of this State, in the place of C. SPAIGHT, Esq. dec'd. In consequence of

Edenton Gazette and Farmer's Palladium 30 November 1831

this determination on the part of Mr. **G.**, Mr. Edward **STANLEY**, who before had offered as a candidate, has declined. ...

[716] *Kentucky.*—We learn that the election for U. S. Senator from this State, took place in the Legislature on the 10th inst., and resulted in the election of the Hon. Henry **CLAY**, by a majority, in joint ballot, of nine votes over Col. R. M. **JOHNSON**, the **JACKSON** candidate.

[717] MARRIED, On the 3rd inst. by Rev. H. G. **LEIGH**, Rev. G. W. **NOLLEY**, to Miss Martha R. B. **NICHOLAS**, of Northampton County, N. C.

On the 24th inst. by Dr. J. B. **BAKER**, Riddick **GATLING**, Esq. to Miss Edith, youngest daughter of Col. Wm. **GOODMAN**, dec'd. all of Gates County.

[718] DIED, At Tarborough, on the 31st ult. Mrs. Martha **LAWRENCE**, wife of P. P. **LAWRENCE**, Esq. formerly of this place.

[719] FOR SALE At the Store on the wharf, recently occupied by Wm. R. **NORCOM**, the following articles wholesale or retail, viz: 2000 bushels Turk's Island Salt, 4000 lbs cotton Seine Twine...6 Tons Rigging, suitable sizes for Seine hauling and made expressly for that purpose, 15 puncheons N. E. Rum, 30 bbls of Apple Brandy...Sugar...Coffee... Charles **FOWLER**. ALSO, The Schr. VISITER, 99 Tons burthen, low deck, a good vessel for the West India Lumber Trade, can be fitted for sea at little or no expense, and will be sold extremely low. A liberal credit will be given if required—apply as above, or to Samuel **FOWLER**. Edenton, Nov. 30, 1831.

[720] Cullen **BUNCH** vs. Nathaniel **MILLER**. NOTICE is hereby given that Humphrey **WRIGHT**, Constable, levied an execution for the sum of $46, 67 cents, on the Lands of Nathaniel **MILLER**, (granted by Wm. **WALTON**, Esq. one of the Justices of Chowan County.) adjoining the Lands of Peter **WHITE**, John **NIXON**, and others, for want of chattel property, and returned the same in the last county Court of Chowan, September Term, 1831. Test, Edm. **HOSKINS**, *Cl'k*. Edenton, Nov. 30, 1831.

[721] NOTICE. As I am desirous of closing my accounts at the end of every year, I have employed and authorised Capt. H. D. **JONES** to collect or bond such as it may be inconvenient for me to attend to myself. J. R. **HERNDON**. Nov. 30th 1831.

Edenton Gazette.
Vol. XXVII.....No. 49. Edenton, N. C. Wednesday December 7, 1831. Whole No. 1401.

[722] [p. 2] The Raleigh Register says, "We understand that it is highly probable that General James **MC KAY**, the Representative elect to Congress, from the Wilmington District, will send in his resignation before the meeting of that body takes place, in consequence of the infirm state of his health.

[723] [p. 3] Edenton: Wednesday, December 7, 1831. ... The Legislature. This body according to appointment met at the Government House on the 21st ult. in Raleigh, and after the qualification of members, proceeded to its organization by the election of Officers, &c. In the Senate, Messrs. D. F. **CALDWELL**, of Rowan, and W. D. **MOSELEY**, of Lenoir, were nominated for Speaker...Mr. **CALDWELL** declared duly elected by a majority of 18 votes. ... After which, S. F. **PATTERSON** was chosen Clerk, and Wm. J. **COWAN**, Clerk Assistant; Thos. B. **WHEELER**, Door-keeper, and Green **HILL**, Assistant Door-keeper. ... Messrs. Jno. W. **COVINGTON** and Daniel **COLEMAN** were elected Engrossing Clerks. ...

In the Commons on the 21st ult. Messrs. Charles **FISHER**, of Salisbury, S. T. **SAWYER**, of this place, and L. D. **HENRY**, of Fayetteville, were put in nomination for Speaker. ... Mr. **SAWYER** thereupon returned thanks for the support he had received, and withdrew his name. Another balloting...resulted in the choice of Mr. **FISHER**. After which, Charles **MANLY** was chosen Clerk, and E. B. **FREEMAN**, Clerk Assistant; Richard **ROBERTS**, Door-keeper, and John **LUMSDEN**, Assistant Door-keeper. ... John W. **COVINGTON**, Daniel **COLEMAN**, and T. G. **STONE**, were elected Engrossing

Edenton Gazette and Farmer's Palladium 7 December 1831

Clerks.

[724] MARRIED, At Philadelphia, on the 24th ult. by the Rev. Mr. **BARNES**, Andrew **JACKSON**, jr. Esq. [adopted] son of the President, to Miss Sarah , daughter of the late Peter **YORKE**, of that city.

[725] DIED, In Eliz. City, on the 27th ult, Mrs. Mary Ann **ESKRIDGE**, in the 24th year of her age, wife of Rev. Vernon **ESKRIDGE**, of the M. E. Church.

At his residence in Halifax county, on the 10th ult. in the 65th year of his age, Gideon **WATSON** [?] Esq.

[726] ATTENTION! CHOWAN GUARDS! You are notified to attend at the regular parade ground before the Court-House, prepared for drill, on Friday evening next, at 3 o'clock precisely. All the members of the company are particularly requested to attend on that occasion, as business of importance will be submitted to their consideration. By order, A. **SPENCE**, O. S. Dec. 7th 1831.

[727] Call and examine for Yourselves. The subscriber has just received from New York, a new and well selected assortment of fashionable and CHEAP GOODS. ... Wm. H. **GRIMES**. Decr. 7th 1831.

[728] NOTICE. The subscriber is under the disagreeable necessity at this time, of earnestly soliciting all persons having unsettled accounts with him, to call and settle them either by paying the Cash or closing them by note, as his situation will not admit of farther indulgence. He also wishes to remind them of a former notice, that all accounts not settled, six months standing, interest will be charged on them from that date, as he has to submit to the same regulation with his creditors. Joseph **MANNING**. Dec'r. 6th 1831.

[729] Oxford Male Academy. *Arrangements for the year* 1832. The Trustees have again engaged Mr. James D. **JOHNSON** to take charge of this Seminary. The winter session will open on the second Monday of January. ... Oxford for health, morality, good society, and religious privileges, suited to the leading denominations in this country, can compete with any other village in the State. ... Mr. **JOHNSON** had the charge of this Institution for eight years preceding the year 1830, and during that period a number of his pupils entered our University. ... Jas. M. **WIGGINS**, Sec'y. Oxford, 24th Nov. 1831.

[730] NOTICE. The subscriber very respectfully informs his customers and friends and the public generally, that he has just returned from New York with a fresh supply of LEATHER, and an assortment of Shoes of every description... John **COUNCILL**. Dec. 7th, 1831.

Edenton Gazette.
Vol. XXVII.....No. 50. Edenton, N. C. Wednesday December 14, 1831. Whole No. 1402.

[731] [p. 3] Edenton: Wednesday, December 14, 1831. ... MARRIED, In Washington, on the 21st ult. by Rev. Wm. N. **HAWKS** [or **HANKS**,] Mr. Samuel **MASTERS**, of Hyde County, to Miss Mary Jane **QUIN**.

[732] OBITUARY. Departed this life, after a severe and protracted illness, on Sunday night last, Mrs. Chloe Little **FARIBAULT**, consort of Joseph F. **FARIBAULT**, Esq., of this County. Seldom indeed, is it the lot of friendship, to record the decease of an individual, in whom personal virtues and excellence were so conspicuously exhibited, as in the life and conduct of the subject of this notice. Possessed of a sweet and amiable disposition, she had naturally secured the esteem and regard of every one within the range of her acquaintance; and the suavity and liveliness of her manners, and the correctness of her deportment towards her fellow beings, always rendered the social circle pleasing and interesting, wherever she was to be found. It may truly be said in regard to her, "to know her was to love her." In her domestic relations she admirably sustained the character of a prudent and economical matron; dispensing alike to all around her the blessings of life. She was in all respects a fond and affectionate companion and tender mother; a firm and unwavering friend and pleasant associate. The vacuum which has been made in her

Edenton Gazette and Farmer's Palladium 14 December 1831

domestic circle, by the nipping hand of death, will not be easily filled; and they to whom she was most closely allied, while they remember her affection, her fondness, her kindness and her devotion to their interest, have the consolation, that tho' they are now deprived of her company, she has gone "Far from a world of grief and sin, Eternally with God shut in."

[733] *Cheap for Cash!* R. T. **HOSKINS**, & co. Offer for sale at their store, corner of Broad and King Streets, a large and general assortment of Dry Goods, GROCERIES, HARDWARE, &c. at a small advance on New York prices. ... Edenton, Dec. 14th 1831.

Edenton Gazette.
Vol. XXVII.....No. 51. Edenton, N. C. Wednesday December 21, 1831. Whole No. 1403.

[734] [p. 2] *Georgia, the Missionaries and the Supreme Court.*—The correspondent of the Savannah Georgian, writes from Milledgeville under date of Friday, 25th inst. that a message was received in the legislature from the Governor, enclosing a citation to the state to appear before the Supreme Court, in January next, pursuant to a writ of error, filed in the Superior Court of Gwinnett county, on the part of Samuel A. **WORCESTER** and Elizur **BUTLER**, (the Missionaries) Plaintiffs in error, to show cause why the judgment rendered against said plaintiffs should not be corrected, &c.—signed Henry **BALDWIN**: and a notice of application for such citation, from Wm. **WIRT** and John **SERGANT**, counsel for the plaintiffs; and recommending resistance to any measure of interference with the criminal jurisdiction of the state.

[735] Wm. W. **MONTGOMERY**, Esq. has been unanimously elected President of the United States' Branch Bank of the city of New Orleans, in place of Beverly **CHEW**, Esq. resigned.

[736] [p. 3] Edenton: Wednesday, December 21, 1831. To afford those persons engaged in the Office the usual respite during the Christmas holidays, the GAZETTE will not appear next week. This number will therefore complete the twenty-seventh and last year of the existence of the "Edenton Gazette;" as it is about to change hands and assume a new name. For farther particulars we refer the reader to our advertising columns, for the prospectus of the "North Carolina Miscellany."

Since we have held the Proprietorship of this paper, we have had in common with our co-labourers in the service of the people, much to encounter;–we have thus far however, survived the storms of opposition and censure, without much disparagement to our little bark. Those who have sustained us thus far by their patronage and punctual pay, are entitled to and have our warmest thanks; while they are ready and waiting to be bestowed on those who have not, as yet, paid us their dues, but intend doing so as early as possible. N. B. It is earnestly requested that those persons who are in any manner indebted to this Office, will, without further notice, take immediate steps towards settling up their accounts, as we are determined to close the business of the establishment forthwith.

[737] Gov. Montfort **STOKES**, the present incumbent, has been re-elected Governor of this State, for the ensuing year. He was opposed by R. D. **SPAIGHT**, Esq. On the first balloting there were for **STOKES** 98, for **SPAIGHT** 83 votes.

[738] The National Republican Convention assembled at Baltimore, on the 12th inst. We learn that Hon. Henry **CLAY** has been nominated for President, and Hon. John **SARGEANT**, of Pa. for Vice President of the United States.

[739] MARRIED, On Sunday the 11th inst. by Rev. Miles **WELCH**, Mr. Seth N. **PARKER**, to Miss Mary **TOPPING**, all of this County.

In Currituck County, on the 15th inst. by the Rev. P. B. **WILEY**, C. R. **KINNEY**, Esq. Attorney at Law, of Eliz. City, to Miss Sarah E. F. **DAVIS**, of Washington Point, Norfolk County, Va.

In Perquimans County, on the 11th inst. John N. **M'PHERSON**, Esq. of Camden County to Miss Pherebe **BAGLEY** of the former county.

Edenton Gazette and Farmer's Palladium 21 December 1831

[740] DIED, At Wilmington, on the 21st ult. Washington **LAZARUS**, Esq. aged 23 years.

[741] NOTICE. The subscriber again has the pleasure of informing his friends and the public, that he has just received from New York…a new assortment of *GOODS*. He deems it unnecessary to add, that he will sell his Goods "at much lower prices than they have been in the habit of giving for them" in Edenton, but respectfully invites purchasers to call and examine for themselves. Wm. H. **GRIMES**. Dec. 21st 1831.

[742] Prospectus Of The NORTH-CAROLINA MISCELLANY. The subscribers propose to issue at Edenton, a weekly paper, bearing the above title, and designed to succeed the "*Edenton Gazette,*" about to be discontinued.

The primary object of this publication is, to contribute to the amusement, convenience, and improvement of the community, to which it is offered. Accordingly, in addition to *advertisements*, and the various *news* of the day, it shall contain such articles of a *political, literary, religious, commercial* and *agricultural* nature, as shall correspond with the end proposed. It shall be appropriated to the exclusive interests of no party, either political or religious; but shall be made a medium of general information, and free discussion, respecting any question, which may properly claim the attention of the public.

The Miscellany shall be printed with good type, on a fair sheet and be furnished to subscribers at $2 50, if paid in advance, or in 3 months from the time of subscribing; and at $3 if payment be made at the end of the year. The first number shall appear as early in January next, as the acquisition of the necessary materials will admit. Thos. **MEREDITH**, Wm. E. **PELL**. Edenton, N. C. Dec. 20th 1831. Those Editors with whom we exchange, will do us the favor to give the above a few insertions in their respective papers.

[743] Constable's Notice. All persons who are aware that I have in my hands claims against them, which are now due, are hereby notified to come forward and make immediate payment, as further indulgence will not be given; and a refusal to do so will place me under the necessity of exposing to public sale their property without delay. N. B. As I am determined to close my business as fast as possible, it is my particular request that the Plaintiffs in all cases attend my sales as advertised. H. D. **JONES**. Edenton Dec. 21, 1831.

[744] State of North Carolina, *Perquimans County* Court of Pleas and Quarter-Sessions, November Term, 1831. **SPEAR & PATTEN**, vs. F. J. **KELENBERGER**} Original Attachm't levied on the Boo__ &c. of said **KELENBERGER**. It appearing to the satisfaction of the Court, that the said Frances J. **KELENBERGER** is not an inhabitant of this State: It is therefore ordered that publication be made in the Edenton Gazette for six weeks, admonishing the said Francis J. **KELENBERGER** to appear at the next term of this Court, and plead, answer or demur, or final judgment will be entered up against him. By order, Test, John **WOOD**, *Clerk*. Hertford. Dec. 21, 1831.

[745] New Washing Machine. The subscriber is authorised to sell, on very accommodating terms, the Patent Right of **APPLETON**'s New WASHING MACHINE, for the Counties of *Currituck, Camden, Pasquotank, Perquimans, Chowan, Gates, Hertford, Northampton, Halifax, Bertie, Martin, Washington, and Tyrrell.* Certificates from respectable citizens of this State, Norfolk and Richmond, Va., recommend it to be preferable to any other Machine yet invented. Orders for single Machines, inclosing *eleven* dollars, post paid, will be supplied. Edmund **HOSKINS**. Edenton. Dec. 21, 1831.

END OF BOOK

NOTES

FEMALE INDEX
Including both maiden and married names of brides.

Abagail
WOOD 670
Abigail
SHERLY 187
(SHERLY) SWAIM 187
SHIRLEY 201
(SHIRLEY) SWAIM 201
Adoris
PARRIMORE 43
Ann
AIRS 394
BUXTON 400
C. BOND 345
Collins PAGE 342
COX 127,315
D. BOZMAN 588
JOHNSON 193
Louisa ELY 480
Louisa (ELY) ARMISTEAD 480
NORCOM 573
NORFLEET 195,436
PETTIGREW 245
RIGHTON 127
ROYALL 711
SINGLETON 315
W. WILSON 155
W. (WILSON) LAND 155
Anna
BOND 127
Anne
ROYAL 392
Betsey
SKINNER 43
Carolina Virginia
JOHNSON 245
Caroline
EAGLES 410
EAGLES WINDER 410
L. HENTZ 642
Catharine
ELLIOTT 316
(ELLIOTT) SATTERFIELD 316
GARDINER 670
GARDNER 518,639
HANKINS 7
TORRANS 399
TORRANS WILLIAMS 399
VAIL 316
(VAIL)

Catharine
MIDDLETON 316
WHITE 670
WHITEHEAD 633
Cela [See also Sely]
JORDAN 518
Ceney
FOSTER 369
FOSTER ELLYSON 369
Charlotte
Catharine M'NIDER 476
LASSITER 227
(LASSITER) WELCH 227
Chloe
Little FARIBAULT 732
Clarissa
COFFIELD 109
(COFFIELD) LILLYBRIDGE 109
Louisa Ryan JORDAN 631
Louisa Ryan (JORDAN) GOODMAN 631
Clarkey
AIRS 519
Cornelia
WHITE 589
Darcise
BENBURY 43
Deborah
LASSITER 691
(LASSITER) GASKINS 691
Edith
GOODMAN 717
(GOODMAN) GATLING 717
Edney
M. BLAKELY 47
Elenor
MONTGOMERY 38,39
Eliz.
LITTLEJOHN 315
Eliza
A. HAUGHTON 701
A. (HAUGHTON) BLOUNT 701
ELLIOTT 531
HARRIS 340
HARVEY 322
J. HARVEY 14,231
J. JONES 436
L. SMALL 400

Eliza
NORFLEET 436
POOL 96
(POOL) ELLIOTT 96
Elizabeth
A. WALL 47
ALTER 294
(ALTER) ELLIS 294
B. GRAHAM 62
B. (GRAHAM) DAVES 62
BOND 702
EVANS 72
IRELAND 499
(IRELAND) SMITH 499
KING 670
LASSITER 275
LASSITER REED 275
LITTLEJOHN 127
PETTIJOHN 132
ROGERSON 442
STRONG 315
SUTTON 15
WILSON 139
WILSON NEWBY 139
WOOD 109,422,528
(WOOD) BEASLEY 109
WOOD GILLIAM 422
YOUNG 670
Emeline
WAFF 127,315
Emily
E. CHRISTIAN 43
BRICKHOUSE 436
Evelina
CHURCH 237
(CHURCH) STATE 237
REA 361
(REA) LAMB 361
Fanny
FORBES 445,517
WRIGHT 92
Frances
Ann GRAY 588
JONES 147
OUTLAW 71
OUTLAW HARTMUS 71
P. TREDWELL 246,340
SATTERFIELD 181
(SATTERFIELD) SPENCE 181
TOMKINS 585
TOMKINS ALEXANDER 585

Frances
  WILDER 340
  WRIGHT 120,173
Francis
  LAWRENCE 490
  (LAWRENCE) RAYNER 490
Freeza
  HARRELL 275
  (HARRELL) JONES 275
Grace
  LITTLEJOHN 436
Grizelle
  P. FLETCHER 490
  FLETCHER JACOCKS 490
Harriet
  HARDY 88
  (HARDY) WILDER 88
  LEARY 347
  SKINNER 127,315
Hester
  BROWNRIGG 588
  C. LEE 43,340
  K. LEE 340,436
Hetty
  JAMES 519
Huldah
  G. WRIGHT 246
Isabella
  NEIL 6
  (NEIL) DEAN 6
  POTTER 664
Jane
  BONNER 315
  Caroline LANSTON 625
  LADLING 436
  POPELSTON 315
  SMITH 399
  (SMITH) GOELET 399
  W. TYLER 308
  W. (TYLER) GREGORY 308
  YEOMANS 324
Johannah
  KEYS 437,519
Julia
  LENOX 298
  (LENOX) KEEP 298
Lavina
  M'GUIRE 436,518
Lavinia
  JONES 38,39
  WELCH 72

Letitia
  CORNICK 416
  (CORNICK) MORGAN 416
Louisa
  A. SAWYER 518,588
  KNOX 127
  MOORE 594
  (MOORE) ALBERTSON 594
  R. CROSS 475
  R. (CROSS) BARNES 475
  SAWYER 670
  TOMS 244
  (TOMS) WHITE 244
Louisia
  LUTON 459
  (LUTON) BEEMAN 459
Lucy
  D. HAYWOOD 105
  D. (HAYWOOD) BRYAN 105
Lydia
  G. JONES 432
  G. (JONES) SHEPARD 432
  PHILLIPS 63
Margaret
  BRANCH 369
  (BRANCH) DONELSON 369
  DONNELL 653
  FLURY 246
  HOLLIDAY 256
  (HOLLIDAY) SANDFORD 256
  NEIL 132
  SATTERFIED 668
  SHERWOOD 643
  (SHERWOOD) REED 643
  WELCH 588
Maria
  CHESSON 672
  HILL 519
Mariam
  M'GUIRE 246
Martha
  A. COOK 393
  A. (COOK) SIMMONS 393
  A. W. NASH 530
  A. W. (NASH) YEOMANS 530
  Ann BATEMAN 43

Martha
  Ann MATHIAS 175
  Ann (MATHIAS) SIMONSON 175
  PERRY 96
  (PERRY) NEWBY 96
  B. HARVEY 340
  BENBURY 246
  BLOUNT 428
  COWPER 369
  (COWPER) CAPEHART 369
  FORGERSON 566
  Henrietta GREGORY 276
  HOSKINS 127,315
  LAWRENCE 718
  NIXON 355
  (NIXON) LONG 355
  R. B. NICHOLAS 717
  R. B. (NICHOLAS) NOLLEY 717
  REA 518
  TURNER 109
  (TURNER) SHEPPARD 109
  W. JONES 445
  WHITE 97
  WILDER 355
  (WILDER) JONES 355
Marthyann
  MATTHIAS 246
Mary
  A. BISSELL 43,132,246, 340,670
  Ann ESKRIDGE 725
  Ann EURE 620
  Ann MC LIN 38
  Ann (MC LIN) ESKRIDGE 308
  BLOUNT 315
  BOND 653
  BROUGHTON 453
  (BROUGHTON) SITTERSON 453
  BROWN 168
  (BROWN) WHEELER 168
  C. GILLIAM 309
  CARTER 608
  CLUFF 110
  CUTRELL 340
  D. HARRELL 341
  D. (HARRELL) HARRELL 341
  D. HOSKINS 315
  DANIEL 670

Mary
  E. JENNINGS 202
  E. (JENNINGS) SHANNONHOUSE 202
  E. SMITH 376
  E. SMITH MASSIN 376
  Eliza MARTIN 238
  Eliza (MARTIN) WOOD 238
  Elizabeth RIGHTON 632
  HOLMES 620
  Jane QUIN 731
  Jane (QUIN) MASTERS 731
  JOHNSTON 246
  JORDON 475
  (JORDON) COSTIN 475
  LASSITER 553
  (LASSITER) PROCTOR 553
  LOUNGE 589
  M. NORCOM 315
  MANNING 127,315
  Matilda M'NIDER 625
  NEWBORN 175
  (NEWBORN) BAGLEY 175
  PIPKIN 62
  (PIPKIN) WYNNS 62
  ROBERTS 619
  ROBERTS ATKINSON 619
  SKINNER 436
  SMALL 132
  SMITH 127,315
  T. WRIGHT 309
  TOPPING 739
  (TOPPING) PARKER 739
  TUMNER 246
  TURNER 109
  WILDER 340,631
  (WILDER) TABER 631
  YOUNGE 589

Matilda
  BRUSH 445

Merriam
  SAWYER 588

Milly
  HAUGHTON 246

Mourning
  BADHAM 423

Nancy
  BLOUNT 340
  HALL 641

Nancy
  HURDLE 355
  (HURDLE) ELLIOTT 355
  M'GUIRE 344
  (M'GUIRE) BADHAM 344
  NEWSAM 43
  P. SKINNER 340
  WALTON 386

Pathenia
  SIMPSON 316
  (SIMPSON) PRATT 316

Patsey
  GREEN 82
  REA 276

Penelope
  CREECY 127,315

Permelia
  CHRISTOPHER 638
  (CHRISTOPHER) HANKINS 638

Pherebe
  BAGLEY 739
  (BAGLEY) M'PHERSON 739

Pherebee
  E. BAGLEY 678

Phillis
  Dominick KING 670

Polly
  FLOYD 436
  HARRIS 43
  REA 475
  REA TAYLOR 475

Priscilla
  BANK 608
  STALLINGS 667
  (STALLINGS) MILLER 667

Rachel
  BEASLEY 330
  (BEASLEY) LASSITER 330

Rebecca
  BAILEY 303
  BATEMAN 256
  (BATEMAN) BLOUNT 256
  FORGERSON 566
  G. SPEARS 96
  G. (SPEARS) EVERETT 96
  SMALL 436

Sally

Sally
  Ann BRITT 672
  ELLIOTT 315
  J. HANDCOCK 586
  J. (HANDCOCK) JONES 586
  Jane MARLEY 589
  PERKINS 43
  THORP 315
  WARFF 246
  WATERS 589

Sarah
  A. THORP 588
  C. JONES 662
  C. (JONES) WALTON 662
  E. F. DAVIS 739
  E. F. (DAVIS) KINNEY 739
  ELLIOTT 608
  FALLAW 379
  GORDAN 533
  GREENFIELD 594
  (GREENFIELD) BEAN 594
  GRIMES 127
  P. KNOX 518
  LEARY 611
  L. WAFF 518
  M. WILLS 410
  M. WILLS WEBB 410
  PETTIJOHN 43
  SKINNER 385
  (SKINNER) HERNDON 385
  THORP 127
  WAFF 315
  WHIPPLE 246,340
  WILDER 6
  YORKE 724
  (YORKE) JACKSON 724

Sely [See also Cela]
  JORDAN 670

Silvery
  JAMES 437,519

Silvey
  HARTHEY 246

Susan
  CLARY 247
  E. HAMPORE 348
  Jane SPARROW 553
  Jane (SPARROW) ANDERSON 553
  M. ARMISTEAD 175
  MOORE 175

Susan
 TURNER 188,607
Tamar
 NIXON 247
Winneyfred
 GREGORY 518

INCOMPLETE NAMES
 ____ GOODWIN 290
Mrs.
 ____ CHAPMAN 282
 ____ GARDINER 581
 ____ GARDNER 469
 ____ HARVEY 402
 ____ HOGG 417
 ____ MONROE 354
 ____ O'BRIEN 456
 ____ PARSONS 340
 ____ ROSS, Michael 218
 ____ SCOTT 285
 ____ VAUGHAN 647
 ____ WARNIER, D. S. 246
 ____ WILLS 4,60
 ____ WOOD 465
 ____ WRIGHT 285

NAME INDEX

A

ABERNATHY
Jacob 696
ADAIR
John 452
ADAMS
___ 236,680
James 589
John Q. 61,427
R. 360
William A. 347
ADDINGTON
Joseph C. 279
ADDISON
___ 667
AIKEN
Wm. 689
AIRS
Ann 394
Clarkey 519
AKERMAN
E. P. 445,608
ALBERTSON
Benjamin 594
ALEXANDER
Chas. W. A. 534
Evan 293
Moses 585
Nathan 43
Reading B. 436
W. J. 293,403
Wm. J. 395
ALFORD
Benjamin 43
Wm. 248
ALLEN
___ 217
James 696
Jas. 597
John M. 304
William 519
Wright 353
ALLEY
H. 107
ALLISON
John 534
Richard 293
ALLSTON [See also ALSTON]
Jos. W. 688

ALPHEUS
Samuel 487
ALSTON [See also ALLSTON]
Benj. H. 263
Gideon 4,431
T. Pinckney 688
Willis
ALTER
Elizabeth 294
ANDERSON
___ 135
Alex. 382
J. 66
John A. 84
Philip 107,553
R. H. 688
Robert H. 92
William 107
ANDRE
___ 636
ANDREWS
Edmund 147
APPLETON
___ 745
ARCHIBALD
William H. 293
ARMISTEAD
Anthony 303,480, 491
John 175
Stark 84,90,340
Starke 641
Susan M. 175
Wm. 43
ARMSTRONG
___ 586
ARRINGTON
J. 280
Joseph 696
ASBELL
Jesse 518
John 518
ASHLEY
Jeremiah 678
ASKEW
Geo. O. 280,397
George O. 616, 696
ASKO
Joseph 672
ATKINSON

ATKINSON
___ 101,576
Irvine 619,638
Irwin 107
AVERY
___ 175,207, 399,400
Alex'r. 307
John 435,436,518

B

BACKHOUSE
John A. 259
BADGER
___ 650
George E. 360, 601
BADHAM
Miles 572
Mourning 423
Myles 423
Starke 460
Starky 344
Wm. 349,525, 703
BAGLEY
___ 436,445
D. W. 84
Pherebe 739
Pherebee E. 678
Wm. 175
BAILEY
Jacob W. 597
Rebecca 303
BAILY
Benjamin 93
Robt. 107
BAIN
Geo. A. 107
BAKEMAN
John 147
BAKER
___ 557
Baker 518
J. B. 717
Jacob 518
John B. 267
Thomas W. 65, 126,132

BALCH
L. P. W. 552
BALDWIN
Archibald P. 688
Henry 35,734
BALLAD
___ 649
BALLARD
___ 283,495
Henry E. 36
BALLENGER
Allen S. 284
BALMORE
John 463
BANCROFT
Thomas P. 688
BANK
Priscilla 608
BANKS
Hardy M. 489
James 678
Linn 688
BARBER
John D. 437
BARBOUR
James 93,326,389
P. P. 679
Philip P. 350,688
Phillip P. 579
BARCLAY
J. M. 688
John 696
BARCLIFF
Wilson 107
BARHAM
B. A. 430
BARNARD
Jona. G. 597
W. D. 280
BARNES
___ 724
Benjamin 519
Benjamin M. 107
C. W. 284
Joseph J. 475
BARNETT
J. 293
BARNEY
G. W. 268,584
George w. 85,263
BARNHARDT
John C. 293

BARNSWELL
Thomas 246
Thomas R. 246
Thos. 132,436
Thos. R. 43
BARNUM
___ 298
Thomas 107,410
Thos. 316
BARRINGER
___ 5
D. M. 696
Daniel L. 614,630
Daniel M. 293
BARROW
Lemuel 517
BARTEE
Robert 340
BARTON
___ 633
Robert 264
BASS
Rowland G. 107
BASSETT
Burwell 679,688
Eleza 100
H. W. 383
BATEMAN
D. N. 696
Daniel M. 84
Daniel N. 293
Dan'l. N. 293
Geo. D. N. 626
Jno. M. 589
John 519
John M. 518,672
Jos. 519
Martha Ann 43
Rebecca 256
BATSH
M. D. 328
BATTLE
Wm. 311
BAXTER
Isaac 280
BEAL
Albert 519
BEAN
George 660
William 594
BEASLEY
___ 397
John 109,293,303, 397

BEASLEY
John B. 161
Nat. J. 22
Nath'l. 436
Nath'l J. 518
Rachel 330
Richard 42,43, 132,246,518
Robert 330
BEASLY
Nat. J. 41
BECKWITH
Waters 696
BEDELL
Gregory T. 360
BEELY
Thos. 436
BEEMAN
Levi 459
BELL
B. W. 314
Benjamin 451
Hayw'd 622
Haywood 696
John 440
Jos. W. 107
S. T. 696
T. 622
Thomas 463
Thos. 284
BELLANGEE
Wm. 709
BENBURY
Darcise 43
Jos. C. 518,670
Joseph C. 246
Martha 246
R. W. 518
Richard 315
Richard W. 127
Rich'd. W. 381
Thomas 15,363
Thos. 363
Wm. 518
BENJAMIN
S. C. 712
BENNETT
John D. 37
W. W. 436,582
Washington W. 582
Wm. F. 46,145, 177,278,288,365, 371,472,484,645,686

BENT
Jas. R. 588
BENTON
John T. 571,572, 591
BERGH
Edwin 688
BERNARD
John H. 688
BERRIEN
J. Macpherson 688
John M. 679
BERRY
Ancrum 285
Benj. 348
Nathan 148
BETHELL
Joshua 107
BETHUNE
___ 618
Lauchlin 614
BETTS
___ 503
BIBB
B. S. 688
BIDDLE
___ 661
Clement C. 679, 688
N. 167
Nicholas 93
Thomas 92
BIGGS
Asa 84
BINGHAM
Danl. H. 463
BISHOP
C. C. 43
Charles C. 132
BISSELL
Mary A. 43, 132, 246,340,670
BLACK
Duncan 463
John 47,293
BLACKFORD
___ 66
BLACKMAN
Calvin R. 284
BLACKNALL
George 534
BLACKWOOD
J. 293,397
BLAIR
F. P. 427
George 199,213, 242,246,303,309,

BLAIR
George 340,430, 518
James Iredell 309
BLAKE
Bennet T. 107
BLAKELY
Edney M. 47
BLAND
T. J. 425
BLOODWORTH
Timothy 264
BLOUNT
___ 647
Benj. H. 47
C. H. 363
Charles 437
Clement B. 98
Clement H. 59, 171,363
Frederick S. 263
James, Jr. 82
James S. 641
John 256,436, 518,588
John G. 431,441
John H. 247,608, 626
Martha 428
Mary 315
N. 340
Nancy 340
Nat. G. 47
Thomas H. 103
Thomas M. 670
Thos. M. 132
William 264
Wm. A. 679,688
Wm. S. 701
BODDIE
George 696
W. W. 280
Willis W. 696
BOGART
___ 435
BOGGS
Chas. S. 359
BOGLE
Jos. 293
Joseph M. 696
BOGUE
Joseph 608
BOND
Ann C. 345

BOND
 Anna 127
 Edwin 345,455, 702
 Elizabeth 702
 Lewis 280,518
 Mary 653
 Nath'l., Jr. 518
BONNER
 Ezekiel 583
 Jane 315
 John 518
 Richard H. 696
BOOKER
 Richard 688
BOORAUM
 Henry 359
BOORMAN
 Jas. 688
BOOTH
 J. B. 642
BORDEN
 D. W. 284
BORLAND
 Roscius 254
BOULTON
 ___ 532
BOURNE
 Nathaniel 340
BOUSH
 Nathan B. 284
BOUTWELL
 Edw'd. 359
BOWEN
 Nathaniel 552
BOWNE
 Walter 54
BOYCE
 Benj. 518
 Jacob 522
BOYD
 J. 107
BOYLAN
 Wm. 234
BOZMAN
 Ann D. 588
 Charles 43
 James 15,17,85, 441,495,512,513, 670
 Jas. 194,239,270, 379
 Joseph 495
 Wm. A. 588

BOZMAN
 Wm. R. H. 518
BRACKENBRIDGE
 Alexander 384
BRADBURY
 John 246
BRADDOCK
 ___ 123
BRADEN
 John 66
 Robert 66
BRAGG
 Jno. 280
 John 696
BRAME
 T. R. 107
BRANCH
 John 153,254,263, 267,369,548,614, 616,630
 Margaret 369
 William 280
BRANDER
 James S. 688
BRATTEN
 Wm. 436
BREED
 Ebenezer 688
BREVARD
 J. 696
BRICKELL
 ___ 478
 Thomas 236
BRICKHOUSE
 ___ 588
 Emily 436
 Nathan E. 43,518
BRIDGES
 H. D. 293
BRIDSON
 John C. 43
BRIGGS
 ___ 435
 E. 348
BRINKLEY
 Edmund 518
 Jethro 353
BRITT
 Hardy 566
 Sally Ann 672
BRITTAIN
 Mark 696
BRITTON
 William 641

BROADHURST
 John 696
BROCK
 John 678
 M. 107
BROCKENBROUGH
 J. 688
BRODHEAD
 ___ 205
BRONSON
 Isaac 688
BROOKS
 J. 696
 Joseph J. 293
BROUGHTON
 Mary 453
BROWER
 Abraham 293
BROWN
 ___ 80
 Archibald S. 47
 Bedford 436
 D. P. 642
 Ezekie 463
 Ezra 147
 J. A. 297
 James 93
 Jas. 427
 John 285,293,340, 463,588
 John A. 489,688
 Joseph A. 107
 Mary 168
 N. K. 247
 O. B. 168
 Peter 488
 Sam'l. 132
 Silvester 470
 Thomas 47
BROWNLOW
 Tippo S. 63
BROWNRIGG
 ___ 132
 Hester 588
 John 572
 R. T. 340,518,567, 572,600,670
 Richard T. 27,84,696
 Rich'd. 132
 Rich'd T. 246,588
 Thomas 132,518
BRUER
 N. 43,124,132,136,

BRUER
 N. 246,323,332, 340,373,436,518, 543,551,567,588, 590,627,655,670, 694
 Nathaniel 635,643, 688
 Nath'l. 160
BRUMLY
 Rich'd T. 47
BRUSH
 Matilda 445
BRYAN
 ___ 445
 J. 58
 John H. 601
 John M. 280
 John S. 105
BRYANT
 Wm. 248
 Wm. S. 445
BRYCE
 Archibald, Jr. 688
BRYSON
 James 47
BUCHANAN
 ___ 180
 George W. 384
 James 680
BUCK
 A. P. 359
BUCTROUT
 Horatio N. 107
BUIE
 Alexander 293
BULLOCK
 ___ 600
 William 572,591
 Wm. 532,567,595, 695
BUNCH
 Cullen 720
 Cullin 436,518
 Elijah 663
 Isaiah 663
 James 445
 Jas. 517
 John W. 518
 Julian 518
 Paul 334
BURBAGE
 J. R. 247,445,517, 608,678

BURDRALL
A. 678
BUREAU
___ 652
BURGEN
Alney 696
BURGESS
C. 303
BURGIN
Alney 304
BURKE
Elisha 293
Thomas 264
BURNETT
S. P. 534
BURNHAM
William 445
BURT
Robert 688
BURTON
Albert G. 107
R. H. 429
Robt. H. 414
BURTT
Stephen 248
BUSANCH
Marco D. 588
BUSBEE
Johnston 529
BUSH [See also BOUSH]
Richard 70
BUTLER
A. P. 688
Elizur 674,734
William C. 304
William E. 679,688
Wm. 688
BUXTON
___ 139
Ann 400
Jarvis B. 400,547
BYNUM
A. 284
Jesse A. 291
BYRNE
Edmund 153
BYRUM
William 572,591
Wm. 199,213,246, 571

C

CAIL [See also CALE, KAIL]
Amariah 300,313, 368
Amariah B. 302
John 247,300,302
CAIN
Samuel 304
CALDWELL
___ 427
D. F. 293,395,723
David F. 696
G. W. 534
Hiram 293
Pinckney 293,696
CALE
A. B. 246
CALHOUN
John C. 191
CALLOWAY
James 314,696
CALVERT
George 339
CAMERON
Alexander 589
Duncan 488
John A. 493,507
CAMPBELL
James 93
John 613,710
M. W. 696
Robert 641
CAPEHART
Cullen 246
F. M. 369
CAPRON
___ 633
CARLISLE
Burrel 588,670
CAROW
Isaac 688
CARPENTER
Josh. 679,688
CARR
Dabney S. 159
CARRINGTON
Wm. C. 108
CARROLL
Charles 326
John B. 436
Thomas King 36
CARSON
Jos. 107
Robert J. 107

CARSON
Samuel 630
Samuel P. 614
William 314,463
CARTER
Isaac 284
Jesse 259
John 688
John J. 107
Mary 608
Perry 311
Thomas M. 124,246
CASEY
Anthony 614
Willis 284
CASS
George W. 597
Lewis 605
CASWELL
Richard 264
Samuel 518
CAUSLER
Henry 696
CHAMBERS
___ 285
E. F. 91
Samuel C. 246
Thomas 135
Thos. 518
CHAMBLEE
___ 626
E. A. 622
Elisha A. 696
CHAPEL
G. 518
James 518
Joel 518
CHAPMAN
___ 281
CHAPPEL
Jesse 517
CHARLTON
___ 633
T. I. 582,611
Tho. J. 25
Thos. I. 22,553
Thos. J. 160
CHASE
Jeremiah 43
Remark 519
CHEAIRS
Joseph H. 534
CHERRY
___ 210

CHESHIRE
Alex. 55
Alexander 47
John 81,89,134,135
Joseph B. 127,315, 340
Thomas Cox 81
CHESSON
A. 152
Andrew L. 672
Hezekiah 672
James A. 329
Maria 672
William L. 338
William M. 329
Wm. M. 589,641
CHESTER
Samuel G. 518
CHEVES
Langdon 128,688
CHEW
Beverly 162,735
CHILDS
John W. 107
CHILTON
Thos. 260,558
CHISOLM
___ 113
CHRISTIAN
Emily E. 43
CHRISTOPHER
Joseph 589,638, 672
Permelia 638
CHURCH
Evelina 237
CHURCHILL
Charles 436
CHURRY
Roderick 696
CHURTON
Alfred 43
CITIZEN
Chas. 518
Wm. 518
CLANTON
Wm. C. 280
CLAPP
Chas. Q. 679,688
CLARK
David 641
Elijah 303
J. S. 273
John 463

130

CLARK
W. 273
William 61
CLARKE
Joshua S. 519
CLARY
Charles 247
Jordan 247
Susan 247
CLAXTON
Alexander 75
CLAY
____ 301,326,427, 452
H. 570
Henry 326,597, 716,738
John Randolph 216,458
CLAYTON
J. 696
CLEMENT
W. 273
CLEMENTS
George W. 347,589
Moses 489
Wm. 518
Woodson 529
CLEVELAND
____ 43, 157
CLINTON
De Witt 150
CLOMAN
John 696
CLOW
Henry 688
CLUFF
Mary 110
Matthew 110
COBB
James 519
COBBS
Enoch 641
COCHRAN
J. W. 688
COCKRAN
Thomas 518
Thos. 436
COFFIELD
Bennett 518
Clarissa 109
Henry 518
James 28,535,584
Jas. 572

COFFIELD
John 518
Josiah 572,584,697
William 73
COKE
Charles 688
COLDEN
Cadwallader D. 427
COLE
James C. 280
COLEMAN
Daniel 397,723
COLLINS
H. W. 584
Josiah 84,603
Josiah, Jr. 603
COLMAN
Moses R. 589
COMBS
____ 612
Jesse 665
COMPTON
Wm. 107
CONNOR
Henry W. 614
CONSTABLE
Jno. 688
COOK
Charles 589
Jno. D. 43
Martha A. 393
COOMBS
John S. 248
COOPER [See also COWPER]
____ 622,633
Jesse 293,696
Rich'd. M. 284
W. W. 626
COPE
Thomas P. 679
Thos. P. 688
COPELAND
A. 674
Thomas 347
CORNELL
____ 603
C. 589
John 437
P. 561
CORNICK
Letitia 416
CORRY
Joseph 501

COSTIN
James 475
COTTLE
Caleb W. 436
COTTON
Godwin 257
COTTRELL [See also CUTRELL]
Thomas 529
COULTER
John 463
COUNCILL
John 325,730
COURTS
D. W. 696
COVINGTON
Calvin C. 534
Jno. W. 723
John W. 723
COWAN
Thomas L. 47
Wm. J. 723
COWEN
W. S. 359
COWPER [See also COOPER]
____ 64, 403
L. M. 38,39,296,297
Lewis M. 489
Martha 369
R. G. 111
Wells 397
William W. 696
Wm. W. 293
COX
Ann 127,315
John 85,134,135, 420,435,466,512, 513,520,588,641
Owen B. 696
Owen W. B. 284
Thomas 84,147, 229,641
COXE
Daniel W. 367
CRAIGE
____ 235
CRANCH
Wm. 191
CRAWFORD
Wm. 293
CREECY
Charles 436,518
James R. 45

CREECY
Joshua S. 318
Penelope 127,315
R. B. 127
Richard B. 127, 315,588
CREIGHTON
John O. 504
John Orde 75
CROCKETT
Davy 659
Robinson 147
CROSS
Louisa R. 475
Richard T. 566
CROWDER
Thomas 140,220, 505
Thos. 107,295
CROWNINSHIELD
Geo. 409
CRUFT
Edw'd. 688
CRUGER
Henry N. 688
CRUMP
John 304
Richard, Jr. 696
CRUTCHFIELD
P. T. 530
CUMMING
John 688
CUNNINGHAM
A. 696
CURRELL
Thomas 519
Thos. 437
William 437
CURTIS
George 608
CUSAC
James 486
CUTHBERT
Jas. 688
John 388
CUTRELL [See also COTTRELL]
Mary 340
CUTT
Erastus 174

D

DABNEY
  Benj. F. 688
  Wm. Beverly 263
DAIL
  Stephen 144
DALTON
  Robert H. 534
DAMERON
  Sam'l. 43
  Samuel 588
DAMON
  Jas. 589
DANDRIDGE
  Wm. 255,263
DANIEL
  ___ 690
  Beverly 382
  John R. J. 696
  Mary 670
  Wm., Jr. 688
DAUGHERTY
  James 696
DAVENPORT
  Frederick 293,626
  S. 397
  Sam'l. 329
  Samuel 696
  Walter 284
DAVES
  John P. 62
DAVEZAC
  Auguste 93,689
DAVIDSON
  Geo. F. 696
  J. E. 107
DAVIE
  F. W. 688
DAVIS
  ___ 42
  Jas. 696
  S. H. 688
  Sarah E. F. 739
  Thomas 303
  Warren R. 91
DAWES
  Robert 503
DAWSON
  Moses 185
DE ENDE
  ___ 652
DE LA RUA
  John 198
DEAN
  ___ 41

DEAN
  Stewart 6
DEAS
  Henry 408
DEBERRY
  Edmund 614,618
DELANO
  Benj. 641
DELK
  James 348
DELOSIER
  Edward 674
DENN
  Clarkson 63
DENNIE
  James 116
DENNY
  Harmer 54
DENSON
  Matthew 146,240,
  336,340,518
DESHONG
  L. 696
DESLA
  ___ 557
DEVANY
  Benj. 107
DEVEREAUX
  T. P. 601
  Thomas P. 126,154
DEVERSON
  Jno. 518
DEW
  Phil. A. 688
  Thos. R. 688
DEY
  James 6,107,369
DIBBLE
  Anthony 107
DICK
  John M. 293,397,
  696
DICKINSON
  John 688
  M. 273,397
DIETSCHY
  Rudolf 66
DOAK
  James W. 293
DOBSON
  Wm. P. 293,696
DODGE
  Pickering 688
  Reuben F. 82

DODSON
  Stephen 293
DOGGETT
  David S. 107
DOLBY
  S. 518
  Stephen 43
DONALDSON
  Jno. J. 688
DONELSON
  S. 369
DONNELL
  ___ 137,556
  John R. 653
  Margaret 653
  William 304
DORSEY
  Jeremiah P. 443
DOUB
  Peter 107
DOUGLASS
  John 518
  Wm. 669
DOWD
  Dickerson 293
  P. W. 246
DOWDY
  Samuel 303
DOWNING
  H. 347
DOZIER
  ___ 622
  Dennis 303
  Thomas 84,696
  Thos. 284
DRAKE
  Ethelbert 263
DRAYTON
  William 198,301
DRINKWATER
  William P. 517
DROMGOOLE
  Geo. C. 688
DUANE
  William J. 93
  Wm. J. 494
DUCACHET
  ___ 109
DUDLEY
  ___ 539
  C. 549
  E. B. 427
  Edw. B. 688
  Edward B. 549,614

DUDLEY
  S. 347
DUER
  John 121
DUMAS
  Isham A. 293
DUNLAP
  Andrew 116
  James A. 689
DUNMAS
  ___ 463
DUNN
  ___ 92
  William B. 529
DUNSTAN
  E. 303
  M. 303
DURANT
  ___ 631
DURYEE
  Charles H. 153
DUTTON
  Wm. F. 670
DYE
  George W. 107

E

EAGLES
  Caroline 410
EARLY
  John 107
  Joseph 66
EASON
  ___ 210
  Jesse 556
EASTWOOD
  James 463
EATON
  ___ 178,183
  J. H. 53
  Surcy 674
ECCLES
  John D. 382
EDMONDSTON
  Ninian 321
EDMONSTON
  N. 696
EDWARDS
  John D. 688
  John H. 259
EEOTT

EEOTT
Stephen 518
ELLERY
Frank 359
ELLIOT
___ 633
ELLIOTT
___ 436,445
Alex. 641
Benjamin 696
Catharine 316
Eliza 531
Ephraim 495,550
Exum 96,531
Henry 316
Job S. 348
Joseph 348
Miles 628
Myles 96
Sally 315
Sarah 608
Silas W. 246,517
Silas W. F. 355
Stephen 154,518, 538
Stephen, Sr. 436
Theophilus 6
Willis 518
Wm. 550
ELLIS
Elisha 294
Ezekiel 47
Josiah 688
William S. 82
Willis 518
Wm. 518
ELLISON
___ 293
Joseph 696
ELLSWORTH
H. L. 165
ELLYSON
Zachariah 369
ELMORE
John A. 688
ELY
Ann Louisa 480
Francis 347
Horace 347,480, 641,704
EMERSON
William 162
EMLEN
Geo. 688

EMMIT
W. C. 696
EMORY
John 708
R. 708
Robert 708
EMPIE
Adam 259
EPPES
___ 647
EPPS
___ 648
ESKRIDGE
___ 202
Mary Ann 725
Vernon 107,308, 619,725
ETHERIDGE
Jeremiah 155
EURE
Hillory H. 620
Mary Ann 620
Sam'l. 247
EVANS
___ 572,602
Elizabeth 72
Henry J. 107
Jacob 518
Jos. R. 688
Joseph R. 679
Z. 572
Zachariah 72
Zech. 518
Zecheriah 436
EVERETT
Alexander H. 93, 128
Charles 688
Richard 589
Thomas H. 96
EVERITT
Hardy 519
Josiah J. 437
Nath'l. 437
Richard 147
EWELL
Benjamin S. 597
EWING
Thos. 452
Wm. L. D. 458

F

FADDIS
Thomas J. 696
FAGAN
Enoch 347,519
Levi 103,147,303
FALLAW
Sarah 379
FARANGE
Wm. 312
FARIBAULT
Chloe Little 732
Joseph F. 732
FAULKNER
___ 30
FELLOW
___ 61
FELTON
Whitmel 436
FENNER
James 76
FEREBEE
George 152
FESSENDEN
Wm. B. 347
FIELD
B. 107
FINLAY
___ 407
FINLEY
Thomas 458
FISH
Preserved 688
FISHER
___ 47
C. 293
Charles 395,450, 696,723
D. 107
FISK
Wilbur 326
FITZGERALD
___ 659
Edward 359
John 198
FLANETT
Cornelius 264
FLEETWOOD
Ashley 587
FLEMING
Mordecai 293
FLEMMING
Mordecai 696
Thos. 688
FLETCHER

FLETCHER
Grizelle P. 490
John 660
Zechariah 247
FLOWER
Hardy 280
Josiah 248,437
FLOWERS
Hardy 696
Josiah 303
FLOYD
Jesse 518
John 36,117,473
Polly 436
Wm. 518
FLURY
Henry 43,518,542, 565
Margaret 246
Thomas D. 132
Thos. D. 497
FONVIELLE
Bryce 293
FORBES
Alpheus, Jr. 669
Fanny 445, 517
FORCE
Peter 76
FORD
Charles M. 445
Henry D. 107
Jas. L. 608
Wm. 518
FOREHAND
Wm. 518
FORGERSON
Caswell 566
Hardy 566
Martha 566
Rebecca 566
FORNEY
Daniel M. 4,431
FORSYTH
John 91
FOSTER
Ceney 369
FOWLER
Charles 719
Jos. S. 236
Sam. 43
Sam'l. 29,596
Samuel 19,21,31, 719

133

FOWLKES
Jeptha 84,267
FOX
William 501
FOXWELL
Stephen 501
FOY
Frederick 293
Miles 107
FRANCIS
___ 648
FRASER
John 688
FREDERICK
Wm. K. 304
FREEMAN
David C. 696
E. B. 723
Ed. B. 242
Geo. W. 105
J. P. 247
Russell 104
FROST
Edw. 617
FROTHINGHAM
___ 255
FULFORD
Absalom 284
FULLER
___ 255
John 252
Thos. 158
FULTON
Hamilton 130

G

GAINES
___ 4
E. P. 60
GALES
J. 372
Joseph 226
GALLATIN
Albert 679,688
GALLAWAY
Rawley 259
GALLOP
Willis 303
GALT
William 580
GAMBILL

GAMBILL
John C. 314
GANN
Thomas 674
GARDINER
___ 581
Catharine 670
J. B. 185
GARDNER
___ 469
Catharine 518,639
Jno. L. 688
Wm. 589
GARLAND
John T. 696
Landon C. 708
GARLINGTON
John 247
GARNETT
James M. 679
Jas. M. 688
GARRARD
Thompson 107
GARRETT
Everard 436,572
J. W. 347
John W. 589
Joseph 589
GARRISON
J. S. 633
Wm. Lloyd 683
GARY
R. B. 284
GASKINS
Dow 691
GASTON
Alex'r. F. 280
Wm. 601,715
GATLIN
Alfred M. 517
John 465
GATLING
John 528
Riddick 717
GAUSE
J. P. 696
GAUZE
John P. 338
GAVIN
Edward C. 304
GAYLE
John 470
GEE
Nevil 63

GIBBS
Charles 503
GILASTER
Robert 678
GILBERT
___ 222
GILCHRIST
Robert B. 617
GILES
Thos. T. 688
William B. 196
Wm. B. 36
GILLESPIE
Jos. 696
GILLIAM
H. 267
Henry 309,422
James 148
L. 280
Mary C. 309
GILMER
Thos. W. 688
GILMORE
John T. 696
GLASS
E. P. 696
GLENN
Gideon 280,696
GLOVER
J. H. 688
GODDARD
William 688
GODFREY
Hugh 348
Samuel 261
GOELET
Edward H. 588,670
Jno. B. 670
John 437
John B. 399
GOLDTHWAITE
H. 679,688
GOODE
William O. 688
GOODENOW
___ 198
J. M. 92
GOODHUE
Jonathan 688
GOODMAN
D. S. 626
Daniel H. 631
Edith 717
J. 107

GOODMAN
J. R. 432
Wm. 717
GOODWIN
___ 289
James M. 517
John 43
Wm. P. 517
GORDAN
John D. 533
Sarah 533
GORDON
John C. 626
Nathan 246
GORHAM
James 24,122,143,
387,438,527
Jas. 506
GOVERNOUR
Samuel L. 609
GRAHAM
Daniel 463
Edward 62
Elizabeth B. 62
GRANBERRY
___ 132
Jos. 132
GRANBERY
Joseph T. 628
GRANBURY
Jos. T. 608
GRANDY
___ 622
A. 696
Abner H. 284
GRANGER
T. 347
Thomas 246
GRANOR
H. 66
GRANT
James 414,529
Jas. 4
Solomon E. 47
GRANTHOM
John 132
GRAY
Alexander 4
Frances Ann 588
Geo. R. 359
GRAYBEAL
David 463
GRAYHEAL
David 47

GRAYSON
R. O. 688
GREEN
Duff 262
Farnifold 569
J. 696
Patsey 82
R. M. 343
Richard W. 93
Rigdon M. 343
Solomon 463
W. M. 249
Wm. M. 439
GREENE
C. R. 446
GREENFIELD
Sarah 594
GREGORY
___ 556
Benj. 348
George N. 107,308
Lemuel 445
Mackey 132,276
Martha Henrietta 276
Nathan 436
Nathan D. 43,246
Providence A. 340
Samuel 28
Thomas 436,518,588
William 109,330
Winneyfred 518
Wm. 43,227,436,691
GRENNEL
George, Jr. 388
GRICE
Charles 125
GRIMES
___ 239
Sarah 127
William 491
Wm. 16
Wm. H. 676,727,741
GRIMHALL
J. Berkley 688
GRIST
Allen 112,284
GRISWOLD
Alex'r V. 63
Geo. 688
GRONLUND

GRONLUND
Geo. W. 251
GUDGER
Jas. 314
GUIN
James W. 314
GUINN
Jas. W. 696
GWYNN
Littleton 293
Littleton A. 696

H

HABERSHAM
Rob't. 688
HACKETT
James 102
Jas. 43
HALEY
James 284
HALL
___ 285,630
Benjamin K. 248
Dan. 107
E. P. 285
John H. 382,690
Nancy 641
T. H. 128,626
Thomas H. 614
William R. 696
Wm. R. 338,397
HALLSEY
Joseph 161
HALSEY
Myles 436
R. S. 501
HALSTEAD
John D. 519
HAMILTON
___ 178,183
Alexander 36
James 178,519,589
James A. 121
Jas. 347,427
Sam'l. S. 339
William S. 36
HAMMETT
John A. 670
William 107
HAMPORE
Susan E. 348

HAMPTON
William 304
HANDCOCK
Richard 127,315
Sally J. 586
Wm. 586
HANDY
William W. 688
Wm. W. 679
HANKINS
Catharine 7
John 247
John G. 7,246,340,518,638
HANKS
Wm. N. 731
HARDENBURG
C. L. 688
Cornelius L. 679
HARDISON
Ezekiel 437
Hardy 248
HARDY
Benjamin 303
Edward 275
Harriet 88
Henry 82,437
James F. 534
HARE
Jacob 269,284
HARMAN
Abraham 508
Parker 508
HARPER
___ 92
Charles Carroll 93,388
James 284
Jas. 696
William 679
Wm. 688
HARREL
___ 114
HARRELL
Abram 107
Arail 348
David 341
Dempsy 517
Freeza 275
James 518,670
John 114
Mary D. 341
Samuel 107
HARRIS

HARRIS
Eliza 340
Henderson 670
Polly 43
R. 293
Ransom 397
Samuel D. 116
HARRISON
___ 647
Aaron 589
Nathaniel 314
Randolph 688
Stephen 43
HART
B. 69
John 696
N. 69
HARTHEY
Silvey 246
HARTLY
Abner 696
HARTMUS
James H. 71
HARVEY
___ 402
E. B. 247
Edmund B. 322
Eliza 322
Eliza J. 14,231
Isaac 411
James H. 396
Jas. H. 670
Martha B. 340
Matthew 76,388
HASKETT
Davis 327
HASKIFT
William 517
HASSELL
___ 626
HATCH
Durant 156
HATHAWAY
T. V. 230,327
Thomas V. 124
Thos. V. 518
HAUGHTON
Charles 132,246,518
Chas. 584,670,701
Eliza A. 701
J. 588
J. H. 418,537,559,565,644,693,713
John 84

HAUGHTON
Jon. H. 568
Jona. 133,544
Jona H. 9
Jonathan H. 603
Jos. 246
Joseph M. 18
Mal. 160
Malachi 124,241, 411,610
Milly 246
Thomas B. 84,347, 436
Thomas G. 127, 315
Thos. B. 437,698, 714
HAWES
Walker 688
HAWKES
Francis L. 464
HAWKINS
Benjamin 264
Jno. H. 280,397
John H. 397,696
Micajah T. 680
HAWKS
Cicero S. 259
Francis L. 339
Wm. N. 731
HAWTHORN
Samuel 519
HAY
George 350
HAYDOCK
___ 30
HAYES
Thomas S. 660
HAYLEY
James T. 696
HAYNES
Isaac 107
HAYWARD
Elijah 92
HAYWOOD
John 535
Lucy D. 105
Sherwood 105
William H. 529
Wm. H., Jr. 529 696
HEAD
Jno. J. 107
HEARD

HEARD
James 688
HEATH
R. R. 246,437
Robert R. 347
HEATON
Albert 66
Townsend 66
HEDRICK
Thos. 436
HEDRICKS
Samuel 522
HENDERSON
Lawson F. 534
HENLEY
Osborn 383
HENRY
L. D. 723
Louis D. 293,696
HENSHAW
David 159
HENTZ
Caroline L. 642
N. M. 259
HERNDON
___ 444,482
J. R. 721
John R. 385,584
Zach P. 688
HEWES [See also HUGHES]
Joseph 264
Josiah 411
HICKERMAN
Benj. 518
HICKS
J. J. 107
HIGASON
David C. 246
HILL
Green 723
Isaac 159,208
J. A. 549
James 303
James K. 304
John 123,304,397, 696
Joseph A. 293,539, 549
Maria 519
Richard K. 259
Thomas 293
Whitmel 264
William R. 32,47

HILL
Wilson 696
Wm. 4,529
HILLARD
R. C. 280
HINDS
___ 289
HINTON
Charles L. 397,529, 656
Jos. B. 397
Joseph B. 280
Ransom 47
William R. 529
HITCHCOCK
J. Irvine 320
HOBART
___ 360
HOBERT
Henry 331
HOEL [See also HOWELL]
Welcome 347
HOELL
Welcome 147
HOFFMAN
Geo. 688
HOFNER
Thomas 326
HOGAN
John 696
William L. 534
HOGG
Gavin 417
HOKE
Daniel 314,397,696
HOLDEN
Josiah 284
HOLDER
Josiah 696
HOLLAND
David 529
HOLLIDAY
Margaret 256
Rob't. 256
HOLLOWAY
Henry 247
HOLLOWEL
Luke 281
HOLMES
G. 293
Gabriel 5,285
George W. 588
Henry 27,620

HOLMES
Mary 620
Richard 96
Step. 132
Wm. 107
HOLSTEAD
John D. 107
HOLT
___ 87
Wm. R. 688
HOMER
Henry 670
HOOPER
___ 285
Archibald M. 285
Elias 304
Obadiah 502
William 78,264
HOOVER
Charles 696
Geo. 293
HORAH
William H. 440
HORN
Henry 367
HORNER
Thomas 326
HORNIBLOW
Jos. 518
HORNSBY
Samuel M. 248
HORRY
Elias 113
HORTON
James 314
William 304
HOSKINS
___ 511
Baker 404,485,532, 572,584,698
Charles 518
Chs. W. 246
Edm. 720
Edmund 15,573,745
Fred. 436
James 315
James W. 127
Jos. N. 497,532,567, 584,709
Joseph N. 448,646
Martha 127,315
Mary D. 315
R. T. 695,733
T. S. 627,635

HOSKINS
Thomas S. 49,473,
567,584,627,635,688
Thos. S. 132,482,
584
HOUGH
William 463
HOUSE
___ 633
HOUSTON
___ 217
George, Jr. 461
Samuel 61
HOWARD
Benjamin C. 172
Jas. 696
Peter 328
HOWCOTT
John L. 347
Nathaniel 44,146,
518
Nath'l. 44
HOWELL [See also
HOEL,HOELL]]
S. 293
Shadrac 696
Shadrach 397
Welcome 248
HOWES
Edward 147
Zechariah 519
HOWETT
John L. 347
Richard 403,434
Silvanus 481
Thomas 315
Thomas B. 127
HOYT
___ 494
Jesse 427
HUBBLE
Wm. 194
HUDSON
Uriah 203
HUGER
Daniel E. 679,688
HUGGINS
Wm. 284
HUGHES
Matthew M. 47
HUNT
Jas. W. 696
Thos. P. 242
William L. 672

HUNT
Wm. L. 347
HUNTER
Charles G. 131,153
Edward R. 84
Isaac R. 626
William 679
Wm. 688
HUNTINGTON
S. 30
HUNTOON
John G. 92
HURDLE
Nancy 355
HUSKE
Jno. 382
John 690
HUTCHINS
Merritt 47
HYBART
Thos. L. 493

I

INDIANS
PUSH-MA-TA-HA
209
TUSKINA 182,197
INGRAHAM
Edw. D. 688
IREDELL
___ 5,80,414
Ja.. 656
James 44,624,635,
656,670,679
Jas. 635,688
IRELAND
Elizabeth 499
IRION
Philip 304
IRVING
George W. 494
John B. 538
Washington 93,617
IVES
Levi S. 564
Levi Silliman 577

J

JACKSON
___ 76,121,183,
367,570,584,613,647,
659,710,716
A. 584
Abner S. 82
Andrew 153,489,
529
Andrew, Jr. 724
David 289
W. 359
William 253,572,
591,696
Wm. 571,670
JACOCKS
Jon. H. 608
Jona. H. 397,588
Jonathan 247
Jonathan H. 490,
628,678
JAMES
Andrew 437,519
Hetty 519
Silvery 437,519
JARVIS
___ 248
Foster 304,696
Leonard 305
JASPER
S. L. B. 347
Seldon 519
JEFFERSON
Thomas 196
JEFFREYS
George W. 4,431
JENNISON
James 107
JENKINS
___ 359
Joseph F. 688
JENKS
S. H. 191
JENNINGS
Lemuel 284
Mary E. 202
Robert C. 678
JERNIGAN
R. 347
JOHNS
___ 109
JOHNSON
___ 406
Ann 193
C. E. 520,572,602

JOHNSON
Carolina Virginia
245
Charles 633
Charles E. 213,340
Chas. E. 132,232,
Chas. E. 245,283,
567,602,627
D. E. 315
Daniel E. 315
James D. 729
Job 688
Josiah S. 464
R. M. 92,716
Richard W. 489
Thomas 588
Thos. 147
W. 383
JOHNSTON
Asa 248
Jas. C. 119
Mary 246
Samuel 264
Wm. 641
JONES
___ 147,235
A. D. 679
Alfred 431,656
Allen 264
Arnold D. 688
Cadwallader 35
Edmund 304,397
Edw'd S. 446
Eliza J. 436
Frances 147
Frederick 432
H. D. 211,560,567,
572,721,743
Hamilton C. 710
Hend. 436
Hend. D. 211
Henry 529
Jacob 36
James 662
James C. 38,39
James S. 39,303
Jas. 688
Jno. B. 616
Jno. F. 696
John B. 696
John F. 284
John H. 246,275
John M. 141,219,
357,404,483,586,654,

JONES
John M.
677,685,687
John W. 679,688
Kimbrough 529
Lavinia 38,39
Lydia G. 432
Martha W. 445
Roger 101
Sarah C. 662
Seaborn 688
Stephen W. 107
Thomas Ap.
Catesby 83
Walter F. 405
Wesley 529
William 355
Willie 264
Wm. 394,518
JORDAN
Cela 518
Clarisa Louisa Ryan 631
John 276,366
Joseph 265
Matthew 604
Richard 436
Sely 670
Thomas 246,588
Thos. 284
JORDON
Mary 475
JOY
Daniel 132
JOYCE
R. A. 588
JUDKINS
Thomas J. 696
JUDSON
Chas. 30
JUSTICE
James D. 47

K

KAIL [See also CAIL,CALE]
Amariah B. 290
KEATING
Robert 518
Robert, Sr. 43

KEATING
Rob't. 588
KEATON
William 641
KEEP
Samuel 298
KEININGHAM
Wm. W. 107
KEITH
M. J. 689
KELENBERGER
F. J. 744
Frances J. 744
Francis J. 744
KELLENBURGER
Lewis 247
KELLY
___ 657
John 690
KENAN
Thomas 4
KENDALL
Amos 185
L. 359
Reuben 304,696
KENNEDAY
William 293
KENNEDY
Edmund P. 83
Morris W. 436
Wm. W. L. 259
KENNON
Beverly 83
Wm. 463
KENT
Orrin 222
KERR
James 293,696
John 107
William 242
KEYS
Johannah 437,519
KIDD
Benjamin 107
KILBY
___ 633
KILGO
Wm. 415
KIMBROUGH
Elijah W. 303,391
KING
Elizabeth 670
Jas. G. 688
John 588

KING
Myles 206
Phillis Dominick 670
Rufus 597
KINGS
Edward VI 127
George I 123
George II 123
George III 123,127
KINGSMAN
Freeman 589
KINNEY
C. R. 739
KIRKPATRICK
J. Bayard 688
KITERELL
Geo. 563
KITTERELL
___ 275
KNAPP
Isaac 683
J. F. 301
J. J. 409
Jno. Francis 339
John Francis 352
KNEELAND
H. 688
KNIGHT
Alfred W. 132
KNOX
Alex. Gordon 688
Andrew 160,246
Louisa 127
Sarah P. 518

L

LA FAYETTE
___ 584
LADLING
Jane 436
LAMB
Geo. 518
Isaac N. 433
Jacob 608
John 247
Luke G. 284
William G. H. 361
Willis 517
Wm. G. H. 518

LAMBERT
___ 588
Ephraim A. 589
John 43,340
LAND
Benjamin 155
LANGDON
___ 285
Samuel 285
LANGHORN
Geo. W. 107
LANSTON
Jane Caroline 625
John 303,625
LARKINS
William S. 293,696
LARY
Hoff 608
Hugh 608
LASPEYRE
Samuel A. 696
LASSITER
Allen 227,330,553, 692
Charlotte 227
Deborah 691
Elizabeth 275
Mary 553
Thomas 248
LATHLEY
Lewis 518
LATHROP
Samuel 680
LAUGHBOROUGH
H. 597
LAWRENCE
___ 87
Alex. J. 529
Alexander J. 529
Francis 490
Martha 718
P. P. 718
Reuben 369,490
William Beach 93
LAWSON
Thomas 293
LAZARUS
Aaron 690
Washington 740
LEA [See also LEE, LEIGH]
George G. 259
Jas. N. 107
Lorenzo 107

LEACH
___ 553
C. 107
LEAK
Walter E. 696
LEARY [See also LERRY, LURRY]
Harriet 347
John 611
John H. 318
Richard 672
Sarah 611
Thomas H. 43
Thos. 340
William R. 246
LEDBETTER
Rufus 107
LEE [See also LEA, LEIGH]
___ 17
Albert M. 597
Henry 94,679,688
Hester C. 43,340
Hester K. 340,436
John F. 597
Leroy M. 107,308
Michael 17
Roswel W. 597
William 303
LEGARDE
Jacques 641
LEGARE
H. S. 538
Hugh S. 688
LEIGH
H. G. 717
Hez. G. 107
James 247
Josh. 107
Samuel J. 152
LELAND
John 406
LENOX
Julia 298
LEONARD
Benjamin 338
J. 688
LEONIDAS 209
LEROY
Lewis 5
LERRY [See also LEARY, LURRY]
___ 303
LEWIS

LEWIS
Malachi S. 84
Richard 259
William B. 121
LILLY
James M. 304
LILLYBRIDGE
Clark 109
LINDEMAN
D. 47
LINDSAY
Jonathan 280,616
Jonathan J. 696
LINN
William 458
LIST
Frederick 388
LITCHFIELD
Mebzas 589
LITTELL
E. 688
LITTLE
Alexander 696
Gray 280
LITTLEJOHN
Eliz. 315
Elizabeth 127
Grace 436
J. W. 125,126
John W. 303
W. A. 127,315
William A. 127,315
LIVINGSTON
___ 427
Edward 150,172
LLOYD
___ 326
J. R. 626
Jos. R. 242
Joseph R. 614
Saltar 304
LONG
Henry W. 111
James 284,355
Jas. L. 166
John 147,519,589
Joshua 672
Thomas 628
Thos. 628
William L. 284,696
LORANE
Edward 162
LORD
Wm. C. 285

LORETZ
Andrew H. 314
LORILLARD
Jacob 688
LORMAN
William 91
LOUNGE
Mary 589
LOVE
James R. 321
LOVE
Robert 407
LOWRIE
John 47
LOWTHER
William D. 246
LOYD
Jos. R. 630
LUCAS
Robert 121
LUKE
John 486
LUMSDEN
John 723
LUND
Oliver 646
LURRY [See also LEARY]
Wm. R. 132
LUTON
Louisia 459
LYON
Robert 696
LYONS
Jas. 688

M

MAC RAE
John 463
MACBETH
Charles 688
MACDONALD
___ 91
MACFARLAND [See also MC FARLAND, M'FARLAND]
Malcolm 688
MACKENZY
John 588

M'AFEE
Robert 314
MAFFIT
John N. 2
MAGRUDER
James 688
MAHOOD
George 107
MAITLAND
B. 498
Benj. 704
MALL
Jacob 47
MALLARY
Rollin C. 536
MALLETT
C. P. 690
MALLETTE
Charles P. 382
MANGUM
James M. 529
Willie P. 414,635
MANLY
Charles 395,723
MANN
E. 293
Ephraim 161
MANNING
Jno. 359
Jos. 85,435
Joseph 20,192,728
Mary 127,315
R. J. 427
MANSON
John 519
Nehemiah 519
MARKLY
Philip S. 61
MARKS
James 588
MARLEY
Sally Jane 589
MARRINER
Demsey 347
MARSHAL
Thomas 696
MARSHALL
C. 304
Clement 696
Clem't. 397
James W. 580
John 584
MARSHALL
Thomas 284

139

MARTIN
____ 299
James 670
James H. 463
James, Jr. 301
John 696
Mary Eliza 238
Robert 304,397,696
Thomas D. 127, 238,315
MASK
Pleasant M. 696
MASON
____ 374
Littlebury 303
Richard S. 138
William J. 688
MASSEY
H., Sr. 696
Howard H. 293
MASSIN
____ 374
Peter 376
MASTERS
Samuel 731
MATHIAS
Martha Ann 175
MATTHEWS
Isham 284,397, 696
MATTHIAS
Marthyann 246
MAURICE
A. J. 204
Alexander J. 446
MAXCY
Virgil 205
MAXEY
Bennett T. 107
MAXWELL
Wm. 688
MAYO
Samuel 674
M'BRYDE
Archibald 4
MC ADEN
Jas. 107
MC DONALD
Phails 107
MC ENTIRE [See also MC INTYRE, M'ENTIRE, M'INTYER]

MC ENTIRE
John 696
MC FARLAND [See also M'FARLAND]
Tryam 696
MC GEHEE
Thomas 696
MC ILHENNY
William 688
MC INTYRE
Wm. 690
MC KAY
James 630,722
MC KENNEY [See also M'KENNEY]
T. L. 339
MC LANE
____ 61
Louis 93
MC LAURIN
Duncan 696
MC LEAN
John 386
MC LIN
John J. 308
Mary Ann 308
MC MILAN
John J. 696
MC NEILL
Alex'r. 293
David 696
MC PHERSON
Wiley 294
MC QUEEN
Hugh 696
MC RAE
Duncan 690
M'CAIN
Geo. W. 696
Nathaniel H. 259
M'CAULEY
Charles S. 83
Robert 608
M'CLEESE
Charles 626
Chas. 626,696
M'CLURE
Ezekiel H. 49
MC'NEILL
Alex. 397
M'CONNICO
A. J. 405
Andrew J. 400
M'COY

M'COY
____ 303
M'DANIEL
Risden 696
Risden M. 284
M'DONALD
D. 135,435,623
Duncan 126
James 107
M'DOWELL
D. 333
Daniel 132,518,588
MEAD
Abraham 248
Jacob 246
MEARES
Wm. B. 293,397
MEBANE
Alexander 280
Alexander W. 84
James 696
Jas. 234
MEDLEY
C. J. 304
MEEKINS
____ 200,236
Daniel 236
MEIGS
Jonathan 615
R. J., Jr. 615
Return Jonathan 615
MELCHOR
Christopher 293,696
MENDENHALL
G. C. 427
Nathan 234
M'ENTIRE
J. 314
MERCEIA
Wm. A. 30
MERCEIN
Thos. R. 688
MEREDITH
____ 376,385,422, 584,701
Thomas 181,361, 695
Thos. 238,256,742
W. 411
MERRYMAN
Joseph 518
MESSER

MESSER
Asa 76
MEWBORN
Joshua 671
M'FARLAND [See also MC FARLAND]
Tryam 293
Tryan 397
M'GEHEE
Henry 529
M'GHEE
Thomas 293
M'GUIRE
Lavina 436,518
Mariam 246
Nancy 344
MHOON
James G. 242,291
Wm. 280
Wm. S. 414,429,529
MIDDLETON
H. A. 688
Henry 688
R. H. 23,56,170,374, 433
Richard H. 316
Rich'd 518
Wm. 518
MILLEN
Geo. 87
MILLER
A. E. 538
D. H. 367
E. 246,340
Elisha P. 303
George 47
H. M. 529
Henry M. 529
John A. 107
Nathaniel 720
Silvanus 95
Stephen 304,397, 696
Stephen D. 688
Thomas J. 667
Thos. 688
William, Jr. 131,153
William L. 696
MING
John 608
MINOR
Raymond R. 107
MINTON
Peter B. 514

M'INTYER
George 589
M'INTYRE
Geo. 246
George 132
J. 397
MISHET
James K. 534
MISKELL
John B. 518
MITCHEL
Lugar 247
MITCHELL
Samuel L. 659
Samuel V. 588
Stephen T. 292
Thos. R. 688
Wm. 247,348,517,678
MIXSON
Charles W. 85,453,475,641
Chas. W. 212,246,567
M'KAY
___ 539
James J. 304,614
M'KEE
James 47,321
M'KEEL
Jos. 124
M'KENNEY [See also MCKENNEY]
Thomas L. 326
Wm. 200
M'KEVER
Isaac 83
M'KIEL
Josiah 333,516
M'KIM
Isaac 91
M'LANE
Louis 617
M'LEAN
William
M'LELLAND
N. E. 534
M'MILLAN
John J. 304
M'NEILL
Alexander 293
Daniel 293
Neill 293
M'NIDER

M'NIDER
Charlotte Catharine 476
George W. 443
James 247
Mary Matilda 625
Wm. 43,340,443,476,479,516,545,625
MOFFATT
James 7,10
Jas. 43
MONDRYER
Allen 445
MONK
Archibald 696
Archibald C. 304
MONROE [See also MUNROE]
___ 354,609
James 54,593
MONTGOMERY
___ 397,626
B. J. 152,269,622
Bridger J. 463,696
Bridjer J. 50
Elenor 38,39
J. B. 359
W. 397
William 293,696
Wm. W. 735
MOODY
John M. 696
Wm. 317
MOORE
___ 186
Alexander 409
Alfred C. 293
Allen 147
Aug. 627
Augustus 175,567,627
Cornelius 247
Edwin 247
G. C. 622,626
Gabriel 521
Godwin C. 696
Henry 594
James 517
John, Jr. 137
John W. 688
L. C. 188
Lem. C. 607
Lemuel C. 188,607
Louisa 594

MOORE
Sam'l B. 470
Samuel D. 521
MOORMAN
Charles P. 107
Samuel T. 107
MORFITT
H. M. 83
MORGAN
___ 64
Abram 588
Chas. W. 83
Horatio 481
J. 296,297
James 35,84
Wm. P. 416
MORISEY
Thomas K. 304
MORISSEY
___ 657
MORRIS
___ 304
John 164
Wm. A. 696
MORRISON
Jas. 107
MOSELEY
W. D. 723
MOSELY
William D. 696
Wm. D. 284
MOYE
Alfred 696
W. 397
Wyatt 284,696
M'PHERSON
___ 303
John N. 739
M'REA
J. W. 147
MUDGE
S. H. 688
MULLEN
___ 348,445
Benj. 247,284,293,626
Joseph 203
MULLIN
James 517
MUMFORD
John I. 679
MUNDAY
Jesse 517
MUNROE [See also

MONROE]
Thomas 339
MURCHINSON
W. 397
MURCHISON
Alexander 47
Duncan 47
William 47,293
MURPHEY
James 293
MUSE
Henry 103
Jno. B. 49,656
John B. 447,449,463,656
MYDGETT
Jacob 246

N

NASH
___ 664
Abner 264
E. P. 462
Fred. 427
Martha A. W. 530
Miles 462
NAUDAIN
Arnold 61
NAUMAN
___ 131
NEGROES
CORNISH
Sam'l. E. 343
DAY [See also WILSON]
Aquilla 463
ERSKINE
___ 66
HASSELL
Tom 544
PRICE
Jim 705
Josiah 705
Peter 705
SAMPSON
Henry 285
TREDWELL
Isaac 544
TURNER [See also NAT]
Nat 648,675

WILSON
  Aquilla 463
WOOD
  Jim 229
  ABNER 212
  ABRAM 428
  AZZY 595
  BILL 28
  CARY 391
  DAVE 657
  DAVID 657
  DERRY 310
  DRED 647
  FRED 368
  GILES 28
  HARK 647
  HENRY 27
  ISAAC 544
  JERRY 485
  JIM 42,229,657
  MOSES 303
  NAT 647,657,666, 675,700,706
  PRIMER 212
  ROSE 670
  SAM 648
  TOM 544
NEIL
  Horatio 6
  Isabella 6
  John F. 347
  Margaret 132
NELSON
  Wilie M. 696
NEWBERN
  Henry 509
NEWBORN
  Mary 175
NEWBY
  ____ 424
  Exum 84,139,424
  Francis 149
  Joseph 445
  Sam'l. 96
  Thos. 247,518
NEWHALL
  Isaac 688
NEWLAND
  David 304,397, 431
NEWSAM
  Nancy 43
NEWSOM
  James D. 529

NEWTON
  ____ 633
NICHOLAS
  C. J. 167
  Martha R. B. 717
NICHOLS
  Cyprian 165
NICHOLSON
  Alex. 47
  Joseph I. 83
  Thos. 284,696
NICKLIN
  Philip H. 688
NIELL
  ____ 62
NILES
  Nathaniel 388
NIXON
  B. 572
  Elijah 43
  Henry D. 127
  John 670,720
  John, Sr. 436
  Martha 355
  Nelson 347
  Robert 436
  Tamar 247
NIXSON
  B. 96
NOAH
  M. M. 185
NOBLE
  James 492
NOLAND
  George 246
NOLLEY
  G. W. 717
NOLLY
  George W. 107
NORCOM
  Ann 573
  Benjamin R. 127
  Caspar W. 315
  Casper W. 127
  Frederick 15,658
  J. C. 466,583,669
  James 12,15,84,303, 567
  James, Jr. 584
  Jas. 282,310,584
  Jno. 518
  Jos. 518
  Joseph 573
  Joseph C. 574,669

NORCOM
  Mary M. 315
  W. R. 466
  Wm. R. 84,98,171, 270,363,603,719
NORFLEET
  Ann 195,436
  Eliza 436
NORMAN
  A. 107
  S. 107
  Thomas 61
NORRIS
  Isaac W. 688
NORTON
  John H. 289
NORWOOD
  ____ 353
  Walter A. 534

O

O'BRIEN
  ____ 456
  Spencer 280,456, 696
OGDEN
  H. W. 208
OLIVEIRA
  S. R. 524,588
OLIVERA
  S. R. 436,670
  Simon R. 340
ONDERDONK
  Benjamin F. 360
ORR
  Wm. 314
OSBORNE
  James W. 259
OSKE
  John B. 264
OTIS
  H. G. 427
OUTLAW
  David 616,624,688, 696
  Frances 71
  Joseph B. 4
  Joshua 303
OVERMAN
  Thomas 284
OVERTON

OVERTON Wm. G. 688
OWEN
  ____ 234,490
  John 549
OWENS
  Stephen 284

P

PAGE
  Ann collins 342
  M. 342
PAINE
  ____ 569
PAINE [See also PAYNE]
  Jno. 518
  John 436,572
  Robert F. 445
  Thomas 398
PALMER
  Amos 303
  James 119,535
  N. J. 710
PARHAM
  L. W. 696
PARK
  Roswell 597
PARKE
  Thos. D. 534
PARKER
  ____ 132,647
  David 57,267
  Elisha 176,232
  J. N. 572
  Jacob 232,266
  Jacob N. 355, 572
  Job 246,572
  Job, Sr. 436
  John 280
  Peter 436
  R. E. 535
  Richard H. 84
  Seth 132
  Seth N. 739
  Willis 246,436,509
PARKMAN
  ____ 589
  Henry S. 518

PARKS
M. P. 708
Marshall 258,287
Martin P. 107
PARMLY
L. 511
PARRIMORE
Adoris 43
PARSONS
___ 340
Enoch 679,688
PATCH
Sam 128
PATTEN
___ 744
PATTERSON
S. F. 723
PATTON
Alexander 679,688
PAXTON
Richard 127,315
PAYNE
Geo. M. 688
PEABODY
George 688
PEACOCK
Richard 248
PEAKS
Martin T. 589
PEARSON
Richmond 293
Richmond M. 696
Stephen 47
PEASE
Calvin 198
PECK
Isaac O. 132
PEDRICK
___ 79
PEEBLES
Etheldred J. 303
PEEK
James H. 180
PELBY
___ 642
PELL
Wm. E. 1,426,434, 742
PENDLETON
W. H. 383
PENN
Abram 107
PEOPLES
Allen 293,696

PERCIVAL
J. 359
PERKINS
Caleb 284
Job 678
Sally 43
PERRY
___ 208
Algernon S. 534
Decatur 541
Elisha 247,348
Josiah 96
Martha Ann 96
Thos. 112
PERSON
Presley C. 47
PESCUD
Edward 458
PETERS
Richard 116
PETERSON
John H. 458
PETTERICK
Samuel 347
PETTIFORD
Reuben 340
PETTIGREW
Ann 245
Ebenezer 161,245
PETTIJOHN
Elizabeth 132
Job 518
John 436
John C. 82
Sarah 43
PETTIS
Spencer 661
PETTY
Eli 696
PEYTON
H. S. 107
PHELPS
Chas. H. 82,248
Chas L. 588
Hardy J. 589
Hardy S. 248,437
Jordan J. 82
PHILIPS
Jas. 259
Jas. J. 489
PHILLIPS
Benjamin 247
Lydia 63
William 293

PHILPOT
S. 664
PHIPPS
___ 700
PHYSICK
___ 279
PICKARD
David 3,246
John L. 386
PICKENS
John 688
PICKETT
J. C. 93
PICOT
Julian 52
P. O. 583
Peter O. 4,248
PIKE
___ 21
John 641
PINCKNEY
H. L. 319
Henry L. 408
Thos. 688
PIPKIN
Isaac 303
Mary 62
PITTMAN
Redding J. 696
PLATT
___ 30
PLAYER
Thomson T. 688
PLUMMER
Franklin E. 289
PLUMSTEAD
Joseph 464
POINDEXTER
Geo. 679,688
George 360
POINSETT
J. R. 172
Joel B. 150
Joel R. 224
POINTER
Phillip 436
POLK
Leonidas 186
Thomas G. 696
Thos. G. 293
POLLY
Henry 390
POMEROY
T. S. 688

POOL
Eliza 96
John 152,622,696
Josh. A. 284
POPE
Curran 597
Wm. 688
POPELSTON
James W. 127
Jane 315
John 135,411,588
PORTER
David 121
Wm. 445
PORTINGTON
John H. 147
POST
___ 369
POTTER
Isabella 664
John 688
R. 664
Robert 189,614, 630,664
Rob't. 664
Robt. 680
Wm. 570
POWELL
Alfred H. 637
Marmaduke 304, 696
Thomas 514
POWERS
J. 107
PRATT
Jos. 518
Joshua 316
Nathan 518
Zeb. 518
Zebulon 363
PREBLE
William Pitt 93
PRENTICE
Geo. D. 326,427
PRENTISS
Henry E. 597
PRESTON
Wm. C. 688
PRICE
___ 675
Isaac 712
Richard 688
PRICHETT
Abeishai 589

PRINCE
___ 675
PRINGLE
James R. 319
PRITCHARD
Absalom 67
Robert C. 678
PRITCHET
Ashbee C. 248
PRITCHETT
Abishai 347
Abishui 519
PROCTOR
___ 443
John 553
PRUDEN
Jas. 517
PUGH
W. E. 473
W. H. 641
William 247
Wm. E. 68,267
PURCELL
John 293
PURSER
Churchill 112

Q

QUIN
Mary Jane 731
QUINCY
Josiah 61

R

RAGUET
___ 679
Condy 335
Coudy 688
RAMSAY
Jos. A. 397
RAMSEY
Joseph 293
RAND
Nathaniel G. 529, 696
RANDOLPH

RANDOLPH
___ 216
J. 279
John 208,599,680
RANSOM
John K. 38
Wm. J. 489
Wm. S. 489,570
RANSON
Thomas S. 107
RASCOE
Jacob D. 631
Thos. W. 82
William D. 246
Wm. D. 65,163, 230,253,266,286, 554,603,641
RAVENSCROFT
___ 207
John S. 118,564
RAY
James 475
Jno. 696
John 314
RAYMOND
Peter 82
RAYNER
Henry A. 248
James 490
REA
Evelina 361
Martha 518
Patsey 276
Polly 475
Samuel 276
Willie 518
Wm. 518
RECTOR
Wharton 205
REDDICK [See also RIDDICK]
Lemuel 696
REDWOOD
Wm. H. 673
REED
___ 459
James 518
Jas. 135
John 388
Nathan D. 643
Samuel 463
William 275,348
Wm. 631
REID

REID
___ 132
J. 107
Thomas B. 92
REISSE
___ 633
RENCHER
Abraham 614,630
William 696
RHODES
James 28
RICH
Daniel 519
RICHARDS
Thos. 30
RICHARDSON
Edw. 688
RIDDICK [See also REDDICK]
___ 622
A. 311
Abraham 311,467
Abram 348
Elisha N. 152
James R. 293
James W. 454
Jos. 341
Lem'l. 626
W. 626
Willis 293
RIDGELY
___ 91
Charles G. 83
Nicholas 165
Noah 17
RIDPASS
Ransom 437
RIGHTON
Ann 127
Mary Elizabeth 632
William 132
Wm. 518,632
RILEY
James 47
RIM
John 264
RING
Zebedee 688
RINGGOLD
James G. 689
RINKER
J. M. 359
RIPELY
James W. 128

RIPLEY
E. W. 237
James W. 305
RISH
George 47
RISQUE
Ferdinand W. 688
RIVES
William C. 93
ROANE
Wm. H. 688
ROBARDS
___ 414
Wm. 4
ROBERTS
___ 239
Asa 236
Baker 347
Charles 695
Frederick L. 127
John W. 315
Martin 304
Mary 619
Mills 267
Richard 447,463, 723
Thos. V. 489
William C. 7,74
Wm. 43
Wm. B. 27,436,518, 595,621
Wm. C. 8,48,619
ROBERTSON
James 179
Jos. 696
ROBINSON
Anthony 263
John 689
K.E.V. 383
RODGERS
Sam'l. 293
ROGERS
Allen 529
Daniel 552
Darrell 529
David 463
Nehemiah 641
Wm. B. 688
ROGERSON
Asa 312
Elizabeth 442
Isaiah 13,47,247, 442
RONALDSON

RONALDSON
James 682
ROOT
Samuel 436
ROPES
Joseph 688
ROSE
Howell 688
James 688
ROSS
Michael, Mrs. 218
ROULHAC
J. B. G. 85,624
Jos. B. G. 688
Joseph B. G. 624
ROUNDTREE
Moses 247
ROWAN
A. H. 208
John 409,470
ROWE
James 293
ROWLAND
William S. 696
ROWZEC
Wm. B. 107
ROYAL
Anne 392
ROYALL
Ann 711
ROYCROFT
Thomas 529
RUFFIAN
___ 49
RUFFIN
Thomas 624,635
William K. 259
RUSSEL
Tho. B. 518
RUSSELL
Chas. H. 688
RUST
Geo. 92
RUTGERS
Henry 106
RYAN
David L. 303

S

SALINGER
Kennith 589

SANDERLIN
Charles 670
SANDERS
A. 696
Abraham 608,678
Jas. 597
SANDERSON
Thomas 641
SANDFORD
John W. 256
SANDS
___ 383
SARGEANT [See also SERGANT]
John 738
SASSER
John W. 284,696
SATTERFIED
Margaret 668
SATTERFIELD
Alfred 316,436,518
Frances 181
George B. 315
Henry B. 370,472, 668
Thomas 572
Thos. 518
SAUNDERS
R. M. 529
Romulus M. 529, 656
SAVERN
Isaiah 132
SAWYER
___ 43,157
Caleb 517
Isaac 517
Jas. 517
L. A. 132
Lem'l 132
Lemuel 340,670
Louisa 670
Louisa A. 518,588
M. E. 146,239,603, 670
M. E., Jr. 378
Merriam 588
S. T. 567,627,635, 688,723
Sam'l T. 627
Samuel T. 199,213, 246,518,575,576,591,
Samuel T. 635,696

SCARBOROUGH
Peter 608
SCHOOLFIELD
William M. 107
SCOLFIELD
Wm. M. 147
SCOTT
___ 285,415,675
A. M. 659
Alfred V. 688
J. 66
John 664
Robert 107
SEABURY
___ 245
SEAWELL
___ 664
Gideon 696
Henry 696
SEDGWICK
Henry D. 679
Theodore 679,688
SELBY
William 304,696
SERGANT [See also SARGEANT]
John 734
SETTLE
Benjamin 696
SHANNONHOUSE
Robt. A. 202
Thomas L. 303
SHARKEY
Wm. L. 289
SHARP
___ 626
Elisha H. 38
SHARPE
William 264
SHAW
James 248
Jas. 347
John A., Sr. 161
Thomas 489
SHEPARD
___ 616
Charles 49,651
Charles B. 432
Chas. H. 449
W. B. 130
Wm. 670
Wm. B. 507
SHEPHARD
William B. 614

SHEPHARD
Wm. B. 267
SHEPHERD
Charles B. 259
Sam'l. S. 293
SHEPPARD
Augustine H. 109
SHEPPERD
Augustin H. 614, 630
SHERARD
Gabriel 284,696
SHERBURNE
John S. 388
SHERIDAN
Lewis 328
SHERLY [See also SHIRLEY]
Abigail 187
SHERMAN
___ 66
SHERRARD
Gabriel 397
SHERWOOD
___ 416
Daniel 696
Jas. 132
Margaret 643
Nath'l. 588
SHIPP
Bartlett 314,614
SHIRLEY [See also SHERLY]
Abigail 201
SHORTER
Eli S. 679,688
SHUBRICK
Wm. B. 83
SIDELL
Wm. H. 597
SIKES
Benj. 293
Benjamin 293
SILKMAN
Chas. H. 583
SIMMONS
Benj. 616
Benj. T. 152
Benjamin T. 280, 696
James 284,393
L. R. 397
Luke R. 304,696
SIMONS

SIMONS
  William 246,356
SIMONSON
  Jordan 175
SIMPSON
  Exum 246,436, 572
  Josiah 147
  Pathenia 316
  Philip 132,436
  Phillip 394
  Sam'l. 80
  Samuel 641
  Stephen 367,427, 494
SINGLETON
  Ann 315
  T. D. 688
  Thomas S. 304
  Thos. S. 696
SITGRIOUR
  John 264
SITTERSON
  Chas. 587
  Willis 340,436,453
SKIDMORE
  Lewis 107
SKILES
  William W. 672
SKINNER
  ___ 397,444
  Benjamin S. 653
  Betsey 43
  Charles W. 385, 628,678
  Chas. W. 246,518
  Edmund B. 43
  H. 622
  Harriet 127,315
  Hen. 626
  Henry 96,247,284, 293,355,397,678,696
  J. A. 246
  J. S. 320
  John M. 284,622, 696
  Jos. B. 572,635, 695,698
  Jos. C. 132
  Jos. H. 74,363
  Joseph B. 84,688
  Joseph H. 84,567,
  Joseph H. 571,584, 591,696

SKINNER
  Joshua 518,653
  Josiah 43,246,518
  Lem'l 705
  Lemuel 43,436,518
  Mary 436
  Nancy P. 340
  S. 602
  Sam'l. 518
  Sarah 385
  Stephen 602
SLADE
  Jeremiah 704
SLATER
  Fielding 293
SLAVIS
  Joshua 589
SLOAN
  D. 696
  David 348
  Dickson 304
  John 293
SMALL
  Benj. 518
  Benjamin 246
  Daniel 194,519
  David 43
  Eliza L. 400
  John G. 518
  John H. 194
  Josiah 344,400, 572
  Mary 132
  Rebecca 436
  Reuben 156
  Thomas 270
SMALLWOOD
  ___ 280
  John 152
SMITH
  ___ 615
  Alex. 169
  E. 563
  Fred'k A. 597
  G. B. 320
  J. G. 157,364,412, 515,523,526,582,606, 676
  J. L. 696
  James 225
  Jane 399
  Joel 274
  John 127,315
  John Adams 93

SMITH
  John Aug. 679
  John H. 499
  Lemuel 223
  Mary 127,315
  Mary E. 376
  Miles C. 688
  Nathan 303
  Nathan'l. G. 293
  R. H. 157,364,399, 412,435,515,523, 526,582,606,676
  R. P. 642
  R. W. 376
  Robert H. 127,315
  Robert V. 597
  Sam'l. 91
  Sam'l. F. 688
  Samuel 208
  Thomas 299
  Thos. P. 670
  W. A. 107
  William 597,688
  Wm. R. 132
SNEED
  William M. 51, 696
  Wm. M. 280,397
SNELL
  Silas 437,687
SOULE
  I. 107
SOUTHALL
  Daniel 370
  John W. 489
SOUTHARD
  Samuel L. 165
SOUTHERLAND [See also SUTHERLAND]
  Tho. 437
SOUTHGATE
  J. 250
  W. 250
SPACKMAN
  Sam'l. 688
SPAIGHT [See also SPEIGHT]
  C. 715
  Charles G. 280,639, 696
SPAIGHT
  R. D. 395,397,737

SPAIGHT
  Rich. D. 280
  Richard D. 430
  Rich'd. D. 696
SPANN
  Jas. G. 688
SPARKMAN
  Wm. 266,271,340, 436
SPARKS
  ___ 128
SPARROW
  Susan Jane 553
SPEAR
  ___ 744
SPEARS
  Rebecca G. 96
SPECK
  Henry 107
SPEIGHT [See also SPAIGHT]
  Arthur 696
  Jesse 614,630
  Jessee 189
SPENCE
  A. 41,346,584,681, 726
  Alexander 181
  Robert 670
SPENCER
  ___ 239
  Ambrose 326
  Edward Douglas 663
  H. S. 304
  John 436
  John C. 663
SPIER
  Miles 112
  Robert 112
SPIERS [See also SPEARS]
  Chas. 489
SPIVEY
  Aaron J. 259
SPRUILL
  H. G. 626,696
  Hezekiah G. 293
  S. B. 626
  Samuel 473
SPURGIN
  Joseph 293
STACY
  John 246

STALLINGS
Priscilla 667
Simon 667
W. 622,696
Whitmel 626
Whitmell, Jr. 546
STALLINS
Jesse 445
STAMBAUGH
S. C. 494
STANDLEY
John 568
John W. 568
STANLEY
Edward 651,715
John 518
John C. 328
STANLY
W. 293
STAPLES
Isaac 501
STARR
Jos. 82
T. J. 107
Wm. H. 107
STATE
George 237
STAWNSON
John 517
STEDMAN
Elish. B. 259
Elisha 690
John C. 430,529
John M. 259
Wm. W. 152,267, 293
STEPHEN
Caleb 304
STEPHENS
Caleb 696
Henry 641
STEPHENSON
Rowland 87,326
STEVENS
Jno. A. 688
STEVENSON
Andrew 629
STEWART
G. L. 303
STILWELL
Silas M. 688
STOCKARD
J. 293
STOCKTON

STOCKTON
R. F. 688
William S. 388
STOKES
Montfort 304,429, 450,737
STONE
D. W. 11,401,496, 567,627,635
Salathiel 304
T. G. 723
Thos. G. 395
STORR
John 501
STORROW
S. A. 688
STOVER
Josiah 660
STRANGE
Robert 242
Wm. F. 493
STRONG
Elizabeth 315
STROUGHTEN-BOROUGH
W. 30
SULLIVAN
____ 299
SUMMER
James 641
Seth 641
SUMMERFIELD
____ 30
SUMNER
J. 57,514
Seth 608
SUMNOR
Benjamin A. 696
SURRY
Wm. R. 132
SUTHERLAND [See also SOUTHERLAND]
Joel B. 367
SUTTON
____ 670
Elizabeth 15
Henderson 15
James 15
Jas. 43
Joseph 228
Richard 517
Sam'l 42
William 15

SWAIM
William 187,201
SWAIN
David L. 35,234
SWAN
Benj. L. 688
C. V. 236
John 264
SWANNER
Henry 347
Uriah W. 82,329, 437,519,696
SWETT
Sam'l. 688
SWIFT
Swain 672

T

TABB
John 688
TABER
Charles 340, 631
TALIAFERRO
A. R. 359
TAPPAN
Arthur 388
TARKINTON
Wm. A. 519
TATE
William C. 534
TATHAM
Thomas 696
TATHEM
Thomas 314
TAYLOR
____ 113,463,664
Jno. 688
John 475
John L. 47
John W. 284
Lewis 664
R. B. 633
Robert 664
Robert B. 535
Rob't. 664
W. V. 664
Ward 688
Wm. 507
Wm. D. 514
Wm. P. 688

TAZEWELL
____ 180
John N. 598
TEASDALE
Richard 588
TELFAIR
Alex'r. 688
TERRY
Benj. F. 259
THACHER
H. R. 359
THATCH
Thos. W. 315
THOMAS
Benj. 608
D. L. 215
Isaiah 413
J. M. 696
William 47
Wm. 348
THOMPSON
Benjamin F. 674
G. A. 696
G. M. 436
J. P. 696
James A. 674
John 672
Lewis 616,696
Thomas 33
THOMSON
David 696
John R. 688
THORNTON
James B. 208
THORP
George 127,315
Sally 315
Sarah 127
Sarah A. 588
TIBBITTS
____ 285
TIDYMAN
Philip 688
TIERNAN
Luke 91
TILLETT
Durant 469,471
TIMBERLAKE
____ 53
TOMKINS
Frances 585
TOMLINSON
Gideon 198
TOMPKINS

TOMPKINS
  Samuel D. 107
TOMS
  Francis 244,400,477
  Louisa 244
  Nathan 348,445
TOOLE
  Henry 696
TOOMER
  John D. 696
TOPPING
  Mary 739
TORRANS
  Catharine 399
TOWNES
  Wm. 688
TOWNSEND
  ____ 622
  J. 696
  J. W. 628
  Jos. W. 626
  Joseph W. 68,628
TOXEY
  Joseph 519
TOY
  Daniel 132
TRADER
  Wm. 489
TRAPIER
  Paul 552
TRAVIS
  ____ 633,647
TREDWELL
  ____ 303
  Benjamin 245
  Frances P. 246,340
  J. I. 10,190
  Ja. I. 221
  James I. 518,641
  Jas. I. 436
  Sam'l. 518
TRENT
  William H. 534
TRIMBLE
  Geo. T. 688
TROTT
  James 674
TROUP
  G. M. 76
TROY
  Wm. E. 440
TRUE
  Henry 248,347

TUCKER
  Gideon 688
TUDOR
  Elihu 552
TUMNER
  Mary 246
TURNER
  Alfred A. 188,607
  Martha 109
  Mary 109
  Susan 188,607
  Thomas 338
  Thos. 90
  Thos. H. 437
  W. A. 82,519
  Wm. A. 90,147, 248,347,437,589, 650,672
TYLER
  Jane W. 308
  John 308
TYSON
  Josiah 696

U

UNDERHILL
  Joseph 337
UNDERWOOD
  David 696
UPHAM
  Timothy 76
UPSHER
  Littleton 688
USHER
  ____ 657
UZZLE
  Elisha 284

V

VADIN
  Joseph M. 436
VAIL
  A. N. 589
  Aaron 617
  Abner N. 437,519
  Catharine 316
  Thos. 316
VAN BRUNT

VAN BRUNT
  J. G. 359
VAN BUREN
  ____ 191
  Martin 617
VAN DYCK
  J. C. 688
VAN NESS
  Cornelius P. 93
  John P. 226
VAN SCHAYCH
  Wm. 588
VANHOOK
  Robert 293,397,696
VANN
  John 475
VASS
  Phillip P. 390
VAUGHAN
  ____ 633,647
  Henry B. 647
VENABLE
  Sam'l. L. 688
VERAL
  Lewis 519
VERMULE
  Cornelius 259
VERNELSON
  Samuel 589
VETHAKE
  Henry 679,688
VEZZEN
  Wm. 43
VICK
  S. W. W. 280
VINAL
  Levi 589
  Lewis 589
VOLAVER
  Asa 519

W

WADDEL
  William 293
WADSWORTH
  William 293
  Wm. 696
WAFF [See also WARFF]
  Emeline 127,315
  George 695

WAFF
  Sarah 315
  Sarah L. 518
  Thos. 325
WAINWRIGHT
  ____ 633
WAIT
  ____ 132
WALKER
  ____ 225
  David 328
  Jordan 498,519
  Ranson 280
  Taylor H. 147,347
  Thomas 47,474,498
WALL
  Elizabeth A. 47
  Ezekiel H. 47
WALLACE
  Horatio 362
  Rufus A. 534
WALLER
  Wm. J. 107
WALLERS [See also WALTERS]
  Levi 633
WALLIS
  Shadrach 517
WALMSLEY
  Thomas 503
WALTERS [See also WATERS]
  Levi 633
WALTERSTON
  George 76
WALTON
  Nancy 386
  William 152,199, 213,662
  Wm. 132,144,246, 265,366,375,386,518, 571,572,591,600,720
WANER
  Benjamin 248
WARD
  Edward 47,293,397
  Francis 147
  Geo. W. 597
  Thomas 314,678
  William 152
WARFF [See also WAFF]
  Sally 246
WARING

WARING
Arthur 328
WARNIER
D. 588
D. S. 246,340
WARREN
Henry 529
WARRINGTON
___ 633
WASHINGTON
___ 35,578,584
James 57
WATCHMAN
Anthony 589
WATERS [See also WALTERS]
D., Jr. 107
Francis 388
P. 688
Sally 589
WATFORD
William 303
WATKINS
Henry E. 688
Tobias 92
WATMOUGH
John G. 367
WATSON
___ 147
Alexander 696
George 463
Gideon 725
Henry R. 688
Jno. W. 107
R. C. 624
Reddick 437
Robert C. 624
Wm. 478
WATTS
___ 660
Thomas W. 84
Thos. D. 293
William 293
WEATHERLY
Henry 107
WEAVER
Amos 293,397, 427,696
James 314
WEBB
James M. 314,696
John 410,490
Thos. V. 107
Zechariah 377

WEBBER
Richard W. 289
WEBSTER
___ 116,162
Daniel 91,351
Jno. A. 398
John A. 184
WEIRICH
Christian 233
WELCH
Andrew 47
John 72,227
Lavinia 72
Margaret 588
Miles 514,572,739
Myles 649
William 397
Wm. 321,670
WELLER
Sidney 117
WESCOTT
Hampton 153
WESKETT
Sam 147
WESSON
James 517
WEST
Emanuel J. 154
Jas. C. 34
WESTON
Thomas 518,670
WHEATON
___ 208
WHEDBEE
James 641
WHEELER
___ 616
John F. 674
John H. 84,168,269, 284,430,489,507,510, 614
Thos. B. 723
WHIDBEE
Addison 247
James 684
James P. 348
Jas. P. 517,608
Richard 246
Rich'd H. 436
WHIPPLE
Sarah 246,340
WHITAKER
James 314
Jas., Sr. 696

WHITAKER
Willis 529,656
WHITE
___ 301,304,409
Alexander W. 588
Andrew 97
Benj. 698
Benjamin 340
Catharine 670
Cornelia 589
David 348,424
Edmund 244,628
George 518,588
George, Sr. 670
Hugh L. 579
James 264
John 445,588
John W. 107
Jos. D. 624,688
Luke 369
Martha 97
Peter 720
Philo 235
Solomon B. 347, 437,589
WHITEHEAD
Catharine 633
Foster 247
Williamson 382
WHITFIELD
Nathan B. 431
WHITING
H. 132
WHITLEY
Kedar 284
WHITTLESEY
___ 100
WICKER
John 348
WIGGINS
Jas. M. 729
Mason L. 242
WILDER
Frances 340
Hillary 284
Martha 355
Mary 340,631
Miles 247
Nathaniel 43,631
Richard 88
Rich'd 43,132,246
Sampson 641
Sarah 6
Thomas 6

WILEY [See also WILLEY]
Philip B. 547, 594
WILKERSON
Wm. W. 518
WILKIN
___ 54
WILKINGS
Edward W. 382
WILKINS
Anderson 529
James C. 289
WILKINSON
Luke 147
Thos. 147
W. 688
WILLETT
Marinus 306
WILLEY [See also WILEY, WILLIE]
John 293
P. B. 739
WILLIAMS
___ 54,104,264, 280,452,633
Absalom 47
David 636
H. G. 280
Henry 688
Isaac 436,678
J. J. 397
Jacob 633
James 334
John 112,519
John M. 589
Jonathan 107
Jos. J. 397
Joseph J. 291,293
Lewis 91,614,630
Nathaniel F. 91
Thomas P. 410
Thos., Jr. 688
W. P. 280
William 87,588
Wm. P. 397,696
Wright 399,410
WILLIAMSON
George 293
Hugh 264
Joshua 304
WILLIE [See also WILLEY]
John 626

WILLIE
Lewis K. 664
WILLS
___ 4,60
Henry 438
James 26,85,99,142, 277,410
Jas. 358,371
Sarah M. 410
WILSON
___ 233,348,622
Alden 248
Ann W. 155
Charles 164
Elizabeth 139
George 243
Hugh 688
J. 445
Joshua 463
Louis D. 280,397, 688,696
T. 696
Thomas 236,247, 293
Thos. 167,284,626
Turner 246
Willis 303
Wm. 139
WINBOURNE
Stephen W. 107
WINCHELL
Alfred 480
WINCHESTER
___ 494
Geo. 427
WINDER
John H. 410
WINGATE
Edward 588
WINSLOW
John 259
Nathan 348,368
WINSTON
___ 66
Joseph 696
Joseph W. 304
WINTHRAWP
Charles Archibald 445
WIRT
Wm. 734
WISEMAN
J. 588

WISEMAN
William W. 293
WITCHER
Toliver 696
WIXEN
James
WOOD
___ 465
Abagail 670
David 107
Edward 422
Elizabeth 109,422, 528
H. 246
James 229
Jno. E. 678
John 744
John E. 247,348, 584,628,688
John S. 238
Jordan M. 670
Jos. H. 284
Newton 529
Richard 340
Rich'd 518
Rich'd. 109
WOODALL
Absalom P. 529
WOODARD
John M. 43
WOODLEY
John 347
WOODWARD
John M. 517
WOOTEN
Allen W. 284,696
Councel 284
Shadrac 696
WORCESTER
Samuel A. 674,734
WORMELEY
J. S. 250
WORTH
___ 633
Jonathan 293,696
WRIGHT
___ 285,293,657
Bryant 657
Fanny 92
Frances 120,173
Huldah G. 246
Humphrey 436,720
Jordan A. 84
Mary T. 309

WRIGHT
Miles 239
Minton 356
Nathaniel 356
Nathaniel D. 309
W. 696
William 259
Wm. 304
Wm. J. 696
WYATT
Richard 40
WYCHE
James 696
Jas. 280
WYNN
James D. 475
William 662
WYNNE
Benj. 518,670
Benjamin 436,588
Jeremiah 161
WYNNS
Benj. 436,699
Benjamin 248
James D. 303
William 303
William B. 62

X

None

Y

YANCEY
Bartlett 707
Charles 688
YEOMANS
Jane 324
William T., Jr. 530
YORKE
Peter 724
Sarah 724
YOUNG
Elizabeth 670
Henry C. 688
J. P. 340
YOUNGE
Mary 589

Z

ZEIGLAR
Leonard 304
ZIGLAR
Leonard 696

MISCELLANEOUS INDEX

AGRICULTURE
Board of 450
Grape vine 535
Livestock 448
Peas 404
Pumpkin 381,451
Radishes 396
Rice, introduction of 299
ALMANACK
1831, for 425
Farmer's 413
ANIMALS
Rhinoceros 214
APPRENTICES
JONES, John M. 687
PRICE, Josiah 705
ARMY
___ 101,597
U. S. 4,60,182,410
United States 237
CANAL BOAT
Experiment 478
Favorite 41
CASTRATION
664
CENSUS
1830 152,375
CLERK & MASTER
BOZMAN, Jas. 194,379
James 15
HOSKINS, R. T. 695
CLERK OF COURT
CHESSON, William L. 338
COWPER, L. M. 38,39
HOSKINS, Edm. 720
MOORE, Lem. C. 607
Lemuel C. 188,607
NORCOM, J. C. 583,669
Jos. C. 574
Joseph C. 574,669
SUMNER, J. 57,514
TURNER, Thomas 338
WOOD, John 744
COMMISSIONERS
Town
BRUER, Nath'l. 160
CHARLTON, Thos. J. 160
HAUGHTON, Mal. 160
COMPANIES
Amos PALMER & 303
BAGLEY & ELLIOTT 436, 445

COMPANIES
BROWNRIGG & REID 132
BRYAN & MULLEN 445
Cape Fear Navigation 234
CORNELL's, Messrs. 603
E. P. NASH & 462
J. Irvine HITCHCOCK & 320
J. & J. BRYAN 58
J. &. W. SOUTHGATE 250
J. C. & W. R. NORCOM 466
J. GALES & Son 372
John WHITE & 588
JONES & CRAIG 235
JONES & WATSON 147
MASON & MASSIN 374
Michael LEE & 17
MORGAN & COWPER 296,297
MORGAN COWPER & 64, 297
MULLEN & WILSON 348
N. & B. HART 69
P. CORNELL & Bros. 561
PARKER & GRANBERRY 132
PLATT & FAULKNER 30
Plymouth Turnpike 574
R. H. & J. G. SMITH 157, 364,412,515,523,526,582,606, 676
R. T. HOSKINS & 733
SAWYER & CLEVELAND 43,157
SPEAR & PATTEN 744
Thos. & Wm. A. TURNER 90
Thos. FULLER & 158
Virginia and North Carolina Transportation 79
Wm. DOUGLASS & 669
Wm. M'KENNEY & 157, 200
CONFERENCE
Methodist 107
CONSTABLES
GRIMES, William 491
JONES, H. D. 743
WRIGHT, Humphrey 720
CONVENTION
Free Trade/Anti-Tariff 624,

CONVENTION
627,628,635,656,679,682,688
Methodist 388
National Republican 738
Protestant Episcopal Church 564
State 601
CORONER
HATHAWAY, T. V. 327
COURT
Martial 101,504
DEATHS
5,7,48,59,61,67,72,81,89,
97,102,106,110,114,118,131,
149,153,154,156,164,165,169,
176,203,210,215,218,223,228,
245,257,276,281,290,298,306,
309,318,322,327,331,342,345,
352,354,356,362,370,377,383,
386,390,391,394,400,405,409,
415,417,421,423,428,433,442,
454,460,464,467,469,471,474,
476,481,486,487,491,492,495,
502,520,522,531,533,536,541,
542,552,557,558,573,585,587,
593,611,612,620,625,632,633,
636,637,639,653,657,659,660,
661,663,668,684,692,702,712,
714,718,725,732,740
DEBT
Imprisonment for 261,351
DECLARATION
independence, of 326
DISEASES
[Stroke] 239
Gravel 279
Small Pox 36,76,86,469
Varioloid 86
DIVORCE
188,607
ENGINE
Steam 650
FIRES
3,30,48,59,69,129,160,209,
285,420,447,463,508,562,566,
567,568,572,578,697
HOLIDAY
Christmas 419,736
HUNTING
546
INDIANS
197

INDIANS
  Cherokee 47,76,674
  Creek 182
  hostile 615
  Memoninee 494
  Southern 162
  Tuscarora 47
INSURRECTION
  633,634,640,647,657,666
JUDGES
  BALDWIN, Henry 35
  BARBOUR, Philip P. 350
  BETTS, ____ 503
  GOODENOW, ____ 198
  J. M. 92
  HARVEY, Matthew 388
  HAY, George 350
  HAYWARD, Elijah 92
  HOLT, ____ 87
  MARTIN, James, Jr. 301
  MORFITT, H. M. 83
  NORWOOD, ____ 353
  PARKER, R. E. 535
  PEASE, Calvin 198
  RUFFIAN, ____ 49
  RUFFIN, Thomas 624,635
  SHERBURNE, John S. 388
  TAYLOR, ____ 463
  R. B. 633
  Robert B. 535
  WASHINGTON, ____ 35
  WHITE, Hugh L. 579
  WILKINS, ____ 54
  WILLIAMS, ____ 54
JUSTICES
  CHARLTON, T. I. 582
  ELLIOTT, Ephraim 495
  FOWLER, Jos. S. 236
  MARSHALL, John 584
  WALTON, Wm. 720
LIGHT BOAT 487
LODGES, MASONIC
  Albemarle, No. 77 517
  Grand 430
  Grand Chapter of North Carolina 242
  Grand Royal Arch Chapter, United States, of the 150
  R. A. Chapter, United States, of the 172
  Unanimity, No. 54 10,221, 418,559,565,576,693,713
LONGEVITY
  106,123,176,245,261,306

LONGEVITY
  307,326,499,636
MACHINES
  Cotton Cleaner 148
  Cotton Gin 697
  Steam Engine 650
  Washing 745
MANUFACTORY
  Boot and shoe 146,240
MARSHAL
  District of North Carolina 152
  HARRIS, Samuel D., of Massachusetts 116
MENAGERIE 77
MILITIA
  13TH Brigade of North Carolina 4
  Chowan 333
  Chowan Guards 681,726
  Edenton Guards 346
  Green hall District 211,560
  Independent Volunteers 633
  Norfolk Junior volunteers 633
  Richmond Troop of Cavalry 647
  Tyrrell Regiment 403
MARRIAGES
  6,62,71,88,96,105,109,139, 155,168,175,181,187,201,202, 227,237,238,244,256,275,294, 298,308,316,330,341,344,355, 361,369,376,385,393,399,410, 416,422,432,453,459,475,480, 490,499,530,553,585,586,594, 619,631,638,643,662,667,691, 701,717,724,731,739
NAVY
  2,206,235,359
  U. S. 153,208,569
NEWSPAPERS
  Alexandria Gazette 326
  American Farmer 320
  BADGER's Weekly Messenger 650
  Balt. Gaz. 167
  Baltimore American 660
  Baltimore Patriot 661
  Banner of the Constitution 335
  Boston Bulletin 191
  Boston Manufacturer 351
  Boston Pat. 298

NEWSPAPERS
  Cape Fear Recorder 285
  Carolina Sentinel 204,446
  Carolina Watchman, The 710
  Ch. Cour. 87
  change of issue day 500
  Charleston City Gazette 198
  Charleston Courier 113
  Chas. Courier 148
  Cherokee Phenix 76
  Christian Advocate and Journal 563
  Cin. Amer. 217
  Cincinnati American 388
  Columbian Gazette 94
  Compiler 107
  Daily Journal 427
  Eliz. City Star 547
  Elizabeth City Star 149,594
  Fayetteville Journal 328,618
  Fayetteville Observer 78
  Frederick (Md.) Examiner 552
  Fredericksburg Arena 178
  Freeman's Echo 108
  Globe 680
  The 427
  Greensboro' Patriot 201
  Greensborough Patriot 187
  Halifax Minerva [Roanoke Advocate] 115
  Hartford Times 165
  Liberator, the 683
  Louisville Daily Journal 326
  Louisville Public Advertiser 61
  Lynchburg Virginian 599, 708
  Mer. Adv. 503
  Mercury 224
  Middlesex Gazette 406
  Milton Gazette 164,390
  Milton Spectator 707,710
  Mobile Register 182
  N. Carolina Journal 380
  N. Y. Com. Adv. 223
  N. Y. Cour. 183
  N. Y. Journal of Commerce 712
  N. Y. Mer. 499
  N. Y. Mercantile Advertiser 154
  Nat. Int. 205,216

NEWSPAPERS
Nat. Intel. 185
Nat. Intelligencer 367
National Intelligencer 61, 101,104,150,172,301
National Journal 76,121
New Orleans Bee 69
New York Commercial 255
New York Commercial advertiser 326
New York Evening Post 679
New York Mercantile 609
New York Morn. Her. 245
Newbern Spectator 86,201, 210,236,343,410,415,562,657
Nor. Her. 66
Norfolk Beacon 79,359,467, 533,562
Norfolk Herald 279,283,544
North American Review 128
North Carolina Constitutionalist, And State Rights' Advocate 570
North Carolina Journal 493
North Carolina Miscellany 736,742
Observer 657
Old Dominion 179
Oxford Examiner 664
Paul Pry 711
People's Free Press, The 34
Petersburg Intelligencer 283
Petersburg Times 317
Philadelphia Gazette 173, 679,682,688
Philadelphia National Gazette 131
Phoenix 674
Port. Courier 615
Portsmouth Journal 2
Ral. Reg. 299
Ralegh Star 189
Raleigh Reg, 447
Raleigh Register 33,307, 372,630,722
Raleigh Star 32,50,283, 657
Register 391
Reporter 116
Richmond Compiler 178
Richmond Enquirer 579, 648
Richmond Whig 209,392, 647

NEWSPAPERS
Rights of All 328,343
Roanoke Advocate [Halifax Minerva] 115
Royal Gazette 501
Savannah Georgian 734
Savannah Republican 87
Southern Review 538
St. Louis Times 661
Tarboro' F. Press 548
Tarborough Free Press 128, 614
Telegraph 100
U. S. Telegraph 53,93,305, 367,452
Union, The 461
United States Telegraph 189
Washington Globe 579
Washington Times [Freeman's Echo] 108
Western Carolinian 166,235, 301
Wheeling Gazette 233
Wilmington Recorder 328
Wilmington Reporter 69,76
Windsor Herald 710
Zion's Herald 563

OCCUPATIONS
Attorney 223,433,482,664
Blacksmith 42,124
Booksellers 462
Boot and shoe maker 240
Bootmaker 146
Carpenter 428
Clock and Watchmaker 44
Constable 491,720,743
Counsellor at law 30
Dentist 511,709
Editor 128,187,204,285,320, 326,426,530,538,594,710
Entry taker 463
Farmer 7
Grocer 30
Jailor 491
Laborer 239
Merchant 11,105,110,238, 433
 Commission 673
 Tailor 30
Music, Professor of 251
Physician 239,245,378,444, 534,659
Printer 1,30
Saddler 325

OCCUPATIONS
Shoemaker 325,687
Stationers 462
Surveyor 463
Tailor 20
Teacher 283
Watch maker and jeweller 30
Wire manufacturer 30

POSTMASTERS
BRUER, N. 43,132,246,340, 436,518,588,670
BURBAGE, J. R. 445,517, 608,678
DE LA RUA, John 198
ELLIOTT, Ephraim 495
FITZGERALD, John 198
JONES, Walter F. 405
JORDAN, Matthew 604
M'CONNICO, A. J. 405
 Andrew J. 400
MEIGS, Return Jonathan 615
MUNROE, Thomas 339
TURNER, W. A. 82,519
TURNER, Wm. A. 147,248, 347,437,589,672
WEBB, John 410
WEIRICH, Christian 233
WELLER, Sidney 117
WOOD, John E. 247,348

RACE
Horse 698

RANGER
CARTER, Perry 311

RECORDS
Burned, Hertford Co. 129

REFINERY
Steam sugar 215

REGISTER
GARDINER, J. B., of Land Office, Tiflin, Ohio 185
LITTLEJOHN, J. W., of U. S. Court of Admiralty 125, 126
MOFFATT, James 7

SHERIFFS
ALLEN, John M. 304
ARCHIBALD, William H. 293
BALLENGER, Allen S. 284
BARNETT, J. 293
BAXTER, Isaac 280
BELL, B. W. 314
BLACK, John 47,293

SHERIFFS
BLACKMAN, Calvin R. 284
BOND, Lewis 280
BRIDGES, H. D. 293
BUTLER, William C. 304
CAIN, Samuel 304
CALDWELL, Hiram 293
CARSON, William 314
CHESSON, William M. 329
  Wm. M. 641
CLANTON, Wm. C. 280
CLARK, Elijah 303
  J. S. 273
COLE, James C. 280
COOPER, Rich'd. M. 284
CRAWFORD, Wm. 293
DAVENPORT, Walter 284
DENNIE, James [Dep.] 116
DOAK, James W. 293
FONVIELLE, Bryce 293
FULFORD, Absalom 284
GAMBILL, John C. 314
GILLIAM, L. 280
GRIST, Allen 112
HAMPTON, William 304
HARRISON, Nathaniel 314
HILL, James K. 304
HOLMES, G. 293
HOOVER, Geo. 293
HUGGINS, Wm. 284
KENNEDAY, William 293
LAMB, Luke G. 284
LONG, James 284,355
MANN, E. 293
MEDLEY, C. J. 304
M'KEE, James 47,321
M'NEILL, Daniel 293
MORISEY, Thomas K. 304
OWENS, Stephen 284
PARKER, John 280
POOL, Josh. A. 284
RASCOE, William D. 246
  Wm. D. 65,163,266,286, 554
RIDDICK, James R. 293
ROBERTS, Martin 304
SHEPHERD, Sam'l. S. 293
SIMMONS, James 284
SLATER, Fielding 293
SLOAN, John 293
SPENCER, H. S. 304
STONE, Salathiel 304
TAYLOR, John W. 284

SHERIFFS
VICK, S. W. W. 280
WARD, Thomas 314
WATTS, Thos. D. 293
WILLIAMS, H. G. 280
WILLIAMSON, George 293
  Joshua 304
WOOD, Jos. H. 284
WRIGHT, ____ 293

SOCIETY
Bible, North American 161
  State 427
  Tyrrell 161
Missionary
  Basle, Switzerland, of 66
  Edenton 434
  Gates Circuit 563
Vance Circulating Library 47

STEAMBOATS
Constitution 633
Hampton 633
N. Carolina 79

UNION
the 2

WAR/REVOLUTION
100,149,156,176,306,615, 636
last 237
late 51

WATCHERS
Town 555

WEATHER
272,415,468,540,568,592, 652,660

WHEEL
Spiral 47

LOCATION INDEX

ACADEMY [See also COLLEGES, SCHOOLS, UNIVERSITY]
the [Edenton] 379
Brinkleyville 117
Edenton 127,315,435
Hyde Park Female 231
Lavallee 63
Oxford Male 729
West Point 597,647
Williamsboro' Female 456

AMERICA
Danish 127
North 127
South 127

ARMORY
HARPER's Ferry, at 92

BANKS
___ 107
North 541

BAY
Chesapeake 70

BRIDGE
BALLADs 649
BALLARD's 283,495
BOULTON's 532
NEWBY's 424

CANAL
cross 47
D. S. 425
Dismal Swamp 13,200,236
Great 47
North Carolina 312
Ohio and Chesapeake 70
Virginia 312

CAPE
the 66,258
Fear 234,285

CAPITOL
___ 601

CHURCH
BALLADs Bridge 649
Baptist 7,218,276,576,584, 620
Christ 63,138,564
Christ's 400,547
Episcopal 562,578
of North Carolina 118
Lebanon 267
M. E. 220,295,505,553
Methodist 434,562
Associated 388

CHURCH
E. 576
Episcopal 2,263,308,481,
Methodist Episcopal 619,708,725
Monumental 186
Presbyterian 562
Protestant Episcopal 207, 331,552,564,577
St. James 339
St. John's 547
St. Luke's 564
St. Stephen's 464
Trinity 138

CITIES
Baltimore 36,91,102,167, 172,215,272,298,320,332, 388,427,536,551,660,661, 738
Boston 116,125,159,191, 205,237,252,274,298,328, 351,427,683
Charleston 113,128,148, 154,198,224,225,319,469, 538,552,603,617,689
Cincinnati 92,388
Cincinnatti 185
Louisville 61,326
Mobile 182
New Orleans 69,92,120, 328,501,652,735
New York 20,22,23,26,30, 36,54,55,93,95,99,106,121, 122,142,143,145,154,157, 161,170,177,183,185,192, 208,219,223,245,255,258, 272,277,278,288,306,326, 335,349,357,358,360,365, 383,387,412,415,421,427, 438,446,464,483,484,499, 501,523,525,543,564,590, 593,597,609,645,654,659, 676,677,679,685,686,694, 712,727,730,741
Norfolk 13,34,41,66,69,73, 75,79,107,109,114,140,187, 200,206,220,250,279,283, 359,400,405,462,467,479, 487,524,533,535,544,545, 562,603,633,647,673,745
Philadelphia 61,92,93,128,

CITIES
Philadelphia 131,153,157,165,173,200, 216,258,272,279,335,339, 357,360,411,427,446,504, 577,624,627,628,635,642, 656,679,682,688,712,724
Pittsburg 54,233
Portsmouth 2,40
Portsmouth (NH) 76
Portsmouth (VA) 107,200
Raleigh 32,33,50,85,105, 107,118,154,186,189,207, 242,251,283,299,307,360, 372,382,391,395,417,427, 430,447,488,529,564,570, 578,601,630,656-658,683, 690,722,723
Richmond 66,107,167,178, 186,209,255,342,392,547, 579,580,647,648,675,745
Rochester 128
Savannah 87,326,734
Trenton (NJ) 36
Washington 4,51,53,54,61, 76,83,93,109,116,150,159, 168,169,172,209,226,298, 339,369,370,409,427,492, 548,579,711

COLLEGES [See also ACADEMY,SCHOOLS, UNIVERSITY]
Dickinson 360
Geneva 138
Randolph Macon 708
South Carolina Medical 534
Washington 464,708
Washington, Hartford, Conn. 339
Wesleyan 326
William and Mary 259

COLONY
African 66

CORNFIELD
PARKER's 647

COUNTIES
Amelia (VA) 107
Amherst (VA) 107
Anson 304,463,641,696
Ashe 314,696
Beaufort 107,112,280,284,

155

COUNTIES

Beaufort 641,696
Bedford (VA) 84,107
Bertie 84,88,107,152,259, 275,280,291,303,369,410,
Bertie 414,429,473,490,491,612, 616,624,635,641,665,691, 696,710,745
Bladen 304,549,657,696
Botetourt (VA) 84
Brunswick 338,539,696
Brunswick (VA) 84,107
Buckingham (VA) 107
Buncombe 47,49,314,696
Burke 47,303,304,696
Cabarrus 293,696
Camden 47,84,125,152, 284,303,507,510,556,622, 696,739,745
Campbell (VA) 84,107
Caroline (VA) 107
Carteret 33,284,696
Caswell 84,107,259,293, 594,696,707
Charlotte (VA) 84
Chatham 137,293,696
Chesterfield (VA) 107
Chowan 15,28,42,45,65,74, 84,119,124,133,134,144,152, 194,199,211-213,232,239, 246,265,270,275,283,303, 333,334,337,366,375,379, 430,436,472,497,507,509, 510,512,518,532,550,554, 572,582,584,595,602,621, 635,641,649,653,670,671, 681,695,696,705,720,726, 745
Columbus 47,304,696
Craven 280,303,395,430, 601,696
Culpeper (VA) 107
Cumberland 47,293,641, 657,696
Currituck 84,112,152,155, 280,303,471,507,510,541, 616,696,739,745
Davidson 47,293,463,696
Dinwiddie (VA) 383
Dorchester (MD) 236
Duplin 304,657,696
Edgecombe 84,280,696

COUNTIES

Edgefield (SC) 61
Franklin 47,84,107,280, 680,696
Franklin (VA) 84
Fredrick (VA) 637
Gates 47,57,68,84,107,152, 267,275,293,309,341,353, 403,422,454,459,463,475, 507,510,514,541,545,546, 563,620,622,626,667,696, 717,745
Glocester (VA) 107
Granville 51,84,107,280, 456,664,680,696
Grayson (VA) 84
Green 284
Greene 696
Greensville (VA) 84,107
Guilford 61,84,107,293, 427,696
Gwinnett (GA) 674,734
Halifax 14,84,107,117,231, 254,263,284,291,393,641, 696,725,745
Halifax (VA) 84,390
Hanover (VA) 107
Hardin (KY) 260
Haywood 47,234,321,696
Hertford 38,39,50,62,84, 111,114,129,152,257,269, 284,303,311,353,430,475, 507,508,510,566,616,620, 622,626,662,696,745
Hyde 304,696,731
Iredell 107,259,293,696
Isle of Wight (VA) 84,648
Jackson (AL) 521
Jackson (FL) 96
Johnson 284
Johnston 307,696
Jones 284,657,696
Lenoir 284,657,696,723
Lincoln 47,314,414,696
Loudon (VA) 66,92,354
Lunenburg (VA) 84
Macon 47,314,696
Martin 84,152,291,293, 696,745
Mecklenburg 47,259,293, 395,696
Mecklenburg (VA) 84,107, 708
Montgomery 304,696

COUNTIES

Montgomery (VA) 84
Moore 293,696
Nansemond (VA) 84,467, 647,648
Nash 84,280,680,696
New Hanover 293,657,696
Norfolk (VA) 155,739
North 415
Northampton 84,284,303, 317,459,696,717,745
Nottaway (VA) 84
Oneida (NY) 222
Onslow 47,293,696
Orange 84,259,293,656,696
Orange (VA) 107,389
Pasquotank 49,84,119,139, 152,188,203,284,292,303, 310,449,507,510,607,622, 653,696,745
Patrick Henry (VA) 84
Perquimans 6,42,68,84,96, 97,149,152,175,202,203,229, 236,244,275,284,290,293, 300,302,313,355,368,377, 385,394,397,400,424,442, 465,477,490,507,510,604, 622,625,626,628,631,641, 653,678,684,696,701,739, 744,745
Person 84,259,293,656, 696
Pitt 112,210,273,451,696
Pittsylvania (VA) 84,164, 259
Princess Ann (VA) 416
Princess Anne (VA) 107
Randolph 293,696
Richmond 293,696
Robeson 293,696
Rockingham 84,259,304, 696
Rowan 47,166,293,395, 696,723
Rutherford 314,696
Sampson 304,657,696
Schoharie (NY) 636
South Hampton (VA) 640
Southampton (VA) 84,633, 640,647,648,666,675
Steuben (NY) 585
Stokes 84,304,696
Suffolk (Long Is., NY) 499
Suffolk (MA) 116

COUNTIES
  Sumner (TN) 217
  Surry 47,84,107,293,696
  Sussex (VA) 84,107,647
  Tyrrel 229
  Tyrrell 84,152,161,245, 293,403,473,626,696,745
  upper 415
  Wake 47,84,303,396,529, 601,656,683,696
  Warren 84,193,263,280, 680,696
  Washington 52,84,107,152, 229,259,303,329,338,399, 411,474,498,574,583,603, 638,641,657,669,687,696, 714,745
  Washington (VA) 84
  Wayne 284,657,696
  Wilkes 304,429,696
  Wythe (VA) 84
COUNTRY
  Cherokee 674
  western 326
COURT HOUSE
  Columbia, in 161
  Dinwiddie 383
  Edenton 98
    in 124,126,194,695
  Edgefield (SC) 61
  Elizabeth City, in 607
  Gates 705
    in 57
  Gatesville, in 514
  Hertford 269
    in 628
  Onslow 47
  Plymouth, in 574,583
  Raleigh, in 529,656
  Windsor, at 624
  Winton, at 111,129
CREEK
  ADAMS' 236
  ANDERSON's 135
  Machimacomic 532
  NAUMAN's 131
  Old Plantation 236
DISTRICT
  Alabama 679
  Albemarle 125,126
  Camden 125
  Columbia, of 94,501,597
  Darlington 486
  Edenton 111

DISTRICT
  Florida, Middle, of 689
  Green Hall 211,560
  Greenville (SC) 148
  Halifax 291
  James River 107
  Louisiana, lower, of 237
  Maryland, of 458
  Meherrin 107
  Mississippi 679
  Neuse 107
  New Hampshire 388
  New York, Southern, of 503
  Norfolk 107,140,220,295
  North Carolina 125,126, 152,154
  Passamaquoddy (ME) 305
  Pendleton (SC) 502
  Pennsylvania, Western, of 384
  Rhode Island, of 93
  Roanoke 107
  South Carolina 617
  Tennessee 679
  Virginia 350
  Wilmington 427,549,722
  Yadkin 107
FERRY
  DUNMAS' 463
  HARPER's 92
FISHERY
  COFFIELD's, James 535
  JOHNSON, C. E., of 520
FORD
  Shallow 107
FOREIGN
  Abaco Island 501
  Algiers 94,121
  Asia 127
  Aux Cayes 660
  Bahama 699
  Barbadoes 501
  Basle 66
  Brazil 75,383
  Britain, United Kingdom of Great 93,617
  Calcutta 214
  Chili 154
  Columbia 93
  Constantinople 494
  Copenhagen 208
  Cruz, La Vera, Mexico 507
  Denmark 205

FOREIGN
  England 61,127,299
  Europe 70,127,552
  France 93,388,427
  Gaul 127
  Hamburg 388
  Hog Island 501
  Ireland 93,107,617
  Jacmel 660
  Jeremie 660
  Liverpool 208,552
  London 326,680
  Madagascar 299
  Madeira 64
  Mexico 224,407,507
  Monrovia 66
  Nassau 501
  Navarre 93
  Netherlands, the 93,689
  Paris 388
  Port au Prince 120,173,660
  Porto Rico 125
  Rio Janeiro 154
  Russia 208,216,680
  Scotland 6
  Spain 128,494
  St. Domingo 92
  St. Jago De Cuba 660
  St. Petersburgh 458
  Switzerland 66
  Thermophylae 209
  Turks Island 125,501,699
  West Indies 359
    British 699
FORT
  Macon 33
  Monroe 633
HAMPTON ROADS 75,208,633
HEAD
  Naggs 84
HILL
  Shockoe 107
HOTEL
  BARNUM's 298
  Carolina and Virginia 40
  Hygeia 258,287
  Lafayette 234
  Lake Drummond 13,294
  Mansion House 37
  Planter's Inn 443
HOUSE
  Boarding 581
  Government 723

HOUSE
State [Capitol] 578
Light, at the South entrance of Roanoke Marshes 623
Meeting, EVANS' 572,602
Philadelphia 563
Entertainment, of ____ 545
BRICKELL's Tavern 478
Carolina and Virginia Hotel 40
Refuge, of 312
Mansion House 37
Rising Sun Tavern 478
WOOD's Tavern 465
INLET
New 236
Ocracock 184
Roanoke 84,130,267,584
Topsail 107
INN
Planter's, The 443
INSTITUTE
Columbian 191
ISLANDS
____ 107
Long 245,499
SULLIVAN's 299
KEY
Spanish 501
LAKE
Drummond 13,294
Mattamuskeet 107
Ponchartrain 652
LAND
Coffee House 411
Tuscarora 47
LIGHTHOUSE
at the South entrance of Roanoke Marshes 623
LINE
N. Carolina 13
North Carolina 294,312
Virginia 13,294,312
MARSH
Roanoke 236,623
White Oak Spring 47
MILLS
HORRY, Elias, of 113
MINES
Gold 121
NECK
DURANTs 631
Old 604
Scotland 229

OCEAN
the 84
Atlantic 712
PLANTATION
Belvedier 424
Hayes 428
Sandy Point 15
POINT
the 633
Ocracock 415
Old, Comfort 258,287
Sandy 15
Washington 739
POWDER WORKS
ROGERS, Daniel 552
RIVER
Bannister 107
Bay 236
Black 107
Cashie 64
Chowan 64,520,535
Delaware 131
FISHER's 47
Haw 107
James 107
Little, Lower 47
Meherrin 107
Mississippi 162,652
Neuse 47,107
Ohio 61
Pamplico 107
Pedee, great 463
Pungo 463
Roanoke 64,79,107,704
upper 79
Santee 113
Tar 107
Trent 107
Wycomico, Great 236
Yadkin 107
ROADS
leading from Baker HOSKINS' to Jos. B. SKINNER's 698
leading from Fayetteville to Tarborough 463
leading from Wadesboro' in the county of Anson, to DUNMAS' Ferry on great Pedee river 463
Plymouth Turnpike 574
post, main 544
turnpike, from the Lincoln line to Jacob MALL's mill 47

ROADS
Virginia 270
SCHOOLS
[See also ACADEMY, COLLEGES, UNIVERSITY]
Female 14
HARVEY's, Mrs. 402
Hillsboro' Female Seminary 439
Hillsborough Female Seminary 249
Kentucky Asylum 162
Lane Seminary 388
YEOMAN's, Jane 324
public 61
SHORE
Eastern, of Virginia 200, 236
SOUND
the 520,603
Albemarle 84,107,184,411
Croatan 130
Pamtico 184
Roanoke 130
SPRING
Bedford 309
Shocco 193
White Oak 47
STATES
Alabama 78,197,470,521, 688
Arkansas 407,530
Carolinas 61
Connecticut 198,326,339, 596,615
Delaware 61,93,165
Deleware 617
Florida 2,96,481,597,689
Georgia 61,66,91,148,679, 688,734
Illinois 386,458
Indiana 492
Kentucky 162,208,260,409, 427,452,470,481,534,558, 597,642,716
Louisiana 36,93,237,407, 427,464,689
Maine 92,93,128,305,597, 679,688
Maryland 36,91,93,205, 208,236,458,552,660,679, 688
Massachusetts 65,91,116, 301,339,351,388,409,597,

STATES
Massachusetts 679,683,688
Michigan 605
Mississippi 92,289,360, 597,659,688
Missouri 180,530
New Hampshire 76,208, 388,660
New Jersey 36,328,343, 421,427,679,688
New York 93,121,222, 259,326,331,388,503,585, 597,617,679,688
North Carolina 4,5,11,13, 14,37-39,47,57,60,62,66,79, 80,84,85,91,103,108,110,118, 121,125,126,130,152,154, 161,168,187-189,193,194, 236,241,242,251,254,283, 299,308,309,317,328,347, 369,370,372,401,416,437, 461,462,474,478,481,490, 496,507,508,510,514,519, 529,534,535,541,553,555, 563,564,570,574,583,589, 594,597,598,607,613,614, 624,633,635,641,642,660, 664,669,672,679,688,690, 695,710,717,744
Ohio 70,92,100,121,174, 185,198,452,597,605,615
Pennsylvania 35,54,61,92, 123,180,309,326,367,384, 388,407,458,534,679,688, 738
Rhode Island 76,93,261, 594,597,679,688
South Carolina 91,128,148, 154,178,183,198,225,301, 408,409,427,469,486,502, 534,552,617,679,688,689
Southern 162,328
Tennessee 54,61,217,369, 597,659,688
Texas 407,557
United 51,63,65,92,93,116, 125,126,150,153,154,164, 172,179,180,189,197,198, 222,237,243,252,262,274, 301,350,382,384,388,410, 458,489,501,503,507,521, 529,536,549,557,579,584, 617,624,635,679,680,689,

STATES
United 699
Vermont 93,388,536
Virginia 13,36,40,73,79,84, 92,93,103,117,161,169,187, 200,236,255,258,259,263,
Virginia 326,328,342,350,354,355, 383,389,390,416,458,462, 467,473,535,566,580,597, 629,633,637,666,673,675, 679,688,708,739,745
SWAMP
Bear 27
Dismal 13,200,236,633,640
Great 47
TAVERN
BRICKELL's 478
GARDNER's, Mrs. 469
GILLIAM's, H. 267
HOSKINS', ___ 511
 Edmund 15
 Jos. N. 497,532,709
 Joseph N. 646
Rising Sun 478
WOOD's ___ 465
 lately occupied by Mrs. Elizabeth 528
TERRITORY
Arkansas 407,530
Michigan 605
North Western 615
TOWNS
Alexandria 326,501
Asheville 47
Auburn (NY) 331
Augusta 76
Barnegat (NJ) 421
Bath (NY) 585
Beaufort 33,86
Bedford Springs 309
Belleville 343
Bellfield 640
Boydton 708
Brinleyville [Brinkleyville] 117
Bristol 63
Bristol (PA) 326
Carrolton 326
Chambersburg 123
Chapel Hill 642
Charlottsville (VA) 107
City Point 458

TOWNS
Claysville 233
Clinton 657
Columbia (NC) 161
Columbia (VA) 107
Covington 642
Cross Keys 633
Darlington 486
Dennis (MA) 65
Elizabeth City 13,33,79, 107,110,125,149,184,188, 308,312,341,399,400,410, 424,433,479,545,547,594, 603,607,725,739
Elizabeth-town 328
Enfield 242,548
Fayetteville 78,85,121,158, 234,242,251,256,259,293, 328,380,382,507,547,562, 567,572,578,618,657,690, 696,723
Fincastle (VA) 675
Frankfort 452
Frederick 552
Fredericksburg 66,178,328
Gaston 267,309,353
Gates Co. Ho. 479
Gates Court House 267,705
Gatesville 463,475,514
Geneva 138
Georgetown (D.C.) 94
Greensboro' 201,242
Greensborough 187
Greensborough (GA) 66
Greenville 210,451
Greenville (SC) 148
Halifax 63,115,242,284, 291,393,696
Harlaem (NY) 259
Hartford 165,464,596
Hartford (CT) 339
Hertford 96,236,238,247, 256,322,348,355,368,422, 445,465,479,517,528,531, 608,628,678,744
Hillsboro' 249,439
Hillsborough 249,293,696
Hyde Park 14,231,402
Jerusalem (VA) 633,640, 647,700,706
Lewisburg 193
Lexington 708
Little Rock 530
Livingstonville (NY) 636

TOWNS
Louisburg 360
Louisville 326,409,427
Lynchburg 66,107,599,708
Marietta 615
Merry Hill 410
Middlesex 406
Middletown (CT) 326
Milledgeville 674,734
Milneburg 652
Milton 164,390,707,710
Murfreesboro 64,107,296, 297,311,421
Murfreesboro' 269,369, 416,489,507,510,633
Murfreesborough 62,66, 168,254,370,481,613
N. Bedford 104
Newbern 49,62,76,80,86, 107,112,138,156,201,204, 210,236,251,259,263,280, 308,328,343,399,410,415, 432,446,449,470,553,562, 578,586,639,651,653,657, 696,715
Newburgh 552
Newton (R.I.) 594
Nixonton 310
North Hempstead 245
Ocracock 107
Ocracoke 362
Oxford 664,729
Passamaquoddy 305
Pendleton 502
Pensacola 198,298
Petersburg 107,179,283, 317,647
Petersburgh 458
Pittsborough 259
Pittsburg 392
Plymouth 4,37,52,82,90, 103,105,107,147,229,248, 251,347,386,437,466,480, 491,498,519,561,574,583, 589,603,650,672,704,714
Portsmouth 415
Portsmouth (NC) 107
Portsmouth (NH) 208,660
Portsmouth (VA) 236,312, 633
Providence 261
Reedy Fork (SC) 148
Rensselaerville (NY) 636
Roanoke (VA) 599

TOWNS
Salem (MA) 301,339,352, 409
Salisbury 107,293,301,395, 440,696,710,723
Scotland Neck 229
Sha__etown (IL) 386
Skinnersville 411
Snow Hill 107
Somerton 500
South Quay 633
Springfield, West 680
St. Louis 661
St. Mary's 660
Suffolk 107,355,479,633
Tallahassee 481
Tarboro' 242,548
Tarborough 71,128,259, 578,614,718
Terre-aux-Boeuf 652
Tiflin 185
Transylvania 534
Trinity 107
Urbanna 103
Vandalia (IL) 458
Wadesboro' 463
Warrenton 193
Washington 5,60,103,108, 112,236,251,308,335,461, 553,731
South 657
Washington Point (VA) 739
Wheeling 233
Williamsboro' 456
Williamsburg 107
Wilmington 76,207,285, 293,328,382,410,427,539, 549,657,660,690,696,722, 740
Wilmington (DE) 165
Windsor 58,90,238,242, 478,535,612,624,710
Winton 38,39,111,129, 475,487,545,633
Worburn 61
Yancey 707
UNIVERSITY [See also ACADEMY, COLLEGES, SCHOOLS]
the 641
Alabama, of 78
Brown 76
Harvard 61

UNIVERSITY
North Carolina, of 259
our 78,729
Pennsylvania, of 534
State, of the 315
Transylvania 534
VALLEY
Roanoke, of the 267
WILDERNESS
Western 76
YARD
Navy 504,633